Behavioral Intervention

CONTEMPORARY STRATEGIES

W. Robert Nay *University of Illinois*

Behavioral
Intervention

CONTEMPORARY STRATEGIES

Gardner Press, Inc., New York
Distributed by Halsted Press, Division of John Wiley & Sons, Inc.
New York · Toronto · London · Sydney

020639

GARDNER PRESS, INC.
32 Washington Square West
New York, New York 10011

Distributed solely by the Halsted Press Division
of John Wiley & Sons, Inc., New York

Library of Congress Cataloging in Publication Data
Nay, W. Robert
Behavioral Intervention

Includes bibliographies and index.
1. Behavior modification. I. Title.
BF637.B4N39   361.3   76-7510
ISBN 0-470-15088-2

Printed in the United States of America

1   2   3   4   5   6   7   8   9

To my parents, Bill and Jane

CONTENTS

Preface

In developing curricula for training undergraduate and graduate students to serve as direct agents of treatment within the human services, I could find no text that provided comprehensive, practical coverage of therapeutic procedures relevant across diverse populations of students and professionals as well as being applicable to a wide variety of client groupings. This book was written with these needs in mind.

Within undergraduate pre-professional or "paraprofessional" programs of training, this text would provide a comprehensive informational base upon which the student could be exposed to practicum/ fieldwork experiences. It would be useful in the training of teachers, nurses, rehabilitation counselors, social workers and other human services personnel as primary or supplementary material covering intervention strategies. In fact, many proposed treatment agents at the upper undergraduate level or above should find the material understandable and of practical relevence.

Masters and doctoral level courses or professional consumers might employ the material as a practically written sourcebook of behavioral change procedures. Used in this fashion, the text might usefully augment a literature survey presentation.

The recent merging of "cognitive," "self-control," and other procedures that rest upon a phenomenological base with therapeutic approaches derived from the animal and human learning literature has resulted in an array of well-defined and often effective intervention strategies that largely meet earlier objections that behaviorally oriented approaches are mechanical, reductionistic, or controlling. This text adopts this broad-based view of man, while deemphasizing simplistic, peripheral notions of man's behavior. In addition, contemporary ethical and legal issues suggested by intervention strategies are strongly emphasized.

A comprehensive coverage of behavioral assessment procedures is beyond the scope of this text although certain procedural presentations are preceded by a discussion of assessment procedures and issues. The reader is referred to the author's text, *Behavioral Assessment Strategies* (New York: Gardner Press, 1977) for this information.

I owe much to the many people who have made this project possible. Henry E. Adams' continuing interest and considerable support made this task seem within the realm of possibility. To my former colleagues at Virginia Commonwealth University, particularly Donald J. Kiesler and William S. Ray, I owe many debts. I was fortunate to have been a part of this emerging, excellent graduate training program. I was permitted the freedom to innovate and learned much from the innovations of my colleagues. I appreciate the competent assistance of Linda Brudvig, who transcribed hours of audiotape, Karin Yoch, Inez Hendrick, Lynn Beal, and Yuki Llewellyn, my secretary. I thank Gardner Spungin, my publisher for this project, for his confidence and advice. I am particularly indebted to James C. Melvin, who permitted me to learn most of what I know about institutions.

My students have been an incalculable source of learning and stimulation, particularly the often "forgotten" undergraduates with whom I have had the good fortune to work.

Finally, I thank my wife Joyce for her encouragement, understanding, and love throughout this project.

Chapter 1

Behavioral Intervention
DEFINING CHARACTERISTICS

We live in an age where the prevailing view seems to be that everyone is entitled to be comfortable, to be efficient in his daily pursuits, and to reach the highest potential in social and vocational activities. Within the largely agrarian extended family of the past, educational, medical, vocational, and religious services were delivered in the home, and it was rare that help was sought from outside agencies. The advent of a sophisticated technology for providing services, as well as extensive media that have popularized such services, has led people increasingly to seek out "professionals." In fact, most of us seek out such services as a means of preventing future discomfort or inefficiency in the regular medical and dental checkups that we undertake each year.

In medical science, rapidly emerging technology has been largely successful in meeting the health needs of much of our society, and the average life-span has steadily increased since the turn of the century. Most of us feel certain that if some problem develops, professionals will be able to detect its cause and perhaps provide a program of treatment to alter the underlying disease or bodily insult. Bandura (1969) has pointed out that our orientation toward defining a "disease process" that underlies such "symptoms" has extended from the earliest of times.

1

In analogous fashion, we have also come to view discomfort, inefficiency or bizarre behavior as the result of some "disease" process that must only be discovered to be cured. We often label such behavior as "abnormal" or "deviant" and from earliest times treatment has been directed at exorcising demons, performing rituals, devising various tonics or potions, or intervening surgically. While ritualistic approaches to altering abnormal behavior were soon supplanted by the view that such problems in living were the result of disease (Szasz, 1961) and thus beyond the control of the individual, this "medical model" has continued to dominate our conception of such social/psychological problem behaviors.

While such physical diseases as paresis do indeed provoke behavior that might be viewed as "abnormal," research into the biochemistry of clients experiencing problems in living has been overwhelmingly unsuccessful in discovering physical disease processes. Yet, clients who have been labeled variously by our society as "delinquent," "psychotic," "depressed," "psychopathic," "neurotic," "alcoholic," or "drug addicted" are among those whose problems in living are often viewed as a "sickness." Such persons are considered as diseased or sick even when a thorough physical examination reveals that no known neurological or physical process underlies their problem behaviors. Viewing problems in living as a "sickness" which must be treated within a medical context, this model suggests that the "patient" is suffering because of forces that are beyond his control.

In recent years models that rest upon different assumptions have increasingly directed theoretical thinking and practical applications. Perhaps the best known proponent of one of these is B. F. Skinner (1953, 1957), who views the individual's behavior as the result of differential positive and negative feedback, or "reinforcement," that he receives from the environment. While not questioning the fact that each individual's behavior may be limited by cognitive abilities and physical structure, this model proposes that each individual learns to behave in a particular way in response to environmental events that impinge upon him. Thus, events extrinsic to the individual come to control his behavior through the learning process.

Another model for viewing man often described as a "humanistic" or "existential" approach, emphasizes self determination. Deemphasizing early learning experiences or disease conceptions, this model suggests that the individual is capable of becoming aware of himself and aware of the choices and limitations that his environment places before him. Appropriate or inappropriate behavior is defined by the kinds of choices the individual has made in directing his own behavior. Often notions of "self-actualization" (Maslow, 1962) or "ideal-self" (Rogers, 1951) suggest that the individual strives toward some potential level of self-determination that presumably defines his boundaries of development. Individuals are thus seen as making wise or unwise decisions that may or may not ultimately lead toward this state of "actualized" existence.

Because each of these models holds important implications both for understanding man's behavior as well as in suggesting treatment possibilities, each will be discussed in further detail, followed by an explication of a proposed phenomenal-behavioral model that incorporates features from two and serves as the underlying model for the present text.

MAN AS "DISEASED"

This model might be subdivided into the biological and the intrapsychic. A biological disease model would attempt to define the physical disease that underlies a specific social-psychological problem. While no one would attempt to explain all deviant behavior as a result of such processes, many investigators have focused their research efforts on hypothesized biochemical explanations for such problem behaviors as "psychotic depression" or "schizophrenia" (Woolley, 1962; Heath, 1960). While certain investigators have provided evidence that links such brain catecholamines as norepinephrine or serotonin to states of elation and/or depression, and while others have "discovered" biochemical agents in the blood of particular diagnostic categories (e.g., Heath, 1960), these results are only suggestive at present and have not led to any consistent body of treatments. While certain chemotherapeutic agents (e.g. tranquilizers) seem to alter the biochemistry of the brain, a relationship between these drug-induced changes and possible biochemical etiology remains to be determined. In the main these exclusively biological approaches have been focused upon an extremely delimited set of problem behaviors and have produced largely inconsistent findings.

Of much greater relevance to a "disease" model is the notion that problems in living are the direct result of energy systems, forces, or hypothetical personality structures of which the individual is often unaware. Early experiences within a person's life, particularly within the first five or six years, alter these underlying energy systems in ways that are beyond the control of the individual. Often, early stress, or "trauma," is deemed responsible for a "fixation" of "psychic energy" at a particular stage of psychological development (e.g., Freud, 1955). Problem behavior that an individual exhibits as an adolescent or adult is viewed as "symptomatic" of unresolved conflicts between hypothetical structures (such as "ego," "id," and "shadow"), which have resulted from early traumatic experiences. Examples of "symptoms" of underlying forces are a client's fear of open spaces, height, or social situations; a depresssed person's lethargy and frequent negative self-statements; or the compulsive rituals displayed by an individual who must touch his wallet fifty to sixty times each hour. Merely treating these symptomatic behaviors (e.g., assisting the client to feel more comfortable when out of doors) would be viewed as counterproductive, since the "real cause" of his behavior has not been dealt with.

Because such "forces" or "conflicts" (the causes) lie within the individual's "unconscious," this approach virtually demands that the individual seek a therapeutic medium so that this information may be uncovered, or "worked through" within a relationship that promotes "insight." Often, the therapist is viewed within a parental role ("transference"), and treatment is directed at the past and is focused on the "unconscious." Therapy is often a time-consuming and lengthy process that requires rather highly developed verbal skills on the client's part.

It is strongly emphasized within this model that each individual can be defined by certain "traits" or "personality structures" that he consistently and characteristically displays to others. Thus, a given individual might display "dependency" or "authoritarianism" or whatever. An array of paper-and-pencil measures, which have dominated the practice of psychology for many years, have been directed toward defining an individual's "personality." Some of these measures attempt to define personality in relation to behavior displayed by criterion populations such as "depressives," "hysterics," or "psychotics" (e.g., the Minnesota Multiphasic Personality Inventory, or MMPI). Others expose the subject to increasingly less structured stimuli such as pictures of persons or objects in particular positions (e.g., the Thematic Apperception Test or TAT) or highly unstructured stimuli (e.g., the Rorschach test). The individual is asked to "make up a story" or "tell what you see" within the stimuli. The underlying rationale is that he will project important information that lies within his unconscious upon the test stimulus, thus enabling the examiner to define or diagnose his psyche in some fashion. While many practitioners place much faith in the personality profiles gleaned from such test responses, many researchers have found their relationship to what the client does (e.g., behavioral referents) to be less than adequate (e.g., Mischel, 1968).

Even if such tests were good predictors of hypothesized personality traits, global personality diagnoses (e.g., "chronic undifferentiated schizophrenia," "latent homosexuality") often have little implication for treatment planning. The author has participated in many clinical staffings in which professional colleagues have spent much time labeling an adolescent as "psychopathic" or a middle-aged housewife as "psychotic depressive," yet failed to make any specific recommendations for treatment.

Bandura (1969) is among those who have pointed out that the vast majority of problem behaviors that currently face the treatment agent seem to be beyond the scope of psychotherapeutic techniques that call for a "relationship," "personality diagnosis," and well-developed verbal skills. He has stated:

In the first place, most antisocial personalities, who constitute a sizable portion of the deviant population, simply serve time in penal institutions or remain under legal surveillance. Since such persons generally prove unresponsive to traditional techniques, many psychotherapists have become pessimistic about the value of psychotherapy for modifying psychopathic or antisocial deviant behavior. In the case of younger delinquents, correctional institutions, though often providing a more structured and non-punitive environment than the children have formerly experienced, rarely offer systematic programs that are efficacious in producing enduring behavioral and attitudinal changes. Similarly, most persons exhibiting gross behavior dysfunctions, who also derive relatively little benefit from conventional interview approaches, are provided mainly with medication, occupational therapy in the form of carrying out institutional routines, recreational activities, and custodial care in "mental" institutions where they become intermittent or permanent residents. Nor have conventional methods of behavioral change had much beneficial impact upon the widespread problems of alcoholism, drug addiction, and a host of other major social problems, which, in some instances, require modification of social systems rather than behavior of isolated individuals. (p. 52)

While it is beyond the scope of the present text to critically evaluate the effectiveness of the "disease" model for treating problems in living, it is obvious that the long-term, individualized, verbally oriented approaches that the model often predicts are irrelevant to the needs of a large majority of clients. Perhaps the most limiting manifestation of this model is that it takes the responsibility for treatment away from the individual and gives it to the "medical practitioner" or "clinician," who presumably has the diagnostic skills to assess the nature of the "disease" and provide a program of treatment. In fact, the vast majority of patients that this model treats within the institutional setting are placed on a program of drug treatment that largely sedates them so that they can be better managed. Because of the often poor ratio of staff members to clients within such settings, individualized, one-to-one treatment is just not feasible. In addition, the dependency relationship potentially established within this "doctor-patient" context is not promotive of the kind of self-directed behavior or "self-control" that many individuals should be capable of displaying following a regimen of treatment.

Although the designation of problems in living as caused by "disease" may have initially resulted in more humane treatment of clients it is no longer productive. While the disease model has been of major benefit in treating those physical problems that have their roots in disease, it has been inappropriate and often irrelevant in treating problems in living. Perhaps the current drive to treat clients within the community in outpatient or halfway house environments, as well as the emergence of the paraprofessional as an agent of treatment, is an indication of the contemporary movement away from a disease approach.

EXTRINSICALLY CONTROLLED MAN

Extending from the early work of Pavlov (1927), Thorndike (1932), J. B. Watson (1914), as well as B. F. Skinner (1953), this model views man as the sum product of his previous experiences within the environment, limited only by the cognitive and physical characteristics that he has inherited. Based primarily upon the training, or "conditioning," of infrahuman species, this model emphasizes the consequences that follow the individual's behavior and alter its probability at some future time. In addition, stimuli in the environment associated with such consequences often come to assume controlling properties. Within animal research, a highly complex technology has been developed suggesting that certain kinds of consequences lead to certain kinds of behavior (more will be said about these methodologies in Chapter 2). This model rejects the notion of unconscious processes or internal determinants of behavior in its most extreme point of view; however, Skinner emphasized that thoughts, cognitions, or other internal phenomena could be affected by consequences in the same way as overt verbal and motor behaviors. The individual is consciously aware of all aspects of his behavior and may self-design strategies for altering it; however, environmental contingencies are often beyond the person's control and may come to limit his choices.

In his books *Walden Two* (1948) and *Beyond Freedom and Dignity* (1971) Skinner attempted to apply the technology of the animal laboratory to altering the behavior of people for the betterment of society at large. Skinner has maintained that when control is left to the vicissitudes of the environment, it is often haphazard, thus permitting grossly deviant and unproductive behavior to be reinforced and thus enhanced. He has suggested that society has an obligation to exert more consistent and comprehensive extrinsic controls, and that such engineering could do away with the problems of alcoholism, drug addiction, and other anomalies that society has been unable to control in the past. The extreme points of view of Skinner and other adherents of the "extrinsic" model have generated much hostility and debate. Who decides what the goals of such control are? Who controls? What of self-determinism?

A purely "extrinsic" point of view is often linked with current treatment modalities which have been variously called "behavior modification," "behavior therapy," or "behavior technology." These approaches have been accused of adopting the "extrinsic" model to the exclusion of other models and of viewing man as a "machine" (Shoben, 1963). Chapter 12 will address some of the implications of this assumption more thoroughly.

SELF-DIRECTED MAN

In suggesting that each man has the potential to be aware of himself, define his goals and make choices to achieve those goals, this model has often been linked with "humanistic" or "existential" models of man. It rejects intrapsychic as well as behavioral terminology, and often employs such terms as "phenomenology" (man's subjective view of things), "self," or "self-actualization" to describe its operations and goals. Within this model treatment often involves a warm relationship between "client" and "therapist" that occurs exclusively within the clinical setting and at a verbal level. While perhaps defining the individual in terms of certain "personality" dimensions, this model rejects the idea of underlying energy systems, structures, and the role of early experience as the major determinants of behavior. In fact, the emphasis is upon the here and now, and the client is required to take a major role in defining the goals of treatment. Particular modalities within this model (e.g., Rogers, 1951) are called "nondirective," because the therapist provides little overt direction to help the client make choices. While such directives are not in the form of definite statements, many of the subtle verbal ("Uh-huh," "yes") and nonverbal (nods, eye contact) actions of the therapist no doubt communicate a good deal of information to the client regarding therapist preferences.

While it is often assumed that each of the preceding models offers a discrete, monolithic approach to viewing man (e.g., Breger and McGaugh, 1965), no one model can predict the variety and complexity of human behavior. Viewing the client who has problems in living as "diseased" may offer much face validity and be conceptually quite appealing—locate the disease process and cure the "sickness". However, the array of hypothetical constructs, underlying or unconscious processes, and supposed developmental etiologies that underlie most approaches within this model rest on a shaky foundation of empirically derived data and offer little in the way of treatment possibilities for a large majority of clients who would be viewed as unsuitable for treatment. Although no one can deny that early, perhaps "traumatic" experiences may have an important impact upon an individual's later behavior, it seems that an exclusive focus upon the past as an explanation for all problems in living is unproductive and naive. Many clients have a circumscribed set of problem behaviors that they wish to be the focus of intervention. Often determinants within the contemporary environment have an important impact upon the client's current behavior; to ignore such phenomena in favor of hypothetical processes would seem impractical. Providing a client with "insight" as to his past experiences may promote behavioral change for persons who have the ability to self-modify current behavior; however, most clients do not possess such skills. Learning that a young man's "height phobia" is "symbolic" of some unresolved conflict with a parent is not likely to assist him to drive across a bridge or climb a flight of stairs. While there may be circumscribed cases where an historical-insight-oriented approach is in order, it would seem much more practical to look within the contemporary environment and the self-report of the individual for clues to those variables that maintain his behavior.

An "extrinsic" model that views man as purely the end result of a series of environmental manipulations would seem to be as limited as the "disease" approach. For example, it might not account for the reader's decision to look to the bottom of this page, put the book down, or reach for a bag of "munchies." While keeping snack foods close to the arm of one's reading chair may make consumption more likely (an environmental elicitor), the decision to place them there was no doubt a voluntary and perhaps even novel act. Other chapters explore the important role of covert phenomena and intrinsic events generally, in maintaining an individual's behavior; however, it is obvious that the cognitive decisions, self-statements, imagery, and physiological events that we experience have as much to do with our overt behavior as the consequences that others apply to it. To ignore the importance of either extrinsic or intrinsic events is to ignore the obvious complexities of man's behavior. The emphasis upon clearly defined events, as opposed to mystical, hypothetical personality constructs, as well as its delineation of the ways in which stimuli in the environment may come to control man's behavior, are among the major contributions of this "extrinsic" model; however it becomes obvious that any comprehensive approach to therapeutic intervention must include some provision for self-directed and implemented behavior.

It is unfortunate that the concept of self-directed man has been linked with verbally oriented, one-to-one therapeutic procedures often labeled as "humanistic," when in fact the goal of "self-regulation" (Kanfer and Phillips, 1970; Karoly and Kanfer, 1974), "self-instruction" (Meichenbaum, 1971), or "self-control" (Bandura, 1969; Goldfried and Merbaum, 1973; Mahoney, 1972, 1974) has been adopted by an array of writers who are described as "behaviorists" and publish their findings in such journals as *Behavior Therapy* or *Behaviour Research and Therapy*. Many investigators have succeeded in artfully bridging the gap between an "extrinsic" and a phenomenological, "self-directed" point of view. These change agents would view the clinical setting as one of *many* potential settings within which assessment and treatment might take place, depending upon the nature of those variables that control a client's problem behaviors. Verbal behavior within a positive relationship would be as heavily emphasized as covert phenomena (e.g., thoughts, feelings, physical sensations) or overt motor behavior, with emphases depending upon the specific focus of treatment, as decided mutually by client and therapist.

This merging of phenomenological and more traditionally "behavioral" (e.g., extrinsic control) models rests upon a set of assumptions that form a foundation for the material that follows.

A PHENOMENAL/BEHAVIORAL APPROACH

The merging of phenomenological and behavioral points of view, as defined by the recent literature, would seem to offer seven basic assumptions:

1. The individual is seen as *capable of being aware* of those events that come to define and control his behavior, and *capable of making deliberate choices* to alter them. The relative importance of the extrinsic environment or intrinsic phenomena in controlling behavior might vary across persons as well as across specific behaviors. Thus, while an individual may consciously and voluntarily decide to stop smoking, an array of stimuli in the social environment may come to elicit this behavior (e.g., others that smoke, ads that tell the reader how nice it is to smoke, talking on the telephone), because of the individual's previous experience with such events or because of their very nature. The extent to which extrinsic events come to control a behavior perhaps depends on the degree to which the individual is aware of their controlling properties, can make a conscious choice, and has developed a sufficient behavioral repertoire to alter them.

In addition, *cognitive and physical capabilities provide important limitations* to potential choices. While an individual may cognitively decide to become a basketball player, his current repertoire of physical behaviors (e.g., coordinated arm and leg movements, speed, and agility) may well restrict him from achieving this goal. Thus, a complete analysis of the array of events that come to exert controls upon the individual's behavior must be viewed within the context of his current repertoire.

2. This approach *deemphasizes the role of unconscious processes, fixed traits, or other personality dimensions* as predictors of man's behavior. Such hypothetical constructs may operate in a fashion similar to the theorist's speculations, but they often become much less parsimonious ways of describing behaviors that may be carefully defined in simple and operational language. When clients are asked to monitor specific overt or covert events as a prelude to intervention, they need clear and

concise definitions, not global and imprecise jargon. Thus, a negative self-statement may be much more readily discriminable as a "target" than a "poor self-concept," "depression," or "neurosis." Global personality descriptions often hold surplus meaning and become a convenient way of explaining a client's behavior without focusing on clearly defined goals that the client and others can understand.

3. The client's *contemporary behavior in the here and now is the primary focus*, and case history information is often employed to better understand the development of present behavior and to provide clues that might assist in defining treatment. While the past cannot be changed, this approach requires the client to accept responsibility for his behavior in the present.

4. *Client verbal behavior (e.g., self-report) is viewed as only one of many potential sources of information in defining the goals and outcome of intervention.* To the extent that clients are reliable self-observers, their reports may provide useful data regarding the variables that control their behavior. Most client verbal reports, however, are not sufficiently accurate or comprehensive to define such variables, and one major goal of a phenomenal/behavioral approach is to train clients to be more reliable self-observers (e.g., Kazdin, 1974). Client verbalizations as self-reports or as the primary behavior to be altered are thus placed within the context of an array of other behavioral modalities that are the concomitant focus of intervention. Comprehensive analyses of verbal, nonverbal, and paralinguistic behaviors that a client emits are often monitored by independent observers who employ a systematic approach to observation (Lipinski and Nelson, 1974; Kiesler and Bernstein, 1974). In addition, physiological indices are often monitored and may be the focus of intervention efforts. Following a thorough collection of information, the goals of treatment may be to alter client behavior within one or more of these behavioral modalities.

5. If the client is capable, this approach *encourages his participation in defining goals and choosing from among potential treatments*. The client and therapist together define goals in specific language and decide upon methods and individual responsibilities necessary to achieve those goals. In addition, every attempt is made to provide services efficiently, and often a time frame is projected within which desired behavioral changes should be expected to occur. Thus, the client is offered an active role in all aspects of the assessment and treatment process.

This approach would not deny treatment to those incapable of taking an active role due to cognitive impairment, age, or other limiting factors. Many such persons reside in institutions and over time have lost their ability to function on an independent basis. In these cases, where individual, verbally oriented treatments may be irrelevant or inappropriate, the phenomenal/behavioral approach has often been employed to provoke behavioral change in line with consensually validated societal norms in quite successful ways (Kazdin and Bootzin, 1972; Atthowe, 1973). In defining goals for such clients, the treatment agent obtains the recommendations of other professionals, relevant members of the institutional staff, and members of the client's family when feasible, to assure that goals are purposeful and provoke behavioral changes that are consonant with the client's ordinary environment. Any program of intervention *should encourage client self-directed control as its optimal goal, and methods should be devised that foster such self-controlling behaviors to the extent of the client's capabilities.*

In addition, a phenomenal-behavioral approach does not encourage the development of a therapeutic relationship which *is itself* the goal of treatment and rejects client dependence upon the therapist (e.g., "transference," parental-child relationships). While a warm and positive relationship is not the exclusive goal of treatment, the *relationship is seen as an important medium* within which the client may divulge information to the therapist confidentially, may test out hypotheses, design and evaluate treatments, and generally receive the active support of the therapist for his efforts.

6. *Careful and systematically gathered records of client behavior are maintained as a means of defining the success of treatments* and to ensure that the client benefits from the therapy. Both client and therapist often take an active role in collecting such information, and whenever possible they rely upon data gathered from independent, objective observers as a means of checking on the reliability of their observations. Research is seen as a continuous effort at establishing the utility of methods employed, and whether conducted within a systematic case study or in a well-controlled between-groups analysis, it is an integral part of evaluating methods and outcomes. Such data-collection procedures are performed with the client's knowledge and participation.

7. This approach *sees man as capable of achieving "self-actualization" or his "self-ideal" in the context of the foregoing assumptions.* Self-actualization is not viewed as some mystical process, perhaps innately defined for each individual, nor is the self-ideal viewed as a hypothetical personality construct or undifferentiated energy system. To the extent that the individual is able to become aware of the extrinsic and intrinsic events that define and control his behavior and to set specific goals for himself the basic requirement for achieving "ideal" goals is met. The therapist is a resource for the client, a source of information, who may be of assistance in defining goals or suggesting alternative methods of achieving them. However, his role is not that of "sage" or "doctor," but more that of guide and educator. A warm and positive relationship may provide a medium in which this role is best undertaken; however, client behavioral change is not seen as exclusively the result of empathy and understanding between client and therapist.

It is difficult to see how the foregoing approach could be described as "mechanistic," "perpheral," or "inhumane." The author strongly suggests that the reader evaluate the methods and procedures presented in the following chapters and evaluate their congruence with the above assumptions. It is his contention that those persons who work with clients develop a basic orientation for viewing client behavior, and it is hoped that elements of this model will instigate the reader to evaluate his own assumptions. In addition, the author emphasizes that many of the "be-.havioral" treatment methods that follow are in fact based upon this phenomenal/behavioral approach and *not* upon the purely "extrinsic" model previously discussed. It is hoped that those who evaluate this text would do so within this context, and not in terms of a model that holds more historical than contemporary significance. Chapter 11 will attempt to bring into focus some of the issues often directed at behavioral approaches.

In recent years an ever-expanding array of treatments has sprung from the assumptions of the phenomenal/behavioral model. While emphases upon extrinsic versus self-regulated control, upon learning, social learning, or cognitive supposed underpinnings, have varied considerably, those methods that have emerged have often been described as "behavioral." Rather than attempt to categorize and present every specific treatment that has been directed at some particular class of problematic behavior, this text will present those methods that seem to offer discrete alternative treatment possibilities across widely divergent categories.

While these methods may be employed in isolation, it should be emphasized that they are often combined into treatment "packages" (such as "assertive training exercises" or "thought stopping"), which themselves become a focus for evaluation. Because such "packages" are often tailored to a particular class of problematic behavior, the focus upon major classes of methods that may be applied across client populations and specific problematic events thus would seem to be a more reasonable approach.

Because of the vast variety of personnel to whom this material might be of interest, the term BCA (behavioral change agent) will be employed to define any person who offers services directly to clients. While the institutional setting often employs the BCA, it is difficult to define the requirements and limits of such roles. The BCA is often employed as primary case monitor or therapist and asked to perform training with clients using such procedures as modeling and role-playing (Scopetta, 1972; Gutride, Goldstein, and Hunter, 1973; Baker, 1973). In some cases the BCA's role is that of "counselor" or "teacher" (Allen, 1973; Rawson, 1973).

Because of the lack of consistency in approaches to training and employment of the BCA as an agent of intervention, it is hoped that this text will present an informational base upon which a program of training might be devised. Its primary emphasis is upon a detailed explication of methods, not upon a thoroughgoing review of the literature. An array of graduate-level texts (Kanfer and Phillips, 1970; Bandura, 1969; Rimm and Masters, 1974) have presented comprehensive literature surveys, and there have been many new primary texts as well as edited books of readings. Of course, a comprehensive review of the literature underlies each presentation, and research findings and issues will be presented as relevant. Chapter 10 discusses procedures that might be incorporated into a program of training to ensure that the informational base presented in the chapters is translated into behavior. No written text is sufficient to provoke behavioral change; there must be a rigorous and systematic approach to training that permits the trainee to behaviorally practice important elements in an organized fashion.

PLAN OF THE CHAPTERS

Following a presentation in Chapter 2 of those variables that might control a client's behavior and place limitations upon therapeutic efforts, Chapter 3 considers the manipulation of extrinsic consequences as a means of gaining control of client behavior—when this approach is suggested by assessment efforts. The emphasis is upon approaches to positive as well as aversive control that may be offered by important others within the environment, as well as mediated by the client himself. Chapter 4 will be directed at approaches aimed at some groupings of clients (e.g., a ward, cottage, classroom), and discuss some of the important issues that specifically relate to group-directed methods.

Covert or private events that a client phenomenologically assesses (e.g., imagery, feelings, cognitions, physical sensations) are often systematically manipulated by the client within treatment, and Chapter 5 will focus upon approaches to cover positive and negative control, followed by a discussion of the important limitations imposed by the nature of such private phenomena.

It has already been emphasized that the training of staff members should include some provision for client practice in a systematic fashion. Often, important targeted behaviors are modeled for the client by relevant, competent persons, after which the client has an opportunity to practice or role-play those behaviors presented. Because of the importance of modeling and role-playing in instigating and maintaining an array of skill behaviors, these "social learning" approaches will be presented within Chapters 6 and 7.

The establishment of client self-control is of primary importance within any program of treatment, although it is often limited by client resources. Many investigators have developed treatments that attempt to induce client control of important events by employing multiple procedures in a concerted fashion. These approaches, as well as a means of communicating the goals and methods of treatment to clients within a contractual agreement, will be the primary emphasis of Chapter 8.

When procedures are combined into a program to increase a client's approach of certain objects or situations, the goals often include training a client to be more assertive or to approach some previously feared stimulus event. Based upon the the early formulations of Wolpe (1958), who developed the procedure of "systematic desensitization," multiple options are available to the BCA for reducing avoidant behavior and increasing client approach of such stimuli. These approaches will be presented in Chapter 9, along with a discussion of recent issues regarding the manner in which they may effect behavioral change. The role of relationship and nonspecific variables that might operate within any therapeutic strategy will provide a focus.

The important role of a carefully planned and systematic approach to training clients and staff members to assume assessment and treatment roles, as well as specific procedures that provide options to the trainer, will be presented in Chapter 10. An effort will be made to integrate these various procedures into a proposed training vehicle. The importance of training, which is often deemphasized within the literature, is underlined by a chapter that is directed specifically toward it. Because of the dearth of systematic, well-controlled literature regarding training possibilities, it is hoped that Chapter 10 will serve as a stimulus for others in developing a more extensive compendium of training options for the BCA.

The manner in which the BCA delivers assessment and therapeutic services to clients often suggests certain ethical considerations. Within the literature, as well as within the courts, such issues are increasingly the focus of discussion. An attempt will be made to relate relevant issues to the functioning of the BCA within the institution in Chapter 11, which also discusses important issues suggested by a phenomenal/behavioral approach to treatment.

CHAPTER SUMMARY

Man's behavior is explained within three rather distinctive models, each of which holds important implications for treatment.

In viewing *man as diseased,* two major approaches have been employed. The biological disease model attempts to define some physical disease process that underlies certain delimited "symptomatic" behaviors such as depression and schizophrenia. While certain physical diseases provoke behavior that might be viewed as abnormal from a social/psychological point of view, investigators have been largely unsuccessful in relating problems in living to biological disease. More significant within the disease approach is the view that man's social/psychological problems are "symptoms" of underlying conflicts, forces, or energy systems of which the individual is not conscious.

In viewing man as a function of the *extrinsic environment,* a second model *emphasizes the positive and negative feedback each individual receives from his environment* as the primary determinant of his behavior. Based upon investigations of infrahuman species, an elaborate technology suggests that man's behavior may be predicted by gaining control over extrinsic stimuli, particularly those that hold reinforcing or punishing properties. Intrapsychic events as well as personality constructs are deemphasized within this approach.

In viewing man as *self-directed,* a third model suggests that *each individual is capable of being aware of those events that come to control his behavior and of making deliberate decisions to achieve an ideal state of "actualization."* Based upon a phenomenological point of view, which emphasizes man's subjective view of reality, this approach deemphasizes both intrapsychic phenomena and "conditioning" explanations for man's behavior. Often termed "humanistic" or "existential," this approach often involves the development of a warm, one-to-one relationship between client and therapist, couching the coals of treatment in rather abstract language ("self," "ideal self," "self-actualization").

A proposed phenomenal/behavioral approach upon which this text is based would make the following assumptions: man is *consciously aware of those intrinsic and extrinsic events that come to control his behavior;* while the total life-span of the individual may provide important information, the *"here and now" is emphasized* within assessment and treatment; assumptions regarding *hypothesized structures, personality systems, or unconscious processes are deemphasized* in favor of phenomena that may be described and understood by client and therapist; the client is seen as being *capable of asserting self-control* over his behavior—this model would attempt to move the individual from extrinsic to self-mediated control if feasible; the importance of *carefully defining and assessing client behavior prior to, during, and following treatment* as a means of evaluating the effectiveness of methods is emphasized, as well as case study and more formal, well-controlled investigations; while this model does not typically speak in terms of "self-actualization" or "ideals," *each person is seen as capable of reaching ideal goals through a systematic program of self-mediated behavior.* This phenomenal/behavioral approach does not view man as sick or "diseased," and its procedures are opened up to an array of professional and paraprofessional personnel.

Finally, a review of material to be offered in the chapters that follow was provided for the reader, with some rationale for the emphases of the presentation.

CHAPTER 2

Controlling Variables

Three primary goals confront the behavioral change agent in dealing with client behavior.

First, *an increase in the frequency of some behavior that a client currently exhibits* may be in order. For example, a client may engage in some desirable behavior only on rare occasions, possibly at inappropriate times. Regarding social skills, a seven-year-old boy may sometimes be able to answer yes and no and say simple phrases appropriate to the classroom, but his teacher may observe that he rarely speaks to her or to the other children. We might say that the ordinary rate of speaking behavior is very low for this child compared with other children in the class. Because his failure to answer questions, participate in oral reading assignments, and generally low level of interaction with others inhibits his learning within the classroom, the teacher might realistically desire to increase this child's rate of speaking. More specifically, the teacher might wish to increase the likelihood that the child will answer questions with a yes or no as an initial step toward increased use of speech.

The teacher's goal is to increase the occurrence of a behavior—answering yes or no—that he has previously learned but fails to use with great frequency. We might say that the use of yes and no in response to the teacher's questions are behaviors chosen, or "targeted," for change, and in this case the targeted behaviors are already within the child's repertoire. Increasing the frequency of toothbrush or comb use, attendance at meals, or increased use of greeting statements like "Hello" are all examples of targeted behaviors that might already be within a client's repertoire.

A second goal of behavioral change might be to incorporate some new behavior within a client's repertoire. In this case the client has not previously exhibited the target behavior. For such novel behaviors, the change agent must first get the client to perform the behavior, then find some means of maintaining the behavior after its initiation.

The teacher cannot expect children to spell CAT if they have not previously learned the letters of the alphabet. Thus, in the classroom as in all areas of learning, certain basic information must be learned before more sophisticated material can be taught. The procedures for expanding a client's repertoire to include novel information or skills may be very different from procedures that merely attempt to encourage the use of current repertoire behaviors. Thus, the BCA must carefully assess the current behavior of a client—as well as previous historical experiences with a particular behavior—before formulating a plan to promote an increment in its frequency.

A third goal of treatment might be to *reduce the frequency of a behavior* in a client's repertoire. For example, children might be expected to reduce the frequency of calling out, getting out of their seats, without permission, or loud talking within a classroom setting. Making noise, leaving a setting without permission, or loud talking within a classroom setting without permission, or failing to participate in accordance with rules are examples of behaviors that might be defined as disruptive. The *reduction* of an adult client's avoidance of height situations, public speaking, or exposure to some feared animal might all be goals of a treatment plan, as well as decreasing self-mutilation, window breaking, or verbal and physical aggressiveness within a population of adolescents.

Too often, the BCA will fortunate a treatment plan to accomplish one of these goals without first evaluating the array of variables which might control the current frequency of the behavior. As an example, there are many factors that could control the high degree of self-critical statements made by a "depressed" client. The client may have been previously exposed to some person of influence (say, a parent) who also used a high degree of self-criticism. We could say that this powerful influence "modeled" self-critical statements for our client, who now might be "imitating" the model's way of dealing with his environment. It might be that relatives and friends provide much attention and support to our client whenever he makes such statements as "I always goof up" or "I'm just not good enough." Offers of assistance or such statements as "Don't be upset, everyone feels that way sometimes" and "You really *can* do it" might very well provide much attention from others, who unwittingly encourage this negative behavior. In fact, even professional staff within an institution may provide similar support and sympathy for such statements. Only a careful evaluation of the development of this behavior and community as well as institutional support for it can provide the BCA with sufficient information to construct an adequate plan of treatment.

Because of the importance of defining those variables that might come to control the frequency of targeted events as a precursor to treatment, this chapter will focus upon such potentially *controlling variables*. Verbal self-reports and behavioral observations within and outside the interview situation, self-monitoring and independent observational assessment, physiological measurement, and objective test responses are among ways that such variables may be assessed. While a presentation of these and other assessment procedures is beyond the scope of this text, the manner in which they might be employed as a prelude to intervention will often be discussed.

Regardless of the specific goals of treatment, careful consideration of potential controlling variables often suggests a plan to be followed, carefully defines a client's resources, and is usually an excellent means of instigating a positive relationship with a client.

CLIENT RESOURCES

Could we develop a treatment plan that would train a retarded child (with an IQ of, say, 50) to perform algebra problems, or a brain-damaged, hyperactive client to remain seated for long periods of time, or a six-year-old to operate a lathe? Such questions are of course absurd, yet they illustrate in gross terms the importance of designing therapeutic goals to meet the resources of the client. "Resources" is defined very broadly to include the behavioral possibilities that the client offers to the BCA, and these are certainly influenced by the intellect, and interests as well as the physical capabilities of the client.

In defining targeted behaviors for a particular client, a careful assessment must be made of his resources so that goals of treatment that fall within these resources may be defined. Often a thorough medical examination, case history, and perhaps intellectual evaluation precede the targeting of certain client behaviors for change. In working with children, a careful assessment of developmental level ensures that the BCA will not target goals that are unattainable. Failure to tailor goals to client resources not only leads to disappointments but may well discourage the client from future participation in any therapeutic endeavor.

PREVIOUS EXPERIENCE

Although the BCA does not take past history as the primary emphasis within treatment, it is obvious that past experiences with a behavior affect the probability of its future occurrence. A child who is vigorously doused by a friend subsequently fears the water; a housewife who finds that complaints of aches and pains allow her to avoid housework subsequently increases her complaining; a child who gets some candy or a toy by hitting another child will probably take a similar approach in the future with other children. It is a basic truth that our previous experiences have something to do with the way we currently behave, yet in many cases therapeutic goals are formulated and treatment plans developed that do not take these historical experiences into account. Kanfer and Sasow. (1965) have proposed a system of behavioral analysis that includes an evaluation of many of the controlling variables discussed in the present chapter. While deemphasizing the traditional importance placed upon verbal report of historical information, the authors suggest that a "developmental analysis" of past experiences be undertaken by the BCA:

A developmental analysis suggests consideration of biological, sociological and behavioral changes in the patient's history which may have relevance for his present complaint and for a treatment program. (p. 443)

An evaluation of a client's previous experiences with the behavior of interest provides important clues to the following: the current *strength* of the behavior (resistance of the behavior to change over time); the client's *previous successful and unsuccessful approaches* to dealing with the behavior (or similar behaviors); *incentives* that have motivated the client in the past and may currently hold some value; important *elicitors* of the behavior (e.g., specific persons, situations, times, bodily states such as sickness or fatigue); as well as the *client's own view* as to why the behavior occurs. This information may be gathered from both client verbal reports as well as the reports of others who have had occasion to observe the client over time. The BCA will often have access to comprehensive case history information within most institutional settings, and should supplement this information with data gathered from a careful questioning of the client regarding past events relevant to his current "problem."

EXTRINSIC INCENTIVES

When we engage in certain behaviors we often receive positive and negative consequences that may affect the probability of our engaging in that behavior at some future time. Often such consequences come from the external environment, and they take many forms. In his work with pigeons and other infrahuman species, B. F. Skinner (1953, 1957) and his colleagues have systematically evaluated a number of ways that the current rate of a targeted behavior *(operant level)* may be increased or decreased by the consequences that follow it. These procedures have been called *operant conditioning;* consequences are *reinforcements*. When a one-year-old knocks a bowl of soup onto the floor and older children laugh and make much of the infant's behavior, this laughter and attention would be considered a *positive reinforcement if the probability of the infant's pushing the bowl on the floor is increased in the future*. In fact, any event that follows a targeted behavior is termed a positive reinforcement if its presentation increases the probability of the target occurring again at some future time. In our present example there is a good chance that the infant may engage in the "mess-making" again, to achieve the attention from his older siblings. Importantly, according to Skinner's definition, the laughter and attention would not be considered a "reinforcement" if it had no affect upon the probability of the infant's future behavior.

Skinner uses the term *negative reinforcement* to define the situation where *punishing consequences are removed contingent upon some desirable targeted behavior*. For example, a child sent to his room for "being bad" begins to make a great ruckus, tossing objects about the room, crying, and generally making noise. Sending the child to his room, in this case, is a punishment. The mother might say to the child, "As soon as you stop all that racket, you may leave your room." (The punishment will be terminated), and when the child quiets down the mother goes to him and tells him to come back outside and play. Thus, a state of punishing consequences is terminated contingent upon a targeted behavior (being "quiet"). Negative reinforcement is rarely used within treatment paradigms because it requires that the client already be exposed to punishing consequences or that such punishing consequences be delivered to a client so that they may be terminated as a reinforcement.

When negative consequences are employed, they are most frequently presented within a punishment paradigm. A *punishment or punisher is any event that follows some behavior that decreases the possibility of the behavior at some future time*. Thus, a punishment immediately *follows* a targeted behavior. In our example, the mother's use of a spanking, verbal yell, or other aversive event contingent upon her child's talking back or misbehaving would be termed a punishment. Chapter 3 will have a good deal to say about some of the important issues that underlie the use of punishment and the important ethical considerations suggested by the use of aversive control.

While infrahuman subjects are often reinforced using edible reinforcers, a vast array of additional positive and negative consequences are available to the human organism. Extrinsic consequences for one's behavior fall into two general categories: material and social/activity. A *material consequence is a tangible object that is either provided to a client for some appropriate behavior or removed following some inappropriate behavior*. Thus, a material consequence must have some physical properties. Examples of positive material consequences that have been employed are: foods; cosmetic and health care items; trinkets; cigarettes; toys/craft items; as well as that "great American standby," money. Chapters 3 and 4 define in detail many categories of material consequences that have been employed both with individuals and within group settings. Often, rather than providing some specific material consequence contingent upon a behavior, a BCA will provide a *generalized reinforcer*, or "token" (e.g. poker chip, check mark, punch on a card), which clients may trade for "back-up" material consequences of their choice. There are many of advantages to employing a generalized reinforcer within group treatment, and these will be discussed in Chapter 4. Negative material consequences most often involve the removal of some material incentive contingent upon some negative targeted behavior, and most treatment programs use some combination of positive and negative control.

Social consequences make up the next category. A *social consequence is any verbal or physical behavior on the part of one person—for example, a staff member or parent—that either increases or decreases the probability of a client engaging in a targeted behavior.* Obviously, this is a very broad definition; however, it is extremely difficult to categorize the possible social reinforcers that might operate to influence a client's behavior. Often social consequences are very subtle. A smile, a glance, a touch on the shoulder, a word stated with a certain inflection—even the body stance of the person—may define whether the communication is viewed as being positive or negative by the recipient and predict its subsequent effect upon behavior (e.g., Kiesler and Bernstein, 1975).

Of course, there are a number of more easily observable social consequences that most of us would agree upon. Among such popular positive consequences are verbal statements like "Good job," "I like the way you ____," "Right on," or any other statement that provides positive feedback to the recipient. Then there are physical behaviors—a pat on the back, a kiss, a hug, a smile, an up-and-down nod of the head, and in fact any nonverbal gesture the recipient finds positive.

Negative social consequences include such verbal criticisms as "Poor job," "I'm very unhappy with the way that you ____," and any other remark that provides negative feedback to the recipient about his behavior. There are also physical negative consequences, including a shove, slap, hit, horizontal shake of the head, a frown, the failure of the initiator to maintain eye contact with the recipient, or other physical gestures that communicate to the recipient that the initiator is displeased with his behavior.

In summary, social consequences are often difficult to define, and their value depends totally upon how the recipient evaluates them. Sometimes what an independent observer might think is a negative social communication (e.g., a push or a shove) might very well be viewed positively by the recipient. The author remembers one family whose members used physical raps and hits as signs of affection. For example, rather than verbally tell his son that he approved of his performance in a baseball game, the father reached over and lightly slugged his son on the arm during a therapy session. This was obviously viewed by the son (recipient) as a positive communication. Within this family past experiences had made it clear what kinds of social communications were positive and very clearly what kinds were negative.

Finally, *activity* consequences provide access to some desired activity or event contingent upon some targeted behavior of interest.

In employing positive and negative consequences the BCA must either wait for some targeted behavior to occur naturally and then follow it with an appropriate consequence, or, more likely, attempt to instigate important behavioral events so that they may be reinforced and maintained at a more acceptable frequency. One manner of instigating a target is to begin by *reinforcing some approximation of the targeted behavior, then sequentially rewarding those successive approximations until the client emits the desired behavioral event.* This procedure has been called "shaping" or "successive approximations." This approach is often employed in experiments on animals. When directed at the terminal response of a rat pressing a bar, it might involve first reinforcing the organism's turning toward the end of the cage that contains the bar. Responses of looking toward the bar, making movements toward the bar, and placing a limb upon the bar are all reinforced, as the organism is successively trained to press the bar. Successive approximations are particularly useful with an organism that cannot understand verbal speech or symbolic nonverbal language. Among human organisms, however, successive approximations are a costly and inefficient means of instigating many targeted behaviors. Most often, a targeted behavior is *modeled* for the client, and his subsequent imitation of that behavior is then reinforced. The behavior may also be instigated through verbal prompting or cueing on the part of the BCA. In some cases the environment is altered to increase the probability that the targeted behavior will occur, so that it may be followed by an appropriate consequence. Chapters 6 and 7, which discuss social learning approaches to modeling and role playing, will provide an array of options to the BCA for instigating important targeted events by way of "vicarious" or "imitative" mechanisms.

Often, when working with infrahuman subjects, a *continuous schedule* of reinforcement (after *each* response) is followed until the frequency of the organism's behavior moves from operant to some asymptotic level. Once the organism is shaped up to perform the targeted behavior at a sufficient rate, some *partial schedule of reinforcement* (after particular responses or time periods) is often employed. Many investigators have found that organisms kept on a partial schedule emit the targeted behavior for long periods following the termination of reinforcement—a compared with organisms maintained on a continuous schedule. *Two major categories of partial schedules* have been employed: *interval schedules* (reinforcement is delivered at intervals of, say, every five seconds) and *ratio schedules* (reinforcement is delivered contingent upon the organism's making a particular number of responses, (as, say, following every fifth response). In addition, interval and ratio schedules are often delivered according to a *fixed format* (for example, every five seconds, every five responses) that is invariant over time, or presented within a *variable format,* which varies the specific schedule around some preset mean (that is, the organism is reinforced after one second, ten seconds, three seconds, seven seconds, and so on). While moving from continuous to partial reinforcement might be appropriate in maintaining an animal's behavior, the manner in which schedules of reinforcement affect the behavior of human organisms has not been adequately determined at this time (e.g., Kazdin and Bootzin, 1972). While certain partial schedules lead an infrahuman organism to respond for long periods of time following the *termination of reinforcement (extinction),* it seems likely that the human organism, most particularly the adolescent or adult, would stop responding as soon as he was told that reinforcement was to be terminated. The cognitive capabilities of the human organism would predict that such schedules, if they do hold predictable effects, might operate in a manner different from those of infrahuman organisms.

Another category of learning has to do with the manner in which stimuli within our environment become associated with involuntary responses. In the early 1900s the Russian neurophysiologist Ivan Pavlov (1927, 1928) noted that his laboratory animals (dogs) often salivated upon the rattling of the food dish, prior to the actual presentation of food. Pavlov reasoned that a food dish does not innately elicit such salivation, and postulated that the organisms had learned to respond to the food dish in much the same manner that they had previously responded to the food alone. In later experiments Pavlov attempted to evaluate how neutral stimuli come to be associated with such involuntary responses as salivating to a food stimulus. Pavlov was primarily interested in involuntary responses that might be elicited by a standard stimulus. Because the properties of food reliably and involuntarily elicit salivation on the part of most organisms prior to any conditioning, he termed such stimuli *unconditioned stimuli;* we will use the term UCS. The *involuntary response elicited by an unconditioned stimulus was termed an unconditioned response,* or UCR. When some neutral stimulus that had not previously elicited a response came to elicit a response similar to the UCR via association with the UCS, Pavlov called this stimulus a *conditioned stimulus,* or CS. A response that this CS the elicited by way of its association with the UCS would be called a *conditioned response,* or CR. Pavlov found that an array of previously neutral stimuli that were presented just prior (about .5 seconds) to a UCS would come to elicit a response similar to the UCR (the CR).

For example, a dog is harnessed in a training apparatus that contains a small light bulb and a food dish. Turning the light on and off would of course produce no salivation from the dog; the light is a "neutral stimulus." However, by turning on the light for a very brief time just prior to presenting food in the dish over a number of pairings or *trials,* the

light source would come to elicit the salivation response. A diagram of this exercise, often called *classical conditioning, respondent conditioning,* or *Pavlovian conditioning,* is illustrated in Fig. 2.1.

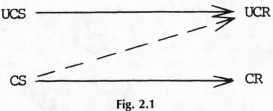

Fig. 2.1
Paradigm for classical conditioning.

Later investigators extended the work of Pavlov to other animals, often employing unconditioned stimuli such as electric shock or aversive noise, and this research further illustrated a number of important characteristics of classical conditioning. One important finding was that not only does the CS come to elicit the CR, but stimuli that are similar to the CS may also elicit a CR which is often not as fully elaborated or intense. For example, let us assume that a tone of 1,000 cycles per second has been paired with a shock (UCS) that produces a leg flexion when applied to the foreleg of an experimental animal. Following repeated pairings of tone and shock, the tone may come to elicit the leg flexion response, and we would now classify the tone as a CS. Importantly, while the 1,000-cps tone elicits the maximal CR, tones of 900, 1,100, 700, or 1,200 cps might also elicit leg flexion, though probably not as intense as the response to the original 1,000-cps stimulus. Thus, *the properties of a CS may generalize to other stimuli that are similar; this process has been called stimulus generalization.* In addition, while the animal may move its right foreleg in response to the CS, it might also move other parts of its body that were not originally the focus for shock; we would call this a *generalization of responding: response generalization.* Just as with operant conditioning, *when the reinforcement (UCS) is no longer provided, the conditioned response will extinguish.* This dissipation of responding typically occurs at a differential rate, depending upon the number and manner of presentation of paired CS-UCS trials.

An array of involuntary responses may be classically conditioned within the human population: eye-blink response to a puff of air, GSR to shock, pupillary response to light and so on. Then, outside the formal laboratory situation, there is a good deal of evidence to suggest that many of the autonomic responses within a client's report of "anxiety" or "fear" may have been learned through classical conditioning mechanisms (Rachman, 1966; Rachman and Hodgson, 1968). Although this is ethically questionable, a number of investigators have in fact induced certain deviant behaviors within subjects using classical conditioning procedures as a means of illustrating the manner in which such inappropriate man-ners may be learned (Watson and Raynor, 1920; Krasnogorski, 1925). The following illustration shows how a classical conditioning model might be employed to explain the development of "phobic" or avoidant behaviors within a child:

When he walked over to his friend's house one day, little Billy decided to cut through Mr. Jones' back yard; climbed over the fence and proceeded to walk toward the back of the grounds. Mr. Jones' rather well-nourished Irish Setter did not appreciate little Billy's intrusion into his "territory," and proceeded to bit Billy on the leg following an abbreviated chase about the grounds. Billy called out in anguish at the pain inflicted by the bite; pulled away from the animal, leaped back over the fence as fast as his little legs would take him, and ran home in a state of frenzy. In the days and weeks that followed, Billy's mother found that he cried at the sight of a dog on the street and immediately asked to leave or more away whenever a dog was seen to approach. On one occasion, when she attempted to force Billy to walk over and touch a dog, he broke out in a "fit of crying," informing his mother that he was "afraid," "please don't make me," etc. In the months that followed, Billy's fear of dogs seemed to generalize to other animals and Billy was found to generalize to other animals and Billy was found to become emotional when exposed to any size dog, cats, and even the animals in the local zoo. Billy's fear of dogs and other animals caused him to avoid wooded areas, closed in back yards, the local park and an array of other locations that had previously been enjoyed because of his reported fear that "a dog might come."

This simplistic example illustrates how the classical conditioning model might potentially explain how a very common childhood fear could be developed. In viewing the example within this model, the paradigm in Fig. 2.2 would seem to describe the generation of Billy's "fear."

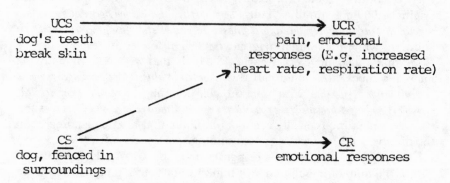

Fig. 2.2
Development of a fear within a classical conditioning paradigm.

In the example the dog bit (UCS) that stimulated pain receptors beneath the surface of the skin led to the involuntary response of pain and a host of other emotional responses associated with receiving a painful stimulus (UCRs). The dog inflicting the painful stimulus was present within the situation, as well as the fenced-in surroundings of Mr. Jones' back yard. Dogs had been a neutral and perhaps a positive stimulus to Billy, but within this context dogs became associated with pain and emotional responding via classical conditioning mechanisms, thus becoming a CS for emotional responding. While a large number of pairing of UCS and CS are often necessary to instigate classical conditioning, a number of investigators have found that such conditioning can occur in just a few trials when the stimuli are very intensive, such as the pain in the present example (Lichtenstein, 1950).

The fact that emotional responding originally associated with the dog generalized to other dogs and animals of similar size can be explained through the process of stimulus generalization already mentioned. It is probable that animals most similar in size and characteristics to a dog would elicit more emotional response than dissimilar stimuli (e.g., a hamster or an elephant). To *extinguish* any emotional response to the CS, the child must now be presented the CS ("dog"), perhaps over some lengthy period of time, with no further presentation of the painful UCS ("bite"). Perhaps the major problem with fears that are generated by classical conditioning mechanisms is that the client avoids the conditioned stimulus (in this instance a dog), and is often unwilling to tolerate its presence even for brief periods of time so that extinction might occur. Possibilities for "desensitizing" or reducing avoidant behavior on the part of the "phobic" client will be presented in Chapter 10. Many of these procedures are based upon a process of extinction within a classical conditioning paradigm.

In summary, the individual may learn a variety of prosocial or maladaptive behaviors by way of operant or classical conditioning mechanisms. Each of these paradigms suggests procedures that may instigate some targeted behavior, as well as approaches to decreasing its frequency (extinguishing) over time. The important concepts of operant control, shaping, reinforcement, punishment, stimulus and response generalization, as well as extinction, will be integrated into discussions of specific treatment procedures in the chapters that follow.

INTRINSIC EVENTS

Early investigators (e.g., Schacter, 1959) suggested that the way one cognitively labels or identifies a state of physiological arousal (e.g., increased heart and respiration rate, sweatier palms) determines whether this "emotion" will be identified as "joy," "anger," "fear," or something else. Thus, one's physiological state and cognitive view of any situation determine how an individual might describe his "emotion" at a given point in time. In a classic study Schacter and Singer (1962) found that subjects who were injected with a drug that increased physiological arousal (epinephrine) identified their emotional state as "angry" when exposed to an "angry" confederate and as "euphoric" when exposed to a "euphoric" confederate. Importantly, the degree of "model" influence depended upon the cognitive set of subjects. Those who were informed of the effects of epinephrine and thus attributed their emotional state to the drug itself were less influenced by the models. Those who were not informed proved to be much more susceptible to influence. Thus, even with a drug that produces relatively fixed physiological effects, the subjective identification of emotion is significantly determined by one's cognitive expectations.

Kanfer and Marston (1963) were among the first to emphasize the manner in which an individual develops internal standards for judging his own behavior and accordingly reinforces himself (e.g., positive and negative self-statements) for performance. Bandura and Küpers (1964) and Mischel and Liebert (1966) are among investigators who have shown that the self-reinforcement standards that individuals adopt are influenced by the standards they observe in others. Thus, standards for self-reinforcement may be learned without any direct contact with an event, but merely by watching someone of influence (model) demonstrate such standards. In fact, Bandura and Perloff (1967) have shown that internal self reinforcement is as effective at controlling children's behavior as are externally administered rewards such as candy or toys. How do intrinsic, self-administered incentives relate to external sources of reinforcement? The author would suggest a sequence of events that might lead to self-reinforcement or self-punishment for a given behavior.

First, a *rule or standard* (for example, Don't lie to others) *is presented* to the individual through a variety of possible mediums: verbal statements by others; another individual modeling the standard; or possibly the standard being presented in some written form (as perhaps, the Bible).

Second, the individual is either *directly or vicariously (through observing a model) exposed to some situation that is directly related to the rule or standard* (for example, a child has the option of lying or telling the truth to his parents about some misdeed). In direct exposure the individual makes some response (lies or does not lie) and receives some form of feedback for his response. Although feedback may be externally mediated—such as receiving a spanking for lying, avoiding a spanking when lying is effective, or praise from parents for telling the truth—some sort of internal feedback must necessarily result from the response. For example, a lie might remove the child from any threat of punishment, thus producing a satisfying internal state of relaxation. Certainly any kind of externally induced punishment such as spanking would induce an internal emotional response—pain, heightened muscular tension, etc.—that might be unpleasant to the individual. Thus, the individual makes a response in accordance with or contrary to the rule or standard and meets with both externally and internally mediated feedback.

Regarding vicarious exposure, a major way we experience such feedback is by observing the behavior of others who in some way have significance for us (models). In the present example the child may experience a physiological response merely by observing another child being punished or praised for standard-related behavior. This standard-related feedback is not directly administered to the individual but experienced vicariously through observing others receiving feedback for standard-related behaviors (e.g., Bandura and Kupers, 1964; Liebert and Allen, 1967).

Third, over repeated exposure to feedback for standard-related responses, the individual may now predict how his environment will respond to pro-standard and contra-standard behavior. *Because he can cognitively rehearse previous externally instigated feedback, he thus experiences this feedback in the absence of the former environmental agents of feedback, and may even experience the concomitant physiological responses previously associated with the externally instigated feedback.* For example, the child can now cognitively rehearse (through, say, imagery) the spanking that his parents previously gave him for lying or that he observed another child receive, and can also experience muscular tension or other physiological responses previously elicited by the event itself.

Importantly, this self-produced feedback may occur *prior to any actual response*, thus affecting the child's choice of responses (to lie or not to lie) in the situation. Thus, this self-reinforcement may occur after the standard-related response or even prior to the response, all in the absence of external feedback. Most of us have experienced anxiety prior to speaking in public, making a date, or some such activity, possibly because of previous unfortunate experiences of our own or of others whom we have observed. Of course, such experiences occur at a private or *covert* level and may greatly influence our decision actually to perform the behavior (e.g., make an *overt* response). Thus, covert processes such as cognitive rehearsals of a behavior and probable feedback we will receive, as well as physiological responses induced by such cognitions, greatly affect what we actually do in any situation. The person who fears heights may in fact avoid all stairs and elevators at some cost to his daily routine. Because he does not currently experience height, we may predict that his avoidance of height situations is now controlled by covert mediators, even though we may trace his fear to some earlier bad experience related to height. The specific category of intrinsic consequences will now be discussed.

Intrinsic consequences

Any *event that occurs within the individual (not directly observable by others) and increases or decreases the probability of some behavior that it follows will be defined as an intrinsic consequence*. This class of "covert" or "intrinsic" behaviors may include an array of cognitive events (thoughts, imagery, fantasy) as well as physiological variables (feelings, sensations, pain). Kanfer (1965) was one of the first behavioral psychologists to talk about the things that happen "inside the black box." Of course, Kanfer was talking about the cognitive and physiological events that might very well have implications for the client's behavior. Thus, the task of the BCA is not so simple as to merely define material and social consequences that are delivered by other "extrinsic" agents.

A couple of examples of the importance of these private or "covert" events might be in order. Let us assume that as a youngster you are paid $3.50 to cut Mr. Brown's lawn. You've been paid $3.50 for your cutting activities for the last two years and have come to count on this income to buy necessary items (gum, candy, etc.). The material reinforcement of $3.50, contingent upon lawn cutting, thus increases the probability that you will mow his lawn on a regular basis (a "positive" reinforcement), and you view this as a fair wage and an appropriate consequence for your efforts. Say that two months ago Mr. Brown began paying $6.00 for the same lawn cutting, and you have received this consequence on four occasions since that time. If Mr. Brown now again offers you $3.50, you may view this formerly positive consequence as negative in the light of your current level of pay, and in fact this lower figure might be viewed by you as a punishment. Your cognitive set now is that $6.00 is an appropriate pay for your performance, and $3.50 might be viewed as signifying a poor job. Thus, the way that you cognitively view the financial consequence is the important determiner of its reinforcing properties.

The harsh words of a father when his son spills the paint are only a negative consequence in that they provoke unpleasant cognitions within the child ("My daddy doesn't love me," "He won't let me work with him again") or physiological responses (stomach tightness, rapid breathing, a slight feeling of nausea, or any of any number of possible physical sensations that we might label "anxiety"). In a very real sense the BCA only has control of extrinsic events. He can provide or remove some material consequences or employ an array of verbal and nonverbal communications as a means of altering some targeted event, but the success of all these communication attempts depends upon the manner in which they are construed by the client.

Perhaps the real value of taking a complete case history, of developing rapport within a positive relationship, and in carefully evaluating the kinds of verbal and nonverbal communications that a client emits (Kiesler and Bernstein, 1975) is in understanding the way that a client labels those events that may come to control his behavior.

In summary, the covert cognitive and physiological responses that we experience are important potential controllers of our behavior and even of the way we identify emotional states. Any evaluation of extrinsic incentives that seem to control some targeted client behavior must be augmented by an evaluation of the way in which the client cognitively construes the incentive. Chapter 5 will show how positive and negative imagery (or coverants; Homme, 1965) have been employed to increase or decrease the frequency of both overt and covert events, such as deviant sexual fantasies and overt sexual behaviors (e.g., Ashem and Donner, 1966; Davison, 1968). Chapter 9 will illustrate the importance of cognitive expectations upon the outcome of therapy aimed at reducing phobic behaviors (e.g., Valins and Ray, 1967; Borkovec, 1973). In fact, because of the increasing use of change procedures directed at covert behaviors (e.g., Goldfried and Merbaum, 1973; Mahoney, 1974), all discussions of behavioral change procedures will include relevant recent "covert" literature.

SETTING SPECIFIC FACTORS

The setting within which a client's behavior occurs (for example, bedroom, office, operating machinery at work, driving an automobile) may exert control upon possibilities for an increase or decrease in its frequency. These controls may relate to the physical constraints of the setting as well as to the physical constraints of the setting as well as to client's previous learning experiences within it. Each class of setting controls will be discussed separately.

Physical constraints

It is most important that the physical characteristics of the setting facilitate desirable targeted behaviors and do not restrict or interfere with their occurrence. Let us imagine attempting to increase the frequency of social interactions of a group of four socially withdrawn five-year-olds during a daily recreational period. In observing them through a one-way mirror, we find that the frequency of physical interactions is about three each hour, and talk interactions are about one per hour. Before developing a treatment plan, we decide to examine the characteristics of the physical setting. The toys and play equipment in the setting are mostly geared toward individual effort (two cannot participate), thus decreasing possibilities for social exchange when they are used. The room itself is large, measuring 30 by 20 feet, making close interaction by chance unlikely and social withdrawal most easy. Thus, two characteristics of our setting do not favor our behavioral goals and in fact favor independent, withdrawn behavior incompatible with our goals.

To determine the effects of manipulating the setting upon social interaction behavior, we place the four children in a much smaller room (15 by 15), to increase the likelihood of physical interaction and thus (we hope) verbal interaction. This is based upon the premise that children must be in close physical proximity before speaking is likely. We also remove all "independently operated" toys and equipment and provide only items requiring at least two to play (e.g., a small seesaw, pushcart, etc.). A noteworthy increase in their physical interactions (the average equaled 13 per hour) and an immediate increase in talk interactions (6 per hour) is observed. Thus, we have provided support for our supposition that the physical setting was exerting a controlling influence upon the probability that the targeted behavior would occur. In fact, it was possible to manipulate the setting to promote behavior change in the desired direction.

As another example, disruptive classroom behavior may be influenced not only by the poor quality of teacher communications to her class, but also by the distracting panoramic view of the playground, interfering noise from the gym next door, or the fact that certain desks are placed so that it is difficult to see or even hear the teacher's presentation. In some cases the setting restricts the opportunities of staff members to observe a behavior (as when a nurses' station is located 60 feet from the clients' lounge) or to carry out treatment plans.

The BCA must carefully evaluate the physical parameters of any setting that is the focus of treatment so that setting constraints may be reduced or eliminated and that treatment makes best use of setting facilitators. In summary, the BCA must ask, "How can I arrange a setting or make use of an existing setting to increase the likelihood of achieving my behavioral goals?"

Stimulus control

Stimuli that are present when an individual is reinforced for some behavior may come to elicit the behavior. For example, many investigators seeking to assist obese persons to lose weight find that many stimuli within the home (e.g., watching TV, reading a magazine, talking on the telephone) have become cues for eating, because previous eating (a pleasurable activity) has occurred in their presence (Stuart and Davis, 1972; Ferster, Nurnberger, and Levitt, 1962). These situational cues may thus prompt the individual to reach for a bag of pretzels or a piece of chocolate cake. The goal of the therapist is to limit the number of stimuli that come to control the behavior (and thus reinforcement for the client) by curtailing situations within which the behavior is permitted. For example, obese clients might be asked to eat only at the kitchen table so that the controlling properties of TV watching, reading, and so on gradually extinguish due to a lack of reinforcement (eating) in their presence. Chapter 9 will present an array of treatment options that attempt to employ stimulus control to facilitate client self-control of targeted events.

MODEL-RELATED FACTORS

Many investigators have shown that *a wide variety of behaviors might be learned by an observer who watches some model engage in the behavior* (e.g., Bandura, 1969; Kanfer and Phillips, 1970). Research has shown that for modeling to occur, an observer must *actively attend* to the behavior of some model (Bandura, 1969). A variety of observer as well as model characteristics such as age, intelligence, dependency, level of status, and power may affect the probability that an observer (O) will imitate some model (M). Chapter 6 discusses each of these important components of modeling as well as ways in which models may be used to promote behavioral change.

Not only may O imitate the behavior of M, but O might also experience an emotion that M displays merely by observing M. Such vicarious induction of emotional states has been studied by many investigators (e.g., Berger, 1968) and serves as the basis for therapeutic procedures that incorporate modeling (e.g., Bandura, Grusic, and Menlove, 1965; Bandura, Blanchard, and Ritter, 1969). Because of the importance of models in promoting and maintaining such a myriad of social and emotional behaviors, it is most important that possible model influences be evaluated in assessing factors that control a client's behavior. In many cases a careful evaluation of model influences may suggest a treatment strategy that includes a reeducation of the inappropriate model as well as the client. As an example, imagine a parent who repeatedly tells his five-year-old son, "Stop hitting your sister," but then spanks or slaps his son for engaging in the hitting. If we assume that the parent is an important model for the son's behavior, the paradox in the parent's approach is obvious. While providing information that basically says, "It's wrong to hit your sister, do *not* hit," the parent concomitantly *models* this very behavior by physically punishing the son. Perhaps the communication of this paradoxical modeling to the son is: "When you want somebody to do something, you hit them and yell loudly." The oft-told example of a parent who tells his child, "Smoking causes lung cancer, so don't smoke," between puffs on a cigarette further illustrates how modeled behaviors may be as important (or more so!) than verbal instructions as controllers of behavior.

Within the institutional setting the BCA must carefully evaluate potential models of influence to the client. While such models may well display behaviors in opposition to treatment goals, they may be trained to model behaviors that promote desired behavioral change. Models might be other clients. For example, it would make little sense to provide praise and other positive reinforcement for reduced consumption of food for an obese client if the client is permitted to eat in the presence of other clients who typically consume great quantities of food. Perhaps until the client alters his eating habits within a setting where such facilitating models are not present, exposure to this group of "energetic" eaters should not be permitted.

It is interesting to consider that many institutions segregate clients with certain problem behaviors because of convenience to staff members providing supervision and care. Thus, a group of hyperactive, retarded children might be separated from the ordinary classroom setting because of their disruptive influence and placed together in another class setting. Or a group of very aggressive delinquents might be segregated from more appropriate peer models because of their disruptive and destructive impact upon less aggressive members of a living cottage. In ordinary academic programs students exhibiting behavior-management problems are often separated from other class members within "special" classes. While this may be justifiable on many grounds (e.g., makes behavioral control easier, allows for specialized training, reduces disruptive effects of the clients upon others) such procedures certainly limit client exposure to appropriate models. In fact such homogeneous groupings increase the likelihood that inappropriate behaviors will be modeled and supported by other clients exhibiting similar behaviors. Such segregation drastically limits the array of social and other behaviors that each member may be exposed to. Regardless of the treatment applied to such a homogeny of "problem" clients, the BCA is necessarily working against the negative effects of the grouping.

There is little data to suggest how particular problem behavior clients might optimally be grouped for most effective treatment. It does seem likely, however, that more heterogeneous groupings increase the array of models exhibiting appropriate behaviors as well as providing more appropriate groups of potentially reinforcing agents. The BCA may very well be faced with constructing a change program for such homogeneously grouped clients, or may be obligated to segregate certain clients for the protection of other clients as well as staff. The problems of negative models and inappropriate peer agents of reinforcement just discussed should be weighed against the gains inherent in such homogeneous groupings.

CHAPTER SUMMARY

Efforts at behavioral change may be directed at *increasing the frequency* of some behavior that the client currently exhibits; at *incorporating some new behavior* within a client's repertoire; or at *reducing the frequency* of some problematic behavior that must already exist within the client's behavioral possibilities. To effect one or more of these goals with a given client, a complete analysis of those variables that control a client's behavior must be undertaken by the BCA. These controlling variables include the following:

Client resources. "Resources" was defined broadly to include the cognitive and physical capabilities of a client as well as the client's interests. It was suggested that the BCA tailor therapeutic goals very specifically to such resources.

Previous experience. While past history is not the primary focus of a phenomenal-behavioral approach, it was suggested that it provides the BCA with clues as to the *current strength* of the target; information as to the client's *previous successful and unsuccessful approaches* to dealing with the behavior; *incentives* that have motivated the client in the past and that may currently be employed as consequences; as well as important *elicitors* of the behavior (e.g., specific persons, situations, times, bodily states).

Extrinsic incentives. Positive and negative consequences within the environment may come to control client behavior. Based upon the "operant" model of B. F. Skinner, "extrinsic" approaches attempt to systematically increase or decrease the probability of some behavior from its "operant" level (pretreatment frequency). An *event that follows some behavior is viewed as a positive reinforcer if it increases the probability of that behavior occurring at some future time. Negative reinforcement involves the removal of punishing consequences contingent upon some desired behavior. Punishment is any event that follows some behavior that decreases the probability of that behavior at some future time.*

Material consequences include tangible objects that hold incentive properties for clients, such as food, cosmetic and health items, money, and so on. A *generalized reinforcer* is a material consequence that may be traded for an array of desirable "backup" material/activity/social consequences of the client's choosing. Among *social consequences,* verbal as well as nonverbal behaviors are included, and are described as reinforcers based upon their effect upon behavior.

One means of increasing the frequency of an event is to reinforce some approximation of it, then sequentially reward successive approximations until the client emits the desired behavior. This procedure has been called *shaping* or *successive approximations.* The client must first exhibit the event, and often such behavior is instigated via appropriate models, verbal prompts, or other cueing methods. While reinforcements might be delivered following each instance of some targeted behavior *(continuous schedule),* particularly with infrahuman species a *partial schedule* of reinforcement (reinforcement after particular responses or times) may produce behavior that is more resistant to *extinction* (elimination of reinforcement). It was strongly suggested that the effects of schedules upon human behavior might be very different from the effect upon animal populations, due to the cognitive capabilities of the human organism.

Another category of learning has to do with the manner in which stimuli within our environment become associated with involuntary responses. An *unconditioned stimulus* (UCS), such as a mild shock delivered to the forearm, reliably elicits an involuntary or *unconditioned response* on the part of recipitent (UCR). A previously neutral stimulus that is associated with a UCS may come to elicit a response similar to the original UCR; this stimulus is a *conditioned stimulus* (CS), and the phenomenon has been called *classical conditioning, respondent conditioning,* or *Pavlovian conditioning.*

Stimuli that are similar to the CS may also come to elicit the CR; this process is called *stimulus generalization*. When the organism elicits responses similar to the CR in response to the CS, we would call this *response generalization*. An array of UCRs have been conditioned to neutral stimuli among human subjects.

Following a review of the importance of cognitive labels that identify emotional states, a model for describing the development of standard setting and self-reinforcement was presented. Such intrinsic phenomena as self-instructions and self-mediated reward and punishment may come to exert important controls over a client's behavior. Examples of *self-reinforcement* were provided, and it was emphasized that the reinforcing properties of any external consequence are dependent upon the manner in which the client cognitively views that consequence. It was suggested that such self-mediated consequences might be useful within treatment.

Because the *setting* within which the client functions may provide important *constraints* to his behavior (e.g., size, noise, distractions), the BCA should carefully evaluate and perhaps modify the setting in line with treatment goals. Also, stimuli that are present when an individual is reinforced for some behavior may come to elicit the behavior (stimulus control). Often, clients are required to narrow or limit the stimuli that control certain behaviors or to enhance learning by facilitating stimulus control on the part of consistently present environmental objects or events.

Finally, the manner in which an *observer* (O) comes to imitate the behavior of some model (M) may explain the development and maintenance of certain client behaviors, and appropriate pro-social models may be employed to facilitate desirable behavioral change.

Chapter 3

Control by Manipulation of Consequences

Often client reports, staff reports, and behavioral observations reveal behaviors that might best be described as negative or problem behaviors. Of course, the goal of any treatment is to decrease the frequency of targeted negative or problem behaviors while correspondingly increasinging more appropriate behaviors on the client's part. It is important that each targeted behavior be carefully defined. Behaviors vaguely described as "being disrespectful," "poor attitude," or "poor self-concept" may have meaning for the BCA but not for the client or for staff members asked to observe and systematically manipulate the behavior. Thus, while it is rather difficult to evaluate any change in patient A's "self-concept," it may be possible to observe and systematically treat the client's negative self-statements; rate of interaction with peers; the client's general appearance and self-care skills, as well as other specific behavioral events that make up this label we call "poor self-concept." Thus, the goal of treatment becomes one of constructing a treatment plan for as many specific behavioral events as are relevant to the client's needs.

One way of planning intervention is to focus exclusively upon problem targeted behaviors in an attempt to decrease the frequency of each of them. *A much different and more preferable approach is to attempt to increase the frequency of behaviors that are incompatible with each of the targeted problem be-*

haviors. An incompatible event or behavior is one that, when it occurs, does not allow the targeted problem behavior to occur. In the classroom situation, for example, sitting at one's desk and giving full attention to the teacher would be incompatible with looking out the window at other classmates in the playground area or playing with one's hands. Raising one's hand as a signal that a student wishes to be recognized is incompatible with "blurting out." Carefully identifying specifically what is liked about a child's performance would be incompatible with a parent's use of vague shrugs or nods. Thus, when a client emits an incompatible behavior, the targeted problem implicitly cannot occur.

In fact, most cases cited within the literature employ some combination of positive and negative approaches to behavioral management. Positive reinforcement is often directed at increasing the probability of some appropriate behavior, while negative control is directed at decreasing the frequency of the targeted problem behavior. This chapter emphasizes the individual client, while Chapter 4 is directed toward groupings of clients within institutional settings.

Five categories of consequation procedures will be discussed: *Extinction; DRO (differential reinforcement of other behavior) procedures; response cost; time out from reinforcement; and approaches to physical punishment.* We will begin our discussion by presenting commonly employed methods for defining such consequences.

DEFINING CONSEQUENCES

Verbal Reports

One obvious way to define consequences that might be useful in treatment is to ask the client. Although verbal information is all too frequently gathered unsystematically, it is nevertheless extremely useful. Information is usually best gathered by asking the client *structured questions* that systematically cover each important category of consequences. Nay (1974) reported the following approach to verbal reports in defining possible consequences for a population of 110 delinquent adolescents:

Sixty girls randomly selected from the population at large met in small groups. A group mediator (consultant) structured this interview to assess possible reinforcers within the following general areas:
  1. Privileges. Students were asked which current privileges they valued most and what privileges they would like to see instituted at some future time.
  ˙2. Activities. An assessment of desired current on-campus and off-campus activities was carried out. Students again were encouraged to suggest novel activities for possible future addition.
  3. Material items. Within this area, group mediators assessed valued items by name brand within each of these areas: food/snack items; recreational/game items; cosmetic/dress items; any others offered by group members.

Group mediators surveyed each of the five girls within the group for their suggestions. (p. 211)

It is important to remember that the usefulness of information about consequences obtained from a verbal report is limited by the comprehensiveness of questions asked of the client population.

Behavioral Observations

Observational procedures can be used to determine *high rate behaviors* that the client(s) engage in. The assumption is made that such behaviors/activities—unless, of course, some controls are exerted—may reveal events that might hold incentive value. Thus, while a depressed client may not be able to tell you verbally about material objects, activities, and privileges that he values, careful observation may reveal that he spends more than half of his waking hours watching television, reading magazines, or looking out the window. Assuming that human behavior is purposeful, these activities may hold incentive properties for that client and may be usefully employed as consequences within a treatment plan. When working with children or adolescents, a verbal interview may produce a dearth of information about events that hold reinforcing properties. Questions like "What kinds of activities do you enjoy?" may often lead to a response of "I don't know," or general statements "Playing outside," which may be difficult to interpret. This is often true of adults, too, probably because most of us are not very good observers of the kinds of things that we do. The author has often heard from institutional staff that client X "doesn't enjoy anything" or that "there are no incentives which work with him." Such statements are often made because staff members have found that commonly valued consequences such as cigarettes, food items, and monetary rewards are not of value to the particular client. Systematic observations of the client may in fact reveal many activities that are consistently engaged in over time. Such activities may indeed hold value as consequences within a treatment plan.

An example of the importance of careful observation in defining possible consequences in treatment is the following case example from this author's experiences. A teacher of 15 educable retarded adolescents reported experiencing considerable difficulty in controlling her class. Students were sent to the principal's office on a regular basis for "offenses" including acts of verbal and physical aggression, out of seat and leaving the room without permission, as well as destruction of classroom materials. To say the least, students were not attending to classroom tasks a large proportion of the time. Both the teacher and principal had previously used a large variety of verbal threats, suspensions from school, isolation in a room adjoining the principal's office, as well as threats of parental reprimand to try to bring the class under some measure of control. Following a severe crisis in which all fifteen students left the class and proceeded to leave the school grounds, a BCA was called in to offer consultation services. The BCA began his task using the independent observational procedures which were previously described in Chapter 4, performing event and time sampling within the classroom for the period of three hours on each of ten consecutive days. Following these rather elaborate observations, the BCA met with the principal, the teacher, and the school counselor to present his information and to discuss possibilities for treatment. While all school personnel could very readily describe and document instances of targeted problem behaviors, they each reported that the students "would not respond to anything." In fact, the teacher had attempted to employ what she considered "behavior modification" in using candy and gum for in seat behavior. She reported that her attempt was successful for a brief period of one or two days; however, these food items did not succeed in maintaining the changes observed. The teacher reported that she felt guilty about using "bribes" with her class, and at this point felt that nothing would work. After explaining that behavior modification was something more than providing food or snack items for appropriate behavior, the BCA proceeded to present in detail his observations as to activities that occurred within the classroom setting. He explained how self-chosen activities, ordinarily available, might be used as incentives for appropriate classroom behavior. For each activity he observed, he also included a brief description of the frequency of that behavior over the period of time that he had observed.

The following activities each were shown to have value to at least one or two class members because of either their high frequency, student self-selection or student statements about their value. These behaviors included: cleaning the blackboards (five or more times per day); operating a movie or slide projector (one to two times per week); maintaining a fishbowl within the class (two to three times per day); handing out classroom supplies (five or more times per day); collecting papers (five or more times per day); taking materials to the principal's office and elsewhere within the school (two to three times per day); handing out milk and snack items (once per day); cleaning desk tops (once per day); being first in line (two to three times per day); choice of seating within the cafeteria (once per day); choice of seating within the classroom (students frequently reported the desire for this); playing with a tape recorder (two to three times per day); equipment monitor for recreations (once per day); distributor of reading texts and other textbook materials (five or more times per day); being first to present in "show and tell" (once per day); distribution of student newspapers (once per day); first in line for bathroom (twice per day); distributor of art supplies and music supplies (two to three times per week); "leaders" in mathematics contests, spelling bees, geography run-offs and other classroom competitions with educational importance (five or more times per week); bulletin board monitor (once each day); as well as many other classroom events.

Thus, within a classroom where staff members reported that students "responded to nothing," the BCA was able to determine well over 25 activities that held incentive properties for one or more children within the class.

If the students had been *asked* to define the sorts of things that they enjoyed within the classroom, it is probable that few of these activities would have been described. Only through careful behavioral observations can such information be obtained.

Written Reinforcement Surveys

Another way to obtain information from clients about incentives is to present them with a written questionnaire. Although such questionnaires vary in format, most include a list of material objects, activities, privileges, positive self-statements, scenes, or other events of interest to the assessor, and the respondent is asked to endorse those items that he most highly values in some way (Kleinknecht, McCormick, and Thorndike, 1973). Some formats use the forced-choice technique, in which the respondent is asked to choose between two possible incentives. Others present each incentive and ask clients to rate on a Likert-type scale (e.g., 1–5) the attractiveness of each item. Sometimes respondents are given the opportunity to provide open-ended responses about each event category following their written endorsement of items. Unfortunately, few reinforcement surveys that are used within the literature are published intact. In fact, most investigators develop their own written surveys, which often present highly idiosyncratic questions to some specific population of interest.

Standard procedures are generally employed in constructing such surveys. First verbal interviews are often conducted with clients to determine possible incentives of value. Questions are asked within content areas as was previously described. Items that are frequently endorsed in the interviews are included within the survey, often within item categories. Usually some agreed-upon cutoff is used to establish inclusions of items (e.g., 75 percent or more of the clients reported interest). The items are then described within the survey, and some system is devised for the respondent to endorse his preferences. Although simple yes or no responses are often used, some system that enables the respondent to place a numerical rating on each item is probably superior. Thus, comparisons can be made within and across item categories, and an overall numerical score can be obtained. This system enables the BCA to establish mean numerical scores for each item and numerical means within item categories (e.g., for snacks, cosmetic items, off-campus versus on-campus items, intrinsic versus extrinsic items).

There are a number of considerations to keep in mind in constructing such a survey. First, items should be easily read and understood by the population of interest. With younger children or specialized populations such as retarded or blind people, items may be presented on audio tape or

verbally and subjects may make verbal responses. It is particularly important that the language match the level of verbal skills of the population of
interest. The questionnaire should present items within categories, which
might include: foods; snacks; cosmetics; health and personal-care items;
handicrafts; reading materials; indoor activities; outdoor activities;
privileges; games; positive imagery; negative imagery; and so on. By presenting items within categories the reader is given a consistent set within
which to discriminate among items.

Instructions should encourage the respondents to respond to the questionnaire freely, not limited by existing regulations or traditions. *Whatever
kind of rating system is employed, careful attention should be given to providing
descriptive examples of what each numerical rating means: 1= do not like, probably
would never seek out; 5 = enjoy very much, would seek out compared to most other
activities.*

An example of a reinforcement survey is presented in Appendix A.
Notice how this survey, geared to a psychiatric population, meets the
criteria previously described.

One popular written survey is the Reinforcement Survey Schedule
(RSS) developed by Cautela and Kastenbaum (1967), found to be reliable
over one to five weeks following initial administration (Kleinknecht et al.,
1973). While items are typically included in surveys based solely upon the
BCA's speculations (face validity), Thorndike and Kleinknecht (1974)
statistically evaluated the RSS and found 13 separate clusters or
categories of items (e.g., "sports"). This kind of research (replicated
across diverse client groupings) may ultimately assist the survey construc-
tor in choosing items representative of all relevant classes of reinforcers.

In summary, the written reinforcement survey is an efficient, eco-
nomical, and speedy means of collecting important information about
possible positive consequences. Surveys can be followed up by written
interviews of clients for further information or may be augmented by
careful and systematic behavioral observations. Perhaps the greatest
value of the written survey approach is that it provides the subject with a
clear set for responding, allows for more specific comparisons among
reinforcement items, and provides a format for the translation of responses
to numerical scores.

IMPORTANT ISSUES REGARDING INCENTIVES

After a systematic assessment of possible consequences that may be
used in treatment, the BCA must decide which of those desired items to
employ. Although many items may hold incentive properties for the
client(s), a consequence must meet certain criteria before it can be useful
within treatment. Although these criteria are rarely specifically stated,

most investigators implicitly evaluate incentives in terms of four factors:

Practicality and Availability

While cigarettes might be highly popular among delinquent females, it may be impractical to use cigarettes because of laws that limit the availability of tobacco products to those above the age of 16. Cigarettes may also be impractical if there are not sufficient funds to purchase cigarettes to be used as consequences. Another example is the impracticality of requiring parents of limited social skills and vocabulary to employ highly communicative positive statements as reinforcement for appropriate child behavior. The author can remember one program that was terminated abruptly when administrators ran out of sufficient funds to maintain a token store. Thus, any consequence must be practically suited to the particular setting in which clients function.

Also, a consequence must be immediately available for dispensing to clients who emit some desirable targeted behavior. Sole reliance on food as positive consequences within a treatment program may provide a minor upset for a deserving client when foods are not available on the athletic field or in other settings within the institution. Although it may be desirable to ask a teacher to frequently praise *each* student in her class for some appropriate on-task classroom behavior, it may be impractical for the teacher to meet both the academic and program needs of some 30 students within a classroom setting. It may be impossible for her to provide such consequences in a consistent fashion. Thus, the choice of consequences must be limited by the practical possibilities of the setting. The BCA may want to consider planning for backup and alternative consequences when items initially chosen are depleted or become impractical. Of course, proper planning in defining incentives decreases this possibility.

Consonance with Treatment Goals

A consequence should not contradict the goals of the treatment plan. Although cigarettes may be very reinforcing for a smoker, they would not be the consequence of choice when nonsmoking was the goal of treatment. Food, of course, would be an inappropriate consequence to reinforce avoidance of eating. Whenever possible, a consequence should promote behavior consonant with treatment goals. For example, consequences involving social interaction, visits and trips into the community, games that provide social interaction, books, handicraft kits, and arts and crafts items are among possible consequences that might be facilitative of adaptive pro-social and/or task-related behaviors among institutionalized youngsters. In their haste to define consequences, treatment planners often do not evaluate the possible treatment value of projected consequences.

Intrinsic to Setting

Many investigators have suggested that only those items that naturally occur in a setting be used as consequences (Kazdin and Bootzin, 1972). Materials and activity/privilege items that may be currently administered in a noncontingent fashion may in fact have incentive value and may be useful as consequences within treatment. One approach is to systematically observe clients and define those behaviors/activities that occur at a high rate, given client freedom of behavior. According to Premack (1965) these high-rate events (HR) may be employed to contingently reinforce treated low-rate behaviors (LR), even if the HR events don't have obvious reinforcing qualities. Thus, a depressed patient may be required to speak to other persons once each hour (LR event) in order to earn time alone (HR event). This "Premack Principle" has been increasingly employed in clinical settings (see Danaher's review of the literature, 1974), particularly as a means of controlling certain "covert" events (see Chapter 5).

The major justification for attempting to define naturally occurring incentives is so that as treatment mechanisms are systematically faded out, those incentives that have begun to maintain a client's behavior remain and may promote transfer of newly learned behavior to nonprogrammed conditions. Also naturally occurring consequences are often more practical and are readily available within the setting. Naturally occurring incentives have already demonstrated their value to motivate clients.

Adaptation

The effectiveness of a consequence should not decrease over time. Foods and certain leisure activities (games, trinkets, craft items) are among items that may become less valuable to clients as they become more familiar. The old saw that "familiarity breeds contempt" may well apply to many consequences chosen for treatment. Although the program designer cannot know for certain which consequences will maintain their value, emphasis upon naturally occurring incentives that have previously demonstrated their incentive value over time may reduce the possibility of adaptation effects. Careful records of client self-selection of incentives should be kept to evaluate potential adaptation effects.

APPROACHES TO CONSEQUATION

In describing the ways that positive and negative consequences might be applied within a treatment program, many authors have reviewed such approaches for specific client populations such as the retarded, psychotic, or delinquent (Yates, 1969; Ulrich, Stachnick, and Mabry, 1970, 1974).

Certainly, careful specification of client needs must be made prior to any specification of treatment. Most of the treatment procedures to be discussed have been applied across an array of client populations, although the specific nature of application may vary somewhat depending upon such client variables as IQ, socioeconomic level, age, and previous history. In presenting each area of application, examples will be drawn from numerous client populations. Thus, the focus for discussion will be upon specific treatment approaches, not upon the interaction of approaches with specific client populations. Once specific targeted behaviors have been chosen, the range of approaches for accomplishing behavioral change vary from strict reliance on punishment to decrease inappropriate targeted behaviors to total reliance on positive consequences to increase appropriate behaviors. Most treatment plans include some combination of these techniques, and approaches will be presented in order of increasing use of punishment as a means of decreasing problem targets. Because of important practical as well as ethical issues that are suggested by the use of punishing agents, an extensive discussion will be included. Use of covert events as consequences is presented in Chapter 5.

Extinction

As the reader will recall from Chapter 2, extinction of a targeted behavior may be brought about by terminating all reinforcement for that behavior. Although we typically see a gradual and systematic reduction in responding when we extinguish the pecking response of a pigeon or other laboratory animal, it is difficult to apply a pure extinction approach to decreasing some human behavior. To extinguish, the treatment agent must remove all possible sources of reinforcement for the targeted problem behavior. Often this becomes extremely difficult or impossible, because any one of an array of material, social, or intrinsic consequences might maintain the behavior. Even if a delineation of reinforcers were possible, it may be difficult or impossible to control all avenues of reinforcement. For example, Becker, Madsen, Arnold, and Thomas (1967) found that when a classroom teacher systematically ignored inappropriate behaviors on the basis that her attention was maintaining these behaviors, there was an increase in these behaviors. The authors surmised that peer reinforcement maintained many of the targets. Thus, an extinction approach is successful only if all avenues of reinforcement are terminated. Although some authors have reported the successful use of extinction, usually as a beginning point in a treatment program (Ayllon and Michael, 1959; Ayllon and Haughton, 1962), there are a number of problems attendant in using a pure extinction approach (Kanfer and Phillips, 1970).

1. It may be impossible to identify and remove all reinforcementmaintaining problematic behavior. Subtle social cues or intrinsic reinforcements may be impossible to define by observation.

2. Extinction requires complete environmental control. Even though a parent is trained to systematically ignore her son's whining and attention-getting behavior, other adults and his peers may provide attention for such behavior. It may be difficult or impossible to gain sufficient control of all of the social agents that the client interacts with daily. In extinguishing delusional speech on the part of a psychiatric resident, the treatment agent might have to train a large number of nurses, aides, other patients, and relatives to systematically ignore the client's verbal outbursts. The only alternative to such control is to limit the client's social interaction in some fashion until extinction of the behavior is completed, then systematically reintegrate the client into the more frequent interactions of the ward setting.

3. Because extinction provokes an initial sharp increment in problem behavior, and because its effects in decreasing the frequency of behavior may take a rather long time, staff members, parents, and other agents of treatment may not be willing to go alone with this method. In a sense the BCA may be asking the treatment agents to "put up with" the client's deviant behavior for some long period of time, with "no end in sight."

4. Practical and ethical considerations preclude the use of extinction for certain targeted behaviors. It is obvious that suicidal acts of self-destruction, the self-mutilation seen within many psychotic and autistic children, or behavior that is destructive to others or to the environment are among behaviors that cannot be permitted to occur without controls. Such behaviors must be dealt with using procedures that provoke a rapid change in frequency (e.g. Lovaas, 1967).

5. Extinction does not ensure that more appropriate behaviors will take the place of those extinguished. Because no systematic approach is employed to increase the probability of incompatible and appropriate behavior, a client may employ a more deviant problematic behavior in place of the extinguished target. If the client is not provided with a clearly defined, alternative means of gaining reinforcement, extinction leaves this endeavor to chance. If the therapist views human behavior as exhibiting lawful properties, it makes good sense that merely extinguishing some problem behavior does not provide for the reinforcement needs of the client. Also the array of variables that have come to provoke the problematic behavior, such as a lack of parental verbal and nonverbal affection or deficient tangible reinforcers for client appropriate behavior, have not been dealt with using this approach.

Differential Reinforcement of Other Behavior (DRO)

This approach augments the pure extinction approach in that appropriate and incompatible behaviors are systematically reinforced while targeted problematic events are ignored to extinguish them. This approach has been used much more frequently within the literature than the pure extinction approach and overcomes many of the criticisms directed at extinction. An early investigation by Allen, Hart, Buell, Harris, and Wolf (1964) provides an excellent example of DRO.

A four year old girl was found to spend most of her time with teachers in a nursery school setting. The child engaged in a variety of behaviors to attract the teachers' attention and rarely interacted with other children of similar age. A time sampling observational system showed that the child spent about 40 percent of her time with adults while spending only 10 percent with children over a five day baseline period. Assuming that the child's teachers were the sole agents of reinforcement for her "isolated" behavior, the BCA instructed the child's teachers to provide immediate attention to the child whenever she interacted with other children. For example, the teacher might go over and sit down with the child within the play group. Whenever the child was seen to be alone or interacting solely with adults, the teachers were instructed to ignore her behavior. Thus pro-social behavior was systematically reinforced using teacher social reinforcement, while isolated and dependent behavior was systematically extinguished. During a five day period while these contingencies were in effect, the child's interaction with peers increased to 60 percent of the time while adult contact consisted of only 20 percent of the time. Reversal of the contingencies (e.g., teachers behave in pre-treatment fashion) produced an increase in isolate behavior, suggesting that the DRO program was responsible for the increase in social interaction. DRO was resumed and follow-up checks at 13, 15 and 26 days following termination of treatment revealed the child was still interacting at a high rate with her peers.

Twardosz and Sajwaj (1972) used a similar procedure to increase sitting behavior in a four-year-old retarded boy. The child's teacher was instructed to place one or more toys on his table and whenever the child sat down to provide tokens that could later be exchanged for candy and trinkets. Social reinforcement in the form of verbal praise was also provided for in-seat behavior. If the child left his seat, the teacher was instructed to ignore him until he began to approach the table. Then she was instructed to take him by the hand, praise him for returning, and to provide consequences as before. The child's sitting behavior rose from a frequency of 0 percent at baseline to 62.5 percent following the implementation of treatment. As in the previous study, Twardosz and Sajwaj presumed that the teacher was the primary source of reinforcement and that her ignoring of the child's out-of-seat behavior provided sufficient control for extinction to take place. Similar DRO procedures have been successfully employed, typically in the classroom setting (e.g., Ward and Baker, 1968; Buell, Stoddard, Harris, and Baer, 1968; Brown and Elliot, 1965; Brooks and Snow, 1972). An excellent example of defining DRO procedures for staff members is provided by Madsen, Becker, and Thomas (1968), who presented the following to teachers:

Teachers are inclined to take good behavior for granted and pay attention only when a child acts up or misbehaves. We are now asking you to try something different. This procedure is characterized as "catching the child being good" and making a comment designed to reward the child for good behavior. Give praise, attention, or smile when the child is doing what is expected during the particular class period in question. Inappropriate Behavior would not be a problem if all children were engaging in a great deal of study and school behavior, therefore, it is necessary to apply what you have learned in the workshop. Shape by successive approximations the behavior desired by using praise and attention. Start "small" by giving praise and attention at the first signs of Appropriate Behavior and work toward greater goals. Pay close attention to those children who normally engage in a great deal of misbehavior. Watch carefully and when the child begins to behave appropriately, make a comment such as, "You're doing a fine job, (name)." (p. 145).

The teachers were also instructed to ignore deviant behavior and to repeat the rules of the classroom several times a day. As in previous studies, the authors found that merely providing rules for appropriate behavior or rules plus pure extinction for inappropriate behavior did not produce a significant decrease in problem behavior. When rules plus praise and extinction (DRO) were employed, problem behavior dropped very low compared with baseline.

Note again the importance placed by the authors on the teacher as a source of reinforcement. Most of the studies that incorporate a DRO approach are applied to young children for whom the teacher is no doubt an important source of reinforcement. But what of the situation where the staff member is not the primary source of reinforcement, where peers and other intrinsic incentives provide reinforcement for problem behaviors? In this situation the DRO approach will not be effective unless all sources of reinforcement for the problem behavior are terminated. Thus, merely asking a staff person to "ignore inappropriate behavior" may not provoke extinction if that agent is not the primary source of reinforcement for the targeted behaviors. Unfortunately, many educators are trained to ignore all deviant behavior and to selectively reinforce appropriate behavior, regardless of the locus of reinforcement.

O'Leary, Becker, Evans, and Saudargas (1969) found that DRO in combination with rules and classroom structure did not provoke a significant decrement in targeted problem behaviors. Only when a token program was incorporated did these behaviors decrease. Legum and Nay (1973) report on a teacher who was unsuccessfully using a variety of approaches including DRO to attempt to manage a classroom of educable retarded adolescents. The scene of this teacher "ignoring all deviant behavior" while students ran madly around the room, hung out of the windows, threw wads of paper at one another, and shouted obscenities suggests the real limitations of the DRO approach. It was apparent that attention from other peers, avoiding class work, and the reinforcement that accrues when a student is allowed to move freely were much more potent maintainers of behavior than the teacher's attention.

In delineating a list of guidelines for dealing with inappropriate child behavior, Becker, Thomas, and Carnine (1971) state: "Ignore disruptive behaviors unless someone is getting hurt. Focus your attention on the children who are working well to prompt the correct behaviors in the children who are misbehaving. Reinforce improvement when it does occur" (p. 162). Regarding negative consequences they state: "Punishment is most likely to be required when the unwanted behavior is very intense (so that there is a potential danger to self or others) or very frequent so that there is little, positive behavior to work with" (p. 163). Thus, the authors qualify the use of the DRO approach by suggesting that some form of punishment for inappropriate behavior be combined with praise when "ignoring" does not seem to be an effective approach.

In summary, DRO has the advantage of systematically reinforcing appropriate incompatible behavior while concomitantly decreasing the frequency of inappropriate targeted behavior, *when the BCA can control the locus of reinforcement.*

Response Cost

In both extinction and DRO procedures inappropriate behavior is not followed by any systematic response from the environment. It is hoped that a lack of environmental response will result in an extinction of such behavior. As was pointed out, procedures that incorporate extinction will be successful only when the BCA has control of all reinforcers maintaining the inappropriate behavior. In many, if not most cases, the BCA does not have such control and must use some form of negative consequence. Of course, negative feedback is best employed in combination with procedures for positively reinforcing incompatible and appropriate behavior. The classic negative response to some problem behavior is the use of physical punishment, in the form of slaps or hits, or verbal punishment, in the form of threats, criticisms, and other negative statements directed toward the individual. Most of us have been physically punished at one time or another in our lives. A later section defines in detail some of the problems and limitations in using verbal or physical punishment as a means of decreasing some inappropriate behavior. There are, however, alternatives to verbal or physical punishment as a means of providing negative feedback for some inappropriate behavior.

Sherman and Baer (1969) have defined two kinds of punishment contingencies: response cost and punishment. Response cost is defined as a client's loss of some positive consequence after some problem behavior. This cost may include the removal of any material, activity, or social reinforcer that holds incentive properties for the client. It is assumed that the removal of some positive stimulus will weaken the behavior that immediately precedes this cost (Sherman and Baer, 1969). Punishment, on the other hand, is defined as the introduction of some aversive stimulus immediately following the emittance of some negative targeted behavior.

Thus, a punishment is a specific event that is added to the client's situation immediately and contingently following some targeted problem behavior. Response cost and punishment, while both being viewed within the negative sphere, are thus two very different sets of events.

The notion of establishing some cost for behaviors identified as problems is not a new one. Fines have been levied for behavior that society viewed as being deviant even prior to Biblical times, and our own legal history is replete with examples of individuals "paying" for their misdeeds. Often the cost involves some monetary payment; however, societally imposed response costs have often included a person's personal property, loss of privileges (e.g., driving one's automobile), or in extreme cases even loss of children by parents who are determined to be "unfit." Response costs have been imposed upon most of us at one time or another within the home stiuation. Restricting television viewing because of poor academic grades, the loss of a toy when it is improperly used, and the loss of dessert when dinner is not eaten are common components of most parents' catalog of punishers. Adults are faced with possible costs for certain inappropriate behaviors within job and family situations. The loss of a predicted raise due to tardiness, the withholding of social and sexual favors when one spouse displeases another, or the withholding of one's social advances are all examples of response costs that might rather "naturally" be employed. Although many cost procedures are already a part of most clients' repertoire, our definition of response cost will include only those costs that are *clearly defined and systematically applied, contingent upon some client problem behavior.*

In a real sense there are as many potential costs that we could apply to some behavior as there are incentives that have value. Once we have carefully defined reinforcers useful in treatment, we have already implicitly defined a set of possible "costs." Within the literature response costs usually fall into two general categories: *removal of reinforcers that naturally occur* for the client (reinforcers that have value for the client prior to the therapeutic intervention), and *costs that involve the removal reinforcers that have been established as part of a therapeutic contract* (e.g., points, tokens, checkmarks, staff ratings, and other "generalized" reinforcers that may be traded in for valued backups). When the focus of intervention is directed toward one client or a single family, a systematic mechanism of generalized reinforcement is rarely developed and the former category applies. In order for a response cost to be maximally effective, it should meet the following criteria:

1. The reinforcer to be removed must in fact hold incentive properties for the client or group of clients. Only a careful assessment or survey of reinforcers as previously suggested will enable the BCA to evaluate costs that have a chance of being successfully employed.

2. Wherever possible, the client should have a part in deciding which specific cost will be employed. By providing the client with an

investment, there is a much greater chance that the cost procedures will be understood. It is probable that this kind of client investment ensures that the procedure will be viewed as fair and that the client will participate in the cost procedures. Such investment is particularly important within institutional settings, where client acceptance of any plan of treatment becomes a prerequisite for success, and seems more ethically sound.

3. Once decided upon, the specific behaviors that result in a cost should be clearly specified. All clients affected should be informed on a regular basis of the costs for each specific problem behavior. Many clients fail when no precise specification of what is expected of them has been provided, and this is particularly true for very young or intellectually impaired clients.

4. It is important that the response cost include only those positive reinforcers that occur with sufficient frequency that the cost may be applied upon each occurrence of the problem behavior. Also, the cost must be one that can practically be levied by the direct agent within the setting. Examples of less than satisfactory response costs are teachers removing privileges that are strictly monitored by cottage or ward personnel; the loss of low rate reinforcers such as trips and other social activities; or any cost that involves a privilege removal that cannot be enforced by parents or staff members.

5. It would seem that a response cost provides maximum communication to a client if it is directly related to the problem behavior in question. Removing a child's dessert when he does not satisfactorily eat his meal is probably more directly related to eating behavior (target), than would be a cost involving loss of television or a trip. Thus, the cost communicates within the same modality as the behavior to be decreased. Other examples of costs which are more directly related to the problem behavior include removal of a toy for some set period when it is used improperly; loss of the use of articles of clothing when they are strewn around the floor; and loss of television time when it interferes with adequate completion of homework assignments. Although this consonance between the response cost and targeted behavior would seem to provide a more direct communication to the client, Kazdin (1971) has reported that it is not necessary for a response cost to be effective.

6. Whenever possible, response costs should be clearly specified prior to the occurrence of the targeted behavior, rather than allowing the direct agent to determine the extensiveness of the cost after each individual occurrence. By clearly specifying the cost prior to the incidents, the BCA will avoid the possibility of costs being used inconsistently across and even within specific clients. When left a free hand, many direct agents impose excessive costs for some targeted behavior because the cost decision is made while emotions are flaring and judgment may be impaired. The removal of privileges should not be imposed for excessively long periods of time simply to impress upon the client the seriousness of the

response. Although Burchard and Barrera (1972) found that greater response costs tended to produce more suppression of targeted behaviors for adolescents, it is obvious that there is some point beyond which excessive costs only provoke frustrative emotional responses. The fact that very low costs, and even imagined costs (Weiner, 1962), have proved successful in suppressing problem targeted behaviors suggests that the actual amount of the cost is not as important as the feedback the client gains from receiving the cost. Kazdin (1972) has hypothesized that the informational feedback aspects of the response cost may play a more significant role in suppressing behavior than the aversive properties of the cost itself.

7. Every attempt should be made to *encourage and reinforce clients for imposing costs upon themselves* following the emittance of some targeted behavior. For example, rather than immediately imposing a cost upon some client, the direct agent could signal or cue the client that the targeted behavior had occurred and encourage him to self-state the cost contingency. By actively encouraging a client to impose a well-published cost upon himself, his behavior comes under self-mediated regulation (Kanfer and Marston, 1963; Kanfer and Phillips, 1970), which should be the goal of any treatment approach where feasible. Also encouraging the client to self-verbalize the cost may facilitate the development of self-control (Meichenbaum and Goodman, 1971). Immediately upon the administration of some cost, the direct agent should treat any further client behavior in a characteristic way, not prolonging the punishment with continued admonitions, threats or additional punishments.

Any response-cost procedure that is to be effective must be used in combination with some form of positive consequences for appropriate client behavior. Sole reliance upon response-cost procedures puts the client in the unpleasant situation of only being able to lose (Bandura, 1969). The important role of positive incentives in enhancing incompatible and appropriate behavior should be well stated to direct agents, rather than emphasizing the punitive aspects of the cost procedure. In some settings sole reliance upon response cost may train the clients in "what not to do," leaving "what to do" up to chance and circumstance. Highly punitive systems may lead clients to compete for high response-cost rates or to engage in problem behavior solely for the attention gained from the staff member who administers the cost. Obviously, more appropriate avenues for attention from the direct agent must be provided through some combination of positive reinforcement coupled with response cost. Table 3.1 describes response costs that have been effectively used within the literature.

With regard to the maintenance of suppression of targeted behaviors with response cost, few studies have evaluated costs over sufficient follow-up periods. Kazdin (1971) found no recovery of the targeted behavior for as long as ten weeks after response-cost contingencies were lifted, while Azrin and Holz (1966) report that the persistence of response-cost effects may even be comparable to that of electro-shock. Others (Winkler, 1970) have found a recovery of these behaviors suppressed by response cost when the contingencies were lifted, and at present it appears that further research as to the long-term effects of response cost must be performed (Kazdin, 1972).

Table 3.1

Targeted Behavior	Response Cost	Investigators
Self injurious responses in a 9 year old boy	Immediate discontinuation of conversation and physical contact	Tate & Baroff (1966)
Stealing	Removal of attention of a favorate staff member	Wetzel (1971)
Use of "naughty finger" in the classroom	One minute of recess time for each incidence of the behavior	Sulzbacher & O'Leary (1972)
Inappropriate classroom behavior (e.g., talking out, out of seat, etc.)	Loss of recess time	O'Leary & O'Leary (1972)
Failure to clean up in a classroom setting	Any objects not put away are locked up for 5 school days	Clarizio (1971)
Lack of attendance of termination of therapy	Loss of a monitary deposit	Kazdin (1972)
Violent arguments	Client burns a valued book after an argument	Manthie (1971)
Speech disfluencies in college students	One cent fine following each disfluency	Siegel, Linske & Broen (1969)

"Time Out"

Time-out procedure is very similar to response cost except that the reinforcer that is removed contingent upon some inappropriate behavior is the client's access to the environment itself. While response cost allows the individual to remain within the environment and continue interaction, time out assumes that the environment itself is reinforcing, and that termination of access to it will hold aversive properties. In simple words, time out most often involves clients being moved from some environment they enjoy to a dull, presumably nonstimulating location within the setting. Thus, upon each occurrence of the targeted behavior, the client is sent to a time-out place. Investigators have used time out from reinforcement with a wide variety of clients (Sherman and Baer, 1967; Tyler and Brown, 1968; Patterson, Cobb, and Ray, 1973; Hanf, 1969; Burchard and Barrera, 1972; Kendall, and Nay and Jeffers, 1976), but the way in which it has been employed has varied considerably. Among the variations in the time-out procedure are the manner of communicating the time-out contingencies to the client; the institutional locations used as time-out areas; the duration of the time-out period; contingencies for dealing with disruptive behavior while a child is in time-out; and the demographic characteristics of client populations to which time out has been applied. We will consider each of these dimensions separately along with a number of practical as well as ethical problems that arise from the use of time-out.

Communication of Time-Out Contingencies—Although it may seem to be a simple matter to instruct a client to go to a time out location following a problem behavior, the manner of communicating time out to clients may significantly predict the success with which it is employed (Nay, 1974). Whether time-out is employed with a single client or with some group of clients in an institution, the usual first step is some clear specification of the behaviors that will lead to a time-out. These rules may be presented verbally and reviewed frequently, or they may be visually posted in the form of paper handouts or signs that hold cue properties for clients (Burchard and Barrera, 1972; Kendall, Nay and Jeffers, 1976). Optimally, an "if-then" statement is communicated to the client(s) involved: "If you (get out of your seat, hit, push, yell, curse), you will be sent to the time-out place for —— minutes of time. When your time out is finished, you may return to the setting." Ideally, this contingency is reviewed with the client(s) prior to actually using time out within the setting, so that all clients fully understand. As with response cost, time-out is most often used in combination with some system of positive reinforcement for incompatible and appropriate behavior.

Most investigators worked on the basis that any infraction of the posted rules resulted in an immediate client time-out; however, some investigators gave the client an opportunity to respond to a warning prior to imposing time out (Hanf, 1969; Nay, 1974; Kendall, Nay and Jeffers, 1976). Based upon earlier work by Hanf (1969), the present author has employed a three-step contingency in training direct agents to employ time out (Nay, 1972; Nay, 1974, 1975). A handout that describes this three-step communication process is given to the parent or institutional staff member to read, followed by a paper-and-pencil test on the material.

The content of this pamphlet, directed at a population of parents, appears below:

Many parents warn or threaten their children with some negative or unpleasant consequence for a "problem behavior." In fact, many homes are characterized by high-pitched screaming and yelling, demands and threats made by parents to attempt to control a child. Although these procedures sometimes work; if you yell loud enough you can ultimately overpower the most persistent 5-year old, they are very inefficient, time consuming and exhausting procedures to employ. In addition, such procedures are usually only temporarily effective, and soon after the yelling stops, the child is likely to behave in the "problem" fashion again. One major problem with multiple threats is that many times they are empty—that is, the parent does not fulfill the consequence. Once the child learns that threats have little meaning, the "threat procedure" will be of little value in influencing the child's "problem behavior."

Time out procedure is not complicated and most report success in using it within 2-3 days. The three steps of the procedure are:

1. *providing information* about what you want the child to do or stop doing; i.e., "Johnny, pick up your toys right away."

2. the *time-out warning*—should the child not comply with your command, you warn the child of the consequence of continued non-compliance; i.e., 'Johnny, if you don't pick up your toys right now, you have to go sit on the time out 'chair' (room, place, etc.).' Importantly, the parent does not scream, yell, beg, physically threaten, etc., the child. The consequence is stated *non-emotionally* but firmly.

3. *time out*—if the child does not comply following the time out warning, the child is then placed in "time out." The parent states the reason, then sends the child to the time out place, i.e., Johnny, since you didn't pick up your toys when I asked you to, you have to go to time out (go sit on the chair, etc.). Again, the parent instructs the child to go to time out unemotionally and with little verbal interaction between parent and child.

The most important feature of time out is that when the child ignores the time out warning, the consequences of being placed in time out must *immediately* follow. In addition, *each* and *every* time the child does not comply following the warning, he must immediately be placed in time out.

The time out place to which a child is sent should be a very non-stimulating, uneventful, dull place. The important feature to remember here is that in using time out you are punishing your child, so the location of time out should be one the child does not enjoy. Following the initial novelty of the procedure, the child soon finds "time out" from his activities a very unpleasant experience. Thus the child's room, where his toys are available, etc., the living room watching TV, any place where he is free to look at or interact with parents, siblings or others should *not* be used for the time out place.

Many parents place the child on a chair facing the wall in a non-stimulating area such as the parents' bedroom, the dining room, the hall (if you are sure other family members won't be walking by) or the bathroom. The child should never be "locked in" or placed in closed-in or poorly ventilated locations.

The first question most parents ask is: "how long do I keep the child in time out?" There is no set answer to this question, as the length of time necessary varies with the child. With the child under 5 years of age, it is best to begin by placing him in time out for five minutes or less; with the over 5 child, begin with ten minutes. If you notice that following this initial period the child is still unconcerned or not at all bothered by the time, it is wise to lengthen it by another five minutes. To many children five minutes or ten minutes alone is most unpleasant and seems like an eternity, and these times can be used regularly. The important thing to remember is that the length of time must be unpleasant for *your* child. Once you have decided on a time, you instruct the child: "You stay here until I tell you to come out."

There are a number of situations which are bound to arise when parents beging using "time out procedure." Some of the more common of these situations will now be discussed.

A) The child cries and whines and generally makes a great fuss over being placed in "time out"—this is a usual response of the child to time out, particularly the very "out of control" child. Here the parent is instructed to make only one reply to the child: "Your time doesn't start until you are quiet." This is stated *once*, firmly, to the child, after which he is ignored. Once the child has stopped crying, the parent then waits the standard duration (five or ten minutes, etc.) before informing the child that he/she can now come out and join the rest of the family. Once the child is placed in time out, the parent must never argue, scold, plead, etc., with him.

B) the child leaves the time out area, gets off the chair, etc.—Obviously the "time out procedure" would not work unless the child learns that he/she must remain in time out once placed there. Each time the child leaves the time out area, he must be immediately returned, spanked twice on the bare bottom or the back of the legs very firmly, and told: "Because you left the chair (room, etc.), you now get a spanking." This is the *only* time physical punishment is used, and only to teach the child that he must remain in time out. After 3-4 spankings, most children learn to remain in time out. The "time out" area itself becomes punishing for the child, without the parents being forced to use physical punishment every time the child misbehaves.

Physical punishment should be used at no other time than when the child leaves the time out area, and should be discontinued immediately after the child learns to remain in time out.

C) The child in some fashion makes a mess (or damages) the time out area— for example, if the parent returns to the bathroom and finds towels and other objects thrown on the floor, etc., the parent informs the child that he has earned another five or ten minutes in time out which will not begin until the mess is cleaned up. Importantly, the child must *remain* in time out until he has cleaned up and the full time has elapsed.

D) Meal time or bathroom—when the child is in time out he/she should not be permitted to leave the time out area except to use the toilet until his "time" is up. In allowing the child to go to the toilet, the parent must insure that the child is returned immediately to time out for the full duration of his time.

E) Interference by other siblings—under no circumstances allow the child in "time out" to interact with a brother or sister. Siblings should be told that the child is being punished and to leave the time out area immediately.

F) Others—never bring the child water or allow him to drink or snack while on the chair, as this certainly interferes with the unpleasantness of the "time out." For the same reason, reading, objects to play with, or other stimulations should not be allowed while "time out" is taking place.

If used consistently and immediately as outlined, this technique is very effective. The child soon learns that when his parents ask something of him, they firmly "mean business." No one desires to punish a child, but by using "time out" as outlined, the child soon learns that certain behaviors lead to an unpleasant consequence (time out). When used consistently, the child receives a clear communication from his parents about what he can and cannot acceptably do, thus making him more secure in his parents' expectations of him. (Partially reproduced in Nay, 1975, p. 16.)

The reader may notice that this pamphlet includes a spank contingency as suggested by Hanf (1969) for use with parents in a home situation. Of course, for time out to be effective the client must remain in the time-out location for the specified period of time, and the spank is usually effective after about three to four spanks. Within the institutional setting, however, spanking may be against regulations or generally not feasible. Also, many BCA's are opposed in principle to spanking, and some alternative form of response cost is typically employed—instead of the spank. This author has employed a fine per minute in points for client refusal to go to a time out location (Nay, 1974), as well as loss of some desired privilege when the child would not participate in time out (Kendall, Nay and Jeffers, 1976). Any response cost that the child views as aversive might feasibly be employed contingent upon a child's refusal to go to time out. This contingency should be clearly communicated to the client(s) prior to using time out. It should also be pointed out that most investigators find that clients rarely refuse to participate in time out (Patterson et al., 1973).

Establishing a Time Out Location. Obviously, for time out procedure to be effective clients must be removed to some location that does not hold reinforcement properties for them. Bedrooms, game rooms, TV-recreation rooms, locations where other children are able to interact with the client, or any locations where clients are permitted to engage in some reinforcing activity would not be desirable time out places; however, they are often inappropriately used by well-meaning parents (as well as professionals). The important defining characteristics of a time out place is that it be dull, nonstimulating, and devoid of any manipulanda or stimulation that might hold incentive properties for the client. A variety of time out locations has been reported within the literature. As many investigators have reported the use of time out within the school setting, some of these studies will be presented initially.

Patterson and Gullion (1968) suggested that the cloakroom of the public school setting might be an ideal location for time out. LeBlanc, Busby and Thompson (1974) removed the child from a play area after an act of aggression and placed him on a chair in the back of the room for a period of one minute. If the child refused to sit in this location, he was sent to a small, empty, but lighted room with the door closed. Of course, if an available room can be designed to meet the criteria of a time out location, it may be the ideal setting. A room should be devoid of furniture except for a chair for the child to sit in, and lacking in windows that would provide the child a view of courtyard goings on. The room should be well-lighted and large enough to be nonthreatening; most investigators report that the door is closed or left ajar, but *never locked.*

A separate room is an ideal location for time out, but most institutional settings do not have sufficient space for this. Also, when several students are sent to time out, additional rooms would be needed, and this is out of the question in most institutional settings. For that reason teachers and staff within academic settings often make use of a variety of rather creative means of isolating a child.

Time out areas might include a corner of the room hemmed in by bookcases or cabinets (Wilson, 1973); a specially designed cubicle (Hawkins and Hayes, 1974); home-made screens made of a sheet spread across two coat racks or a cardboard placed between two wooden supports; or even a large cardboard refrigerator box or furniture box that has sufficient room, lighting, and ventilation. In the nonacademic institutional setting more permanent time out locations may be possible, such as an unused room under a stairwell, *large* unused closets, or the corner of a large room. Kendall, Nay and Jeffers (1976) were faced with the prospect of devising time out areas within a 30-by-100 foot room that housed 35 young boys in a delinquent training school. Because only one staff member was present to monitor student behavior (unfortunately, often the case in institutions), use of a separate room was out of the question. Two large, hoop-shaped metal frames were mounted on the wall in different locations within the room, and curtains were hung on the hoops, thus providing a circular closed-in area within which a chair was placed. These time out locations proved to be very effective and were constructed at a cost of under $15.

In summary, it would seem that an ideal time out location should have the following characteristics:

1. To be as devoid as possible of furniture, objects that might be hand manipulated, windows that might provide an interesting view of the outside, and sounds, particularly from the television, radio, or record player. This location should be as dull and nonstimulating as possible.

2. Large enough (more than 4 by 4 feet) to provide a nonthreatening environment, well lit and ventilated, and supplied with a suitable chair for the client to sit in.

3. Well removed from the usual pathways traveled by institutional staff and clients. Areas such as halls, foyers, dining rooms, and recreation areas are frequently traveled locations and thus often unsuitable.

4. In close enough proximity to staff members so that the client within time out might be checked on periodically. This is particularly important when time out is employed with autistic, retarded, aggressive, or delinquent clients or populations capable of inflicting harm to self or to property.

5. It should *not* be the "locked room" or "isolation area" that we have seen so often in the past within institutional settings. The author sees no reason why a client should be locked into a time out area. Should the client leave the time out area prior to the completion of his time, response cost in the form of privilege losses, loss of desirable activities, increased

duration of time within the time out area, movement to a more nonstimulating time out area (LeBlanc et al., 1974), or some other sanction would be preferable to locking the client in.

Length of Time Out—Although not much research has evaluated the specific components of time out procedure (e.g., means of communication; different time out locations), a number of investigators have evaluated the duration of time out. Time out durations that have been reported include fixed intervals of 30 seconds (McReynolds, 1969), 2 minutes (Boston and Bailey, 1969; Pendergrass, 1971; Zeilberger, Sampen, and Sloan, 1968), 5 minutes (Ramp, Ulrich and Dulaney, 1971), and 15 minutes (Tyler and Brown, 1967), as well as intervals varying from 15 seconds to the entire length of a meal (Barton, Guess, Garcia, and Baer, 1970) and from 30 minutes to 2 hours (Hamilton, Stephens and Allen, 1967).

Most investigators have employed time out ranging from about 5 to 20 minutes, and probably any period over an hour would better be described as "institutional isolation" rather than time out. Some institutions have abused time out procedures, labeling programs of long-term (24 to 48 hours) isolation in a locked room as "time outs." It is the author's view that such long-term periods of isolation go well beyond the immediate feedback and "cooling off" that a time out permits and do not place the client back in the natural environment so that he might learn new behavior.

A few studies have systematically compared various intervals of time out to determine the most effective duration. Pendergrass (1971) found that durations of both 5 and 20 minutes did not differ in suppressing classroom misbehavior; however, consistent application of one duration seemed superior to an intermittent schedule involving both durations. White, Nielson, and Johnson (1972) found that a 15- or 30-minute time out duration seemed to produce equal suppression of child deviant behavior and was superior to a one-minute time out. Burchard and Barrera (1972) found that a 30-minute time out was superior to a 5-minute time out in reducing personal assaults, property damage, and swearing behavior in a population of delinquent adolescents. It would seem that there are many factors that might predict how successful a given time out duration would be in suppressing problem behavior in some client population.

One interesting factor to emerge from the present research is the possibility of contrast effects; that is, shorter durations of time out seem to have less suppressive effects when followed by longer durations. For example, White et al. (1972) found that the one-minute time out was most suppressive when it preceded the use of longer durations. When one minute followed longer durations, its suppressiveness became less reliable. The authors state that "The sequence effect concerning one minute time out is perhaps the most interesting finding of the investigation." Burchard and Barrera (1972) found a similar "contrast effect" in comparing 5 and

30 minutes of time out. In a study to test the possibility of such contrast effects, Kendall et al. (1976) introduced the following experimental sequence to a population of delinquent adolescents: baseline, rule presentation, rules plus 5 minutes of time out, rules plus 30 minutes of time out, rules plus 5 minutes of time out, and return to baseline. In contrast to previous findings (O'Leary et al., 1969) the presentation of rules regarding four targeted behaviors (using highly discriminable posters and a frequent verbal recitation) resulted in significant reduction in three out of four targeted behaviors (aggressive verbal, aggressive physical, noncompliance, and out-of-the-area behavior). The introduction of a 5-minute time out contingent upon violation of one of the four rules resulted in even further reduction of two of the four targeted behaviors. Following the presentation of 30 minutes of time out, the second presentation of 5 minutes of time out resulted in paradoxical elevations in three of the four targeted behaviors, suggesting that when the second 5 minutes of time out was contrasted with the previous 30 minutes, it produced significantly less suppression, and in fact an elevation from baseline. Several explanations were offered by the authors for this phenomena, but it becomes readily apparent that no simple statements can be made about the "most effective" duration of time out.

Also, it seems rather obvious that the duration of time out must be carefully tailored for the specific population to which it is applied. While one-minute time outs might effectively suppress some targeted behavior for two- through five-year-old children, it seems reasonable that such a short duration may not be as effective with an adolescent population, although White et al. (1972) report some suppression even with a one-minute time out. In fact, no investigator has systematically evaluated time out duration across age groups and across important diagnostic differentiations such as retarded, delinquent, normal classroom, and psychiatric.

Populations—As alluded to in the previous section, the utility of time out for any given population must be functionally demonstrated; that is, time out should work. The vast majority of the investigators who describe the use of time out employ the procedure with children between the ages of about two and twelve (e.g., Patterson, Cobb, and Ray, 1973; Tyler and Brown, 1967; Hamilton, et al., 1967; Wilson and Williams, 1973; Nay, 1975; Kendall et al., 1976). The use of time out with older adolescents or adults is less frequently reported, probably for a variety of reasons. It becomes difficult for the direct agent to "insist" that older clients, particularly delinquents, physically relocate to a time out area. While the issue of control usually does not arise with younger institutionalized clients, a forced time out might be viewed as repugnant, overcontrolling, or even unethical when applied to adults. In short, the effectiveness with older individuals has yet to be determined, though it would seem that the procedure would be impractical and possibly unfeasible with most older persons.

One of the troubling aspects of time out is the possibility of its abuse. It has already been stated that some institutions have called long-term isolation a "time out." When one thinks of the ethical implications of forcing clients to remove themselves from the natural environment to a small and isolated setting; of the possibility of abuse by overzealous, punishment-oriented staff members; of the possibility that time out locations may be constructed to include threatening properties, and of abuses regarding its duration, it soon becomes obvious that time out must be carefully presented to change agents. The "control" issue applies not only to time out but to other procedures, and will be dealt with in Chapter 11 in some detail.

While time out does provide a kind of response cost with as little attention to deviant behavior as possible, another drawback is that it removes the client from the natural environment for a set period of time. During this period, particularly with regard to the classroom setting, the client is not in a position to behave, make mistakes, and learn new behaviors, or generally interact in a more natural fashion. It would seem that, whenever possible, *some alternative procedure of aversive control that allows the client to remain in the natural setting should be considered prior to employing time out*. For example, this author and his colleagues (Nay, Schulman, Bailey and Huntsinger, 1976) found student loss of self-chosen and labeled "territories" (desk chairs demarcated on the floor with duct tape) contingent upon specified targets (e.g., out of seat) was most effective in reducing two classes of problem behavior. Territory loss meant that students were required to sit in a nondemarcated unlabeled desk chair ("no-man's land") located *within the classroom*. Thus, class participation remained unhampered.

PHYSICAL PUNISHMENT

While extinction, response cost, and time out all involve the removal of positive reinforcement, physical punishment is characterized by *the administration of some aversive stimulus to the client contingent upon the problem targeted behavior*. As with the reinforcer, the aversive properties of a punishing stimulus must be defined by the manner in which the client cognitively construes that stimulus. A teacher's or parent's shouting at an unruly teenager, while ostensibly aversive, may serve as positive reinforcement by the recipient, particularly if the youth's behavioral goal is to provoke such a response. Although the way that we cognitively label a stimulus is an important determinant of its aversive properties, there are stimuli that rather consistently hold punishing properties for most of us—high levels of electric shock, nausea-provoking chemicals, criticism and other verbal reprimands from individuals we esteem, as well as many other forms of verbal and physical abuse. Even a lack of stimulation may hold punishment properties for a client, as is demonstrated by the literature regarding time out procedure.

Although the use of physical punishment has often been employed within behavior therapy procedures (e.g., McGuire and Vallance, 1964; Bancroft, 1966, 1974; Feldman and McCullough, 1965; Greene, Hoats, and Hornick, 1970; Whitman, 1972; Merbaum, 1973), *its use has typically been restricted to decreasing the frequency of behaviors for which extinction or removal of positive reinforcement is not effective.* Behaviors that must be immediately interrupted—for instance self-mutilation (Lovaas, Freitag, Gold, and Kassorla, 1965; Risley, 1968; Tate and Baroff, 1966)—have often been dealt with using mild forms of aversion in the form of slaps and electric shocks; permitting them to extinguish would lead to a possibility of severe damage to the client. Certain behavioral categories that offer a high degree of immediate reinforcement to clients (e.g., certain sexual behaviors, alcoholism and drug addiction, smoking, control of eating) have also been dealt with using a punishment approach, typically coupled with reinforcement for incompatible appropriate behavior. In recent years aversive imagery, negative self-statements, and other covert aversive consequences have been employed in lieu of physical punishment (Cautela, 1967). These procedures are discussed in some detail in Chapter 5.

Although an exhaustive presentation of the theoretical underpinnings, procedures, research, and significant ethical implications that underlie punishment is beyond the scope of this text, the author will attempt to provide the background of the important theoretical issues involved in using punishment, the major areas of application, and certain "key" issues, using citations from the literature to illustrate important points.

Background: Important Issues

Most of the research evaluating the effects of punishment has employed animals as subjects, and it remains to be seen whether or not these findings will be validated with human populations. The problems in using punishment with humans are obvious, and for that reason a reliance on animal research has been necessary. Probably the most important controversy within the area of punishment has to do with the permanence of its effects upon behavior. Early work by Estes and his colleagues (e.g., Estes, 1944) indicated that punishment delivered contingently upon an animal's response (e.g., a bar press) produced only a temporary suppression of response. Another controversy involved the manner in which punishment suppressed behavior. Researchers asked, Does punishment *work by associating emotional responses with the specific behavior punished,* or by associating emotional responses with *the environmental stimuli present* during the original presentation of punishment? (Azrin, 1956) Other issues: How does one ideally deliver punishment? Is there a difference between punishment administered early in a response sequence as opposed to late in a response sequence? How does the intensity of punishment effect response suppression? (Azrin and Holz, 1966; Powell and

Azrin, 1968) Other issues have been nicely summarized by Bandura (1969).

Although many investigators have maintained that physical punishment only temporarily suppresses behavior (Skinner, 1938; Estes, 1944), Skinner has probably made the most eloquent attack upon the use of punishment (Fantino, 1973). In his well-known book, *Science and Human Behavior* (1953), Skinner made his views on punishment known:

> The commonest technique of control in modern life is punishment. The pattern is familiar: if a man does not behave as you wish, knock him down; if a child misbehaves, spank him; if the people of a country misbehave, bomb them. Legal and police systems are based upon such punishments as fines, flogging, incarceration, and hard labor. Religious control is exerted through penances, threats of excommunication, and consignment to hell fire. Education has not wholly abandoned the birchrod. In everyday personal contact we control through censure, snubbing, disapproval or banishment. In short, the degree to which we use punishment as a technique of control seems to be limited only be the degree to which we can gain the necessary power. All of this is done with the intention of reducing tendencies to behave in certain ways. Reinforcement builds up these tendencies; punishment is designed to tear them down. . . .
>
> More recently, the suspicion has also arisen that punishment does not in fact do what it is supposed to do. An immediate effect in reducing a tendency to behave is clear enough, but this may be misleading." (pp. 182-183)

Skinner's views on punishment have had a great impact on its consideration within the field of psychology. His criticism falls into three major categories: (1) the effects of punishment are transient, producing no long-term suppression of punished behavior; (2) punishment is relatively ineffective when compared with positive reinforcement; and (3) there are many troublesome by-products of punishment, which may produce behavior that is more inappropriate than the behavior to be eliminated. As a good bit of the research on the effects of punishment seems to be focused around these three critical issues, the present discussion will attempt to evaluate each area of criticism prior to a presentation of specific techniques and procedures currently employed.

The "Transient Effects" issue.—Following Thorndike's initial statement regarding the "law of effect" (1913), he sought to evaluate the differential effects of reward and punishment upon human verbal behavior. He found that while words that were followed by "right" on the part of the experimenter tended to increase in probability, words followed by "wrong" also increased in frequency, thus seemingly confirming that punishment does not weaken responding. Thorndike then rejected his earlier view that punishment correspondingly decreases the frequency of behavior as reward increases frequency. Skinner (1938) found that when punishment (a hard slap to the foot) followed lever pressing for rats, a significant depression in rate of responding was noted. However, when comparing rats who were punished during the training situation with those who weren't, no differences in time to extinction were noted, suggesting that punishment produced no permanent effects in bar pressing rate. In similar and more comprehensive studies of the effects of punishment on responding and extinction, W. K. Estes (1944) found that punishment produced only short-term effects in a variety of rat training experiments. The short-term suppressive effects of electric shock seemed to be independent of whether the organisms were shocked for the specific response of lever pressing or on some random schedule, suggesting that punishment creates an emotional state that interferes with learning. Previous research had found that for positive reinforcement to be effective, it must contingently be related to the targeted response. These findings thus suggested that reinforcement and punishment operate in a very different fashion.

These early findings to the contrary, many more recent investigations have found that punishment can indeed produce lasting effects upon the behavior of a variety of organisms. Importantly, however, it seems that the manner in which punishment is presented to the organism is the important determiner of its utility in suppressing behavior. Results summarized by Bandura (1969) from a large body of evidence with animals (Azrin and Holz, 1966; Church, 1963), children (Parke and Walters, 1967) and adults (Powell and Azrin, 1968) have demonstrated that punishment may indeed produce lasting and stable reductions in behavior. It seems that the degree of response reduction is an increasing function of the intensity of punishment. Most importantly for the present discussion, responses that allow some clients to avoid potential punishment (e.g., a fearful client who avoids height situations) seem to be extraordinarily resistant to extinction even when there is no obvious reinforcement occurring to account for their longevity (Solomon, 1964; Rimm and Masters, 1974). Perhaps the most eloquent statement about the effects of punishment was made by Lichtenstein (1950), who found that the delivery of massive shocks to dogs, contingent upon eating, produced animals that would starve themselves rather than approach the food box again.

The "Punishment Is Relatively Ineffective Compared with Positive Reward" Issue.—The data so far presented seem to indicate that punishment can very clearly produce permanent changes in behavior. Contrary to early evidence, punishment does seem to operate in a fashion similar to that of positive reinforcement. It seems to be most effective in suppressing behavior when it is delivered contingent upon some specific response and on a consistent basis over time (Fantino, 1973). While punishment seems capable of inducing lasting behavioral change (issues 1 and 2), perhaps the "unfortunate effects" issue is of most contemporary relevance to the BCA who considers a punishment approach to treatment.

The "Unfortunate By-products" Issue.—In our everyday lives it would seem pretty obvious that when we experience pain or the threat of bodily harm, we probably do not pay maximal attention to material that someone is asking us to learn. While there seems to be some optimum level of arousal for learning (Malmo, 1957), the high emotions often generated by punishment may induce the individual to avoid or escape from the punishment situation, using novel behaviors. As such responses often occur on a trial-and-error basis, some of them—such as fleeing the situation; completely withdrawing by making no response; lashing back in a counterattack at the punishing agent; using crying and other behaviors to elicit sympathy—may well be incompatible with treatment goals. Solomon (1964) in summarizing the effects of punishment, has made the following observations: (1) the use of aversive stimuli alone may not be sufficient for the development of maladaptive emotional responses, and such responses seem to develop most often when the organism cannot escape (e.g., is restrained in some fashion); (2) the danger of emotional disturbance in using punishment is remote; and (3) punishment will be most effective, with the least possibility of generalized emotional responses, when the client is offered some positively rewarded alternative that is clearly defined for him as an alternative to his inappropriate behavior. Thus, it is not a simple matter of punishment being more effective or less effective, but that punishment is maximally useful when combined with reinforcement for some incompatible and appropriate behavior that is clearly defined for the client.

There are some other "unfortunate" effects of punishment that should be considered prior to its use. While punishment is directed to some specific maladaptive behavior (e.g., targeted child hitting another child), its effects may in fact generalize to other more socially desirable behaviors of the clients (e.g., children's general repertoire of the assertive behaviors that are necessary for ordinary interaction with peers). Although the case made by Stanley Kubrick in his film "A Clockwork Orange" may be an extreme one, the reader may recall that punishments in the form of nausea-producing agents directed at suppressing the protagonist's deviant aggressive behaviors generalized to other behaviors in his repertoire to the extent that he could not engage in socially acceptable acts of aggression (e.g., defend himself against an attacker). Bandura (1969) makes the point that punishment must always be presented in a highly discriminable situation, where contingencies are clearly stated and the behavior that punishment is directed toward is unambiguous.

... a change agent who wishes to restrict the range and direction of behavioral suppression should not merely apply negative sanctions to undesirable response patterns, but should arrange different consequences for related forms of behavior in different social contexts. For instance, physically assaultive behavior may be punished but desirable assertiveness rewarded. In addition to selective reinforcement, discrimination is greatly facilitated by the use of verbal aids. By clearly labeling the modes of behavior that are permissable and those that are punishable, and by specifying the times and places at which certain courses of action are appropriate or unsuitable, greater specificity of punishment effects can be insured. (pp. 309–310)

Another problem with the presentation of punishment is the possibility of its abuse by the punishing agent. Parents or others who have dealt rather intensively with children may realize that their emotional state at a given time can be translated into the way they deal with youngsters. The father who has experienced a hard day at the office may tend to be.ave differently in response to a child's inappropriate behavior than he would under more relaxed conditions. Providing punishment when the punishing agent is emotionally aroused can lead to inconsistent, poorly communicated contingencies; it may also lead to an overresponding, since this emotional state may be translated into the punishment delivered. Particularly where potentially damaging physical punishment is employed, this potential for inconsistent responses should be of concern to the behavioral change agent.

One might consider a situation where a parent or staff member providing punishment actually models behavior that is maladaptive or undesirable. The parent who pulls little Sally off her sister and then proceeds to slap or in other ways physically punish Sally is clearly (and paradoxically) modeling the very kind of physical aggressive behavior that he wishes to suppress. This communication may not be lost on the child. The staff member interested in decreasing the level of noise, verbal threats, or other forms of verbal aggressive behavior in a setting of institutionalized youngsters clearly would be behaving contrary to treatment goals by using verbal threats, insistent commands, or other obnoxious verbal behaviors to suppress behavior. In a sense this kind of staff behavior communicates: "When I want you to do something, I yell."

Another problem pointed out by Rimm and Masters (1974) is the possibility that punishment will suppress certain behaviors to the extent that the client behaves in a rigid fashion. Certain behaviors that punishment may suppress earlier in one's development (e.g., engaging in or talking about certain sexual behaviors such as mutual manipulation, fondling, or intercourse) are important repertoire behaviors for the adult. In fact, if these and other sexual behaviors have been sufficiently suppressed by previous verbal threats and punishments by well-meaning (if misdirected) parents, we speak of a pathological situation and talk of sexual "dysfunctioning" or "deviancy" or employ some other negative label. Often, assertive behaviors such as making verbal demands, using threats, certain facial expressions, and other acts of aggression are severely punished in childhood only to be perfectly appropriate aspects of an adult's repertoire, being of value in certain social situations (eg., dealing with an unscrupulous merchant). Many psychologists have in fact developed programs to train individuals to be more assertive. Fortunately, the effects of punishment are not often long-lasting, because punishment is most often delivered at mild or moderate levels of intensity and over brief durations of time.

Punishment may in fact produce conditioned emotional responses associated with behaviors that are punished and the situation within which punishment occurs, which may prove to be maladaptive. From the early work of Watson and Rayner (1920) we know that the kinds of emotional responses that we speak of as "fears" may be systematically learned. These investigators found that they could condition fear of a white laboratory rat in an eleven-month-old child named "Little Albert" if a loud sound made by striking a steel bar was associated with the rat in a classical conditioning paradigm. The striking of the steel bar held aversive properties for the child prior to treatment and was used here as a punishing/aversive stimulus (UCS). Not only did the child become "afraid of" the rat, he also showed emotional responses to other similar furry objects, presumably through a process of stimulus generalization. The literature describing "experimental neuroses" (Pavlov, 1928; Masserman, 1943; Gantt, 1944) shows that animals have exhibited an array of emotional behaviors (e.g., trembling, making stereotyped responses, exhibiting rage, withdrawal) when placed in situations that have often involved punishment: forcing the animal to make difficult discriminations; increasing the intensity of aversive stimuli such as shock; providing intensive punishments for high-frequency behaviors that had previously been reinforced). This "neurotic" behavior often endures for long periods of time and in some cases it is irreversible. The most important feature that seems necessary for the development of "experimental neuroses" is that the animal be unable to escape the situation, but is forced to endure the treatments described under some kind of restraint. It is clearly possible that some of the fears and inappropriate emotional responses that we see on the part of adults and often label as "phobias," "free-floating anxiety," or "depression" are a result of previously administered punishments under conditions of physical or even psychological restraint. Because of the ethical issues involved with experimentally testing procedures for inducing such neurotic behavior, the animal literature presented is clearly only suggestive, but it should provoke the thoughts of those behavioral change agents who employ punishing agents in treatment.

To make a summary statement regarding the "unfortunate" effects of punishment, it would seem that the BCA should be very cautious in employing punishment as a mechanism in treatment, and should ensure that punishment is employed only under the following conditions: highly discriminable appropriate behaviors should be concomitantly reinforced, so that the clients may readily discriminate those targeted behaviors to be increased; maladaptive and socially undesirable behaviors should not be modeled for clients; mild or moderate levels of punishment intensity should be self-determined by the clients; clients should be provided with readily understandable methods of avoiding the punishment agent if they so desire (e.g., engaging in some incompatible behavior). Also, the behavioral change agent should seriously question the use of punishment as a means of decreasing those behaviors that might prove socially desirable and have importance for the client at a later period of development. When such behaviors (acts of physical aggression and verbal aggressiveness) are to be decreased using punishment, appropriate discriminative responses (e.g., appropriate use of verbal and nonverbal warnings and other assertive responses) should be systematically reinforced in combination with the punishment. Finally, it is the viewpoint of the present author that the BCA should seriously question his use of physical punishment on each occasion prior to its use. Whenever possible, procedures for providing negative feedback should employ extinction, response cost, and time out procedures prior to the use of physical punishment.

The immediate cessation of some classes of behavior such as self-destructive acts (e.g., Lovaas, 1967), acts of violence, or physical aggressiveness that may cause damage to others is often necessary. Punitive control may become necessary to interrupt such events immediately. When punishment is used to achieve such a goal, it should be used only when positive alternatives are systematically reinforced.

There are many options available in employing punishing agents. Most of the treatment procedures employing physical punishment have used either drugs or electrical stimulation in either a classical conditioning or operant-punishment training situation. More recently additional stimuli have been employed as physical punishers. For that reason the present discussion will present an overview of the literature and general format for treatments in the following categories: aversive drugs, electrical approaches, and a rather loose, inclusive category of "other" approaches.

Aversive Drugs

Procedures employing some sort of aversive pharmacological agent have most often been used when other less intensive consequences prove to be ineffective in the face of the great amount of immediate reinforcement the problem behavior brings. The use of alcohol, drugs, cigarettes, as well as certain "deviant" sexual behaviors are among such classes of behavior. For the present discussion a few representative reports of drug-induced aversion will be used to describe usual methodology, followed by a fairly intensive critique.

Because of the immediate and potent social and physiological (e.g., feeling relaxed and "good") effects of alcohol, Lemere and Voegtlin (1950) opted for an aversive approach to reducing consumption among over 4,000 alcoholics treated during a period of some 15 years. Although their program of research may be criticized on a number of grounds, it is rare to find any systematic treatment applied to such a large population of clients by a homogeneous group of investigators within any treatment area. As the reader may recall from Chapter 2, in classical conditioning we associate some neutral stimulus with an unconditioned stimulus that produces a characteristic response. In the present case the authors paired the sight, taste, and smell of alcohol (conditioned stimulus = CS) with the drugs apomorphine and emetine (unconditioned stimulus = UCS), which produce nausea and vomiting (unconditioned response = UCR). The classical conditioning paradigm that they employed is shown in Fig. 3.1.

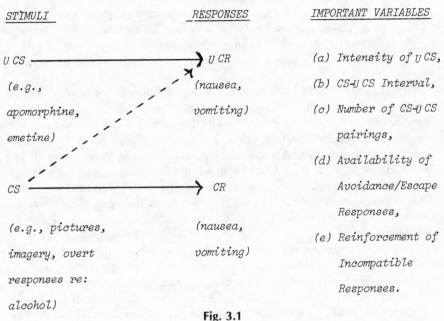

STIMULI	RESPONSES	IMPORTANT VARIABLES
U CS	U CR	(a) Intensity of U CS,
(e.g.,	(nausea,	(b) CS-U CS Interval,
apomorphine,	vomiting)	(c) Number of CS-U CS
emetine)		pairings,
		(d) Availability of
CS	CR	Avoidance/Escape
		Responses,
(e.g., pictures,	(nausea,	(e) Reinforcement of
imagery, overt	vomiting)	Incompatible
responses re:		Responses.
alcohol)		

Fig. 3.1

Classical conditioning paradigm most often employed with aversive chemicals.

Thus, after repeated pairings the alcohol-related stimuli (CS) would ideally come to induce nausea and/or vomiting (CR).

In actual practice treatment included the following steps:

1. The patient was administered emetine hydrochloride (UCS) orally or by injection, which provokes first nausea and then vomiting. It is important to note that the effects of emetine or other drugs employed in this paradigm often vary due to such variables as previous food intake, fatigue, or other factors. Also, different clients vary considerably in the UCRs produced.

2. An alcoholic beverage (CS) desirable to the patient was held in front of his face and he was asked to smell deeply. The patient was then asked to take small sips of the beverage, focus upon its taste, and swish it around his mouth prior to swallowing so that its sensory impact was fully developed.

3. The procedure was repeated a second time, and typically by this time (if the drug dosage and timing were correct) the client had begun to feel nauseated and would ultimately vomit.

4. Treatment sessions typically lasted 30 minutes to one hour and were performed on alternate days. Most patients received an average of six sessions.

5. The client was terminated from therapy when the sight of alcohol provoked nausea and/or vomiting.

6. Typically, two to four booster sessions (repeated pairings of CS and UCS) were employed routinely or as often as necessary at standard periods following the termination of treatment.

7. Patients who relapsed were brought in for a second treatment regimen.

From 1935 to 1948 the authors obtained followup data on 4,096 of 4,468 patients. The data show that 60 percent of patients remained abstinent (as defined by no use of alcohol) for the period of one year; 51 percent remained abstinent for two years; and at about five years 38 percent remained alcohol free. A total of 23 percent of the patients treated remained abstinent for ten years or more. Unfortunately, the authors did not provide a population of control clients who were motivated to reduce their drinking but did not receive drug aversion therapy. Thus, a major criticism of these results is that 23 percent of patients who desire to terminate use of alcohol might be able to maintain abstinence for a period of ten years *without having received a regimen of aversion therapy.* When we employ any sort of treatment, an assessment of *base rate* for therapeutic change when no regimen of treatment is employed should be obtained (Eysenck, 1970). One might also question what the effects of mere hospitalization would be for some population of patients that did not receive therapy. This treatment paradigm is very similar to other paradigms that have been used more recently.

Raymond (1956) paired apomorphine-induced nausea with displays of handbags, perambulators, and covered illustrations of desired objects with a 33-year-old male fetishist. The author reports that at the end of only a few weeks of treatment the patient reported that the sight of these objects made him feel sick. A 19 month followup (after a "booster session" at six months) showed that the client was still free of fetishist fantasies and behaviors. Sanderson, Campbell, and Laverty (1963) employed curarelike chemical agents that produced a temporary respiratory paralysis as unconditioned stimuli in a similar aversion paradigm with alcoholics. Respiratory paralysis is a most unpleasant experience. The chemical agent is injected to the point of respiratory failure, at which time the physician holds a bottle of alcohol to the mouth of the patient, allowing a few drops to enter his mouth. During this period of respiratory arrest, the patient is enabled to breathe using a respirator. The beneficial effects of this approach do not appear to be lasting (Farrar, Powell, and

Martin, 1968), and the ethical questions posed are obvious. Many of the problems in using such aversive agents have been ably summarized by Rachman and Teasdale (1969), and these will be summarized.

Choice of an agent.—While a variety of agents produce the often desired effects of nausea and/or vomiting, many of these agents are central nervous system depressants and thus may interfere with any learning that might take place in the conditioning situation. Careful evaluation of the site of action of any pharmacological agent should be determined prior to its use. Also, the potential of many agents to cause unpleasant side effects should be carefully evaluated in the light of the client's current medical history.

Temporal factors.—Perhaps the most potent criticism of the use of drugs in classical conditioning is the difficulty in regulating the time between the conditioned stimulus (CS) and the unconditioned stimulus (UCS). The reader may recall that the "interstimulus" interval (CS-UCS) has been found to be a most important predictor of successful conditioning in a variety of studies with animal and human populations (Chapter 2). Because of the differences in time between injection or ingestion and the occurrence of nausea and/or vomiting, it is difficult for the BCA to regulate the interstimulus interval. Nausea may occur prior to the presentation of the alcohol-related stimulus (CS) in which case, a backward conditioning paradigm (UCS-CS) is operative and conditioning is much less likely to take place, if at all. It would thus seem difficult to control for the temporal effects of such drugs.

In addition, individual clients respond differently to chemical agents at different times due to an array of variables, making it difficult to systematize the interstimulus interval across treatment sessions. Another important limitation of a drug approach is that the effects of such drugs limit the frequency with which classical conditioning trials may be undertaken. There are limited occasions when a client can tolerate the intense bodily response brought on by some drugs. Thus, presentations may be limited to one within any given day.

Unpleasantness and health factors.—Often staff members (you may be one) object to this sort of treatment and carry it out with the gravest of reservations. Also, these drugs may cause physiological damage. Lemere and Voegtlin talked of possible cardiac effects and other side effects as a result of such drugs. Morganstern and Pearce (1963) provided clinical evidence of increases in hostility and aggressiveness on the part of patients who are so treated.

Restriction of setting.—Since such treatment must be performed with a physician present, it cannot be employed by the client on his own in the natural environment, perhaps limiting the generalizability of treatment effects and the frequency of training sessions. It would seem that any treatment technique that can be employed within the natural environment would be much more successful than a purely clinic-based treatment. The covert procedure (Cautela, 1967) discussed in the Chapter 5 offer a very promising alternative to such clinic-restricted treatment approaches.

Electrical Procedures

While most drug-related procedures employ a classical conditioning paradigm, electric shock is typically employed as an aversive stimulus in an operant punishment paradigm. The most usual paradigm for treatment is outlined in Fig. 3.2.

RESPONSE (R)———————→ PUNISHMENT (P)		IMPORTANT VARIABLES
(e.g., imagery,	(presentation of	(a) Intensity of P,
physiological,	aversive electric	(b) Number of
overt behavior)	shock)	presentations of R-P,
		(c) Corresponding
		reinforcement of
		incompatible R,
		(d) Schedule of P
		(e.g., VI, VR).

Fig. 3.2

Punishment paradigm most often employed with shock as the aversive stimulus.

Within this paradigm some aspect of a client's behavior to be reduced is systematically followed by aversive electric stimulation. As with drug aversion, targeted behaviors have most often been those for which client self-control is most difficult, because of the immediate reinforcement that they provide to the client. Thus, alcoholism, certain sexual behaviors, the inappropriate eating habits of obesity, as well as use of cigarettes have been among frequently reported targets for electrical aversion procedures (Rachman and Teasdale, 1969; Bancroft, 1974). An early study by McGuire and Vallance (1964) well illustrates the usual paradigm employed in electrical aversion. Working with a variety of targeted behaviors (sexual, smoking, alcohol) the authors employed the following steps:

1. Clients were systematically trained to imagine themselves engaging in the particular targeted behavior or to imagine some stimulus related to that behavior. For example, the client might imagine himself taking out, lighting up, and smoking a cigarette, or seeing someone else lighting a cigarette. In similar fashion the client might imagine himself reaching for

a glass of alcohol, putting it to his lips, taking a sip, tasting it. Thus, the primary method of presenting the stimulus is in imagination, which is similar to an array of other behavioral treatment procedures (Wolpe, 1958; Cautela, 1967).

2. The client is made familiar with the apparatus that delivers a low-level milliampere shock and is asked to self-determine the level of shock that is most unpleasant, yet nondamaging (an innovative procedure suggested by Tondo and Gill, 1975, relates shock setting to client scores on the Fear Survey Schedule; Wolpe and Lang, 1969). In most treatment paradigms the *client thus determines his own level of punishment* (Marks and Gelder, 1967; Tondo and Gill, 1975). This level of shock is set prior to each conditioning session and sometimes within the session, as clients tend to adapt to particular shock levels over time (Rachman and Teasdale, 1969).

3. After electrodes have been attached to some part of the body (most typically the hand or arm), the client is asked to imagine the stimulus as he has been trained to do and to signal the therapist when the scene becomes fully elaborated in his imagination. With sexual targets the client may be asked to signal at that point when he becomes aroused to the deviant sexual stimulus as defined by self-description of arousal (McGuire and Vallance, 1964; Marks and Gelder, 1967) or when some physiological measure illustrates that the client is aroused (Bancroft, 1966). Autonomic measures of GSR, respiration rate, and heartbeat may be employed to indicate arousal to the imagined stimulus, or some measurement device such as a strain gauge or plythysmograph (Freund, 1963; Barlow, Becker, Leitenberg, and Agras, 1970) may be attached to the male penis to measure blood volume changes as a measure of sexual arousal.

4. When the client signals the therapist, a single shock or train of shocks is immediately delivered on some schedule. Some investigators use an intermittent variable schedule for delivery (Marks and Gelder, 1967; Feldman and MacCulloch, 1965; Blake, 1965).

5. The procedure may be repeated for some systematic number of trials per session, or until the client is no longer able to imagine and/or achieve arousal within the treatment session. Treatment sessions often last from 10 to 30 minutes, and may be administered on a frequent basis within the day.

6. Typically the client is terminated from therapy at that point where the targeted image no longer holds positive properties for him as measured by attitudinal tests, physiological measures, self reports, behavioral observations of the client, report of family members or others important in the client's life, responses on personality measures, or other measures of change.

7. Often some access to therapy in the form of "booster sessions" is available following termination. Most desirably, the client is "followed up" over some long period of time to assess the maintenance of effects.

While imagery may be the behavior focused upon in treatment, many investigators have punished overt acts that the client was encouraged to engage in within the treatment session. For example, Marks and Gelder (1967), in describing the treatment of five subjects described as fetishists or transvestites, shocked actual deviant behavior such as putting on other-sexed garments. Most reports of electrical aversion have been directed at sexual or alcoholic behavior. However, these approaches have been directed at many of other behaviors, and most reports are of the case study type. Use of electrical aversion to disrupt the mental images of obsessive clients has been employed by Marks (1968), Kushner and Sandler (1966), and Marks, Gelder, and Bancroft (1970). More recently, Kenny, Solyom, and Solyom (1973) used electric shock to disrupt the verbal phrases and mental images employed by five chronic obsessive patients. The authors required each client to:

break it [the compulsive or obsessive thought] down into about ten distinct steps which could subsequently be imagined, e.g., ten consecutive steps in the act of compulsive hand washing, from turning on the taps to drying his hands. If a patient's targeted symptoms were obsessive fears, ruminations, horrorific temptations or pervading doubts, he was asked to express these in distinct phrases (as they might come to his mind), e.g., "Thought of touching urine, I'll contaminate others." Ten of these phrases, those rated by the patient as most frequent and severe, were then selected for therapy.

During each therapy session, the patient was seated with his back to the therapist. A finger electrode was attached and a shock pain threshold was determined. If the target symptom were a compulsion or ritual, the patient was asked to imagine the first step and to indicate, by raising his finger, when the image was formed. As soon as he raised his finger, the therapist delivered an electroshock at pain threshold intensity for 0.5 seconds. After a pause of thirty seconds the next image was demanded and the procedure continued until each image on the list had been completed. The phrases describing ruminations, doubts and fears were treated in a similar fashion; except that the patient was asked to repeat the phrase to himself before raising his finger. (p. 451).

The authors report that sessions usually consisted of a repetition of the ten items three to four times every 40-minute treatment session. Measurements of phrase repetition or latency of image formation were taken for each presentation. Sessions occurred at a rate of three to five times per week "so that the patient would not as easily rehearse his obsessive behavior between treatments." Following the third session, the authors employed a variable ratio of shocks (shocks on only 60 percent of trials). The authors report that three of the patients showed great improvement and were very satisfied with their gains. While another patient required further treatment, a fifth patient became psychotic and required a course of electroconvulsive shock therapy to terminate her psychotic episode. Unfortunately, the follow up period was only a mean of 4.8 months across clients. The mixed results presented here seem to be typical of many reports on the use of electrical approaches to treatment (Blake, 1965; Bancroft, 1966; Marks and Gelder, 1967).

Another more recent application of electrical aversion has been directed at suppressing self-destructive behavior such as head banging, clawing of arms, limbs, and face with fingernails, beating or slapping of the body or face displayed by seriously disturbed children. Ivar Lovaas and his colleagues at the University of California at Los Angeles (e.g., Lovaas and Simons, 1969) have assumed a leadership role in combining aversion to reduce such self-abusive behaviors with positive reinforcement provided for more adaptive social behavior with young autistic children. Because these self-mutilating behaviors cannot be dealt with using more traditional sorts of talk therapy, behavior therapists have been called upon to interrupt and terminate these behaviors, often employing aversive control. It is important to note that the kinds of aversion employed (light slaps—Lovaas; unpleasant but nondamaging levels of shock—Tate and Baroff, 1966; Lovaas and Simmons, 1969; Risley, 1968) do not cause physical damage to the child and are terminated as soon as the self-mutilation behavior has been halted. Because these procedures are typically employed within the clinical setting, many investigators find that the decrease in self-mutilation does not automatically generalize to other environments unless those environments are very similar to the clinic (Risley, 1968; Birnbrauer, 1968; Lovaas and Simmons, 1969).

In a more recent study Merbaum (1973) taught a mother to employ shock to punish the face-slapping behavior of a 12-year-old child variously diagnosed as autistic, schizophrenic, retarded, brain-damaged, or some combinations of these. It was thought that if the mother and his teachers could successfully employ this technique, the problem of generalizing treatment effects from the clinic to home and school would be solved. The authors employed a time-sampling procedure to carefully observe the frequency of blows to the face at baseline prior to treatment and following implementation of aversive control. They report:

The punishment contingency was administered by a Hot Shock stop prod. The prod, 18 inches in length with two end terminals about .5 inches apart, is battery operated and gives off 150 to 300 small and large A4 milliamps peak amperage, with output from 200 to 500 volts. The treatment program was arranged as follows. The therapist (the author at the beginning of the project) waited until Andy hit himself and then presented the shock. Andy's initial reaction to this experience was surprise, a cry of pain and immediate fear of the device. Paradoxically, his reaction to the therapist was one of approach and desire for closeness. Tenderness and affection were freely expressed by the therapist and Andy responded warmly to this attention. For the next two hours, with the shock prod visible to him, there was not one instance of self-abusive behavior. Andy's teachers, carefully instructed in the use of the shock device, played an essential role in the treatment program. The shocker, carried around constantly, was immediately available when Andy began to beat his face. On those rare occasions on which he would hit himself a shock was immediately forthcoming along with a resounding "no" from the teacher. It was estimated that Andy received no more than 17 shocks at school before the behavior appeared to be under tight stimulus control. Throughout subsequent weeks the teacher continued to carry the shock prod wherever they went and Andy was constantly exposed to the threat of shock." (pp. 443-444)

Prior to treatment the child's face was terribly bruised and "his cheeks grotesquely swollen." The authors reported a consistent reduction in Andy's self-beating behavior with treatment, even though for the five years prior to aversion therapy many intensive therapeutic programs, including conventional psychotherapy, had failed. The authors also reported that the child's mutilation behavior was reduced to extremely low levels at a one year followup. The mother reported, "When he does start to hit, and this is very infrequently, a strong 'no' is sufficient to stop the behavior" (p. 444).

The authors justified their use of such pain-provoking methods because of the clear threat of harm that the child's behavior predicted, and the previous failure of less aversive approaches. It is very interesting to note that throughout the entire course of therapy the mother reported using the shock stick only about 25 times. The authors pointed out the care necessary in selecting a parent to dispense such aversive contingencies. They would not employ the procedure if a parent had a history of using punishment in a sadistic or tyrannical way. This case study presents a good example of the use of such pain-provoking aversive stimulation by therapists who carefully evaluated the rationale for treatment and clearly traded a brief exposure to systematic punishment for a five-year history of potentially damaging self-mutilation.

Based upon a review of the literature reporting use of electrical aversion, as well as common sense, the following comments would seem to apply to the use of electrical aversion:

Precise control—Use of electrical stimulation as an aversive agent enables the BCA to precisely control the intensity of the unconditioned punishing stimulus, as well as its duration and temporal factors governing its administration. Thus, the punishing stimulus may be applied precisely .5 seconds, 10 seconds, or at any time following the targeted problem behavior. In addition, because shock does not produce the lasting debilitating effects that many drug agents do, the BCA is able to employ frequent trials or repetitions within a given day, thus gaining greater control over the intertrial intervals. It may be that frequent repetitions allow therapeutic progress to be made more rapidly. Also, using a more discrete stimulus, such as electric shock, allows the BCA to measure more precisely which particular elements of the punishment presentation produce treatment effects. Comparisions of such factors as differential shock levels, temporal relationships, and duration of shock allow the therapist using electrical aversion to systematically evaluate the effectiveness of the elements of his treatment approach.

Unpleasantness and health factors.—As with use of drugs, clients as well as staff members often object to the use of shock for perfectly logical and understandable humane reasons. In recommending the use of electric shock as an aversive agent, the BCA must first determine that such treatment is the optimal approach in the situation and that there is some logical justification with regard to the literature to assume that such an approach will be effective for the particular targeted client behavior. No therapeutic agent who behaves in accordance with a high standard of professional and ethical behavior would insist upon the use of shock, or in some fashion coerce clients or staff members to employ such a procedure against their will.

It is of concern to many BCAs that aversive techniques are often employed with individuals who are out of the mainstream of society. In a recent review of behavior therapists who employ behavioral change procedures to alter homosexual behavior, Davison and Wilson (1973) found that therapists as of the summer of 1971 "make considerable use of various aversive techniques with homosexuals, much more so than any other behavioral approach." They point out that, "In view of questions recently raised as to the appropriateness of aversive conditioning to helping homosexuals change their orientation (Wilson and Davison, 1974; Barlow, 1973) this is not a happy situation for the field." Unfortunately, some 13 percent of the respondents said that they had treated or would consider treating homosexuals against their wishes with a goal of changing orientation. The authors see this as an uncomfortably high proportion of therapists who would attempt to coerce homosexuals to change. Certainly, whether aversive techniques are applied to homosexualty, alcoholism, or any one of a number of socially undesirable behaviors (remembering that "undesirable" is defined in the eye of the beholder!) an array of ethical questions must be dealt with by the BCA. It is encouraging that well-known practitioners such as Davison and Wilson are becoming increasingly concerned with the ethical implications of altering many targeted behaviors, as well as with the use of aversive techniques in general.

It is also particularly unfortunate that many recent protests regarding teh use of behavioral techniques (and the cutting back of funding for programs that employ "behavior modification" within several state and federal agencies) have been directed toward the use of aversive conditioning. In fact, the use of aversive procedures is reported less and less frequently in the literature. Because of the nature of procedures that employ physical aversion, the possibility of their abuse, and the real possibility of physical and/or psychological damage when inappropriately applied, the practical and ethical questions being raised may ensure that such techniques are more optimally and benignly employed in future years. It has been common to view behavioral approaches as something of a "fad," with "instant" behavior modifiers emerging from the reading of a textbook article or from participation in a workshop. The use of physical aversion must be more carefully monitored so that it is not abused by individuals who do not have the theoretical, assessment, and practical background necessary to perform any kind of therapeutic intervention.

Along more practical lines, the BCA must ensure that devices that deliver an electrical current are safe. This author strongly urges that a competent electrician be employed to test such devices before use with clients. Also, certain investigators have suggested guidelines for construction (see Butterfield, 1975, and Siddall, Vargas, and Adesso, 1975).

Increased possibilities for self-control.—Perhaps a major advantage of electrical approaches is the ease with which they may be employed outside of the therapeutic situation by the client himself. Any procedure that attempts to induce self-control of targeted behaviors by encouraging the client to manage his own treatment would seem to be superior to procedures that rely exclusively on extrinsic manipulation by some BCA. The preceding case study by Kenny, Solyom and Solyom (1973) is among a number of research efforts recently reported in which portable electric shock apparati have been employed by the client in the natural environment. Such portability would of course be impossible with drug treatments for both practical as well as medical reasons. Thus, the client who receives aversive shock in the McGuire and Vallance (1964) tradition in the clinical situation can systematically shock himself using "personal shocker" when he experiences an urge to engage in the targeted (sexual, alcoholic, smoking, etc.) behavior in the natural environment. Self-control procedures will be discussed further in Chapter 8.

Innovations in Physical Aversive Control

The previous discussion has emphasized drug and electrical approaches because of the frequency with which they have been reported in the literature. Many investigators have experimented with alternatives in the hopes of finding a procedure that has the characteristics of physical aversion, yet can be easily employed within and without the therapy setting, is relatively inexpensive, exhibits no unpleasant side effects, and does not trigger the negative set among clients and staff members often observed with aversive drugs and shocks. An array of these procedures will be presented in the hopes of providing a suggestion of the alternatives the BCA has in choosing a physical punisher or UCS. Perhaps any stimulus that holds aversive properties *for the particular client* may be used in an aversive conditioning paradigm.

One promising area of investigation is the use of aversive odors (Foreyt and Kennedy, 1971) and taste (Whitman, 1972) as aversive agents. Using a classical conditioning paradigm, Foreyt and Kennedy paired the noxious odor of agents such as skunk oil and butyric acid with obese clients' imagery of desirable food items. In actual practice the client imagines some valued food item, and at the point where the client reports well-developed imagery, the therapist administers a noxious odor via a nosepiece. Using a partial schedule, the imagined food (CS) was not followed by the noxious odor (UCS) on all trials. Clients received 15 pairings of CS-UCS per session, several times per week over a period of nine weeks. In comparing the aversive conditioning group with a control group (both groups were part of a Weight Watchers program), the authors found that the aversive group showed a mean loss of 13.3 pounds and the control group showed a mean loss of 1 pound at the end of nine weeks. At 48 weeks, when the authors conducted the important followup necessary to evaluating any treatment, they found that the aversive group showed no change. They concluded that this procedure might be a useful adjunct to a weight-control program. Interestingly enough, the authors found that clients are most willing to undertake this kind of aversive control. Also, the aversive stimulus employed was directly related to the behavior (eating of certain foods) to be reduced. Smell and odors generally are important components of eating, and Berecz (1973) has stated that the ideal aversive stimulus should in some way be related to the targeted behavior to be reduced.

Whitman (1972) employed a pill that, when placed in one's mouth, produced a severe burning sensation and bitter taste after about two minutes contingent upon smoking. Clients were asked to light up a cigarette and inhale when the pill was half dissolved, so that the cigarette (CS) would be associated with the aversive properties of the pill (UCS). This represents an interesting alternative to electrical approaches, but is open to the criticisms previously discussed within the drug category (poor control of temporal variables, difficulty in controlling the intensity of the UCS, and so on).

Other investigators (Solyom, 1972) have employed relief from aversion as a counterconditioning agent to anxiety in desensitization. The drift of this approach is that the termination of an aversive stimulus such as shock leads to a feeling of cognitive and physiological relief or relaxation on the part of the clients. This period of relief might be used therapeutically as a counterconditioning agent (see Chapter 9 on control of avoidance behavior) in desensitization.

Green and Holz (1971) suggest a novel and somewhat paradoxical approach to aversive control. In working with two blind, institutionalized clients who were engaging in inappropriate physical behavior such as head banging, pinching, scratching, and general destructiveness, they employed 3 to 5 seconds of tickling, which they had found to be aversive to the two subjects. Interestingly enough, the tickling in this punishment paradigm served to reduce the frequency of these disruptive physical behaviors. Mervyn Wagner (personal communication) has used a simple, inexpensive, extremely portable approach to aversion to decrease a variety of targeted behaviors. Wagner asked the client to wear a rather thick rubber band around his wrist, and upon experiencing an urge related to the targeted behavior, to punish himself by pulling the rubber band back and letting it go. Not believing in the aversive properties of this arrangement, the present author tried it, only to let out what could best be described as a yell. Perhaps this approach emphasizes the fact than any of a number of agents applied to any body site could feasibly be used as an aversive stimulus, provided that their effects were cognitively viewed as aversive (Berecz, 1974; Hunt and Matarazzo, 1973) by the client recipient.

It is encouraging that investigators are increasingly attempting to define and employ physical aversive agents that may be more readily employed and more easily satisfy the practical and ethical requirements of an ideal aversive stimulus.

The Quest for the Ideal Aversive Stimulus: Important Issues

Following an explication of some of the important background research within the animal literature from which most aversive procedures have been derived, the present discussion has described major drug, electrical, and other innovative approaches to physical aversion, while attempting to provide a critique within each area of application. On a number of occasions the point was made that a careful consideration of practical, medical, and ethical considerations must be under-taken because of the specific characteristics of the aversive agents employed. It is very pleasing to see behavior therapists engaging in a discussion regarding the practical (Berecz, 1973; Danaher and Lichtenstein, 1974; Berecs, 1974), theoretical (Wilson and Davison, 1969), as well as ethical (Rachman and Teasdale, 1969; Davison and Wilson, 1973) issues that underlie the use of physical aversion. A summary of some of the practical suggestions indicated seems in order.

1. Summaries of the theoretical explanations for the effects of punishment (Bandura, 1969; Rachman and Teasdale, 1969) suggest that no one conceptualization does a comprehensive job of explaining the effects of punishment. In fact, the investigator who uses a seemingly pure classical or operant approach is often confounding two or more of these paradigms (Rachman and Teasdale, 1969). An array of consistent findings as to the optimal means of presenting an aversive physical stimulus have been suggested by the animal (Azrin and Holz, 1966) and human (Rachman and Teasdale, 1969) literatures. Although many of these findings have not been experimentally evaluated with human populations, and rest rather heavily upon the animal literature, they will be presented as the "best predictions" in terms of the current literature in the material that follows.

2. The success of suppression seems to increase with the intensity of the punishing stimulus. Obviously, there is a limitation in terms of the amount of aversive stimulation a given client can tolerate and an intensity

beyond which learning would be seriously interfered with due to extremely high levels of emotional arousal. In application, the BCA may best determine this point of maximally intense stimulation by carefully examining the self-report of the client as differential levels of aversive stimulation are experience, to be sure that the aversive stimulus employed is in fact cognitively experienced as aversive by the recipient (Rachman and Teasdale, 1969; Berecz, 1973; Tondo and Gill, 1975). Most investigators report that this optimal level of intensity varies markedly across clients and within clients depending upon such variables as fatigue, cognitive set, current level of emotional responding, and other factors. Inclusion of physiological measure to assess level of arousal generated by differing punishment intensities might enhance our understanding of the aversive stimuli employed (Berecz, 1973). In fact, however, we must ultimately rely upon self-report of the client regarding the subjectively experienced intensity of any type of painful stimulation. Danaher and Lichtenstein (1974) have stated:

Research programs of aversion treatment typically include a preperatory stage wherein the subject is asked to indicate the maximal amount he can tolerate with respect to the particular aversive stimulus being employed. Self-report may again be solicited during intervention in order to check for possible habituation effects. This careful attention to individual differences in reaction to individual stimuli has been witnessed in the application both of electrical shock and ehcmicals in conditioning paradigms. (p. 114)

The authors suggest that additional indications of the aversiveness of some punishing agent may be obtained through observation of various overt indices of unpleasantness, such as dizziness and nausea.

3. Although many investigators vary the schedule of punishment, it appears that *the use of continuous punishment—that is, punishment after each incidence of negative behavior—produces more suppression than does intermittent punishment for as long as the punishment contingency is maintained* (Azrin and Holz, 1966). It would seem that because many targeted behaviors that are the focus of aversive procedures yield a high schedule of immediate, extremely positive reinforcement for the client, a partial schedule might allow the reinforcement that occurs on nonpunished trials to outweigh the effects of punishment.

4. The punishing stimulus, as with a reinforcement in a strictly operant approach, should be *delivered immediately* after the response (Azrin and Holz, 1966; Church, 1963).

5. Whenever possible, therapists should attempt to *decrease or remove to the extent the positive reinforcement that is currently maintaining the undesirable behavior*. Such reinforcement for inappropriate behavior would of course interfere with the potential for response suppression. Unfortunately, as Rachman and Teasdale (1969) have stated:

In the types of behavior to which aversion therapy is applied, the situation is not so simple. Much of this behavior is of a consummatory nature, so that it is impossible to remove the primary reinforcer without destroying the behavior which it is intended to punish, e.g. it would be difficult to punish the response of drinking alcohol without letting the patient drink alcohol. Plus, the drinking behavior continues to be positively reinforced during the punishment procedure. The only thing left to do in such a situation is to allow the maintaining reinforcer to follow the punished response but to try to change its sign from positive to negative. (p. 125)

6. It is extremely important that *positive reinforcement be provided for some incompatible and appropriate client behavior that might take the place of the punished targeted behavior.* In their behavior therapy text, Rimm and Masters (1974) state: "As we must stress throughout this chapter, aversive techniques, especially punishment, are rarely utilized alone; their effectiveness will be maximized but potential problems minimized when they are used in conjunction with other techniques designed to promote more effective behavior patterns" (p. 367). The importance of reinforcing alternative desirable responses cannot be overemphasized.

7. There seems to be disagreement as to whether punishment is most effective when applied early in the response sequence (e.g., following an urge to take out a cigarette but prior to lighting up) or later in the response sequence (e.g., during or following the puffing on a cigarette). Rachman and Teasdale have suggested that "Although punishment early in the response sequence seems most effective in delaying relapse back to the performance of the previously punished behavior, it may be that punishment late in the response sequence, producing more guilt, would be more effective in reducing the overall frequency of the undesirable behavior over an extended period" (p. 128). Although we have little data to suggest an optimal point for physical punishment, it would seem to the author that *punishment should occur as early in the response chain as possible.* When the client is permitted to engage in the undesirable targeted behavior prior to receiving the punishment, he receives the immediate reinforcement for that response, and this may paradoxically interfere with the effects of the punishment that follows. In this situation a learning paradigm might be described as the client being reinforced with the puff on the cigarette, followed by a punishment: an inconsistent communication to the client. It would seem that if the client is provoked into engaging in self-control of the targeted response, he will need to intervene and engage in some incompatible behavior early in the response chain—prior to his receiving reinforcement for the inappropriate behavior.

8. *Because of the usual high rates of reinforcement for the targeted behavior in the natural environment, punishment might best be administered under conditions whereby the BCA can obtain control over these reinforcers.* Treatment sessions employing punishment should be conducted on a *frequent* basis, particularly when mild forms of punishment are employed (Azrin and Holz,

1966), because during the time between extended sessions, a targeted behavior may be reinforced at a high rate. Again, the client receives great amounts of reinforcement for the targeted response in the natural environment, and this competes with limited amounts of negative consequences within the clinical setting on an infrequent schedule. It becomes obvious that under such conditions the probability of successful suppression is remote. Whenever possible, *the client should be encouraged to practice and employ the punishing agent upon each occurrence of the targeted response outside the clinical setting.* It makes sense that the more the client associates punishment with the targeted response out in the natural setting, the greater the chance of successful suppression.

9. Although there is some discrepancy within the literature (Berecz, 1973; Wilson and Davison, 1969; Danaher and Lichtenstein, 1974), it would seem that the punishing stimulus should be related in some meaningful way to the targeted behavior to be decreased. Thus, the use of aversive odors or tastes might be a more effective punisher for responses having to do with the consumption of food or obesity of clients, while rapid smoking or hot smoky air (Schmahl, Lichtenstein, and Harris, 1972) might be the most relevant aversion to employ in decreasing smoking behavior. One might ask, as have Rachman and Teasdale (1969), what pressing a button or lever to avoid being shocked has to do with a complex set of responses involved in avoiding a homosexual stimulus. Unfortunately, many BCAs have rather mechanically employed existing paradigms using shock or drugs as aversive agents for targeted responses that seem topographically dissimilar.

10. Last, the author would like to underscore a point made by Rachman and Teasdale (1969): *"Aversion therapy should only be offered if other treatment methods are inapplicable or unsuccessful and if the patient gives his permission after a consideration of all the information which his therapist can honestly supply"* (p. 174). In addition they state: "The substitution of effective but less unpleasant alternative methods of treatment should be carried out as soon as this is feasible" (p. 174).

The important issue here is the creativity with which the BCA employs aversive techniques. In carefully assessing the variables that control some targeted behavior, it is most important that the BCA carefully tailor an approach that best fits the characteristics of the targeted response to be decreased and best increases the probability that some more adaptable, socially desirable behavior will occur. As previously emphasized, physical aversion should be employed only after the BCA considers alternative methods characterized by less unpleasant effects.

The present discussion suggests rather strongly that the BCA must make many decisions as to the means of presentation, intensity of the stimulus, incorporation of avenues of self-control, as well as a host of other variables in designing a treatment plan employing physical aversion. *Unthinking application of shock, drugs, or any specific physical aversive approach across clients and targeted behaviors may be practically limited and ethically questionable.* The potential for abuse, the general repugnance of the lay public, as well as the discomfort a client may experience make it crucially important that aversive approaches be employed only by the well-trained BCA in a thoughtful and systematic fashion.

CHAPTER SUMMARY

While the goal of treatment might be to reduce the frequency of inappropriate, problem behaviors, a careful definition of alternative and incompatible events that might concomitantly be increased in frequency is emphasized. In fact, most cases cited within the literature employ some combination of positive as well as negative approaches to behavioral management.

In defining consequences, the BCA might ask the clients for a verbal report of those material items, privileges, activities, or other events that they value. Another approach is to observe clients' functioning within the natural environment and to employ as consequences those events that occur at some high rate, suggesting their value to clients. In addition, perhaps to augment verbal reports, written reinforcement surveys might present mulitple items to clients and permit them to endorse those items valued or disliked. Consequences should be practical to the setting and available to the client so that reinforcement may occur consistently and on an immediate basis. Also, consequences should be consonant with treatment goals and intrinsic to the setting within which clients function. Finally, the consequence should not lose its effectiveness over time due to satiation or adaptation effects. Once consequences have been defined, an array of approaches is available for employing them within treatment.

Extinction involves terminating all reinforcement for some targeted behavior. This goal is desirable, but it is often very difficult to terminate avenues of reinforcement that maintain inappropriate client behavior, and so the extinction approach is very limited in its usefulness.

Using a *DRO approach, appropriate and incompatible behaviors are systematically reinforced using positive consequences, while targeted problem events are ignored to facilitate extinction.* This approach is quite limited, particularly with adolescents and adults who are reinforced by multiple agents within the environment.

Response cost is defined as the loss of some postive consequence following the emittance of a targeted client behavior; it may include the removal of any material, activity, or social reinforcer contingent upon some inappropriate event. Response costs are maximally effective when the reinforcer that is removed actually holds incentive properties, when the client has a part in deciding upon costs employed, and when the cost is clearly specified. Response costs should remove reinforcers that occur frequently enough so that the cost may be consistently applied, and the cost should be related to the problem behavior and specified prior to the occurrence of the target, particularly when the client self-imposes a cost upon his own behavior. This approach should be employed with reinforcement for the incompatible event.

Similar to a response cost, *time out involves limiting access to the environment itself contingent upon some inappropriate behavior; the client also may be physically removed from a reinforcing setting.* Time out may be best applied using a clearly defined set of communications (three-step contingency), and its use must be carefully monitored by the BCA as it is often abused by institutional staff or parents.

Physical punishment is characterized by the administration of an aversive stimulus to the client contingent upon targeted problem behavior ranging from verbal criticism and reprimands to hits, slaps, aversive drugs, and shocks. Many stimuli have been employed as physical punishers. Physical punishment has usually been employed to decrease the frequency of behaviors that are difficult or impossible to treat through extinction or removal of positive reinforcement. Such behaviors often provide very immediate, highly intensive reinforcement for the individual (e.g., consumption of alcohol), and physical aversion is chosen because of its immediate, interruptive, and aversive properties.

It was concluded that, contrary to previous findings, physical punishment can promote a permanent change in client behavior. Many problems associated with the use of physical punishment were discussed; among these problems were that physical punishment may produce unfortunate by-products; it may be abused by the punishing agent; and it often requires the BCA to model aggressive behavior, which may be incompatible with treatment goals. Also, punishment may produce conditioned emotional responses that may prove to be maladaptive. When physical punishment is employed, appropriate discriminatory responses should be systematically reinforced in combination with the punishment.

Early studies used pharmacological agents that induced nausea or vomiting within a classical conditioning paradigm to reduce an array of maladaptive targeted behaviors (e.g., consumption of alcohol, inappropriate sexual behaviors), and the problems inherent in using drugs were discussed. Electrical approaches to aversion often involve the presentation of mild, yet unpleasant electric shocks contingent upon some maladaptive response within a punishment paradigm. The use of electric shock provides the BCA with much more control over the aversive agent. These procedures may also be employed by the client in the natural environment. A number of different approaches to employing shock all seem to be effective in reducing particular targeted behaviors. There are ethical issues associated with the use of punishment, and it was suggested that these approaches not be used as the treatment of choice.

Finally, there are alternative approaches to physical punishment that may be more humane ways than a physically punishing agent.

There are many practical ways to increase the chance of success in using punishing consequences: most effective suppression is attained when intensive stimulation is presented within a continuous schedule of punishment; the punishing stimulus should be delivered immediately after the response; whenever possible, positive reinforcement currently maintaining the undesirable behavior should be evaluated and terminated to the extent possible; reinforcement should be provided for some incompatible, inappropriate client behavior that takes the place of the punished target; the client should be encouraged to practice and employ the punishing agent in the natural environment; and aversion therapy should be offered only if other treatments are inapplicable or unsuccessful, and if the patient gives his permission after a consideration of all the information.

Chapter 4

Manipulation of Consequences:

APPLICATION TO GROUPINGS

Within an institution it often becomes desirable to apply many of the procedures presented in Chapter 3 to groups of individuals in some consistent fashion. The usual poor ratio of staff members to clients often makes individual treatment less practical and approaches that apply a standard technology to all the members of a ward, cottage, classroom, or other entity can provide an efficient means of attaining therapeutic goals. Following the early work of Ayllon and Azrin (1965, 1968), investigators such as Atthowe (1964, 1966), Burchard and Tyler (1965), and Meichenbaum, Bowers, and Ross (1968) have applied group contingencies within an array of institutions (Kazdin, 1975). Quite often the public school (O'Leary, Becker, Evans, and Saudargas, 1969; Madsen, Becker, and Thomas, 1968; Walker and Buckley, 1968) has served as the focus for such efforts, and an array of "how to" texts have been directed at teachers (e.g., Becker, 1971).

In contrast to individual approaches, most institutional programs do not rely upon any one reinforcer or class of reinforcement. Instead, clients are informed of behaviors for which they may earn some "generalized" reinforcer such as a token (e.g., poker chip, points, checkmarks on a card), which may be traded in for any one of an array of material, social, or other reinforcements that have been chosen through careful survey procedures as suggested in the previous chapter. Thus, a "generalized" reinforcer is merely something the client receives that may be exchanged for other backup reinforcers. A program employing "generalized" reinforcers or tokens can ensure that each client finds some highly desirable reinforcement to purchase with tokens earned. The term "token economy" is often used to describe such an approach, although the way in which group programs are constructed varies considerably. Kazdin and Bootzin (1972) have presented a number of advantages in employing "generalized" reinforcers within institutional treatment programs. "Generalized" reinforcers: (1) make it easier for staff members to provide an immediate and discrete consequence for targeted behaviors; (2) permit reinforcement to occur at any time; (3) may be used to maintain performance of a behavior over an extended period of time when the backup reinforcer cannot be parceled out; (4) are not dependent upon client deprivation to maintain their incentive properties (e.g., like food); (5) do not lose their effectiveness due to client satiation (e.g., food is less valued as you become "full"); and, (6) provide an efficient means of reinforcement for individuals who have different preferences in backups.

Other important contributions of the token approach include:

1. Most programs clearly specify targeted behaviors that must be increased in frequency as well as those behaviors that should be decreased. Thus, the token approach requires that institutional administrators clearly specify the rules, expectations, and responsibilities defining client behavior. This clear explication of expectations is important in itself as many clients would probably fail if they had no clear idea of how they were expected to respond.

2. Because of its emphasis upon rewarding appropriate behavior, a token program forces staff members to focus their attentions and efforts upon those desirable and adaptive behaviors for which clients may earn tokens, rather than upon maladaptive behaviors that may have been previously punished in a wide variety of ways. Often backup reinforcers are chosen only after clients as well as staff members have had a hand in the decision process, thus increasing their investment within the treatment program as direct agents of treatment, and not mere "caretakers."

3. In many cases important incentives that did not previously exist for clients, such as consistent social approval from staff members, activities within the community, as well as participation in other social and task oriented activities which hold incentive properties (Nay, 1974), come about with the establishment of such a program.

4. The token program provides a record of client progress as its usually elaborate accounting procedures keep track of client earning and spending. When token earning is directly related to specific behaviors within the record-keeping process, and particularly when such records are available to clients, they serve as an important source of feedback as to progress. Often, observational data are also collected as a means of

evaluating the effectiveness of such programs, and this data can be of great importance in redesigning treatment planning.

5. While often accused of being artificial, mechanical, or a system of bribery, the token system may be more like the natural environment than many institutional settings. For example, within such a program clients must monitor their own behavior in order to earn tokens as well as to evaluate progress. There is a payment for services rendered, much like the monetary payments that we all receive in the community, and clients are provided with animportant role in altering their own behavioral patterns. The more traditional institutional environment, where many services are rendered for clients by staff and the client is rendered a "patient" with few responsibilities, is very much unlike the natural environment, and probably does little to promote generalization from the institution to the community. The important issue of generalization from a token program to the community has often been discussed within the literature (O'Leary and Drabman, 1971; Kazdin and Bootzin, 1972; Walker and Buckley, 1972; Atthowe, 1973; Nay, 1974), and a variety of procedures that may increase the probability that behaviors learned within the token economy translate into behavioral gains within the community will be presented in this chapter.

6. Often, token programs serve as a morale booster among clients, not only because of the reinforcement attendant to such programs, but because they offer the clients a means to become involved, and generally provide increased avenues of stimulation. Depending upon the manner in which staff members are provided with a chance to participate in the construction of such a program, are trained in its use, and are in some way provided positive feedback (reinforcement) for their efforts, token efforts may also increase the interest of staff members in promoting positive behavioral change on the part of clients, as well as boosting staff morale.

The token economy approach has been applied to an array of institutional populations, including psychiatric (Ayllon and Azrin, 1968; Atthowe and Krasner, 1968; Schaefer and Martin, 1966; Marks, Sonoda, and Schalock, 1968), mentally retarded (Girardeau and Spradlin, 1964; Birnbrauer and Lawler, 1964; Zimmerman, Stuckey, Garlick, and Miller, 1969), delinquent (Tyler and Brown, 1968; Cohen, 1968; Burchard and Tyler, 1965; Phillips, 1968; Phillips, Phillips, Fixen, and Wolf, 1971; Nay, 1974), as well as classroom settings within both institutions and publ c schools (O'Leary and Becker, 1967; O'Leary et al., 1969; Madsen et al., 1968; Walker and Buckley, 1972; Legum and Nay, 1973). Although the range of settings is quite variable, the present chapter will focus upon the primary steps generally involved in program construction, providing practical recommendations where appropriate, as well as defining the many problems often engendered or encountered in constructing, implementing, and evaluating such a program. Atthowe (1973) has summarized the current status of the token literature very succinctly:

Since the inception of token economy programs with chronic backward psychotics (only because it was felt that nothing would work with this population and any attention was better than nothing), token programs have proliferated to the point that most treatment, rehabilitative, correctional and educational settings use some form of contingent contracting (e.g., Rickard, 1971). Procedures and goals vary considerably. In some token programs the objectives have been to shape individuals to arrest or to overcome their aberrant activities. In others, the objective has been to create new ways of behaving, and, in some cases, to stimulate a greater level of activity. Whether the goals of the token programs have been easier management, habilitation or rehabilitation or whether the population of customers were chronic or acute psychotics, felons, the physically disabled or problem and normal children, the conclusion remains that contingent, token reinforcement programs are powerful techniques for modifying on-going behavior when properly applied. But, like all techniques of change, the persistence of produced changes have been rather short lived. However, a "broad spectrum" token economy program has many of the elements more often associated with generalization and enduring change than has most forms of individual therapy. (pp. 646-647)

Following a detailed discussion of each of the procedures for implementing a token system, alternative group contingency formats (some of which employ token economy features) will be presented. In all cases material will be illustrated using examples from the literature so that the reader may obtain some practical idea of how other investigators have proceeded.

DEFINITION OF TARGETED BEHAVIORS

Many investigators who use a token economy approach fail to explain why certain staff and child behaviors are chosen to be manipulated from the array of possibilities (e.g., Phillips, Phillips, Fixen, and Wolf, 1971; Kaufman and O'Leary, 1972). In addition,

the procedures used to assess the behavioral needs and resources of the institution are rarely described. Without this information, it is difficult to determine whether the token program has effectively dealt with the specific behavioral needs of that institution or has merely manipulated those behaviors which are less difficult, least costly to alter, or more suitable to a research methodology. (Nay, 1974, p. 207)

Client groupings often exhibit an array of divergent problem behaviors, and staff members may view these behaviors with varying degrees of concern. How then does the BCA define behaviors for change that will be imposed upon some large group of clients and manipulated by some aggregate of staff members? To the extent that staff or other potential agents can be trained to carefully observe their setting for potential targeted behaviors, a pooling of data across observers will provide the BCA with some initial notion of which behaviors need to be changed and in what direction. It would seem that staff members who will be asked to carry out program mechanisms should be given input into the choice of targets. It is assumed that many investigators provide staff members with this kind of input even though it often is not specifically discussed in their reports of such programs. By allowing staff members to have a say about what will be changed as well as how, the BCA can ensure that the individuals who are going to carry out the program will make an investment in its goals as well as its mechanisms. Perhaps staff members could be asked "What behaviors do you think clients need to increase in frequency? What client behaviors present problems for you or for the client and should be decreased in frequency?" This data may be augmented by meeting with staff members in a small group so that they might together review their global observations and begin to define some goals for treatment. By allowing staff members to discuss informally and freely their own observations of clients, the BCA not only provides them with an investment, but begins a new program of intervention with a positive atmosphere of cooperation, and sets up a model for close communication as the program is implemented and maintained over time.

Nay (1974) used the small group approach to define a series of goals for a proposed token program in a training school for adolescent delinquent females:

As a first step, a meeting with the superintendent and other key administrative staff was held. An attempt was made to operationally define their goals in seeking consultation services. It was determined that the administration desired some means of exerting control over the inappropriate behavior of students as well as being provided some level of treatment. An initial contract with the administration specified that a two month period would be required to independently assess the needs of the institution. A report to the administrative staff followed this assessment period. A variety of procedures were used to assess the needs of all settings of the institution—school, cottage, and vocational. (p. 207–208)

With regard to the small group meetings he reports:

The goal of the treatment consultants [the author and a team of six graduate students in clinical psychology] was to train the institutional staff as primary agents of treatment no matter what treatment goals were ultimately endorsed. Thus, it was necessary to obtain information from staff regarding treatment needs within their settings. As is typical in the training school for delinquents, many staff members were quite inflexible in their manner of dealing with children and wary of any "new" treatment ideas. In fact, previous treatment programs had failed within the institution due to a lack of staff support. It was thought that meeting with all 87 staff in small groups of five would allow the consultants to learn about behavioral problems, resources, and limitations of each setting and also give the institutional staff an opportunity to meet the consultants. In addition, by giving them such an opportunity over three meeting periods, the staff made an investment in the treatment program. Thus, from the beginning, the consultants made it clear that the staff would have a part in developing the treatment program. Many staff members had never been asked their opinions about anything regarding the care of girls under their direct supervision. To say the least, the small group meetings provided the consultants with practical information as to treatment possibilities as well as a keen understanding of limitations due to staff time available and staff expertise. Perhaps most importantly, these meetings precipitated staff interest in carefully looking at child behaviors and served to establish lines of communication which had not previously existed among institutional settings. (p. 208)

Similarly, clients should be given as much input into this decision process as possible to assure that goals are representative of their needs and to encourage investment in the program. In defining behaviors for change, the BCA might employ the following criteria:

1. Does the behavior occur with sufficient frequency to be considered worthy of change?

2. Does the behavior occur with sufficient consistency across a large enough number of clients within the institutional population to suggest that a group contingency (applied to all clients) is of more utility than defining individual treatment goals for those specific clients exhibiting the behavior?

3. Targets should reflect some consensus among staff and clients about the behaviors to be targeted for change. Strong disagreements as to the practicality, importance, or feasibility of changing specific targeted behaviors will certainly lead to inconsistent support for the program.

Target behaviors must be defined in clearly stated and operational language. Rimm and Masters (1974) make the following statement about specification of targeted behaviors:

Perhaps the most basic recommendation is that the particular behaviors in question, both those to be changed and the eventually desired behaviors, must be specified as concretely and elaborately as possible in ways that require but a minimum of interpretation by staff or patient. For example, uncooperative behavior may be many things; however, when defined as "responds willingly to requests regarding the taking of medication," a certain behavior is clearly specified and differentiated from all manner of other behaviors that are also uncooperative, but are not part of the particular set of problem behaviors characterizing patients on a certain ward. (p. 223)

Schaefer and Martin (1969) carry this point further:

General terminology may be used when forming descriptions for a treatment plan, but its meaning must be clearly specified. If a terminal goal is "good grooming" nursing personnel must describe which grooming habits need to be treated. Hair combing? Dressing? Selection of clothing? Perhaps a desired behavior is that a patient appears more "feminine." Like all adjectives, this one has content meaning which seems quite clear until people are asked to give its definition. No two respondents will use exactly the same terms to describe what constitutes feminine appearance, but many will agree that femininity is associated with attempts to maintain personal appearance. "Attempts to maintain personal appearance" can and should be stated in behavioral terms such as the following: combing hair neatly, wearing non-wrinkled clothing, wearing well fitting shoes, asking about current fashions, reading fashion magazines, and discussing choice of color, length and cut of dresses. (p. 83)

The importance of clearly defining a targeted behavior for clients and staff members cannot be overemphasized. It is implicit that some targeted behaviors are those for which an acceleration in frequency is desirable, while other behaviors demand a deceleration. In attempting to describe the kinds of behaviors that have been targeted within the literature, both classes of behavior will be presented. Of course, any behavior can be stated in either a positive or negative way. For example, clients could earn tokens for the targeted behavior of brushing their hair 50 strokes (positive) as well as lose points for failing to brush their hair the required number of strokes. Behaviors targeted within the literature seem to fall into five major classes, rather arbitrarily designated by the author. Within each class of behavior an array of specific targets will be presented. Many of these targets would seem to apply across diverse populations (such as mentally retarded, psychiatric, delinquent); however, some targets would most appropriately apply to a specific population (such as unusual or bizarre behaviors with psychiatric clients).

Self-Care Behaviors

Targeted behaviors involving skills necessary for adequate maintenance of self in accordance with consensually validated societal norms seem to fall into three categories:

Hygienic behaviors—Behaviors most often targeted within this category include washing hair, face, hands, elbows, and other body parts; applying deodorant; cleaning mouth; brushing teeth; cleaning body cavities (ears, nose, genital area, etc.); cleaning nails; brushing hair; combing hair; maintaining certain hair styles; applying or using certain necessary medications; application of cosmetics.

Dress—This category encompasses the appropriate matching of clothes; appropriate choice of clothing; color coordination; maintenance of clothing: cleaning, pressing, hanging up clothes properly; dressing correctly for various occasions; wearing articles of clothing as they are intended to be worn (e.g., shirt on right side out). Often clients are given the opportunity to vote on or select rules for dress appropriate to the age, cultural backgground, and current styles of the client grouping. One can imagine the problems inherent in asking elderly staff members, for example, to evaluate the jeans and T-shirt fashions of younger clients. It is very important that specific dress behaviors be clearly published for all staff and client members.

Administration of medication or therapy.—Among targets often chosen are taking prescribed medications; applying prescribed medications; performing prescribed exercises; engaging in other prescribed activities such as walks and physical therapy; eating a prescribed diet.

Social Behaviors

A great many social behaviors have been targeted within token programs. The present discussion will not attempt to be all-inclusive, but to present those behaviors most usually manipulated. Social behaviors will be divided into verbal and nonverbal classes.

Verbal Behaviors.—Included in this category are: Responding to name or greeting; initiating conversation; maintaining conversation when prodded to converse; control of pitch and/or loudness of voice; frequency of verbalization (either too much or too little); content of verbalizations: relevant versus irrelevant to ongoing topic of conversation; laughing or giggling or other joyful verbalizations (either too many or too few occurrences); talking to oneself or mumbling; positive/negative self-statements; positive/negative statements to others (e.g., approval, praise, criticism); aggressive (intention of hurting or harming another) verbalizations; profanity; meaningless verbalizations; increasing the frequency of verbal initiations.

Nonverbal Behaviors.—Included are walking skills: head up, back straight, toes straight ahead, nonshuffling; sitting in an array of inappropriate postures (legs not together, back not straight, head hanging down, sitting in a "slumped" position); maintenance of facial expressiveness (eye contact with fellow interactor, smiling, facial movements, facial expressiveness appropriate to situation, smiling when happy, not sad); self-stimulation behavior (chewing gum with mouth open, picking nose, cracking knuckles, making sounds with one's mouth, clicking fingers, etc.), horseplay and aggressive and assaultive behaviors such as hitting, kicking, slapping, pushing, shoving, and throwing things.

Work-Related Behaviors

Within many institutional settings clients work on an informal basis or do specifically jobs that result in token earnings. Many programs provide tokens for such activities as maintaining one's living quarters; providing services to the setting at large (e.g., cleaning, sweeping, dusting); or more vocationally oriented activities such as working in a kitchen, on the grounds, and so on. In many cases such behaviors are reinforced using tokens. When a task includes multiple procedures, requires certain materials for its completion or must be performed within a certain time limit and according to certain criteria, it is important that all relevant information be provided to the client in a clear and concise manner. Nay (1974) employed a "task assignment sheet," which was completed by the staff member and the client prior to initiation of task-related activities. Importantly, this sheet provided the client with a clear specification of the nature of the task, materials required, specific instructions for completion, a time frame for completion, as well as a clear understanding of token earnings that would be received following completion. Fig. 4.1 offers an example of this sheet.

TASK ASSIGNMENT SHEET

NAME: Jane Smith DATE: April 25, 1972

I. TASK DESCRIPTION: Dust and polish furniture in the lounge

II. TASK MATERIALS NEEDED:

1. Clean rags
2. liquid wax polish
3.

III. TASK INSTRUCTIONS: (If I follow these I earn 1-2 points)

CIRCLE those instructions which are correctly followed

If ALL are CIRCLED, INITIAL

1. remove all objects (such as lamps) from area to be cleaned
2. dust surface with rag
3. polish surface with wax
4. replace objects on furniture
5. put all of the cleaning equipment away

ND (1-2pt)

INITIAL:

IV. TASK TIME:

ND (1 pt) 1. If I LISTENED RIGHT AWAY, I earn 1 point for IMMEDIATE POSITIVE RESPONSE.

ND (1 pt) 2. I must BEGIN by 1:00 o'clock to earn 1 point for IMMEDIATE POSITIVE RESPONSE.

(1 pt) 3. I should FINISH by 2:00 o'clock to earn 1 point for COMPLETES TASK.

V. AGGREEMENT: I have no further questions and agree to perform this task the best I can.

Girl: Jane Smith

Staff: Miss Davis

INITIAL:

VI. TASK QUALITY: If my work is:

(1 pt) 1. Average: I do not earn a point.

ND (2 pt) 2. Good: I earn 1 point.

3. Excellent: I earn 2 points.

(1 pt) VII. ENCOURAGEMENT POINTS for IMPROVING: If I improve and do better that my previous work, but do not qualify for points above, I can earn 1 point for this improvement. ANYONE who steadily IMPROVES can earn points.

NOW TRANSFER ALL POINTS TO THE CARD WHEREVER POINTS HAVE BEEN INITIALED.

Fig. 4.1

Task assignment sheet (from Nay, 1974).

A similar task assignment procedure has been employed by Schaefer and Martin (1969). Phillips, Phillips, Wolf, and Fixsen (1973) describe an array of cottage-maintenance behaviors required of a population of delinquent boys in "achievement place," a residential, family-style behavior modification program for predelinquents. Staff members made frequent checks of task performance based upon highly specific criteria that were clearly presented to the boys.

Ayllon and Azrin (1965) offer an extensive list of jobs for which psychiatric clients could earn tokens within a ward setting (see Table 4.1).

Table 4.1

Types and Number of On-Ward Jobs

Dietary assistant

1. **Kitchen chores** (3[a], 10[b], 1[c])
   Patient assembles necessary supplies on table. Puts one pat of butter between two slices of bread for all patients. Squeezes juice from fruit left over from meals. Puts supplies away. Cleans table used.

2. **Coffee urn** (1, 10, 2)
   Patient assembles cleaning compound and implements. Washes 5-gallon coffee urn using brush and cleaning compound. Rinses inside, washes, and dries outside. Puts implements away.

3. **Ice carrier** (1, 10, 2)
   Patient goes with attendant to area adjacent to ward where ice machine is located, taking along 10-gallon ice container. Scoops flaked ice from machine into container and carries it to the kitchen.

4. **Shakers** (2, 10, 2)
   Patient assembles salt, sugar, and empty shakers on table, fills shakers, and puts supplies away.

5. **Pots and pans** (3, 10, 6)
   Patient runs water into sink, adds soap, washes, and rinses all pans used for each meal. Stacks pans and leaves them to be put through automatic dishwasher.

6. **Steam table** (3, 10, 5)
   Patient assembles cleaning supplies. Washes and dries all compartments used for food. Cleans and dries outside of table. Places all pans in proper place on steam table.

7. **Meal server**[d] (6, 60, 10)
   Patient puts food into proper compartments on steam table. Assembles paper napkins and silver on counter placed at beginning of serv-

ing line, puts tablecloths, napkins, salt and sugar shakers on tables. Prepares proper beverage for each meal, putting ice in glasses for cold beverages and drawing coffee from urn. Prepares proper utensils for dirty dishes and garbage. Dips food, places food and beverage on trays. Gives patients their trays. After the meal is over, dietary workers empty all leftover food and garbage, place all trays, glasses and silver used on cabinets ready for the dishwasher.

8. **Dishwasher**[d] (9, 45, 17)

Patient prepares dishwasher, fills automatic dishwasher. Washes dishes, silver, and glasses. Operates automatic dishwasher, washes cabinets, sinks, and tables, and puts everything away. Patient counts silver (knives, forks, and spoons) for all patients and places them in containers ready for next meal.

Waitress

1. **Meals** (6, 10, 2)

Empties trays left on tables and washes tables between each of four meal groups.

2. **Commissary** (3, 10, 5)

Cleans tables, washes cups and glasses used at commissary. Places cups and glasses in rack ready for automatic dishwasher.

Sales clerk asssistant

1. **Commissary** (3, 30, 3)

Assembles commissary items. Displays candy, cigarettes, tobacco, cosmetics, dresses, and other variety store items so that they can be seen by all. Prepares ice, glasses, and cups for hot and cold beverages. Asks patient what she wishes to buy. Collects the tokens from patient and tells the secretary the name of the patient and the amount spent. Puts commissary supplies away.

Secretarial assistant

1. **Tooth brushing**[d] (1, 30, 3)

Assists with oral hygiene. Writes names of patients brushing teeth.

2. **Exercises**[d] (2, 30, 3)

Assists recreational assistant with exercises. Writes names of patients participating in exercises.

3. **Commissary**[d] (3, 30, 5)

Assists sales clerk assistant. Writes names of patients at commissary, records number of tokens patient spent. Totals all tokens spent.

Ward cleaning assistant

1. Halls and rooms (24, 30, 3)
Sweep and mop floors, dust furniture and walls in seven rooms and hall.

2. Special (1, 30, 4)
Cleans after incontinent patients.

3. Dormitories[d] (1, 180, 8)
Supplies each of five dormitories with the necessary cleaning implements. Fills buckets with cleaning water and delivers bucket of water, broom, mop and dust pan to each dormitory at a designated time. Picks up cleaning supplies and implements after a 30-minute interval.

Assistant janitor

1. Supplies (1, 10, 1)
Places ward supplies in supply cabinets and drawers.

2. Trash (3, 5, 2)
Carries empty soft drink bottles to storage area, empties waste baskets throughout the ward, and carries paper to container adjacent to building. Carries mops used during the day outside to dry.

3. Porch[d] (2, 10, 2)
Sweeps and washes walk adjacent to building. Washes garbage cans with soap and water.

4. Washroom janitor (1, 20, 3)
Obtains necessary cleaning supplies and implements from utility room. Cleans four wash basins and four toilet bowls with cleanser and brush. Returns cleaning supplies and implements to utility room.

Laundry assistant

1. Hose (1, 15, 1)
Match and fold clean anklets and stockings.

2. Delivery (1, 10, 2)
Carries bags of dirty clothing and linens from ward to outside linen house adjacent to building.

3. Folding[d] (2, 30, 3)
Folds and stacks clean linens in neat stacks and takes to the clothing room.

4. Pick-up service[d] (1, 60, 8)
Sorts dirty clothing and linens and puts items into bags marked for each item.

Grooming assistant

1. Clothing care (1, 15, 1)

Patient sets up ironing board and iron. Irons clothing that belongs to patients other than self. Folds clothing neatly. Returns ironed clothing, iron, and ironing board to nurses station.

2. Personal hygiene[d] (3, 60, 3)

Patient takes basket with grooming aids, gargle, paper cups, lipstick, comb, hairbrush, and powder into patients' washroom. Patient stays with grooming basket and assists any who need help with their grooming before each meal. Returns grooming basket after the meal has ended.

3. Oral hygiene[d] (1, 20, 3)

Assembles toothpaste, toothbrushes, gargle solution, and paper cups. Pours gargle into cups and dispenses toothpaste or gargle to all patients.

4. Personal[d] (1, 30, 3)

Patient assists selected patients who need extra aid with personal grooming.

5. Bath[d] (2, 45, 4)

Patient assists with baths, washing, shampooing, and drying. Cleans tub after each bath.

6. Beauty aids[d] (1, 30, 4)

Assists in shampooing, setting, and combing hair for patients who desire special service.

Recreational assistant

1. Walks[d] (1, 20, 3)

Assists ward staff when taking group of patients on walks. Walks in front of group.

2. Exercise[d] (1, 20, 3)

Operates record player and leads patients in exercises.

3. Movie projectionist (1, 90, 10)

Sets up movie projector and shows movie to patients. Changes reels and rewinds tape.

Special services

1. Errands (1, 20, 6)

Leaves the ward on official errands throughout the hospital grounds, delivering messages and picking up supplies and records pertaining to the ward.

2. **Tour guide** (1, 15, 10)
   Gives visitors a 15-minute tour of the ward explaining about the activities and token system. Answers visitors' questions about the ward.

3. **Nursing assistant**[d] (1, 10, 10)
   Assists staff with the preparation of patients to be seen by the medical doctor. Assists staff with the control of undesired interaction between patients.

Self-care activities

1. **Grooming** (−, −, 1)
   Combs hair, wears: dress, slip, panties, bra, stockings, and shoes (three times daily).

2. **Bathing** (−, −, 1)
   Takes a bath at time designated for bath (once weekly).

3. **Toothbrushing** (−, −,)
   Brushes teeth or gargles at the time designated for toothbrushing (once daily).

4. **Exercises** (−, −, 1)
   Participates in exercises conducted by the exercise assistant (twice daily).

5. **Bed making** (−, −, 1)
   Makes own bed and cleans area around and under bed.

[a] Number of jobs
[b] Duration (minus)
[c] Tokens paid
[d] Job requires two or more patients for its completions.

There is potential value in providing clients with an array of vocational tasks as a means of earning tokens. To the extent that such tasks are comparable to tasks likely to be performed in the natural environment, they encourage generalization of learned behaviors from the institutional setting to the community—and may in fact provide important training to the client. When a task-assignment sheet format is presented, the strategy of how to organize task materials, follow instructions, time requirements, and so on is learned by the client. Once this strategy is learned for a particular task, it may generalize to the way clients perform other duties both within and without the institution, and is an important source of skill learning.

It is extremely important, and cannot be overemphasized, that any task presented to clients be clearly stated with all expectations for completion carefully defined. Only then does task performance promote appropriate, goal-directed, task-related skills. Earning tokens for task-related activities is very similar to a salary the client will earn upon returning to the community. Unfortunately, within many institutional settings, particularly where funds are lacking, clients perform tasks mainly to perform some service to the institution, with no real opportunities for task specification or for feedback on performance. In this situation the task becomes an "end unto itself" and a service to the institution and may not promote new task-related skills that might foster a client's adjustment to the community setting. Recent legal decisions to be discussed in Chapter 11 have attempted to develop a better definition of a "therapeutic" work activity, and would not permit clients to be used merely as a captive labor force. Unfortunately, institutional administrators often have very little control over the kinds of tasks available to clients.

Table 4.2

Available Patient Positions and Responsibilities

Positions	*Responsibilities*
Clerks and paymasters	Collect or pay tokens
Store clerks	Collect and record number of tokens exchanged for products and recreation facilities
Television monitors	Collect and record tokens paid for TV use
Meal clerk	Collect and record tokens paid for meals
Paymasters	Pay tokens for work accomplished during their shift
Data collectors	Systematically observe ward behavior
Housekeeping checker	Evaluate and record duration of work
Buffer checkers	Record number of rounds per worker
Grader (school)	Correct papers, record work production
Research worker	Record rate of behaviors for behavioral engineer and staff
Behavioral engineers	Training and supervision of patients
Workshop supervisor and assistant	Training, bookkeeping, providing materials, rewarding, checking quality
Store manager	Provide supplies, training, pay and records daily inventory
Toothbrush mentor	Set up materials, pay, record data, and train
Exercise leader	Records attendance and quality of training

Because of the great investment of staff time required to set up and maintain a token program, many program administrators have employed clients to perform important activities related to the program. Kale, Zoutnick, and Hopkins (1968) found that there was never enough staff time to adequately manage a comprehensive token program and carry out other therapeutic work as well. They employed patients to serve as "integral parts" of the project staff. Patient responsibilities are shown in Table 4.2.

Kale et al. (1968) make this important point:

When patient helpers are employed it is important to guard against the temptation to exploit them. Placing a patient in a job he is already capable of handling defeats the purpose for which the system exists. Such an action benefits only the staff and other patients—the helper gains very little. Once a patient has developed as much skill as his particular job assignment allows, he must be advanced to a more demanding position. This project has been a key element in a comprehensive program which has significantly elevated the discharge rate of chronically ill patients. (p. 38)

While the importance of these guidelines cannot be overemphasized, it would seem that employing clients in important program roles not only provides necessary manpower to maintain the program, but offers an opportunity for these individuals to function within levels of increasingly greater responsibility. They begin to deal with institutional staff more at the level of peer than of patient. Feedback in monitoring patient helpers' efforts might be accomplished by way of a careful evaluation of client records, of ratings and systematic observations performed by staff members, as well as helper-generated reports of daily activities in the form of a journal, log or rating sheet (e.g., Panyan, Morris, and Boozer, 1970).

Classroom-Specific Behaviors

A clear majority of reports about the effectiveness of token programs comes from the public school classroom, typically focusing upon younger aged subjects in a self-contained classroom setting. Token programs are rarely directed at "normal" adolescent populations. Perhaps the reasons for this are the difficulty in defining reinforcers for older adolescents, the difficulty associated with designing and evaluating research in a setting where students move from one classroom to another throughout the day, and the inherent difficulties in applying such procedures to older subjects, who might be more difficult to physically control. Most token programs are geared not only toward the self-contained classroom setting, but toward the more traditional student role: in seat, facing straight ahead, actively paying attention, as opposed to the "open classroom," which is increasingly being employed in many educational environments. Thus the list of behaviors to be presented clearly reflects these limitations. Although investigators vary in the specific labels employed to describe these behaviors, the coding system presented by Madsen, Becker, and Thomas (1968) would seem to be inclusive of most behaviors defined as targets within classroom token programs.

Table 4.3

Behavioral Coding Categories for Children

I. Inappropriate Behaviors

A. *Gross Motor.* Getting out of seat, standing up, running, hopping, skipping, jumping, walking around, moving chair, etc.

B. *Object Noise.* Tapping pencil or other objects, clapping, tapping feet, rattling or tearing paper, throwing book on desk, slamming desk. Be conservative, only rate if you can hear the noise when eyes are closed. Do *not* include accidental dropping of objects.

C. *Disturbance of Other's Property.* Grabbing objects or work, knocking neighbor's books off desk, destroying another's property, pushing with desk (only rate if someone is there). Throwing objects at another person without hitting them.

D. *Contact (high and low intensity).* Hitting, kicking, shoving, pinching, slapping, striking with object, throwing object which hits another person, poking with object, biting, pulling hair, touching, patting, etc. Any physical contact is rated.

E. *Verbalization.* Carrying on conversations with other children when it is not permitted. Answers teacher without raising hand or without being called on; making comments or calling out remarks when no questions have been asked; calling teacher's name to get her attention; crying, screaming, singing, whistling, laughing, coughing, or blowing loudly. These responses may be directed to teacher or children.

F. *Turning Around.* Turning head or head and body to look at another person, showing objects to another person, showing objects to another child, attending to another child. Must be of 4-sec duration, or more than 90 degrees using desk as a reference. Not rated unless seated. If this response overlaps two time intervals and cannot be rated in the first because it is less than 4-sec duration, then rate in the interval in which the end of the response occurs.

G. *Other Inappropriate Behavior.* Ignores teacher's question or command. Does something different from that directed to do, including minor motor behavior such as playing with pencil or eraser when supposed to be writing, coloring while the record is on, doing spelling during the arithmetic lesson, playing with objects. *The child*

involves himself in a task that is not appropriate. Not rated when other Inappropriate Behaviors are rated. Must be time off task.
H. *Mouthing Objects.* Bringing thumb, fingers, pencils, or any object in contact with the mouth.
I. *Isolate Play. Limited to kindergarten* free-play period. Child must be farther than 3 ft. from any person, neither initiates nor responds to verbalizations with other people, engages in no interaction of a non-verbal nature with other children for the entire 10-sec period.

II. Appropriate Behavior

Time on task; e.g., answers question, listens, raises hand, works on assignment. Must include whole 10-sec interval except for Turning Around responses of less than 4-sec duration.

Table 4.3 shows this coding system. It should be noted that any of the child or teacher behaviors specified could be targeted for token earning or loss, depending upon the requirements of the classroom. In some cases the categories stated (e.g., gross motor) would be broken down by the program administrator, who might decide "getting out of seat" would be the specific target for intervention. "Running," "hopping," "skipping," and so on might be dealt with as separate targeted behaviors once children had learned to remain seated.

In most cases token administrators begin with a small subset of behaviors that might realistically be brought under control without overloading either clients or teacher. In particularly disruptive classroom settings it is obvious that any attempt to alter all problem behaviors at once, particularly when some behaviors are of very high rate, would be untenable and impractical for teachers as well as students. The order with which certain behaviors are dealt with depends upon their specific characteristics, frequency at baseline, and the degree to which the teacher is willing to intervene. Once a problem target is chosen for deceleration, an incompatible, adaptive behavior should be defined for acceleration, as suggested in Chapter 3. Thus the focus of behavioral change efforts is not merely upon negative control, but upon positive reinforcement of incompatible events.

THE TOKEN ECONOMY: DEFINITION AND MECHANISMS

Choice of Token

A wide variety of token reinforcers has been reported in the literature, including poker chips, metal disks, coins, paper money, points, or checkmarks as well as punch marks made upon some written record. As one might imagine, these forms of token feedback would have little meaning for clients if they were not traded in for "backup" reinforcements desirable to the client. Thus, the "token" may take on reinforcing properties through its association with "backups."

One could make the point that even tokens that were not previously associated with backup reinforcers might hold incentive properties for clients, given that staff members held in high esteem give them out for good performance. The stars awarded by many teachers represent a kind of token that usually has no backup reinforcers associated with it—it is often reinforcing because it is earned in a context of social reinforcement by the teacher and is given in the competitive environment of the peer group. Thus, the extent to which any token might hold reinforcement properties beyond its mere association with some backup reinforcers really depends upon the kind of token, the manner in which it is given (e.g., with or without social reinforcement), and, of course, the way the client views the token feedback.

Perhaps any kind of tangible reinforcement for some client behavior could be considered a token. Within such a broad definition everything from material items to forms of written feedback would all be considered within the token approach. In fact, within the literature this broad definition seems to have been adopted (O'Leary and Drabman, 1971; Kazdin and Bootzin, 1972). One major differentiation among tokens is between *physical objects*—poker chips, money, colored tags, or other material objects, and those approaches that provide some form of *written feedback*. Both the *material* and *written approaches have been widely used*.

Tokens should have the following properties:

1. Values should be readily understood—the client must be aware of the value of the token, and "backups" must be specified with costs clearly presented for each item.

2. There ought ot be some relationship between the number of tokens and the degree of reinforcement provided for some behavior (Ayllon and Azrin, 1968).

3. Tokens should be easily transportable, particularly if clients are asked to move to different settings within the institution. Male clients can have difficulty transporting large numbers of coins or other material objects without the aid of some container. Points and other kinds of feedback written on a card the clients carry with them provide an easily transportable means of token feedback.

4. Tokens should be constructed of a durable material, and written token feedback should be placed upon a paper material that is not apt to fall apart prior to client spending (Ayllon and Azrin, 1968).

5. Token feedback should be easy for staff members to dispense within the limits of their ordinary interaction with clients. Material tokens offer distinct advantages with regard to dispensation, whereas written feedback can often be too demanding a task in training or classroom

situations. In class or training settings the token system should interfere as little as possible with the academic goals of the teacher. If a teacher is asked to provide elaborate written feedback to each child on a frequent basis during the course of class, this reduces time that might be spent in academic pursuits. Staff members asked to devote large amounts of time to token distribution may take a negative view of the program. Consequently, any kind of written token feedback should be limited. A check, a quick punch of a card, a circling of some point value is certainly preferable to providing a written paragraph describing a client's behavior.

6. The token system should require minimal bookkeeping. Written approaches can be constructed so that the record of performance is logged on the card as each client earns tokens. Any token system that requires staff members to spend large amounts of time at the end of the day summarizing token data or transposing it onto ledger sheets takes away from time available for working directly with clients. The author has employed a card punch system for providing token feedback in an institution for "delinquent" adolescent females. Each client's card lists each of the targeted behaviors, and points earned for a particular behavior are punched on the card in the space designated for that behavior. A punch system makes point awarding easy—card can even be stacked and punched as a group. Clients are required to carry the card throughout the day, thus transporting their own records. Prior to bedtime all cards are turned into a night matron, who spends one to two hours recording point performance for the girls in her cottage in record books provided. This system requires no writing or record-keeping by any staff member except the night matron, who has time available while the girls sleep. If records of differential point earnings across settings were required, staff within each setting could be provided with punches with distinctive cuts (all school staff punch hearts; all cottage staff punch diamonds, etc.). These "Gem punches are produced in a variety of cuts by the McGill M.P. Co., Marengo Co., Ill., and may be economically purchased. Fıg. 4.2 illustrates one of these punch cards.

The card enables clients to see how many points are earned or lost for specific behaviors, as well as (in the present program) those behaviors for which points have been lost. This visual feedback occurs each time the clients look at their point record as points are earned throughout the day. Such records increase the clients' role in the program as monitors of their own behavior, possibly encouraging self-control (Kanfer and Marston, 1963).

Tanner, Parrino and Daniels (1975) provide a thorough description of a "punch" record-keeping system that employs automated data summarization. All token data is coded weekly, keypunched, and fed into the hospital computer. The unit psychologist then receives a printout for each client (e.g., amount earned for each behavior; amount spent for specific categories of "backups"; negative point totals, etc.) Similar summary data is printed out for the entire ward unit.

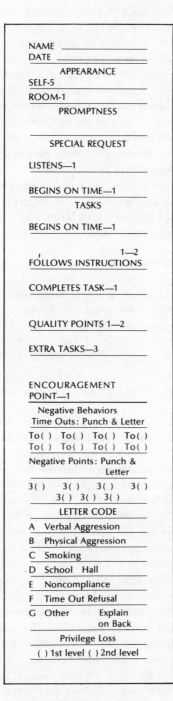

Fig. 4.2
Behavioral recording card.

7. By having relevance to real currency (e.g., token "money"), a token system may encourage the client to learn appropriate money management skills that may be a help upon reexposure to the community.

8. Tokens shoud be nonduplicable and unique so that the BCA may be assured that they are received only in the authorized manner (Ayllon and Azrin, 1968; Tanner et al., 1975). Material reinforcers that are not specifically labeled with a client's name or identified might be readily stolen, employed for gambling, or even offer the basis for a "protection racket." Written records, upon which a subject's name is placed, do much to ensure that these unfortunate events do not come about.

From the preceding criteria it makes sense to employ some form of written feedback whenever possible, particularly because it may provide visual feedback to clients regarding their progress throughout the day. The problems of transportability, gambling, theft, and so on would seem to apply primarily to material tokens.

Definition of Backup Reinforcers

An extraordinary number of items have been employed as backup reinforcers, as one might infer from the kinds of potential backups included in the reinforcement survey presented in Appendix A. In defining backup reinforcers, the observational data with regard to high-rate client behaviors, data from small group meetings with clients and staff members, and reinforcement survey data should be evaluated to ensure a list of backup reinforcers that will in fact hold incentive properties for the population of clients.

With a tremendous number of possibilities available, the program designer is faced with a decision as to what kinds of backups to include. In making this choice, a number of important issues must be addressed.

Most reports of token programs within the literature have been heavily weighted toward using material items as backups, and the point could realistically be made that much of the behavior we engage in within the community results quite naturally in some material reinforcement for us. We earn money for task-related activities, and we spend it on a variety of food, clothing, grooming and cosmetic, recreational, and other items. Most token programs make use of a "store," where material items may be purchased for tokens. This is helpful in many settings, where such activities as trips into the community and increased mobility inside and outside of the institutional setting may not be possible due to institutional regulations, legally imposed placements (often the case in psychiatric and penal settings), or because of permanent placement of clients who will never be able to function within the community (e.g., many retarded clients are permanent residents of the institution). Because of the frequent use of such material incentives (Ayllon and Azrin, 1968; Atthowe and Krasner, 1968; Ruskin and Maley, 1972) it is important to carefully define the items that are most highly valued by the specific client population. Ruskin and Maley (1972) have made the point that there are no guidelines within the literature for stocking stores with preferred items. These authors attempted to evaluate item preferences among a group of 20 "schizophrenic" patients monitored over a six-month period (see Table 4.4). Their finding that tobacco and edible items were the major categories of purchase caused them to suggest:

Perhaps this is explained simply by the immediacy of reinforcement when consuming these items, compared to items such as clothing or cosmetics. However, the fact that tobacco and edibles showed very small percentage increase over the six month time period, while all other categories of reinforcers except "miscellaneous" exceeded a 100% increase, suggests the desirability of using a *wide range of back-up reinforcers.* It would appear that as patients show improvement, their preferences begin to change and items related to grooming and personal attractiveness become more powerful reinforcers. (pp. 375–376)

Table 4.4
Ward Store Items Bought Over a Six-Month Period

Category	Item	Number Sold	Token Cost Per Item	Total Tokens Spent
Edibles	Candy bars	3881	5	19,405
	Penny candy	6620	1	6,620
	Packs of Lifesavers	163	5	815
	Cups of coffee	460	5	2,300
	Bags of nuts	400	15	6,000
	Packs of chewing gum	106	5	530
	Individual cookies	200	3	600
	Packs of crackers	526	5	2,630
				36,900
Tobacco	Packs of cigarettes	886	35	24,410
	State tobacco (bags of tobacco sufficient to make 20 cigarettes)	903	20	18,060
				42,470
Clothing	Sleeping robe	2	400	800
	Dress (rent daily)	60	10	600
	Pairs of shoes	46	50	2,300
Pairs of socks		14	10	140
	Pairs of nylon hose	10	15	150
				3,990

Personal	Pairs of earrings	104	30	3,120
Accessories	Single hair ribbon	10	2	20
	Miscellaneous jewelry	70	5	350
				3,490
Grooming	Toothbrush	146	10	1,460
Aids	Tubes of toothpaste	120	5	600
	Cans of deodorant	45	10	450
	Bars of soap	320	5	1,600
	Bottles of mouthwash	40	10	400
	Hand mirrors	10	20	200
				4,710
Cosmetics	Lipsticks	27	20	540
	Nail polish	21	10	210
	Powder	41	10	410
	Cold cream	30	20	600
	Comb	104	5	520
				2,280
Miscellaneous	Kleenex	62	20	1,240
Items	Envelopes	40	3	120
	Writing paper	20	15	300
	Billfold	10	50	500
	Paintings	10	65	650
	Radio (daily rent)	15	10	500
				3,310
	OVERALL TOTAL			97,150

In designing a token program for a population of 115 female delinquent adolescents, the present author attempted to include material items as well as such activities as visits to other adolescents in similar institutions, shopping excursions, trips to dances and rock concerts in the community, recreational and educational trips, and an array of other activities that *encouraged exposure to the community*. Because getting together with one's peers seems to be so important to high-school-age children, a night spot was created for the girls in the basement of one of the cottages. For a certain number of points the girls could get together in an informal atmosphere to talk, dance, and generally share information of interest.

Representative subjects decorated the setting to suit their tastes. At specified point costs, a soda counter supplied subjects with a variety of desirable food and material items. Since the provision of such material items becomes expensive, regular allotments of canteen funds provided by the state purchased many of the items—with donations and some limited program funds purchasing the remainder. Wise incorporation of existing recreational funds, training funds, and canteen allotments within the token program becomes a necessity when program funds are limited. Also, by requiring a program to make use of existing funds within the institution, the program is not dependent upon external grants which may vanish as state and federal budgets are altered. As trips to the night spot were limited to two each for each cottage, privileges, cottage activities and off campus events which stress social interaction and exposure to the community were emphasized. (Nay, 1974, p. 220)

While it may be necessary to use material backups when clients do not respond to other items, the BCA should employ those items that are ordinarily available in the setting. As token procedures are systematically faded out, those items remain, and they may continue to hold incentive properties for clients (Jones and Kazdin, 1975). The teacher in Chapter 3 who stated that "no incentives were available in my class" discovered a tremendous array of incentives after careful observations of student "high rate" behaviors. Along these lines, McLaughlin and Malaby (1972) found that fifth and sixth grade students in a normal public school setting were able to rank privileges within the classroom. These privileges then were provided for certain point costs, with the most desirable costing the most and the least desirable costing very few points. Among the backups were sharpening pencils, seeing animals, taking out balls, sports activities, engaging in special writing activities on the blackboard, serving on a committee, engaging in special classroom jobs, playing games, listening to records, permission to come in early, seeing the grade book as well, as many special projects. Osborne (1969) found that "free time" served as an effective backup reinforcer to eliminate out-of-seat responses in a classroom of six students.

Barrish, Saunders, and Wolf (1969) divided a regular fourth grade class into two teams to "play a game." Certain defined problem behaviors resulted in a mark being placed on the blackboard for the team with the offending member, and his inappropriate behavior resulted in a possible loss of reinforcement for all members of his team. The team with the fewest marks was permitted to wear victory tags, put a star by each of its members' names on the winners' chart, line up first for lunch, and take part in a 30-minute "free time" for special projects. The team that lost did not receive these privileges and would continue working on an assignment during the last half-hour of the day. Members would have to stay after school if they did not do their work during this last half-hour period. If *both* teams earned fewer than five marks, both would receive the winners' privilege. If a team (or teams) did not receive more than 20 marks in a week, the members would be permitted the extra weekly privilege of going to recess four minutes early. Participating in the "good behavior game" seemed to become as reinforcing to students as the naturally occurring privileges that were employed as reinforcers.

If the goal of employing some group treatment method is to foster changes in client behavior that will be maintained in some other setting within the community, every attempt should be made to include backup items that naturally occur within that setting. It makes sense for the BCA to use incentives that will maintain their value upon a client's return to the community setting. It is hard to conceive of any occasion for which token mechanisms would not be geared toward promoting token-free, intrinsically controlled behavior on the part of some population of clients who were capable of exhibiting such behavior. For that reason the BCA must carefully assess the characteristics of the terminal environment for clients (that is, the environment in which clients will function adequately if the program achieves its goals), and attempt to build as many characteristics of that environment into the program as possible.

As with incentives generated for individual clients, *items chosen as backup reinforcers should be in line with the goals of treatment.* Many reinforcers seem to be more promotive of behavioral change in the direction of treatment goals than others. In working with a group of retarded clients deficient in social skills, for instance, games, outings into the community, privileges relating to group activities, as well as any activity or privilege in which a client came in contact with others might be preferable to incentives that required only individual participation. Material items such as arts and crafts kits, which require careful task planning, motor coordination, and some measure of creative thinking, might be preferable (provided the items were geared to the subjects' capabilities) to candy, gum, and snack items for clients with whom these skills are relevant to treatment goals. Often, incentives that require clients to move into the community—trips home, excursions with staff members of a recreational or educational sort, social interactions with interesting members of the community, involvement in activities such as camping programs, dancing, art, drama lessons, and so on—all would seem to be of assistance in training clients to function better within the community, and would probably be preferable to items that are merely consumed on an immediate basis. Similarly, if the goal of treatment is to promote a more appropriate appearance, pleasurable activities that have to do with choice of articles of dress or in applying cosmetics might be a good choice, along with material items such as clothing, cosmetics, and health-care items.

Whenever possible, *backup items should not promote behaviors that are contrary to treatment goals* or are in opposition to appropriate health care. Reinforcements such as cigarettes (which may foster an array of health problems), snack items (which are high in carbohydrates and often promote obesity among relatively inactive clients), time spent alone (which may in fact be contrary to social skills goals) are all examples of items that may hold high incentive properties for clients but may also promote effects contrary to treatment goals. Of course, if the *only* motivational tool that the BCA can come up with for a specific client is a cigarette or junk food, the issue becomes a rather abstract one. To the widest extent possible, the

BCA should attempt to evaluate the possible therapeutic value of all reinforcers included as backups, and wherever possible attempt to employ such reinforcers as an important part of treatment planning. Chapter 11 will discuss certain legal requirements in defining back-ups.

Distribution of tokens

This section will discuss some of the important issues that must be faced by the BCA in deciding how tokens will be distributed for certain targeted client behaviors.

Parameters of administration—Staff members should be consistent in the manner in which tokens are given. There must be *clearly published* guidelines describing which behaviors earn how many tokens. Whenever possible, the behavioral requirements for token earning, the number of tokens earned for some specific behavior, as well as the list of backup reinforcements should all be posted in prominent locations within the setting or distributed in clearly presented handout form (Nay, 1974) to all staff member and clients. A written communication ensures that all parties involved realize what is expected within the program, and thus serves to increase the consistency among staff members as well as clients.

While the animal literature is replete with carefully controlled experiments that evaluate the way different schedules of reinforcement affect response rate, maintenance of effects, and extinction of effects, there are very few data regarding schedules that might be useful when employed with the human organism. Although some researchers have attempted to study the effects of schedules in highly controlled, machine-oriented laboratory environments (Long, Hammack, May, and Campbell, 1958), we are on firm ground only when talking about schedules related to specific animal populations (Ferster and Skinner, 1957). In their excellent review of the literature Kazdin and Bootzin (1972) have stated: "Although there is an abundant literature on the effects of schedules of reinforcement on extinction, schedules are seldom varied within token economies. Partially, this is due to the fact that it would be uneconomical to monitor the schedules so closely. In addition, intermittent schedules may only delay extinction, rather than prevent it" (p. 363). Investigators who have monitored the effects of different schedules report somewhat inconsistent results (Haring and Hauk, 1969; Meichenbaum, 1971a), and a study of schedule effects is an obvious next step for research in the token area. Often, program designers skirt the difficult problems raised by employing different schedules for different clients by requiring clients to proceed through a series of carefully defined levels, each of which requires more sophisticated and complex patterns of behavior as well as provides different avenues of reinforcement.

Another means of systematically increasing the amount of effort a client must engage in prior to reinforcement involves delay of reinforcement. Here the delay between the response clients make and the delivery of tokens is gradually increased. Atthowe and Krasner (1968) paid clients in tokens for certain behaviors only at the end of a week of behavioral effort, thus attempting to duplicate the kind of delays between behavior and payoff that exist in the community. O'Leary and Becker (1967) systematically increased the number of days prior to point payoff in a classroom token program, thus increasing the amount of work engaged in prior to reinforcement. Kazdin and Bootzin (1972) state that:

Numerous rewards in the natural setting (e.g., grades, money) are delayed. Thus, it seems desirable to train subjects so that they could perform without receiving rewards immediately for performance. It is assumed that training under delayed reinforcement in the treatment setting would generalize to performance in non-treatment settings. It is also hoped that in the treatment setting when extrinsic reinforcement is delayed, behaviors will come under the control of naturally occurring reinforcers, such as praise and attention. Evidence supporting these assumptions is not available. (p. 363)

Following up on this idea Jones and Kazdin (1975) found appropriate classroom behavior was maintained when the following was administered within a token program:

To further reduce reliance upon the token system, the exchange of tokens for back-up reinforcers was only intermittent. Back-up reinforcers were accessible on only 3 of the 5 days. On days 1, 3, and 5 back-up reinforcers were available contingent upon criterion performance. The initial criterion consisted of earning a total of four tokens in the morning or afternoon. On the next day of token exchange students had to earn at least one more token than the previous day to obtain the back-up reinforcer. This strategy was employed to shape increasingly attentive behavior. On days when there was no exchange of tokens, the tokens were merely collected and had no actual back-up value. (p. 157)

Combining social reinforcement with token reinforcement—It would be fair to say that most token program designers attempt to elicit more appropriate and adaptive behaviors by employing material incentives on an immediate basis, in the hopes that these behaviors will ultimately be maintained by the ordinary social reinforcements within the community, as well as the intrinsic reinforcements of "satisfaction in performance" or "feeling good about a job well done." Often, social reinforcement is paired with material token reinforcement in the hopes that it will take on value for a population of clients. This is particularly important when the BCA is working with clients who have not been extensively exposed to social reinforcements, such as those from impoverished backgrounds. For such clients social reinforcement may even be viewed as a punishment, whereby one individual is picked out by the "the man" or "the establishment, " and clients may in fact be suspicious of such feedback. Many subcultural groups find the use of verbal praise or nonverbal communications of affection to be very difficult. However, such clients may respond to a rich schedule of reinforcement by tokens that may presumably be traded in for material items, and this may be *combined with* staff verbal and nonverbal social reinforcement that carefully labels why the tokens are earned.

Among verbal positive social feedback that might be employed in combination with a giving of tokens, Madsen, Becker, and Thomas (1968) suggest the following: "I like the way you're doing your work quietly, *(name);* that's the way I like to see you work, ____; that's a very good job, ____; you're doing fine, ____; you got two right, ____; that's very good (if he generally gets no answers right)" (p. 145). The authors suggest:

Try to use variety and expression in your comments. Stay away from sarcasm. Attempt to become spontaneous in your praise and smile when delivering praise. At first you will probably get the feeling that you are praising a great deal and it sounds a little phoney to your ears. This is a typical reaction and it becomes more natural with the passage of time. Spread your praise and attention around. (p. 145)

Most importantly, praise should be provided in a labeled or direct fashion (Hanf, 1969; Nay, 1972). *Well labeled* means that a *clear definition of what the client did that was on target should be clearly specified,* rather than merely saying the indirect "Good" or giving a nod of some sort. Thus, "Johnnie, I like the way you *cleaned up your room,"* would be preferable to "Good job!" It would seem that when behavior is specifically linked to social reinforcement, the client receives a clear understanding of specifically which aspects of his performance were appropriate and/or inappropriate.

While verbal social reinforcement is often reported within the literature to be a part of token exchange, nonverbal reinforcers are frequently not clearly spelled out. Regarding classroom programs Kazdin and Klock (1973) have stated that nonverbal behaviors are often included in definitions of approval, yet their individual affect on student behavior is rarely evaluated. Perhaps this is because verbal approval, as opposed to facial expressions and physical contact, makes up about 85 percent of teacher behavior, and teacher training is likely to emphasize verbal behavior. Nevertheless, nonverbal staff behaviors may provide an important source of reinforcement. These authors found that nonverbal behaviors such as smiling, extension of the mouth (with or without lips parted) to express pleasure or approval, and any physical contact indicating approval such as patting on the head, back, or shoulder and hugging were a useful means of increasing the frequency of certain targeted behaviors with a population of moderately retarded elementary school students. While the validity of their data is certainly limited to the retarded population they studied, their findings may have important implications for a wide array of client populations. Also, nonverbal reinforcement may be a potent source of feedback for individuals who experience difficulty in responding to language or in processing verbal statements.

Merely asking staff members to increase their use of verbal and nonverbal rewards does not usually promote any significant change in the way that they act. A staff member's ability to employ such feedback may be limited by his repertoire of verbal and nonverbal social behaviors, which is based upon past learning and cultural influence. Training involving modeling and role-playing (practice) social reward styles is most desirable. Thus, the BCA must carefully assess the skill with which staff members can in fact provide such feedback, and provide appropriate training as necessary. Social reinforcements may promote generalization from token to the more ordinary social reinforcement conditions, and may be necessary if a program is to move to a more natural basis (Kazdin and Bootzin, 1972; Jones and Kazdin, 1975). Merely providing tokens without this kind of socially labeled feedback may cause clients to wonder about their progress, as behavior is not clearly tied to consequence. The importance of employing such social reinforcers cannot be overemphasized, and it is strongly suggested that the designer of a token program include avenues of social reinforcement within program procedures and staff training.

INDIVIDUAL VERSUS GROUP CONTINGENCIES

Although most token programs are directed toward a group, reinforcements are typically administered on an individual basis, depending upon the targeted behaviors displayed. An alternative system would specify certain collective goals and only provide reinforcers when all members of the group had met a criterion, or provide punishment when one or more members violate it. Bandura (1969) has emphasized that when mutual responsibility, cohesiveness, commitment, and contribution to a common goal among all members is a goal of intervention, this can be accomplished most effectively by instituting reinforcement contingencies on a group basis. Thus, by sharing in the consequences of their decisions and actions, group members' degree of social responsibility and involvement is increased. Such "interdependent contingency systems" (Bandura, 1969) are employed on a wide scale basis within the Soviet Union (Bronfenbrenner, 1962). Students from the primary grades onward are assigned to a collective unit, and daily records are kept on each unit member's task performance. Grades are based upon the overall performance of a unit rather than on any individual's performance, and competition is introduced to further encourage high rates of performance within units.

Of course, such a system encourages and supports cooperative behavior directed toward group accomplishment, rather than focusing upon outstanding individual performance. Within our own country the tremendous interest in various team athletics is perhaps the best example of our adoption of such group contingencies. A team must work together to earn the reinforcement of ultimate "victory." It is fascinating, however, that certain individuals are picked out as "stars," and often are the envy of their peers as well as the population at large. The American system of capitalism seems to be strongly rooted in the performance of the individual: if one strives, one should be rewarded for his individual efforts. Perhaps this emphasis upon the individual is one reason why purely collective systems are not often employed at any level within society. Use of group contingencies is rarely reported; most often, collective contingencies *supplement* contingencies for individual efforts.

Most investigators who have employed group contingencies (Barrish, Saunders, and Wolf, 1969; Sloggett, 1971; Axelrod, 1973; Phillips, Phillips, Wolf, and Fixsen, 1973; Drabman, Spitalnik, and Spitalnik, 1974) have done so within the classroom token system. Often all group members receive the same reinforcement, based upon the behavior of randomly selected individuals or upon the average of class performance (Packard, 1970; Schmidt and Ulrich, 1969). In another variant, children in a particular group receive backup reinforcement based upon the behavior of certain *targeted* (problem) students who display the most inappropriate behavior within the group (Barrish, Saunders, and Wolf, 1969).

Sloggett (1971) reports upon a group contingency system applied to a population of 24 boys aged 14 to 17 enrolled in a self-contained class within an intermediate school. After the students were matched and then assigned to one of four teams, they were informed that they could earn points by both individual performances as well as participation within the group. For individual performance members could each earn a maximum of 300 points to be applied toward the team total. Points were earned for arriving at class on time, following a set of rules that the students had a hand in making up, bringing appropriate materials to class, and for the quality of task completion. Additional points could be earned for certain group-oriented activities not specifically related to task performance but intended to encourage the boys to help one another .Such behaviors as contacting remiss students about school attendance, tardiness, or misbehavior as well as other helping behaviors (e.g. helping a class member with a task or in solving personal problems) would earn additional points for the team. At the end of each week any team with an average of at least 1,000 points per member earned an "A" and received an award such as an excursion off school grounds during the following week. Thus, each team competed against a published standard, and all, a few, or none might obtain the highest reward. All inappropriate classroom behaviors were ignored, while appropriate behaviors were rewarded either with points or with praise from the teacher. The authors report that not only did classroom performance seem to improve as measured by tasks completed, but here appeared to be an increase of self-imposed peer pressure for good conduct. As a surprising example, class members periodically requested the teacher to take disciplinary action for certain group members.

In contrast Phillips et al. (1973) evaluated a variety of group contingency systems directed at improving cottage-maintenance behavior (sweeping, cleaning, dusting, straightening things up) for a group of delinquent adolescents. The authors clearly found that group consequences were not nearly as effective as individual consequences in maintaining appropriate cottage care behavior. Subjects seemed to prefer conditions where their specific behavior resulted in a consequence, as opposed to group consequences. This well-controlled study also evaluated the utility of engaging one of the subjects as a manager, who would assign cleaning tasks and award or take away points depending upon student efforts. In comparing a variety of methods for assigning subjects the role of manager, the authors found that there was no difference in cleaning behavior whether the managership was purchased or when it was an elective position. However, subjects preferred a system whereby each had a vote in electing the manager. In contrast to previous investigators, the authors thus found that group contingencies were not as effective as individual contingencies, and make the following point: "Thus, it appears that group consequences are effective in some cases, but the present experiments indicate a clear improvement in behavior with individual consequences as compared to group consequences for behavior" (p. 559). The fact that these authors collected information to determine which kind of token approach was most preferred by subjects is highly commendable. They make the important point that it is often easy to overlook the client's satisfaction with the treatment procedures. This is probably less of a problem in treatment settings that deal with clients who voluntarily submit to procedures and who can leave any time they are dissatisfied. In these voluntary programs the clients thus maintain some (at least implicit) consequences for staff behavior that makes them unhappy. However, in treatment settings where the client is not a voluntary participant, the staff must develop other means of evaluating the clients' preferences because they cannot simply drop out of the program or vigorously register their dissatisfaction. By systematically comparing various treatment procedures on both the effectiveness and the satisfaction-preference dimensions, it might be possible to employ procedures that are sufficiently effective in changing client behavior as well as being preferred by clients (Phillips et al., 1973).

In another well-controlled study Drabman et al. (1974) applied one of four distribution systems to a population of 23 first grade schoolchildren who were randomly assigned to conditions. Over time, using a latin square design, each treatment group was provided with token feedback under one of the four conditions. Using individual reinforcement, each child within the group received an amount of free time equivalent to the total number of points that child earned for the day. A second condition awarded reinforcement to the group, determined by the most disruptive child in the group. Children received an amount of free time equal to the lowest number of points earned by any group member. For example, if one child in the group had behaved inappropriately and earned only five of the possible 15 points, the entire group would receive only five minutes of free time. Group reinforcement determined by the least disruptive child in the group was the third condition. With this approach, all groups members received free time equal to that earned by the child with the highest score earned for that day. Finally, group reinforcement determined by a randomly chosen member of the group awarded free time based upon the number of points earned by a child whose name was chosen randomly from a can. Points earned for following classroom rules, were distributed by the teacher every 20 minutes (signaled by a timer) and immediately written upon a highly visible chart placed within the classroom.

Results showed no significant difference in disruptive behavior either among "well behaved" or "disruptive" children across the four conditions, suggesting that distribution systems may be selected for reasons other than effectiveness. For example, group reinforcement determined by a randomly selected member of the group required less teacher time and was the teachers' favorite and the class's second choice. Group reinforcement determined by the most disruptive child was liked least by the class but did lead to some important sociometric changes. The conventional individual system was not popular with the class and was too time-consuming for the teacher. The system in which the group received the amount of free time earned by its least disruptive member was most popular with the children but was usually disliked by the teacher. The results also suggest that teachers need not spend time observing and systematically rating every member of a class, but can effectively select a few or perhaps only one child for monitoring and not inform the class which child is being monitored. Thus, more time would be available for the teachers' academic efforts than in most individually tailored token programs. In support of these findings Rosenbaum, O'Leary, and Jacob (1975) found no differences in effectiveness in comparing individual contingencies with group contingencies determined by the problem (hyperactive) child. Jones and Kazdin (1975) found individually determined token effects to be maintained when group contingencies were successively implemented as a means of fading out the program with young retarded children.

In summarizing these varied findings, the following recommendations are in order:

1. The literature seems to suggest that group contingencies can foster cooperative social skill behaviors that may not be fostered where individual clients are earning and possibly competing with one another to earn tokens. Thus, it makes sense to employ group contingencies *along with* individual contingencies, perhaps thus achieving the best of both worlds. With this kind of program clients might only *gain* by the efforts of other

group members, and cooperative behavior is associated with positivity. Should other individuals exhibit behaviors that do not earn sufficient tokens for some group backup reinforcement, the individual earner is still reinforced for his efforts. The author can think of nothing worse than punishing an individual client who has worked on his behavior over some period of time simply because one member of his group did not do so. Such a system, particularly when punishments are levied on the group based upon individual performance, may result in a paradoxical punishment of appropriate individual efforts.

A practical and ethical issue emerges at this point. Drabman et al. (1974) found that students who were well behaved prior to the program maintained their appropriate behavior, and presumably would have whether or not a program had been implemented. Thus, the primary focus of the program, and too often of all such programs, is to improve the behavior of certain targeted individuals. One might ask if it is fair to inflict group-related punishment on those individuals who are working positively toward treatment goals. Also, an exclusively group-determined program might allow a few targeted individuals to actively control the behavior of some larger group, thus putting them in a position of power that may be paradoxically reinforcing. Axelrod (1973) reports upon a group contingency system in which monetary backups were provided to all the students of a group based upon group functioning. The behavior of one individual, who rejected the procedure as "baby stuff," "stupid," and "dippy" (p. 5), consistently resulted in a response cost for other members of the group. Rather than improving student behavior, the procedure resulted in an increased level of student disruptiveness from a baseline of 47 percent to a level of 73 percent during the program proper. Only by employing the problem student in a special role as consultant to the teacher was his behavior brought under control, ultimately resulting in the class being reinforced at a much higher rate and in an ultimate reduction in problem behavior. Bandura (1969) has said:

Pervasive and unrelenting application of group-oriented systems of reinforcement which stifle autonomy and self determination clearly are antithetical to goals that are highly valued in most societies. Therefore, where interdependent contingencies are instituted to increase group unity and responsibility, each member should also be given opportunities for independent accomplishment. (p. 282)

Thus, it is not a matter of choosing between individual and group contingencies, but in some way combining the two to ensure that individual as well as cooperative group efforts may be reinforced.

2. Based upon the previous discussion, it would seem that group contingencies might better apply to the earning of positive reinforcement rather than the earning of punishments. Those few problem clients who engage in possible aversive manipulation can best be dealt with through individualized programs (as suggested in the previous chapter) rather than group-related contingencies. Of course the data are equivocal here,

and at present no clear findings with regard to the usefulness of group contingencies have emerged (e.g., Phillips et al., 1973; Drabman et al., 1974).

3. Whenever possible the program designer should initially provide rather limited avenues for group reinforcement to determine client and staff members' performance and preferences prior to employing group contingencies on a wide scale.

Extensive additional research is needed before any statements can be made as to which specific client populations, targeted behaviors, or kinds of institutional settings may most appropriately employ group contingencies to advantage. One can think of examples where such contingencies might promote behavior disruptive to treatment goals. For example, among socially aggressive delinquent clients group contingencies that foster high levels of competition might paradoxically increase the frequency of behaviors targeted for treatment. Careful evaluation of the manner that specific populations respond to such contingencies (through collection of data) would be a welcome addition to the literature.

SELF VERSUS EXTERNALLY IMPOSED CONTINGENCIES

While a number of investigators have suggested that clients be permitted to self-determine point earnings as token procedures are gradually faded out, only a few studies have shown that clients maintain low rates of deviant behavior while self-assigning points (e.g. Kaufman and O'Leary, 1972). Santogrossi, O'Leary, Romanczyk, and Kaufman (1973) have criticized this study as well as previous investigations that have found grade school subjects able to set and maintain appropriate standards for their own behavior and very accurately pay themselves off in tokens and other rewards (Bandura and Perloff, 1967; Lovitt, and Curtiss, 1969; Glynn, 1970). Santogrossi et al. (1973) have stated of the Kaufman and O'Leary findings:

Students behaved extremely well during the self-evaluation period, which lasted for seven days, but an even longer period of self evaluation is needed before one would suggest that self evaluation be introduced as the standard procedure in all token programs. One might surmise that at least some children would greatly over-evaluate their behavior in order to receive rewards associated with high evaluations. (p. 278)

In contrast, Frederickson and Frederickson (1975) showed that self-reward conditions (of up to *eight* weeks) maintained appropriate behavior instituted under teacher-determined token earning conditions for a normal grade school class. Also, student evaluations of their own behavior consistently correlated highly with independent teacher ratings over an 11-week period.

Among negative findings are the following. In comparing teacher-determined with self-determined point values for following rules in a classroom of nine adolescent boys selected from a psychiatric hospital school, Santogrossi et al. (1973) found that, while students' ratings of their own behavior correspond quite highly with teacher ratings, self-ratings without token reinforcement did not significantly alter the frequency of deviant behavior from baseline. During two phases when the teacher determined how many points each student earned at the end of 15-minute class periods (student could earn between 0–2 points), the frequency of disruptive behavior showed significant decreases in comparison with baseline. When students rated their own behavior and decided upon a point value to pay themselves, deviant behavior was maintained at low rates for between two and four days, but elevated rather dramatically following this initial period (see Fig. 4.3).

The increases in disruptive behavior obtained in the first self-determined point phase seemed largely caused by two subjects who quickly recognized that the system could be beaten and were quite effective in employing social pressure to provoke other subjects into defiance. By declaring themselves "on strike" and denouncing as "fools" those who did not take advantage of the situation, these pupils instigated much disruptive behavior. The second time students were given control of token determination, these two pupils again urged others not to cooperate. Thus, this investigation suggests that the beneficial reductions in inappropriate behavior seen with self-monitoring may dissipate over time, in direct contrast to the Frederickson and Frederickson (1975) findings.

A similar study by Felixbrod and O'Leary (1973) compared self-determined and externally determined point earning in inducing a population of 24 second grade children to solve arithmetic problems correctly. The authors found that, although there seemed to be no difference in number of problems solved correctly between the self-determined and the externally determined groups, the students in the former group imposed increasingly lenient standards upon their problem-solving performance over time. At the start of the final training session six of seven children in the self-determined condition selected the most lenient standard.

These data suggest that a program designer who wishes to provide some avenue for client self-determination of token earning would do well to evaluate carefully whether or not behavioral changes induced through staff-imposed tokens are maintained when self-imposed tokens are instituted. In the light of published findings as well as common sense, the following statements are offered about the efficacy of permitting clients to self-determine token earnings:

1. While it seems a highly desirable treatment goal to allow clients to self monitor and pay themselves for their behavior, the dearth and inconsistency of the literature and its primary focus upon children as opposed to adult populations make any evaluation of the utility of self-imposed contingencies premature at the present time. If clients are ever to learn self-controlling responses that will enable them to function without

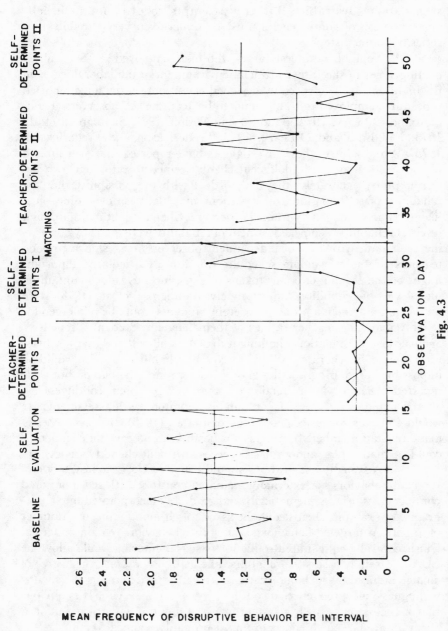

Fig. 4.3

Disruptive behavior of a reading class as a function of experimental conditions (from Santogrossi et al., 1973).

externally controlled sanctions, some effort at allowing clients to "determine their own fate," and test out the accuracy of their self-evaluations seems to be desirable. But any attempts to promote such self-determination of contingencies must be undertaken very carefully in a series of planned steps.

2. None of the investigators who have employed self-determined contingencies in the rather artificial environment of the laboratory or in the highly controlled, specially designed classroom setting have reported procedures employed to train clients to be accurate self-observers (Kaufman and O'Leary, 1972; Bandura and Perloff, 1967; Santogrossi et al., 1973; Felixbrod and O'Leary, 1973; Frederickson and Frederickson, 1975). While some of these investigators have reported that over limited periods elementary and adolescent clients seemed to rate their own behavior pretty accurately, they fail to deal with the possibility that the reliability of self-monitored observations may decrease over time—just like the data produced by trained observers. Clients might maintain high levels of reliability if some assessment of reliability were made by comparing their data with that of independent observers (e.g., staff members, teachers) on some random schedule over time. Particularly important might be the earning of bonus tokens or extra incentives for maintaining high levels of reliability. Unfortunately, Santogrossi et al. (1973) were unable to implement a proposal whereby students would be reinforced for reliably matching teacher ratings of their behavior. Students "rebelled" against this manipulation, claiming it to be too difficult and that teachers' ratings were "inaccurate." Without frequent reliability checks it would be impossible for a program designer to determine whether or not self-reported behavior was a function of progressively lenient contingencies, altered standards over time, or reliably monitored self-assessments. It would seem, as suggested by Santogrossi et al. (1973), that such checks made by staff members or others in a position to observe independently could be made on a random basis, perhaps without client awareness.

3. A system of self-ratings should usually follow the instigation of targeted behaviors via externally mediated controls, with self-monitored contingencies being systematically and gradually incorporated into a program. For example, clients could be asked to self-monitor one of a number of important targeted behaviors, while other behaviors remain under extrinsic control. Sequential introduction of self-monitoring would allow the BCA to carefully assess the reliability of client observations, the degree of change induced by such observations, as well as to determine the clients' willingness and preference to continue with such a system. It is obvious that if clients reject such a system or if self-monitoring is thrust upon a client all at once, such efforts are most probably doomed to fail.

Another way that clients might be induced to self-monitor is to introduce a system of self-government within the token system. Perhaps one of the most complete reports of a self-government system is that of Fairweather (1964), who allowed a group of schizophrenic clients in a psychiatric setting to make treatment decisions regarding the progress of ward members. Participants received certain privileges as well as monetary rewards as they moved through a series of four progressively more complex levels with a token program. At each level the expected behavior of clients included increasingly complex and sophisticated social skills. Client groups met daily to discuss the progress of indivdual group members, to suggest methods of treatment, and to differentially assign the client to a step higher or lower. Staff members served as consultants, supplying useful information to the group as to treatment possibilities, but refrained from recommending specific courses of action. Staff members also either approved or disapproved decisions made by the group. Depending upon the appropriateness of the group's recommendations, all its members could be rewarded or penalized by being raised or lowered one step level. This contingency ensured that the group would carefully attend to its task, and it provided a source of immediate feedback for group members as to the soundness of their decisions.

Within this qualified self-government system staff members moved increasingly into the role of resource personnel and consultants and away from their role as direct agents of treatment. Thus, clients moved from complete dependence upon staff decisions to increasing independence, as their treatment decisions became more appropriate.

When these clients began to function in a cooperative effort, they expressed increased interest in the behavior of others and even assumed full responsibility for providing employment to eligible members graduated from the program. Group members who possessed certain skills offered specialized courses of instruction to those who required such skills for adjustment to the community. The authors report that in comparing the self-government group to a group of matched control clients, the "experimental" clients showed more interpersonal responsiveness, increased verbal communications skills, and a general decrement in the frequency of bizarre behavior, as assessed by staff behavioral ratings, self-evaluations, and other attitudinal questionnaires over a 27-week period.

The previous work reported by Phillips et al. (1973) suggested that clients democratically elected by their peers to make treatment decisions were preferred by a population of adolescent boys, and, importantly, this led to high rates of appropriate targeted behavior. The authors maintain that it might be advantageous for other token programs to employ an elected manager, who might increase the clients' level of satisfaction as well as reducing the amount of direct supervision required by staff members, since some of these duties could be effectively carried out by the manager.

When any form of self-government is introduced, one must expect clients to fail and to make mistakes as they learn the skills necessary to make important decisions. Institutional personnel must be willing to tolerate those few clients who abuse such a system; the problem behavior that may develop as such self-controlling responses are tried out and gradually adjusted by individual clients; and to tolerate the fact that staff members become increasingly less important to decision-making as clients move through the program. Often, in the interests of making an institution function more efficiently, staff members restrict client responsibility and precisely define client roles. Administrators may not be able to tolerate the possibility that clients will make inadequate decisions or that inefficiency will develop as clients try out new approaches. Within many settings this increased risk, regardless of the common sense justification for allowing clients to participate in their own treatment, is too great, and such programs are not permitted to develop or are so restricted as to be indistinguishable from typical staff-client relationships.

Within such settings the introduction of self-controlling behaviors must be gradual and systematic, so that program administrators have time to adjust to client self-governing behaviors and so the chance of major problems developing at once is reduced. As administrators discover that an initial situation of inefficiency may develop into one where staff members have increased time to participate in the important job of consultant or resource person, rather than baby-sitter or full-time monitor, self-controlling programs may be increasingly tolerated.

Often, BCAs become very frustrated when they see treatment possibilities for clients restricted by institutional policy. By realizing that attempts at increasing client responsibilities may be threatening to and have real negative consequences for institutional administrators if they lead to client abuses, the BCA will be in a better position to suggest some initial program of self-control that might prove to be more acceptable to those in authority, and perhaps "open the door" to further attempts to increase client responsibility.

NEGATIVE FEEDBACK PROCEDURES

While the emphasis of most token programs is upon positive point earning for certain targeted behaviors, many programs include some means of providing negative feedback for problem behaviors that often occur at high rate and must be decelerated. Most frequently there is some form of token cost or loss of tokens contingent upon violation of posted rules (see Kaufman and O'Leary, 1972; Phillips et al., 1971; Nay, 1974). As Phillips et al (1971) have stated:

An economy can be "all positive," that is, tokens can be given for certain specified behaviors but they cannot be removed. Or, an economy can be "all negative" where each youth starts off each day with a full complement of tokens and can lose them for certain behaviors. Another possibility is an economy where tokens can be both earned and lost, a "positive and negative" economy. (p. 57)

While some token programs might best be characterized as "all positive," there are few reports within the literature of "all negative" programs. Within a negative system everybody starts off with a fixed number of tokens, and all the clients can expect to accomplish for their behavior is a loss of points. Should clients engage in one or more targeted positive behaviors, nothing happens; they merely maintain their point total. It would seem pretty discouraging to function within this kind of a system, with its emphasis upon point loss or punishment, and the author would recommend that its use be avoided. The "positive and negative" system is the system most frequently employed when some negative feedback is applied, and typically some combination of response cost in tokens and/or time out procedure is employed contingent upon targeted negative behaviors.

A number of investigators have shown that point loss can be an effective way of gaining control of targeted behaviors (Burchard and Barrera, 1972; Phillips et al., 1971; Nay, 1974); however, there are a number of considerations that the program designer must take into account in employing loss procedures. Many authors have spoken of the possibility for abuse when any system of punishment is built into an institutional treatment program (e.g., Walker and Buckley, 1972; Tyler and Brown, 1968). Because many institutions have functioned on a punitive basis prior to program implementation and because of the general emphasis upon punishment as opposed to reinforcement within society at large, many staff members find it much easier to punish clients in an array of creative and sometimes astonishing ways than to provide even the simplest rewards for appropriate behavior. Positive reinforcement often leads staff members to talk of "bribery" and "mechanical and artificial situations," but they may find it very easy to employ a diverse array of punishments at the slightest instance of some negative client behavior. Prior to implementing a large-scale token program the author (Nay, 1974) found an inconsistent and extraordinary array of punishments, employed both within as well as across treatment cottages. In reporting upon these punitive procedures, the author stated:

Since there are marked similarities in training school approaches across localities, a description of treatment before the present program may be useful. A discipline team consisting of a group of staff, selected according to undefined criteria, was the only organized staff approach to behavior management. If a student transgressed one of a multitude of rules and regulations which varied with each classroom and living cottage, a discipline sheet was forwarded to this discipline team. In many cases a student would be required to wait for her punishment a week or more until the team convened. This marked delay between offense and punishment left many students uncertain as to why they were being punished. Among approaches to punishment were frequent use of lengthy solitary confinement, work detail, and a severe curtailment of privileges. Regarding appropriate behavior, a student was called in at irregular intervals (in some cases intervals of six months) for feedback as to her "progress" within the institution. Progress was based on uncertain criteria consisting primarily of global, subjective staff reports. . . . In summary, treatment before the present program might be described as operating within a contingent punishment, non-contingent reward paradigm. (pp. 205–206)

In designing a classroom token program for a group of 48 male and female subjects classified as academic and behavioral problems, Walker and Buckley (1972) did not include aversive control procedures, because their effective use requires a great deal of close supervision by experienced staff. They state: "Time out and cost-contingency procedures are also easily abused and used punitively within the regular classroom setting" (p. 214). Thus, in employing any form of token loss, time out, or other punishment, the BCA must carefully assess the possibility of staff overuse of such punitive approaches, and perhaps limit the manner in which the approaches are employed within the program.

For rule violations within the program described (Nay, 1974) point loss was administered according to a "three-step contingency" similar to that described in the previous chapter for time out. This contingency ensured that the clients realized that they were in violation of some rule, were adequately warned as to what the consequences would be, and that point removal would be undertaken in a manner that would involve minimal amounts of attention for the inappropriate behavior as well as limit staff overresponding to the situation. The three-step contingency was as follows:

Step 1: *Information.* Subject should be instructed in a clear communication to *stop* some specific inappropriate behavior (e.g. verbal or physical aggressiveness).
Step 2: *Warning.* If subject does not comply with the request, she should be told the following: "If you do not stop (behavior clearly specified), you will lose three points."
Step 3: *Point loss.* If subject does not respond to the warning, immediately punch three negative points on her card, carefully explaining why points were lost. *Under no circumstances* should a staff member argue, plead with or berate the girl. Point loss should be undertaken in a calm, matter of fact manner, emphasizing the inappropriate behavior in question. Once points are removed, the matter is settled and no further punishment should be undertaken. Failure to give up a card for punching results in an immediate referral to the supervisor. (pp. 220–221)

Steps 1 and 2 were used on the first incidence of some negative behavior on a particular day, with repeated behavior immediately incurring Step 3.

Problems suggested by experience with response cost within this program including the following:

1. Institutional staff of modest skills and punishment-oriented backgrounds may emphasize point loss, thus providing a greater proportion of staff attention for inappropriate behavior.
2. Institutional subjects, particularly delinquents, may view negative point totals as a measure of status and thus work to increase negative point accumulations.
3. Negative points may reduce the value of positive point earning. A subject

who is sufficiently "in the hole" with negative points gains little from positive point earning. (p. 211)

In order to effectively limit possible overuse of negative points by staff members, negative point earning was limited to 15 per client per day. When the 15th negative point was earned, the student was immediately referred to a supervisor, who would discuss the point losses with the student and remove a privilege appropriate to the situation. Privileges were ordered into levels of value according to the reinforcement survey. The subject was informed that future inappropriate behavior on that day would make her eligible for a higher level of privilege loss. Thus, problem girls were immediately identified and dealt with on a more flexible basis according to their individual needs. Kazdin and Bootzin (1972) as well as others have reported that certain clients are nonreactive to token programs and must be clearly identified and dealt with through individually tailored programs.

While the use of negative points can be effective in dealing with problem client behaviors, careful record keeping and avenues for additional staff training, as well as some system by which negative points per client are limited for any given day might all be ways to decrease the probability of abuse. Just as point loss is employed within many token programs, time out procedure, as reported in the previous chapter, may also be used for certain offenses, particularly those involving active, aggressive responses on the part of child and adolescent clients. By using time out period for these aggressive kinds of behaviors the program designer ensures that staff may be flexible in applying negative contingencies, thus in a sense making "the punishment fit the crime."

It is unfortunate and perplexing that few investigators have attempted to evaluate the various procedures employed in training staff to employ contingencies. Kazdin and Bootzin (1972) have reported upon a diverse array of training procedures and the need for carefully controlled research to examine which procedures might most effectively be employed, in what manner, and with what specific client and staff populations. Unfortunately, most program designers must proceed in training by a series of educated guesses (Grabowski and Thompson, 1972). What makes it very difficult is the fact that few investigators have reported upon the manner in which staff were trained. Even anecdotal case presentations of training procedures would be useful; however, they are rarely provided. Chapter 10 discusses in detail techniques that may be employed in training staff members, as well as the importance of providing avenues of reinforcement for their efforts.

THE STRATIFIED LEVELS APPROACH

Increasingly, program designers are including some form of incremental *levels* that designate client responsibilities as well as reinforcements available, either within the standard token format or as the primary approach to treatment.

Often, clients are required to begin at one level and, depending on their improvement in performance, move systematically through higher levels that required increasingly sophisticated behavior and offer more opportunities for self-directed activities. As the behavioral requirements for the client systematically increase with each level, the array of reinforcers often increases correspondingly. Higher levels may provide the client with reinforcers that permit more exposure to the community as token mechanisms are gradually faded out. Atthowe (1973) suggests the use of a levels approach to individualize a token program:

As a patient moves from the lowest to the highest level, he is required to become more responsible and independent while his potential reinforcers concomitantly increase. The issue becomes one of making each succeeding step that much more reinforcing. The ultimate level may be earning one's way out of the token system (Atthowe & Krasner, 1968), spending more and more time in the community outside the hospital (Henderson & Scoles, 1970), and eventually living as a group outside the hospital (Atthowe, 1973). As the patient progresses through each step, tokens may be thinned out, delayed (weekly paydays rather than daily or immediate reinforcement), and faded into real money and/or social reinforcements. . . . Color coding of each level of responsibility and reinforcement (e.g. Taulbee & Wright, 1971) so that individuals at each step level would have a special colored name tag would make it easier to enlist the help of the entire hospital staff (from treatment specialists to secretaries to maintenance personnel) in treating each patient. (pp. 648–649)

The program previously mentioned (Fairweather, 1964), in which clients in a psychiatric setting were assigned a level of existence by contingent group means, is perhaps one of the earliest and best examples of this approach. The comprehensive treatment program described previously (Nay, 1974) has recently augmented a standard token approach with a system of levels (Nay, Northen, Melvin, and Lawrence, 1975) to deal with problems of variable point earning. Requiring students to spend points earned for backups available that day and evening (to prevent hoarding) resulted in quite variable student performance across days. Earnings seemed to fluctuate with incentives available on specific days (e.g., trips, movies, opportunity to swim), and there was no published scheme for relating daily point accumulation/point losses/time outs to an individual student's progress. In incorporating a levels system, specific earnings criteria were provided to determine a student's progression through four color-coded levels (green, yellow, blue, and red).

While the green level made minimal behavioral demands upon students and provided primarily in-cottage reinforcers, each succeeding level required increased point earning and control of problem behavior, while providing expanded avenues of campus and community privileges and activities (e.g., dances, shopping trips, rock concerts).

Each student was evaluated in a cottage-wide meeting once a week to determine whether she had met level-specific criteria, and thus would receive a promotion (a "GO") to the next week in her level. Fig. 4.4 shows the criteria for each level.

LEVEL	COUNT TIME OUTS FOR THE WEEK	COUNT NEGATIVE POINTS FOR THE WEEK	COUNT POSITIVE POINTS FOR THE WEEK	COUNT TOTAL POSITIVE POINTS FOR THE WEEK	IF YOU EARNED A "GO" INITIAL NEXT TO NUMBER	IF YOU DIDN'T EARN A "GO" INITIAL NEXT TO NUMBER
GREEN	If 5 or less GO	If 24 or less GO	If each school day is 60 or more and all non-school days 15 or more GO	If 350 or more you earn a "GO"	1. ___ 2. ___ 3. ___ Go to Yellow	Just stay in Green until 3 "Go's" are earned
YELLOW	If 4 or less GO	If 15 or less GO	If all school days 70 or more and all non-school days 15 or more GO	If 400 or more you earn a "GO"	1. ___ 2. ___ 3. ___ 4. ___ 5. ___ 6. ___ Go to Blue	1. ___ Go back to Green until 1 "Go" is earned ___ (Initial) when Green "Go" earned. You may continue in Yellow
BLUE	If 3 or less GO	If 9 or less GO	If all school days 75 or more and all non-school days 15 or more GO	If 450 or more you earn a "GO"	1. ___ 2. ___ 3. ___ 4. ___ 5. ___ 6. ___ 7. ___ 8. ___ Go to Red	1. ___ 2. ___ Go back to Yellow (When 2 Yellow "Go's" are earned: 1. ___ (Initial)2. ___ (Initial), you may continue in Blue
RED	STUDENT SELF RATES BEHAVIOR TREATMENT TEAM WILL REVIEW SELF MONITORING CARDS WITH STUDENT				1. ___ 2. ___ 3. ___ 4. ___ 5. ___ 6. ___ 7. ___ 8. ___ Release!! With Court Approval	Any movement back to Blue depends upon self-ratings and treatment team decision 1. ___ 2. ___

Fig. 4.4
Levels assignment sheet.

Successful completion of a certain number of weeks in a level resulted in a promotion to the next level, until the student completed the red level and was released to the community. To "fade out" the specific reliance upon points, students received all " blue" backups without paying points for each item (as they had in green and yellow), and at the red level students functioned without point earnings, with student self-ratings and staff social feedback the only monitoring/treatment mechanism.

Preliminary evaluation has shown that this system of levels significantly increased the consistency of student behavior (reduced the variability in point earnings across days) when students functioning within levels were compared with those in regular point programs. Levels are a means of relating daily and weekly progress to movement through the program, of increasing student responsibility for self-monitoring and self-control, of moving students from token to nontoken functioning, and of permitting staff members to recognize easily (via colored cards) a student's level of progress and eligibility for campus and off-campus activities. More than anything else, levels can provide a clearly published set of goals for clients and staff members, so that daily token earning does not become an end in itself.

The author would urge program planners to consider some modification of levels in devising criteria to regulate client progress within a group management program. It is hoped that additional research will assess the utility of this approach with an array of client populations.

CHAPTER SUMMARY

Consequences directed at groupings of clients often rely upon generalized reinforcers—tokens in the form of chips, points, or check marks that may be traded in for various material, activity, social, or other backup reinforcements. Generalized reinforcers permit immediate and discreet consequences to be applied to client behavior at any time, they may be used to maintain performance over extended periods, they are not dependent upon client deprivation, and they provide an efficient means of reinforcing individuals who have different reinforcement preferences.

Diverse categories of behaviors have been targeted for change within institutional formats. Targeted behaviors should be constructed with client and staff input and clearly defined in explicit, operational language. Self-care behaviors, including hygiene, dress, and administration of medication or therapy, as well as verbal and nonverbal social behaviors are among categories frequently targeted. In addition, an array of task activities including custodial and administrative tasks, serving as a "therapist" for other clients, and monitoring behavioral change within a program have been the focus of token efforts.

Tokens may be physical objects like poker chips or written feedback like checkmarks, but most tokens should exhibit the same properties. Their value should be readily understood, and there should be some relationship between token earnings and degree of reinforcement provided for the target. In addition, tokens should be readily transportable across settings, constructed of a durable material, easy for staff members to administer, and require minimal bookkeeping.

In defining backup reinforcers for clients, most settings have employed material/activity items; more recently, however, items intrinsic to the client's setting or the natural environment have been employed (e.g., free time, "good behavior" game). It was strongly suggested that multiple of backup reinforcers be provided for clients, and that backups be carefully evaluated on an ongoing basis to determine their continued reinforcing properties. Whenever possible, backups should be consonant with therapeutic goals and promotive of adaptive, prosocial behavior.

At present the relationship of schedules of token administration to client performance has not been fully explored in the literature; however, certain investigators have provided an increased delay between token earning and client receipt of backups. Token reinforcement should be coupled with verbal and nonverbal social reinforcement from staff members, delivered in a consistent and well-labeled fashion.

Another option is for the BCA to provide tokens based upon the behavior of some grouping of clients; this facilitates mutual responsibility, cohesiveness, and cooperation among the group. Most often, group contingencies have been employed within the classroom setting, and individuals have earned tokens based on the functioning of the group at large or on the behavior of the most or least disruptive client. While many group systems seem to be as effective as individual systems, the literature suggests that positive individual contingencies be provided along with group contingencies, so that individual performance is not punished by the "worst member" of a group.

While early investigations suggested that clients might self-rate and award tokens in a reliable and consistent fashion, more recent class-room investigations have pointed to a gradual dissipation of behavioral gains over time. While it may be highly desirable to permit clients to self-monitor and reward themselves, they must be carefully monitored, with frequent reliability checks undertaken by independent observers. Few investigators have evaluated self-imposed contingencies for adult populations, and at present no conclusions may be drawn.

An alternative is to permit clients to govern themselves, with the BCA serving in a "consultant" or advisor role. The work of a number of investigators suggests that this approach is valued by clients and promotive of desirable behavioral change. Unfortunately, little systematic research has evaluated such self-mediated contingencies.

Most programs include some means of providing negative feedback to clients, and most usually employ response cost (e.g., loss of tokens) as the punishing agent. Response cost seems to be as effective as positive reinforcement systems in gaining control of important targeted behaviors; however, because of the possibility of its abuse, and the fact that certain unskilled clients may end up receiving more negative than positive feedback, negative feedback must be devised with care and be evaluated on a consistent basis.

Most program designers do not report sufficient information about staff training procedures in their reports, and little research has been directly focused upon training methodologies. Systematic and comprehensive staff training was strongly emphasized as an important predictor of success for such programs.

An alternative to the token approach is client progression through a series of carefully defined levels of responsibility and concomitant reinforcements. Client movement through the levels depends upon highly specific and carefully defined target behaviors. Often, levels are defined by certain labels or color-coded designations to assist staff members as well as clients in identifying levels of progress within the program. Because levels programs have not been comprehensively evaluated within the literature, no conclusions as to their effectiveness may be drawn at the present time.

Chapter 5

Manipulation of Consequences:

COVERT PROCESSES

With the emergence of a behavioral approach to treatment in the late 1950s, the role of thoughts, ideas, sensations, and other private events as relevant targets for behavioral change became the focus for a debate that has only recently subsided. Behaviorists were accused of being very "peripheral" in that they tended to focus their therapeutic efforts upon observable behaviors that could be reliably observed and systematically counted by others (Breger and McGaugh, 1965; Wiest, 1967). In addition, the behavioral approach was called simplistic in attempting to directly translate the experiments of the animal lab to treatment paradigms for human behavioral change.

As outlined by the phenomenal-behavioral model presented in Chapter 1, it is much too simplistic, and a further example of "beating the straw man" (Weitzman, 1967), to insist that behavioral therapists have traditionally turned their backs upon such covert phenomena in favor of overt processes. Wolpe's procedure of systematic desensitization, first reported upon in 1958, stands apart from early attempts at operant shaping of overt behaviors in its focus on covert phenomena. Very simply, phobic clients in a state of relaxation are asked to imagine an array of events around a central theme (e.g., height, animals) that elicit an emotional response. Wolpe felt that the state of relaxation would "reciprocally inhibit" a client's emotional response to the phobic imagery. The process of relaxation is often augmented by hypnotic imagery (Lang, 1967); in fact, many clients are trained to imagine prior to undertaking treatment. After completing an array of scenes constructed in hierarchical fashion, Wolpe found that clients were able to tolerate the previously feared stimuli in the natural environment. Importantly, Wolpe did not work with his clients in the natural environment, but relied exclusively upon their imaginal representation of the "real world" as a focus for treatment. Although desensitization was originally explained exclusively with learning theory terms such as extinction or counterconditioning (Wolpe, 1958), it soon became obvious to researchers and practitioners that no one explanation would suffice for the effects of this approach (Borkovec, 1973; Wilkins, 1971), opening the door to non-specific factors often involving "covert" processes.

In a sense Wolpe was treating clients' mental images in much the same way that others applied treatments to overt behaviors. This was not a new idea, and in fact in 1953 Skinner had made the point that private events obey the same laws as nonprivate events, thus opening up the entire array of covert processes to procedures based upon a learning orientation. To place this discussion in some historical focus Bernstein (1974) makes the following point:

Covert events may be loosely defined as thoughts, feelings, images, and all other behaviors which are directly observable only to the individual engaging in them. Such behaviors have come in and out of fashion as objects of study in psychology. When the science of psychology was first beginning in the late 19th and early 20th century, covert processes were a prime area of research concern. Such noted psychologists as Wundt (1873), Titchner (1898) and James (1884) devoted most of their time to such studies. These investigators trained their subjects to observe their own covert processes by a highly structured process of introspection. Watson (1930) was one of the earliest psychologists to take issue with the study of covert events. He believed that overt and observable behaviors were the only proper variables for psychological study. Watson's influence changed the nature of psychology from a science of inner worlds to a science of behavior. The study of overt events became the rule, yet a number of theorists and researchers felt the need to include private events in their theoretical systems. Tolman (1932) dealt with cognitions and expectations, Guthrie (1935) with the stimulus properties of intensions, and Hull (1952) with fractional anti-dating responses and stimuli (Rg and Sg). These writers all felt that covert behaviors obey the same laws as overt behaviors. More recently Skinner (1953), his associates and students have made a strong case for returning to staunch Watsonian behaviorism. Skinner's influence is still quite strong today; in fact, it is such a powerful current in the mainstream of psychological thought that it seems to detract attention from the fact that the study of covert events has held a reputable place in psychology for many years. . . .
It seems to the present author that research into the role of covert processes is increasing, owing mainly to the introduction of covert paradigms into the mainstream of behavior therapy. This research seems to be proceeding as if these topics were never considered before in the history of psychology. It is interesting to

note that in one well received volume on the role of private events in psychological research (Jacobs and Sachs, 1971) the names of Wundt, James and Titchner are not mentioned, even though the methodologies that they have developed may offer a number of useful insights into the present day study of covert events. (pp. 5–6)

More recently procedures have been developed that specifically focus on covert phenomena as a means of altering both covert and overt behavior. A perplexing variety of terms has been employed to describe these treatment modalities, including *coverant control* (Homme, 1965), self-reinforcement (Kanfer and Marston, 1963), *covert sensitization, covert positive reinforcement, covert negative reinforcement, covert extinction* (Cautela, 1966, 1970, 1971), and *covert modeling* (Cautela, Flannery, Hanley, 1974; Kazdin, 1974).

The present chapter will look at the primary ways in which therapeutic manipulations have been applied to covert phenomena. Beginning with procedures employed primarily to accelerate client targeted behavior, a thorough outline of the component steps of each approach will be illustrated by examples from the literature. Procedures that are primarily employed in the deceleration of problem targets will follow. Finally, important issues suggested by a therapeutic focus upon covert processes will be discussed.

SELF-REINFORCEMENT

Hill (1968) makes the point that all reinforcers "involve an evaluation of the subject, either by someone else or by himself, with positive evaluations functioning as positive reinforcers and negative ones as negative reinforcers. They may therefore by grouped under the term evaluative reinforcers" (p. 132). Kanfer and his colleagues (Kanfer and Marston, 1963; Kanfer and Duerfeldt, 1968; Dorsey, Kanfer, and Duerfeldt, 1971; Karoly and Kanfer, 1974) have viewed this process within the framework of "self regulation," and divide the regulatory process into three phases: self-monitoring, self-evaluation, and self-reinforcement. According to this model the reinforcing or punishing of events follows a discrimination concerning the adequacy of one's current performance as it relates to a subjectively held standard (or performance criterion). Self-reinforcement (SR+) is presumed to follow when performance equals or exceeds the standard. Self-punishment (SR−) is an expected consequence of substandard performance (Karoly and Kanfer, 1974).

With regard to self-evaluation, analog studies conducted in laboratory settings have shown that subjects do in fact adopt specific standards to evaluate their behaviors. A "standard" is defined as some particular level of performance, some criterion beyond which an individual might evaluate his performance as "good" or "acceptable" and below which it might be viewed as "inadequate." Chapter 3 presented certain methods that employ extrinsic controls in the form of reinforcements and punishments to systematically increase certain appropriate targeted behaviors while decreasing socially maladaptive behaviors. It is perhaps through the process of parental/teacher/peer-administered rewards and punishments, contingent upon specific classes of behavior, that standards for self-evaluation and self-reinforcement become set as the child develops. Children who are extrinsically reinforced through praise, physical affection, or material rewards like money or toys might over time internalize their parents' standards so that they evaluate the condition of a living setting in terms of those standards. While standards are learned through direct experiences with reinforcement or punishment, they are probably also learned by observing models reinforced by other important extrinsic agents for certain levels of performance (Bandura and Kupers, 1964; Mischel and Liebert, 1966). Thus, a child observing an adult play a pinball machine and only reinforce himself for a high level of performance may adopt a stringent standard for evaluating his own efforts (Mischel and Liebert, 1966).

The primary focus of self-reinforcement research has been upon that process the individual engages in *following* an evaluation of his performance, that is, the self-mediated consequences administered. The feeling of satisfaction expressed with positive self-directed statements or thoughts ("I'm really doing better," "I did a good job") or the negative self-statements applied to one's behavior ("No good, I've just got to improve," "X is much better than I am") are examples of such self-mediated consequences. Different people no doubt engage in this process of self-evaluation and self-reinforcement in unique ways. The private nature of such events and the fact that these reinforcements are often not verbalized (e.g., a feeling of relaxation, calmness, an overall good feeling following an excellent performance) make research into the components of such self-regulatory processes much more difficult than research that focuses on purely overt phenomena.

The important question for the clinical researcher has been, How might a client be trained to evaluate his own behavior more appropriately, more in line with the way that others evaluate a similar performance? Many of the behavioral problems that clients present may be due to the adoption of inappropriate (e.g., unrealistic, poorly defined) standards for self-evaluation. The "depressive," if viewed along these lines, is an individual who may impose unrealistically stringent standards on his behavior. In a sense the standards are set so high that it is impossible for him to ever deliver a self-reinforcement for a job well done. The client traditionally defined as having "poor self-concept" or "poorly defined ego" may in fact be an individual whose standards for self-evaluation have not been clearly defined. Although this is a rather simplistic explanation for very complex categories of behavior, investigators have increasingly employed some notion of self-evaluation/reinforcement in their analysis of the behavior of certain client diagnostic categories. For example, Lewinsohn (1974) is among investigators who view depression as resulting from lack of extrinsic and self-mediated reinforcements.

Most frequently investigators have employed self-evaluation and self-reinforcement to increase or decrease the frequency of some targeted behavior, as a component of a treatment package that often includes training in self-monitoring, some form of extrinsic control, as well as a host of nonspecific relationship variables such as expectancy and cognitive set (Borkovec, 1973a, b). Also, it should be emphasized that self-reinforcement may be in the form of covert events (e.g., positive and negative self-statements) and/or of extrinsic incentives that clients apply to themselves (e.g., earning of television time, points which may be expended toward desirable activities). In reviewing a large number of studies that have employed self-reinforcement as either the prime method or a collateral method of treatment (e.g., Rehm and Marston, 1968; Kanfer and Duerfeldt, 1968; Marston, 1969; Mahoney, Moura, and Wade, 1974; Mahoney, 1974), the following procedural steps are typically employed:

1. Following a mutual decision by therapist and client as to important targeted behaviors, the client is asked (and in some cases trained) to *self-observe* the targeted behavior within some systematic schedule. Until the client can define *when the targeted response is about to occur or occurs*, it is impossible to attempt any sort of manipulation of consequences. The targeted behavior may either be overt, such as a weighing in to help avoid certain foods (Mahoney, 1974) or covert, such as successfully completing an imaginal step on a desensitization hierarchy, avoiding an "urge" to eat, smoke, drink, or engaging in inappropriate sexual behavior. Because of the previously mentioned finding that self-monitoring alone may cause a change in the targeted behavior (McFall, 1970; Johnson and White, 1971), it is often difficult to separate out the effects of this self-monitoring treatment from the additional effects of applying some sort of self-reinforcement (Kazdin, 1974; Mahoney, 1972).

2. An assessment is made of possible reinforcers (or punishers) the client may administer to himself. Therapists often review either verbally or through a questionnaire (Cautela and Kastenbaum, 1967) those statements a client might make to himself that are either reinforcing or punishing. It is not so easy as merely asking the client to say "Good job" to himself—and many clients have not developed a very extensive repertoire of such reinforcing self-statements. In some cases the therapist provides the client with a list of possible reinforcing or punishing self-statements to review and to practice. In other cases the therapist might model by verbally stating some of the reinforcers and have the client verbally rehearse

each self-statement out loud, as a prelude to self-administering them at a covert, nonverbal level. It is extremely important that the therapist review these self-reinforcers with the client and provide avenues for modeling and practice through role-playing to ensure that clients have mastered the ability to administer them to themselves.

With regard to extrinsic reinforcements suitable for self-administration or self-imposed costs, the therapist and client may devise a list of positive/high-rate activities that the client may be asked to apply contingently upon, or remove following a targeted behavior. For example, after turning down a piece of pie or a cigarette or after completing a certain number of minutes of study (targeted behavior), the client may be asked to reward himself with some reinforcing activity (e.g., watching television for *x* minutes, playing a record album, making a desired telephone call, or engaging in some positive hobby activity). Should the client engage in a targeted negative behavior (e.g., eating a snack food, smoking a cigarette, thinking an obsessive thought), he might be required to terminate some reinforcing activity for a predetermined time.

3. Once client and therapist have decided upon a list of either covert or overt incentives that may be self-applied following some targeted event, the client is then asked to administer the reinforcer immediately and consistently following the targeted behavior. The target could be a covert behavior (thought, image, an urge that precedes some overt behavior) or an overt event. Now that the client has control of the reinforcements, it is hoped that through repeated experiences with self-mediated consequences, he will begin reinforcing himself for prosocial and appropriate behaviors on a continuous basis. Chapter 8, on self-control, further illustrates how self-reinforcement and self-punishment might be incorporated along with other procedures into an overall program that encourages client self-control.

Jackson (1972) used a program of self-reinforcement to increase certain positive, pro-social behaviors on the part of a depressed young woman:

"L.M. was a 22-year old housewife married for two years to a clerical worker. During the last two years she had seen a number of therapists because of feelings of depression, worthlessness, inactivity, and frequent self-denigratory statements. Previous therapeutic attempts had tried to increase understanding of "Why" she was depressed and to get her doing things, and although this would reduce some depression, she reported that invariably it returned. . . . L.M. was extremely harsh with herself to the point of restricting herself from pleasurable experiences. Her activities were carried out in a quasimechanical manner with an apparent unfavorable distortion to feedback in terms of considerable sensitivity only to unacceptable performances. When questioned about rewarding experiences she gave herself, she was quick to reply that this definitely contradicted her upbringing; thus, self-managed consequences were predominantly aversive or, if ever positive, seemed to be random. Generally, the only positive reinforcement she received came from her surroundings, this being infrequent and neutralized by self-devaluating statements. It turned out that, over time, compliments became a discriminative stimulus for self-criticism.

It was decided to select a task that she performed frequently and considered important and to elaborate a self-reinforcement pattern for it. While reviewing her activities, she enumerated relating to people, housekeeping, reading, talking to her husband, watching television, and drawing. When asked to assess them in terms of frequency and their importance to her she chose housekeeping as the first behavior to monitor and she was given three records to keep daily, assessing them at about the same time each evening (between 9–10 P.M.). She was instructed to record the total amount of time per day spent on washing and drying dishes, and dusting. Second, she was asked to rate her depression according to her own criteria on a 10-point scale, 10 being very depressed. She was to record the number of rewards she gave herself throughout the day for housekeeping. A reward was defined as praising yourself, doing something you like, or feeling contented as a consequences for doing housework.

During the second interview the role of positive self-reinforcement was explained in detail to her, especially in maintaining behaviors for which positive social reinforcement is available only intermittently. She was asked to take each chore *separately* and define what she wanted to accomplish in terms of the task and the amount of time estimated to complete it in much the same way that instructional objectives are formulated.

At first it was necessary for the therapist to lower the goals that L.M. had set for herself thus increasing the probability of her attaining success. To provide later reference, each goal was written down specifying the performance before starting the task. When she had completed the task, she was told to assess what she had done in light of what she had set out to do. If she judged that she had matched or surpassed her goals she was told to do something positive or pleasant immediately, such as compliment herself, have a cigarette or telephone an interesting friend. To concretize these operations at first, she was given a box of poker chips and told to take as many as she thought she deserved up to 10 and then record the number she took. The inclusion of the chips was to promote her dispensing consequences to her performance. During the interview the process was modeled by the therapist and then rehearsed by L.M. until she had it mastered.

Beginning the 11th day, she was instructed to reinforce herself positively contingent upon her evaluation of her activity and was asked to continue monitoring her behaviors. . . . Additionally, she spent less time doing housework which she attributed to increased efficiency plus a more easy going attitude towards it. One early outcome was a generalization of gains to other areas such as socializing. Independently, she applied the procedure to behaviors associated with the role of hostess, deciding what behaviors she wanted to manifest, evaluating her performance and then rewarding herself. This innovation received strong approval from the therapist. Interviews were held on the 15th and 21st days, at which time her progress was reviewed and new tasks were assigned. During the fourth interview, Day 21, L.M. reported that her depression had subsided and she ceased the observing and recording but continued the self-reinforcement program. Approximately two months later she was asked to resume the monitoring of frequency of positive self-reinforcement, depression and time spent on housework as previously defined. . . . The positive self-reinforcement now took the form of content or satisfaction in contrast to the initial feeling of "it still isn't good enough" and the subsequent verbal approval. (pp. 302–304)

Fig. 5.1 shows the data collected by this client during treatment and at a
two-month followup.

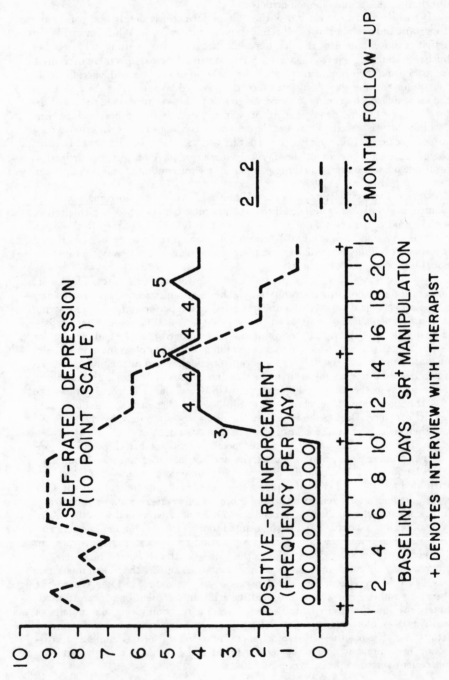

Fig. 5.1

Self-reinforcement in treatment of depressive behavior (from Jackson, 1972).

COVERT POSITIVE REINFORCEMENT

Cautela (1971) employed covert positive imagery as a reinforcer for both overt and covert client targeted behaviors. Covert positive reinforcement, or COR, is very similar to positive self-reinforcement, except that it exclusively involves positive imagery as a reinforcer, is presented by the therapist within the clinical setting, and often incorporates other procedures such as relaxation, thought stopping (Cautela, 1970), and imagery building. The following procedural steps are most often employed in the relatively few published reports of COR (Cautela and Wisocki, 1969; Krop, Calhoon, and Verrier, 1971; Manno and Marston, 1972; Wisocki, 1973; Blanchard and Draper, 1973).

1. Following determination of client-targeted behaviors designated for acceleration, the therapist and client attempt to *define those images that hold reinforcing properties* for the client. This reinforcement survey may be conducted formally, using the Reinforcement Survey Schedule (RSS, Cautela and Kastenbaum, 1967), which lists 54 item categories and requires the client to rate each on a five-point scale, indicating "pleasurable feelings" that the item provokes for the client. After the RSS has been completed those items the client has rated as "very much" are then rank-ordered from least pleasurable to most pleasurable. Items rated "very positive" are then tested according to the following criteria:

a. The client must be able to obtain a *clear image* of a scene focusing on the item.

b. The client must be able to obtain a clear image of this scene *within five seconds* of its presentation. This seems to be important. Data from many experiments indicate that the closer the reinforcement to the response in time, the greater the influence on response rate (Cautela, 1970).

The client and therapist then review open-ended questions on the RSS that define certain high-rate thoughts that may be useful as reinforcing images.

2. Clients are provided with a *rationale* for the events to follow. Very simply, clients are informed that their behavior occurs because their environment provides positive consequences for it. They are informed that a problem behavior may be changed simply by imagining themselves performing certain behaviors and then imagining certain consequences. Thus, the role of imaginal events in altering clients' behavior is stated. Clients are encouraged to ask questions about the basic theory underlying the technique.

3. Some decision is made as to what specific scenes will be worked on in the therapeutic session. Each scene is a representation of an event in the client's life involving the targeted behavior to be increased in frequency. For example, in working with an obese client, scenes of "turning

food down," engaging in alternative and incompatible activities, or any other overt or covert responses that assist the client in avoiding improper foods might be included as imaginal scenes to be reinforced. Cautela (1972) has employed the following scenes with obese clients:

You are sitting at home watching TV. . . . You say to yourself, "I think I'll have a piece of pie." You get up to go to the pantry. Then you say, "This is stupid. I don't want to be a fat pig."
You are at home eating steak. You are just about to reach for your second piece and you stop and say to yourself, "Who needs it anyway?"
Imagine that you have lost 50 pounds and you are standing naked in front of a mirror. You congratulate yourself for getting rid of all the flab. (p. 213)

The scenes are often arranged in the form of a hierarchy with increasingly difficult behaviors included in each hierarchical scene. The first scene to be dealt with in the therapy session (scene 1) would involve some behavior that the client could readily engage in, with the last scene (scene 10) very difficult for the client. While Cautela claims that the use of a hierarchy is not necessary, he often reports breaking scenes down into smaller segments (Cautela, 1971). Chapter 10 discusses the construction of hierarchies in detail.

4. Once the scenes have been decided upon, the client is *trained to imagine*. Often, a practice scene is presented to review the extent to which the client is able to obtain a clear image of the scene. Many clients find it very difficult to obtain clear imagery, and they must carefully practice imagining scenes prior to treatment proper. Cautela encourages his clients to use all senses when imagining a scene. For example, in a scene that involved lighting up a cigarette and then deciding to put it out, Cautela might have the client focus upon how the smoke looks as it is exhaled, the sensation of the smoke in the throat and mouth, sensations of warmth or cold associated with the smoke, any taste associated with the cigarette at the lips or with the smoke in the mouth, the smell of the cigarette, as well as any other sensory experiences associated with smoking a cigarette. The therapist might ideally have the client engage in the targeted behavior (if possible, i.e. smoking) in the therapy session while focusing upon the various sensations that it provides, so that the client will be better able to obtain a clear image of the attendant sensations during the treatment process proper. The therapist might also have the client self-record this information (e.g., what a certain food tastes and smells like; what an urge to smoke feels like) as part of the preliminary data collection prior to treatment. This information may be very useful in suggesting the various cues to be included in a given scene.

Typically, Cautela asks clients to imagine the scene and to close their eyes while he describes the scene in detail, attempting to incorporate many of the cues previously determined through careful questioning of the client. Clients are asked to raise their finger at the point when they clearly imagine the scene, and at that time the therapist questions them about the clarity of the scene and the ease with which they are able to obtain and maintain it. Then clients are asked to imagine a scene by themselves, with additional training sessions provided if they experience further difficulty.

5. Each scene is treated in the following fashion: Clients are given instructions to imagine each scene as clearly as possible, raising the right index finger when they have obtained a clear image. They are then instructed that when the therapist says the word *reinforcement*, they are to attempt to imagine some specific reinforcing scene as previously defined, raising a finger again when the reinforcing scene is clearly defined. Cautela (1971) reports these preliminary instructions:

In a minute I'm going to ask you to try to relax and close your eyes. Then I will describe a scene to you. When you can imagine the scene as clearly as possible, raise your right index finger. I will then say the word "reinforcement." As soon as I say the word, "reinforcement," try to imagine the reinforcing scene we practiced before, the one of swimming on a hot day, feeling the refreshing water and feeling wonderful. Do you understand the instructions? Remember to try to imagine everything as vividly as possible, as if you were really there. All right, now close your eyes and try to relax. (p. 121)

Each presentation of a scene followed by "reinforcement" is considered a trial. Only when the client has vividly imagined the reinforcement scene is another trial begun. As mentioned before, the treatment scene may be broken down into smaller segments, rather than presenting the entire scene as a whole. An example of this (Cautela, 1971) illustrates the COR procedure for a client who is fearful of taking examinations.

It is the day of the examination and you feel confident ("reinforcement"). You are entering the building in which the exam is going to be given ("reinforcement"). You remember that in all the scenes you were trying to feel confident. Now you enter the building and go to the classroom ("reinforcement"). You sit down and kid around with another student who is taking the exam ("reinforcement"). The proctor comes in with the exam. You feel good; you know you are ready ("reinforcement"). The proctor hands out the exam ("reinforcement"). You read the questions and you feel you can answer all of them ("reinforcement"). (p. 122)

Often, covert positive reinforcement is "built into" the scene proper rather than being presented as a separate image. Manno and Marston (1972) employed this procedure with a group of 41 obese clients.

(Session 2): Simple conditioning procedures were explained to the group and *S*s were told about the positive covert procedure, and given simple relaxation instructions. The *S*s were asked to imagine that they saw a high frequency food, reach for it, pick it up and bring it to their mouth. Just as they are tempted to eat it, they say "I don't want it", they put it down and imagine feeling wonderful that they were able to resist. They are thrilled with themselves. A friend whom they want to impress was imagined seated beside the *S* and she (he) is pleased with *S*'s self-control. This was repeated for three more trials using different specific foods on the hierarchy. The *S* was also asked to imagine how wonderful he will look in new clothes. The last part of the hour was devoted to discussion of the food data sheets and any questions that arose. Sessions 3–7 were essentially the same with several exceptions. (Session 3): *S* was asked to see the food item, pick it up (but not bring it to his mouth), say "I don't want it" and put it down. He then feels wonderful and is praised by his friends who notice his self-control. (Session 4): *S* imagined reaching for the food, imagined not really wanting it, imagined himself with the ideal body and other advantages of losing weight *(E* enumerates several of the reasons for weight reductiong gathered from the scales). (Session 5): *S* imagines seeing the food item and being thrilled that he doesn't want it; imagines himself with the ideal body, in a bathing suit and feels wonderful (Sessions 6 and 7): *S* imagined the food, has no desire for it, imagined the dial on a scale showing a five pound weight loss, then a ten pound weight loss, feeling marvelous. (p. 204)

Each of the scenes of the hierarchy employed by Manno and Marston involved increasingly difficult behaviors for this obese group of clients. The reader may notice how the reinforcement was actually built into the scene and was not merely an unrelated positive image.

Anywhere from five to 20 trials have been employed within the session (Cautela, 1971; Wisocki, 1972), with clients taking a major role in imagining the scenes on some systematic schedule. For example, Wisocki (1972) presented every odd scene and the clients self-presented every even scene, for a total of 20 scene presentations. Typically, clients are asked to practice the scenes on their own from two to 20 trials once or twice a day, and are particularly encouraged to apply COR when some positive targeted behavior occurs naturally (e.g., not smoking a cigarette, turning down a fresh piece of pie). Therapy often extends for a period ranging from six to eight weeks, followed by booster sessions at various intervals following termination.

Although a relatively novel procedure, COR has been employed to increase the frequency of a variety of targeted behaviors. Cautela (1970) employed COR to increase the frequency of approach behaviors for test-anxious clients as well as clients fearful of dating. In both instances clients were instructed to reinforce themselves with positive imagery after thinking of an appropriate approach response such as taking an examination or calling a female friend on the telephone. Cautela also has applied the covert positive reinforcement procedure to reduce the frequency of smoking (Cautela, 1972), decrease the frequency of obsessive compulsive behavior (1970), and as an adjunct to treatment designed to reduce homosexual approach behavior (Cautela, 1970).

In these cases COR was used to reinforce incompatible and adaptive events. Blanchard and Draper (1973) employed the COR procedures to increase a client's ability to approach and tolerate rats. Although probably most of us could do without this skill, the client was a 20-year-old female who would be required to handle laboratory animals as part of a graduate program in psychology. Her expressed goal for treatment was to "become comfortable enough around rodents that she could complete courses in experimental psychology" (p. 560). Treatment consisted of the client imagining increasingly difficult approach responses in handling a laboratory rat, with each successful approach response followed by "reinforcement" as described previously. To augment the effects of COR in the therapy situation, the authors made a tape recording of the COR instructions and asked the client to employ this tape to facilitate practice at home. The authors included additional treatments in the form of "support," "insight," as well as exposure to a fearless model. As a matter of fact, most authors combine the COR procedures with other treatments, which makes the determination of the effectiveness of COR in isolation most difficult (e.g., Kendrick and McCullough, 1972; Hall, 1972).

A number of studies have shown that COR may help to successfully alter the attitude of subjects regarding some topic. For example, attitudes toward the elderly (Cautela and Wisocki, 1969) as well as the attitudes of a group of undergraduate students toward the mentally retarded (Cautela, Walsh, and Wish, 1970) were altered in a positive direction using the COR approach. In the latter study subjects were asked to imagine the following scene:

Please sit back in your chairs and relax as best you can, placing both feet on the floor and hands folded in front of you. Now, close your eyes and imagine a mentally retarded person as vividly as you can. By "vividly" we mean really try hard to imagine as many details as possible, i.e., the color of eyes, the expression of his face, the way he talks, etc. When you can do this, please raise your hand. (p. 3)

S's were then asked to immediately "shift" into a positively reinforcing scene:

Okay, fine. Please put the picture of the mentally retarded person out of your imagination for a while. Now, still relaxed and with your eyes closed, try to imagine yourself doing something you enjoy very much and which gives you a great deal of pleasure. For example, some people enjoy. . . . (p. 3)

At this point subjects were given examples of potentially pleasant scenes from the RSS, with each trial requiring the subject to imagine a mentally retarded person and then immediately "shift" to a positive scene, thus pairing positive imagery with the "retarded" image. Subjects were asked to practice this pairing sequence at home at least twice a day. Responses to a Likert-type questionnaire showed a significant increment in positive attitudes toward the retarded following COR.

COVERANT CONTROL

Another procedure employing reinforcing imagery is the "coverant" control procedure developed by Homme (1965), who suggested the application of coverant control within a paradigm described by David

Premack—the so-called Premack principle (Premack, 1959). According to the Premack principle (see Chapter 3) activities that occur at a high rate for an individual are considered to be reinforcers. Given that these behaviors occur voluntarily and that behavior is generally lawful, those things that we do must hold some positive properties for us. According to the Premack principle, *high-rate behaviors may be used to systematically reinforce certain low-rate behaviors* that may be targets within treatment. By making a high-rate behavior (reinforcer) contingent upon a low-rate event, we reinforce the low-rate behavior and increase its frequency. According to Homme, a client might be asked to think some low-rate thought prior to engaging in a typically high-rate behavior. For example, in working with a "depressed" client, the goal might be to increase the frequency of positive self-evaluative statements such as, "I'm doing a good job," "I'm a good person," "I can do this" (low rate events). Suppose a client engages in frequent cigarette smoking (high-rate behavior). In using the Premack principle to obtain coverant control, we might ask the client to think some positive thought about himself each time prior to lighting a cigarette. This paradigm is shown in Fig. 5.2.

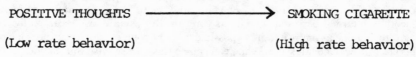

Fig. 5.2
Paradigm for coverant control.

In working with an anxious client, one goal might be to encourage the client to employ relaxation procedures frequently. Homme states:

Suppose lighting a cigar is a high probability behavior in a given instant. Further suppose that the lower probability behavior one wishes to strengthen is the relaxation coverant. Does one light a cigar and then relax? Not if one's intent is to strengthen the relaxation coverant. Instead, one will say to oneself, "As soon as I relax, I may light this cigar." (p. 504)

In another example Homme (1965) uses the high-probability behavior of drinking a cup of coffee to reinforce the low-probability behavior of thinking about writing a paper:

For example, he can say to himself (if getting a cup of coffee is a high probability behavior), "As soon as I think about that paper I am to write, I will get some coffee."

In this example, *S* has self managed his contingencies so that the execution of a high probability behavior (getting coffee) was contingent upon the execution of some lower probability behavior (thinking about the paper). If Premack is correct, the tendency to think about the paper ought to increase in frequency. It is interesting to note that contingencies do not automatically get thus managed. Without keeping the Premack hypothesis in mind, it seems just as reasonable for *S* to say to himself, "As soon as I get my coffee, I'll think about the paper." (p. 504)

Other examples of coverant control might include cigarette smokers who are asked, prior to lighting up each cigarette (high-rate behavior), to think about the way their lungs would look if they had lung cancer. Or obese clients might be asked, prior to eating any form of snack food, to picture themselves as derisive laughter is directed at their size. Thus, the coverant control procedure could be employed to accelerate some social, adaptive behavior or to decelerate some maladaptive behavior, depending upon the specific coverant that the client is encouraged to reinforce using the high-rate event. Todd (1972) reports a case where coverant control was successfully employed with a 49-year-old-woman suffering from "chronic depression" that periodically became quite severe, causing her to attempt suicide on three occasions:

Mrs. M was asked to describe herself by a series of single words or phrases. Her responses were all negative. It was pointed out to her that if a person had only self-denigrating thoughts about herself it would be difficult for her not to be depressed. Therefore, we were going to substitute positive thoughts about herself for the negative ones. With agonizing slowness and much therapist prompting, Mrs. M managed to find six positive statements she could entertain about herself. (With those patients who fail to find anything positive about themselves, it may be necessary for the therapist to reflect honestly good points that he sees in the patient—thus to start the list for her). The six statements were printed in large letters on a sheet of notepaper and in somewhat smaller letters on a card which was trimmed to fit inside of the cellophane wrapper of her cigarette package. Mrs. M was then informed how, according to Premack's hypothesis, a behavior (in her case, thinking positive thoughts about herself) could be increased by being paired with a behavior with higher probability of occurrence (smoking cigarettes, in her case). She was to read one or two of the six positive items before smoking a cigarette. She was to do this without exception, which would require considerable conscious effort on her part. Whenever she put her cigarettes down for any length of time she was to place them on the sheet of notepaper bearing the list of items. When carrying the pack of cigarettes around, the list would be available on the card. In addition, she was to add positive items to the list as they occurred to her.

Mrs. M carried out the instructions faithfully and, within a week, her depression had lifted considerably; moreover, she had increased the number of positive items to 14. After the second week, she reported that she felt better about herself than she had in years. She now had 21 items on her list. The positive thoughts, she said, popped into her head even when she was not smoking or about to smoke. (p. 92)

Mrs. M was followed for a three-year period after treatment. The author reports:

Mrs. M has become active in volunteer work for political and mental health causes, is considered an excellent hostess and enjoys a wide circle of friends. She reports that she has not suffered any serious depression during this time and considers herself a relatively happy person. She admits to bolstering her spirits by thinking good thoughts on those infrequent occasions when she is "down," but has made no systematic use of the Homme technique since the early weeks of behavior therapy. (p. 92)

Todd (1972) reports applying the coverant control procedure to a 27-year-old college student who had serious doubts about his abilities in comparison with other students. From a list of ten items reflecting his past accomplishments, the client was asked to read one or two of the items from a printed list (low-rate behavior to be increased) prior to to making one of many daily telephone calls (high-rate behavior). The author reports a significant increment over a six-month period in the client's view of himself as a competent student.

One important assumption of this approach, as with all covert approaches, is that what one experiences at a covert level has implications for changes in overt behavior. Bernstein (1974) has stated of Homme's position:

Homme also states that coverants may serve as approximations of overt behaviors. He suggests that the more an individual thinks about performing a behavior, the more likely he is to perform that behavior. Granted that this idea is true, though it would be difficult to test, Homme's technique has applications in raising the frequency of overt behaviors of numerous types. Homme states also that his technique may be used to increase self-confidence or happiness by making high-rate behaviors contingent on confident or happy coverants. Perhaps the most important use of Homme's technique is in its combination with other covert techniques, such as covert positive reinforcement. (p. 15)

Very little research has examined the effectiveness of the coverant control procedure in other than case-study fashion. A few studies have compared Homme's coverant procedure with other covert procedures. For example, Tyler and Straughan (1970) compared an aversive control procedure (holding one's breath as an aversive stimulus associated with thoughts of food) with coverant control, in which pleasant thoughts associated with food were used as the high-rate behavior to reinforce behaviors incompatible with eating for groups of obese clients. The authors found no significant differences in effectiveness between the two procedures as compared with no treatment controls. Unfortunately, *S*s were only provided with one training session; thus, it seems improbable that they might have been able to master and systematically apply the treatments to themselves. In summarizing the literature on coverant control, Bernstein (1974) makes the following observations:

Generalizing across studies, it seems that the more training *S*s were given in the coverant control procedure, the more successful the procedures seem to be. . . .

Coverant techniques require a good deal of skill on the part of the therapist in training clients to be aware of their own covert behaviors. It seems logical, though training procedures are seldom specified, that the more training the subject is given the greater will be his ability to observe and control his behavior.

Based on the results of a study by Horan and Johnson (1971) it would seem that the more often the coverant is experienced the more likely it is to influence overt behaviors. Studies have not been done to specifically test out this particular proposition, however. (pp. 19–20)

Although it has been suggested that Homme's coverant control procedure may be employed to decelerate some targeted event, there are covert procedures whose *primary* function is to decrease targeted overt or covert behaviors.

COVERT EXTINCTION

Cautela (1971) has applied extinction procedures to covert imagery with responses that elicit a good deal of reinforcement (e.g., consuming alcohol, taking a drug, or engaging in some sexual behavior). This approach involves terminating all reinforcement for the behavior within the client's imagination. Cautela (1971) asks the clients to imagine engaging in the previously reinforcing activity; however, clients are instructed not to feel or in any way receive the reinforcement previously associated with the behavior. For example, clients addicted to amphetamines (Gotestam and Melin, 1974) would imagine themselves taking the amphetamine and feeling no positive effects. An evaluation of the literature indicates that covert extinction has been rarely employed, and the results of its use are at best mixed. It does represent a procedure that might be artfully employed along with some sort of imaginal or overt consequence, but as a treatment technique in isolation, its effectiveness appears to be limited.

COVERT SENSITIZATION

Cautela (1972) has emphaszied that stimuli presented in imagination by way of instructions may affect the frequency of covert and overt behavior similar to the way stimuli presented extenally would affect behavior. Thus, if you reward a response in imagination, it should increase in probability; if you punish a response in imagination, it should decrease, just as it would if you used external consequences.

In contradistinction to the COR procedures discussed in the previous section, covert sensitization (Cautela, 1966) is a procedure whereby a client's imagination of some problem behavior is followed by an aversive image. The assumption is that a covert punisher that immediately and contingently follows the imaginal targeted behavior will decrease its frequency.

Of all the covert approaches covert sensitization has been most widely employed and most carefully evaluated. It has been successfully employed to reduce the frequency of targets within an array of targeted problem categories, including obesity (Cautela, 1972; Harris, 1969; Manno and Marston, 1972; Stewart, Sachs, and Ingram, 1972); smoking (Cautela, 1970; Sachs, Bean, and Manow, 1970); use of alcohol (Anant, 1968; Cautela, 1966, 1971); as well as of sexual problems (Gold and Neufeld, 1963; Barlow, Leitenberg, and Agras, 1968; Davison, 1968).

In contrast, more recent investigations have questioned the efficacy of covert sensitization in altering eating habits of obese clients. For example, Foreyt and Hagen (1973) employed an attention-placebo control group (exposure to therapy but no covert sensitization) along with a covert-sensitization group and found no difference in weight loss between the two. Diament and Wilson's (1975) replication of this study produced similar negative findings, causing those authors to suggest that covert sensitization may not be superior to mere self-monitoring and/or suggestion. They emphasize that these findings cannot be generalized to behavior categories other than obesity, and suggest additional research.

The major steps included in covert sensitization procedures as suggested by Cautela (1966, 1967, 1971, 1972) and other investigators (Barlow, Leitenberg, and Agras, 1968; Janda and Rimm, 1972; Maletzky, 1973; Diament and Wilson, 1975) are as follows:

1. Definition of Targeted Behavior

Client and therapist together review the targeted behavior to be reduced in frequency. A series of scenes is constructed that depict various aspects of the targeted event. For example, scenes constructed for an alcoholic client might be constructed around themes similar to the following:

a. "You're standing at the bar and you order a Scotch."

b. "You're at a party and (name) offers you a drink."

c. "You reach for a class of Scotch and slowly bring it up to your mouth; you take a sip."

For each of these core themes a scene suggested by the client's past drinking behavior can be more thoroughly constructed.

2. Definition of Aversive Imagery

Cautela often employs the Fear Survey Schedule (Wolpe and Lang, 1964, Chapter 10) as a means of defining objects or situations that are unpleasant for the client (e.g., Cautela, 1970). The client is carefully interviewed to determine such unpleasant sights, objects, sounds, smells, or tactile sensations. Aversive imagery employing nausea and vomiting has been commonly employed (e.g., Cautela, 1967), although aversive imagery of any kind might be used. For example, Wisocki (1972) employed a description of being "attacked by spiders" as an aversive image following drug-related imagery with a heroin addict.

It is obvious that the aversive image chosen should be intensely unpleasant for the client, and this might be assessed by the amount of time that the client can imaginally tolerate a scene prior to experiencing extreme anxiety/unpleasantness (and perhaps signaling the therapist to terminate). Defining and employing aversive imagery for a client is an unpleasant task for the BCA. *Care should be taken to choose an aversive image that is unpleasant yet does not provoke a response that facilitates other maladaptive behaviors on the client's part.* For example, the BCA would want to rule out aversive imagery focused around an historically phobic object or situation. Thus, for the client who reports an intense fear of heights (which has presumably provoked intense discomfort and perhaps behavioral inefficiency such as avoiding height-related situations), height imagery should not be employed. Presentation of such imagery for brief periods of time may augment the client's avoidance of height stimuli. In fact, Binder (1975) suggests that many fears are learned in the natural environment through covert sensitization processes (e.g. individual repeatedly rehearses fearful/aversive stimuli in association with some specific class of stimuli). The creative BCA can ensure that an aversive image chosen is not related to a client's avoidance behaviors (another target), yet provokes sufficient unpleasantness to hold punishing qualities.

Covert sensitization procedures are often employed in place of physically aversive procedures. The reader should review the discussion in Chapter 3, which attempted to define important practical limitations and ethical considerations suggested by the application of punishment.

3. Presentation of Rationale

Clients are told that their behavior occurs because it is reinforced by their environment. If the consequences of the behavior are changed, then as a result the behavior will increase or decrease. The BCA might say something like, "It has been shown that just by imagining oneself performing certain behaviors and then imagining certain resulting consequences, the problem behavior can change". Clients are also told that their cooperation is necessary for success.

4. Imaginal Training

Clients are instructed to use all their senses when imagining a scene, e.g., how the liquor tasted, how the partner smelled, and how the sheets felt. Rather than merely watch what is happening, clients are told to experience the scene. A practice scene is presented to determine how well clients are able to imagine scenes.

a. Clients close their eyes and are instructed to imagine everything described. When the scene is clear, they are told to raise their right index finger.

b. A scene is described in detail.

c. After the clients raise their finger, they are asked about the clarity of the scene and the ease in imagining the scene (perhaps using a well-defined rating scale).

d. They are asked to imagine the scene by themselves. If they encounter difficulty, more imagery training is given before continuing.

5. Treatment

Clients are seated in a comfortable chair, and the BCA presents each treatment scene in the following manner:

a. The scene involving the targeted behavior is presented (e.g., "You reach for a glass of Scotch, and slowly bring the glass to your mouth; you take a sip"). Thus, the sequence of events in approaching or consuming the targeted event is presented. Clients are instructed to imagine the scene as vividly as possible.

b. Once the targeted scene is vividly imagined (client signals using finger), previously defined aversive imagery is presented. In most cases this imagery is presented as an integral part of the scene, although it could be any unrelated highly aversive image. An example is a case of obesity treated by Cautela (1967):

At first covert sensitization is applied to sweets of all types, especially to foods with heavy carbohydrate content, and then to between-meal eating. The amount of food is usually the prime concern after the kinds of food and the time of eating has been considered. If the therapist finds that the patient is eating too much apple pie or pastry for dessert for instance, he can proceed in the following manner:
I want you to imagine you've just had your main meal and you are about to eat your dessert, which is apple pie. As you are about to reach for the fork, you get a funny feeling in the pit of your stomach. You start to feel queasy, nauseous and sick all over. As you touch the fork, you can feel food particles inching up your throat. You're just about to vomit. As you put the fork into the pie, the food comes up into your mouth. You try to keep your mouth closed because you are afraid that you'll spit the food out all over the place. You bring the piece of pie to your mouth. As you're about to open your mouth, you puke; you vomit all over the table, over the other peoples' food. Your eyes are watering. Snot and mucous are all over your mouth and nose. Your hands feel sticky. There is an awful smell. As you look at this mess you just can't help but vomit again and again until just watery stuff is coming out. Everybody is looking at you with shocked expressions. You turn away from the food and immediately start to feel better. You run out of the room, and as you run out, you feel better and better. You wash and clean yourself up, and it feels wonderful. (p. 462)

c. Often covert positive reinforcement is employed to enhance covert sensitization procedures. For the case just presented Cautela (1967) reports:

In addition to the scene (about 10 per session) in which the patient gives in to the temptation and vomits, scenes in which the patient is initially tempted and then decides not to eat the food are also included in equal number. An example of such a scene is as follows: You've just finished eating your meal and you decide to have dessert. As soon as you make that decision, you start to get that funny feeling in the pit of your stomach. You say, "oh no; I won't eat the dessert." Then you immediately feel calm and comfortable. (p. 463)

6. Self-Mediated Practice

The client is asked to practice specific scenes a certain number of times each day in the natural environment (or perhaps on his own, in an institutional setting). Practice trials require that the client present the targeted scene, followed by aversive imagery, just as it was presented within the treatment session.

Also, the client could be asked to use the aversive imagery whenever tempted to engage in the targeted event (e.g., eat a piece of pie, take a drink) in the natural environment.

It is important to note the use of postive imagery associated with turning away from or turning down the negative stimulus. Thus, incompatible, socially adaptive behavior is reinforced following the punishment of some maladaptive response. In fact, many investigators have emphasized that merely punishing inappropriate behavior is not enough; some socially acceptable, incompatible alternative behavior must be concomitantly reinforced so that the client's repertoire is expanded to include appropriate options for reinforcement (Rimm and Masters, 1974).

It is also of interest to note that although many of the covert procedures are called by different names—*coverant control, self-control, covert positive reinforcement, covert sensitization,* etc.—there are many similarities in these approaches. Kendrick and McCullough (1972) are among few investigators who have explicitly stated that their procedures included a combination of covert reinforcement and covert sensitization approaches. In treating a 21-year-old male homosexual who desired to decrease the frequency of his homosexual urges, the authors report:

Covert sensitization was used to decrease the frequency of homosexual urges. The homosexual fantasies were now paired with verbally induced nausea while the heterosexual imagery was reinforced by using highly reinforcing nonsexual imagery from the RSS. Five sensitization pairings and five covert reinforcement trials were administered during each therapy session; and the client also practiced the sensitization pairings ten times daily at home. (p. 230)

COVERT NEGATIVE REINFORCEMENT

As the reader may recall from Chapter 2, the termination of a noxious stimulus may be employed to contingently reinforce targeted behaviors.

Experimental psychologists have often employed shock as the negatively reinforcing agent. Within this paradigm an organism such as a monkey is shocked *until* he makes the correct response (e.g., turns toward the manipulanda, presses the bar) Cautela (1970) describes the use of a negative reinforcement approach at the covert level. This paradigm is shown in Fig. 5.3.

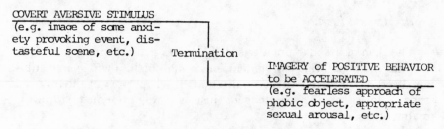

Fig. 5.3
Paradigm for covert negative reinforcement.

In employing the covert negative reinforcement approach, Cautela typically proceeds through five steps:

1. Definition of Targets. Following a careful behavioral assessment of the client's needs, the therapist and client decide upon targets that might be imaginally presented. Among the targeted behaviors that Cautela and others have sought to increase using the covert negative approach are approaching previously feared objects, becoming aroused to sexual imagery that previously did not provoke arousal, or turning away from, refusing, or avoiding some inappropriate stimulus or behavior. Thus, imaginal targets might include engaging in any positive adaptive behavior or avoiding/turning away from any class of negative problem response.

2. Rationale. The client is provided with the following rationale for the covert negative reinforcement procedure (CNR):

"Experiments with animals and humans have shown that if a response is accompanied by a termination of a noxious or aversive stimulus, the probability of that response tends to increase in frequency. Now we are going to use the same procedure except that we are going to do the whole thing in imagination." (Cautela, 1970, p. 274)

3. Definition of Aversive Imagery. Often data from the Fear Survey Schedule (Wolpe and Lang, 1964) is combined with interview data to determine categories of imagery that are aversive to the client. For example, the therapist might ask, "What is the most frightening scene or experience that you can imagine, " or "Tell me something you're afraid of that may not be on the questionnaire I just gave you."

4. Imaginal Training. The client is then trained to carefully imagine the aversive stimulus, and to be able to terminate it and shift to an alternative stimulus (targeted behavior). Cautela (1970) gives an example of the kind of instructions provided during this imaginal training:

"Now close your eyes. I want you to imagine that your girl friend's mother is yelling at you. Try to imagine that you hear her voice and see her face in anger. All right, now try it. Raise you index finger when you feel the scene is clear." (p. 274)

When the patient signals, the therapist inquires, "How clear did you get the scene? Did you become upset when the girl friend's mother yelled at you?" If the answer is in the affirmative, the therapist might say, "All right, now I want you to imagine the scene again. This time when you raise your finger, I will say the word *shift.*" Thus, the client is instructed to imagine the stimulus as well as to "erase" it upon a command from the therapist.

Cautela maintains that a suitable aversive stimulis has the following properties: *(a)* merely saying words associated with the stimulus elicits anxiety; *(b)* the client can clearly imagine the stimulus; *(c)* the image of the stimulus produces responses similar to those produced by external presentation; *(d)* the patient is able to terminate the image immediately at the request of the therapist with little or no residual discomfort. This is necessary to avoid contiguity between the aversive stimulus and the response to be increased, which follows.

5. *Treatment.* The client is provided with the following instructions:

"In a minute I'm going to ask you to close your eyes. I will then ask you to imagine the scene in which you . . . (a description of the particular noxious scene chosen for use). When the scene is clear and you feel upset, raise your right index finger. I will then say the word, 'response.' Then immediately shift to the scene in which you . . . (a description of the response to be increased). As soon as that scene is clear, again signal with your right index finger." (Cautela, 1970, p. 275)

Cautela emphasizes the importance of the client being able to terminate the aversive stimulus upon the therapist's command "Response." It is obvious that if the positive response is associated with the still-maintained aversive stimulus (client cannot terminate), then the procedure will serve as a punishment of the appropriate imagery. This procedure would seem to require rather extensive client training to insure that he may consistently gain control of imaginal processes. In the author's experience many clients experience great difficulty in gaining this kind of control over imaginal processes, and would not be ideal candidates for this sort of procedure. Cautela reports that typically no more than 15 sessions are needed to produce a great improvement in behavior, and estimates that CNR has been successful in 90 percent of treated cases. Unfortunately, there is little data other than Cautela's (1970), 1972) to evaluate the efficacy of CNR. Cautela's reporting of CNR procedures is rather abbreviated, and no evaluative data was presented in the 1970 paper in which the procedure was formulated. A typical case example is presented as follows:

A girl who would not leave her house because of fear of being sexually attacked was asked to imagine she was hearing sirens (which she reported as being highly aversive to her). She then shifted to walking outside her house on a bright sunny day. With repetition she acquired a feeling that it was great and safe to be out and enjoying the world. Removal of the anxiety response to walking outside the house combined with encouragement by the therapist actually to do so led to the performance of the behavior in which she had previously practiced in imagination. A man who was impotent was asked to imagine that his boss was yelling at him (aversive stimulus). Then immediately he switched to a scene in which he was lying in bed naked next to his wife feeling relaxed. A girl who was afraid to say anything at a party when a man walked up to her, imagined that she was just about to fall off a high building (aversive stimulus) and then shifted to responding to a man's questions about her work, hobbies, etc. (Cautela, 1970, p. 275)

Cautela suggests that the CNR procedure should not employ nausea-producing imagery such as that used in the covert sensitization procedure because it is unlikely that nausea will disappear immediately when the patient is asked to terminate the imagery. While recommending the use of COR procedures whenever possible (they are "more humane"), he recommends CNR for clients who claim either a lack of available reinforcers or poor imagery of positive reinforcers. He also points out that CNR might be combined with other approaches, but he presents no data to support this.

COVERT TREATMENTS: IMPORTANT ISSUES

It would seem that virtually every therapeutic procedure employed to alter overt behavior has also been directed at covert phenomena. Thus, we have "covert" positive and negative reinforcement, "covert" sensitization, "covert" extinction and the term "covert conditioning" (Cautela, 1971), which generically applies to any one of the "covert" procedures. Self-reinforcement and coverant control procedures have also been addressed. It has been shown that there are indeed many similarities between these covert approaches, and in summarizing across these various procedures four issues seem to emerge:

There seems to be obvious value in training clients to manipulate private events systematically. By providing the clients with skills that they may direct at their own behavior, it would seem that the possibility of training clients to exhibit self-control of maladaptive behaviors would be enhanced. The lack of generalization from clinical setting to the natural environment has often been reported within the literature as clients perhaps learn to discriminate between situations (e.g., the clinic) in which reinforcers and/or punishers are presented and situations in which such consequences are not systematically presented. Clients trained to self-administer covert consequences could apply them to covert behaviors that precede undesirable overt behaviors (e.g., an urge to smoke, an urge to take a drink), or to the overt event itself, *as these events occur in the natural environment.*

In employing covert procedures, the therapeutic manipulation (e.g., presenting a positive image) cannot be directly observed. Thus, it is impossible for the therapist to determine whether or not the client actually employs the covert technique. Again we have a question of reliability: did the client employ an aversive image? Did the client employ some positive imagery contingent upon "turning down" a glass of alcohol? While some authors have stated that it is impossible to obtain reliability within the covert paradigm (Simpkins, 1971), others have suggested that covert phenomena may be assessed by carefully observing overt referents of covert events (Nelson and McReynolds, 1971). Thus, the perspiration that accumulates on a client's shirt combined with the client's report that he is anxious might be an overt referent underlying covert anxiety. A person's reaching for a pack of cigarettes may be the overt referent of an underlying urge to smoke. While a hypothetical covert-overt chain suggests that a particular covert event is occurring within some client, the BCA must still rely on client verbal report for validation.

It is the opinion of the author that we are unfortunately limited to the client's self-report. One suggestion for increasing the reliability with which the client self-presents covert imagery is to train the client very carefully and systematically to define and employ covert phenomena. It would seem that this training, often mentioned as extremely important by investigators (Cautela, 1966, 1970, 1971), must be emphasized if we are to ensure any systematization of covert treatment efforts. Fortunately, Cautela has made a rather complete presentation of the procedures he employs to train clients, and these have been presented within this chapter.

Perhaps because of the problems of reliability within the covert design, very little research has been employed to carefully test out the "essential" components of covert procedures. So many possible therapeutic components are operating that it becomes very difficult to determine the "live element" of treatment. For example, within the covert sensitization approach elements of punishment, classical conditioning, positive reinforcement, and extinction seem to operate in combination, not to mention expectancy and demand effects. While early studies reported almost uniformly positive findings, more recent research has employed longer followup periods, more subjects and controls for therapist attention and positive expectancy to change. Results have shown covert procedures to be no more effective than control conditions, and Diament and Wilson (1975) suggest the burden of proof now lies with the proponents of covert treatment strategies to evaluate the live elements of their treatments. Hopefully future research will systematically evaluate this potentially important category of procedures more thoroughly and across divergent client populations.

CHAPTER SUMMARY

While a behavioral approach is often denigrated as being "peripheral" or exclusively interested in overt behaviors, there are many of assessment and therapeutic procedures that focus upon covert or private phenomena. Perhaps the key theme of this chapter is that covert events seem to obey the same laws as do overt phenomena and may be readily manipulated as consequences within treatment. The following organized strategies for achieving covert control were presented.

When an individual sets some standard for his performance, monitors his own behavior, and rewards or punishes himself using covert self-statements, we would say that a process of **self-reinforcement** is being employed. Self-reinforcement (SR+) is presumed to follow when performance equals or exceeds the standard. Self-punishment (SR−) is an expected consequence of substandard performance. While standards may be self-generated by the individual, they are often learned by way of feedback the individual receives from important persons within the environment. In addition, standards may be learned vicariously by observing the behavior of important others. An outline of procedural steps typically employed in training clients to self-reinforce was presented.

Covert Positive Reinforcement, or COR, is similar to positive self-reinforcement, except that COR procedures employ *positive imagery as the exclusive reinforcer.* In addition, COR is presented by the therapist within the clinical setting and often incorporates procedures such as relaxation or imagery building. Very little research has evaluated this approach, and most reports are of a case-study nature. Procedural steps include definition of reinforcing imagery; presentation of rationale; definition of treatment scenes; imaginal training; treatment proper. COR has been employed to increase the frequency of a variety of targeted events, and may even be successful in altering the attitudes of individuals.

The Premack principle states that high-probability behaviors may be used to reinforce low-probability events. Homme has applied the Premack principle to covert operants, or "coverants." *Prior to engagingi n some desirable high-rate behavior (e.g., smoking, eating, talking on the telephone), the client is asked to engage in a low-rate, desirable targeted event (e.g., making a positive self-statement or issuing a self-instruction).* The high-rate behavior that follows this low-rate event serves as the reinforcement, and the frequency of the low-rate behavior should increase. Case studies have shown how coverant control can be employed to increase the probability of relaxation, of prompting one's self to perform task behavior, and of positive self-statements by a depressed person. The important assumption is that what one experiences at a covert level has implications for overt behavioral change. Homme made the point that coverants may serve as approximations of overt behaviors, and suggests that increasing one's thinking about a behavior increases its probability. Very little research has evaluated the basic assumptions of the coverant control approach.

Employed with targeted behaviors that result in a high-level reinforcement for clients, covert extinction involves *terminating all reinforcement for some behavior within the clients' imagination*. The clients are asked to imagine a reinforcing activity that holds negative implications for them (e.g., drinking alcohol, taking drugs); however, they are instructed not to feel or in any way receive reinforcement associated with the behavior. This procedure has not been the subject of controlled evaluation within the literature.

Used exclusively to decelerate some problem behavior, covert sensitization involves the *presentation of a problem event within the clients' imagination (e.g., drinking alcohol, reaching for a piece of pie), which is immediately followed by an aversive image*. Using this punishment paradigm, covert sensitization is perhaps the best researched of covert procedures, and has been directed at an array of targeted problem behaviors. Procedural steps include definition of targets, definition of aversive imagery, presentation of rationale, imagery training, treatment, and the possibility of self-mediated practice. Research findings are mixed regarding the efficacy of these procedures.

Similar to Skinner's negative reinforcement approach, *covert negative reinforcement requires the client to imagine an aversive image, which is then terminated upon the imagination of appropriate desirable behavior*. Thus, termination of the negative image serves as the reinforcement. The following procedural steps are most often employed: definition of target, definition of aversive imagery, presentation of rationale, imaginal training, treatment proper. Cautela presents the data from case studies, but no carefully controlled experimental research has examined this approach. Importantly, if the client is not able to immediately terminate the aversive image, the therapist might paradoxically punish the appropriate behavior within the client's imagination.

An array of *important issues* which define covert procedures were discussed.

1. Covert manipulations do seem to provoke a change in overt or covert behavior.

2. Self-administered covert treatments may enhance client's self-control of important targeted behaviors, and may be employed within the natural environment.

3. A major problem with covert events cannot be directly observed by the therapist, suggesting a question of reliability. While recommendations were made for increasing the reliability within this covert design, the BCA must still rely upon client verbal report for validation.

4. It seems that an array of "live elements" is operative within covert approaches (e.g., punishment, classical conditioning, positive reinforcement, extinction), and it was hoped that future research would be directed at relating these treatment procedures to a variety of client populations.

Chapter 6

Modeling

From previous chapters, which have strongly emphasized the importance of defining consequences within treatment, it might be surmised that all behavior is learned through the process of systematic shaping through reinforcement and punishment. Of course, this is not the case, and a vast body of literature suggests that we learn in other ways. For example, if you wanted to train a five-year-old to pick up and properly swing a baseball bat, you might demonstrate the swing and then provide the child with an opportunity to practice what he had observed. In this demonstration you were the "model" and the child was an "observer." Once the behavior of picking up the bat and making attempts to swing was instigated by the modeling, you might provide immediate social consequences to the child for both appropriate and inappropriate bat swinging attempts, until some criterion level of "swinging" was achieved. This chapter will focus upon the special case where the *probability of some specific behavior on the part of an observer (O) is altered through the observation of some model (M)*. The term *modeling* will be employed to describe this process, although a variety of terms (e.g., *imitation, vicarious phenomena, identification*) have been adopted within the literature.

While a number of investigators have presented paradigms to explain modeling (Miller and Dollard, 1941; Mowrer, 1960), Albert Bandura of Stanford University and an array of colleagues (Walters, Blanchard, Ross, Grusec, Mischel, Ritter, and others) have performed the most substantive experimental investigations of modeling phenomena. This research will be referred to at length in the pesent discussion. While a numer of investigators have attempted to classify modeling effects, the categories of Bandura and Walters (1963) as well as Kanfer and Phillips (1970) most comprehensively depict important classes of modeling. Both classification systems will be presented, with illustrative therapeutic examples provided for each.

CLASSIFICATION SYSTEMS

Bandura (1969) has said that "exposure to modeling influences has three clearly different effects, each of which is determined by a separate set of variables" (p. 120).

Observational Learning, or Modeling Effect

When an observer acquires some *new behavior not previously within his repertoire* following his exposure to a model, Bandura would say that "observational learning" has occurred. For example, most of us probably learn the initial sounds that make up our speech through the process of "observational learning." The number of different sounds that the infant can emit grows from very few to well over 1,500 within the first few years of life. This tremendous increment in the infant's vocabulary has not been engendered by systematic shaping and reinforcement of each word, but through the process of hearing important models (such as parents, siblings, peers) emit such words on a frequent basis, possibly followed by positive feedback from others when the infant attempts to employ the new sounds. In addition, as modeled words are employed by the infant to gain certain necessary items from his environment (reinforcement), they become a permanent part of his vocabulary. It becomes obvious that "observational learning" applies most directly to the developmental periods of infancy and childhood, when many novel behaviors are modeled. As the individual moves through adolescence to adulthood, the probability of observing something novel necessarily is reduced by one's previous experiences, and behavior imitated during these later periods may fall into one of the next two classes of modeling effects.

Inhibitory and Disinhibitory Effects

This class of effects applies only to *behaviors that have previously been learned*. If an observer (O) observes some model (M) *undergo punishing consequences for some behavior, inhibitory effects* are said to have occurred if the observer then inhibits that same behavior as a result of the modeling experience. A good example of this might be within a training school, where certain behaviors are targeted for punishment. Often, the effects of punishment are transmitted vicariously through the inhibitory process, and so it is not necessary to systematically punish every child within the setting to achieve suppresssion of the targeted negative behavior. For example, if child A is punished in the presence of peer observers for physically assaulting another child, there is some chance that these observers will inhibit their aggressive physical responses in the future as a result of the vicarious experience. Obviously, the observers have witnessed a punitive outcome for some specified behavior, and this provides them with important information useful in deciding which behaviors are likely to be punished and which reinforced. One would assume that behaviors that are vicariously seen to be punished will decrease in frequency only if the observer views the modeled sequence as bearing some relationship to future consequences for himself. Thus, seeing a cottage parent punish another child in one's cottage for some behavior would be more likely to inhibit the observer's emittance of that behavior than would seeing some actor on television punish a similar behavior. The former situation has immediate consequences for the observer, whereas a TV scene may not be viewed as relevant, and thus may not effect the observer's behavior.

Disinhibitory effects have to do with previously punished behavior

An observer who has been punished for some behavior, and now emits that behavior at a very low rate (inhibits the behavior), may begin to display the behavior at a higher rate following *exposure to a model who engages in the behavior and suffers no ill consequences.* In effect, the nonpunished peer model *disinhibits* the observer, and in all probability will increase the frequency of that behavior. A child who has previously fallen down in the water and now avoids stepping into the water (inhibited) may give the ocean an additional try if she sees a similar peer engaging in fearless splashing and playing at the water's edge.

Therapeutically, inhibitory vicarious effects might be employed to decrease the frequency of some problem targeted behavior by exposing observers to a relevant model experiencing punishment for engaging in the targeted event. Disinhibitory effects are most often employed in increasing a client's approach toward objects previously associated with aversive consequences (e.g., phobic behavior) or in increasing the frequency of social behaviors that for one reason or another have been inhibited (e.g. assertive responses, conversational strategies) because of previous association with aversive consequences. This category of effects has perhaps been most prominently employed within the treatment literature (Bandura, Grusic, and Menlove, 1967; Bandura, Blanchard, and Ritter, 1969).

Response Facilitation Effect

When some *previously learned behavior becomes more frequent after exposure to a model,* Bandura would say that this response has been *facilitated* by the model. In differentiating response facilitation from observational learning and inhibitory and disinhibitory effects, it is important to remember that no new response is acquired (as with observational learning), and the response in question has never previously been associated with punishment (as with inhibitory and disinhibitory effects). A good example of social facilitation would be the classic case where one individual in a crowd looks up and others in the immediate area begin looking up, too. We often see facilitation effects among animals that are eating. There is a good chance that even a satiated puppy will begin eating again when exposed to another puppy that is avidly partaking of the latest dog food. With regard to therapy, whenever clients are exposed to appropriate models engaged in eating, conversation, recreation, task related or other behaviors, the potential for social facilitation exists. Very often within treatment the BCA may attempt to increase the probability that clients will model certain appropriate targeted behaviors by exposing these clients to valued models who are engaging in the behavior.

The Five Categories of Kanfer and Phillips

In their well-known review of the literature Kanfer and Phillips (1970) have presented a schema for categorizing modeling effects that is a bit different from Bandura's, and more comprehensive. They present five categories as representing the range of possibilities of a model (M) differentially affecting the behavior of an observer (O):

1. Matched-Dependent Learning. An observer is *directly rewarded for imitating* the behavior of a model, who is usually serving in a training capacity. This is perhaps the most simple and straightforward approach to inducing change via modeling. Within this situation the behavior to be rewarded is extremely explicit, and the model takes great pains to carefully demonstrate each aspect of the targeted behavior. This kind of approach is often used with young children within the purely educational situation as well as with adult populations lacking certain basic skills, who require a careful and systematic approach to modeling. For example, in treating autistic children and adult schizo-phrenics, a usual goal is to train these clients to expand their repertoires to include certain basic self-management skills. Within this matched-dependent model a trainer-model might demonstrate specific sounds or words for a client who exhibits little or no meaningful speech, immediately reinforcing any approximation of those sounds that the client emits. Using a shaping procedure, the trainer-model continues to model a sound, rewarding increasingly improved attempts by the observer to make the same sound. Once the observer's response is conson-

ant with the model's, the model might then demonstrate another important sound or word, systematically reinforcing the client in a similar fashion for his efforts at imitation. This is an excellent example of modeling
procedures very nicely combined with operant shaping procedures.
Within the task area the trainer-model might carefully demonstrate the
appropriate way to employ a leatherworking tool, then systematically
reinforce the client-observer's attempts at reproducing this behavior. Importantly, when using the matched-dependent paradigm, the trainer-
model should begin with some basic behavior or part of the behavioral
sequence; then, as the client-observer incorporates basic skills into his
repertoire, the model gradually moves on to more complex and sophisticated sequences of responses.

2. *Co-Learning*. Here, two or more individuals alternately serve as
model and observer in carrying out a learning task. Both individuals are
thus learning within the situation ("co-"). In its purest form both "lear-
ners" are clients who work together to learn the requisite behaviors to
perform the targeted task. As novel approaches are tried out, one participant might serve as model and demonstrate some new method for the
other, who at that point serves as observer. Model and observer roles
would interchange as each participant found novel behaviors to demonstrate to the other. Should clients be permitted to work on important
targeted behaviors within a co-learning paradigm, an array of inappropriate, trial-and-error responses would be modeled and of course observed, and these might interfere with goal-directed performance.

Thus, used in treatment, the model is either a staff member or a client
who has already mastered the appropriate skills, and in essence takes the
observer through the task step by step. Although the two are working
together on the task, the sophisticated participant serves to direct the
"co-efforts" toward treatment goals, so that learning takes place in efficient fashion. Inappropriate trial-and-error responses are immediately
discouraged by the sophisticated participant, and appropriate task-
directed behavior is immediately demonstrated. One might ask how the
co-learning situation is discriminated from the matched-dependent learning situation. Within the co-learning paradigm no specific, preprogram-
med reinforcement is provided for matching responses, although, of
course, a good bit of social reinforcement may occur. Also, the client is
given more leeway to try out novel responses, under the guidance and
direction of his sophisticated co-learner; in many cases the client "discov-
ers" appropriate methods of completing the task on his own. This situation would be better geared to more sophisticated clients who have already mastered basic skills. Thus, in the co-learning paradigm the client is
given more responsibility for task completion, with the sophisticated participant working side by side in more of a guidance, feedback role, able to
immediately model the appropriate response when necessary.

An excellent study by Janis and Hoffman (1970) illustrates the co-learning treatment approach, employing client co-learners. Thirty clients who wished to reduce their frequency of cigarette smoking attended five weekly meetings with a treatment consultant. Each client was assigned to another client to make up a treatment dyad, and each dyad was assigned to one of three experimental conditions: high-contact partners, who phoned each other daily; low-contact partners, who spoke only at clinic meetings; or controls who had a different partner for every meeting. The clients in the high-contact group, who were extensively involved in telephoning and monitoring each other's progress, showed the greatest change in their cigarette smoking and the smallest increase in number of cigarettes smoked over a one-year follow-up. Thus, each member of a dyad serves as both model-trainer as well as observer-trainee over the course of treatment. Both roles would seem to have important therapeutic value for clients, and possibly this kind of yoking would reduce the amount of staff time necessary for adequate monitoring of clients.

In group therapy, from three to usually twelve clients meet together to monitor each other's progress, to provide feedback to one another regarding ongoing behavior, and to make suggestions about treatment plan modifications. In the group each observer is exposed to an array of models, with each observer having the opportunity to serve in a modeling role. Perhaps any group therapy situation could be classified within this co-learning paradigm.

Co-learning approaches have also been employed to reduce phobic behaviors (Ritter, 1968; Blanchard, 1970; Ritter, 1969). Within these investigations the therapist works directly with the client in approaching the phobic object. Often, there is a good deal of physical contact between the therapist and client "co-learners." For example, the therapist might prod the client to move gradually closer to the feared object and possibly even guide the client's hand so that it makes contact with the phobic stimulus (Ritter, 1968, 1969). Although the client recognizes the therapeutic role of his "co-learner," the therapist and client participate on a somewhat equal basis in systematically moving through the steps of treatment. For that reason any kind of therapeutic procedure in which client and therapist behave together in carrying out the treatment goals could be considered an example of co-learning.

One application of co-learning not frequently reported is the use of heterogeneous groups of clients who exhibit an array of behavioral deficits as well as strengths, who can thus serve alternately as models and observers. An artful "yoking" of clients with diverse strengths and weaknesses might prove to be an ideal co-learning situation for the promotion of desired therapeutic change. For example, let us assume that client A shows well-developed skills in going up to another, beginning a conversation, maintaining a topic, as well as picking up on important cues as to when to terminate the conversation; however, he has extreme difficulty in forcefully asserting himself in social interaction when this is called for.

Client B, on the other hand, is extremely adept at employing nonverbal and verbal assertive communications, but has extreme difficulty in initiating and maintaining ordinary conversation. In addition, client B usually fails to read important nonverbal and verbal cues that suggest when another wishes to terminate a conversation. Thus, while both of these clients show important skill deficits, each exhibits strengths that would prove beneficial within the modeling situation. For example, client B could model important verbal and nonverbal skills necessary to assert oneself, with client A in an observer role; client A could model approach and maintenance skills within standard conversations, while client B serves as the observer-participant. Both clients not only are exposed to appropriate behavioral models, but both have the opportunity to serve in the trainer-model role, thus enabling them to take a responsible, active part in treatment. Perhaps this kind of "yoking" also fosters cooperation and empathy among clients. It is hoped that future research will more carefully evaluate the possibilities of therapeutic benefits derived from this "yoking" paradigm.

3. Vicarious Classical Conditioning. Many investigators have found that an observer can both cognitively and physiologically experience an emotional response displayed by a model (Bandura and Rosenthal, 1966; Berger, 1962). This is not a new finding. Anyone who has attended a good play or watched a vivid TV drama or movie may have experienced an emotional response while observing actors portray the characters' emotions. Even reading about the emotional responses of others (e.g., a particularly sad story) will evoke an emotional response in the reader, with the written model thus vicariously provoking an emotional resonse in the reader-observer. If a model is classically conditioned, an observer might also be classically conditioned through the vicarious process. Typically, within this paradigm a model is presented an emotionally arousing stimulus (UCS) that evokes an observable emotional response (UCR) in the presence of a previously neutral stimulus (CS). The observer of such a scene may experience a similar emotional response in the presence of the neutral stimulus without ever directly experiencing the unpleasant, painful stimulus. Through the pairing of this vicariously induced emotional response with the observation of the neutral stimulus, the observer may become classically conditioned.

There are many examples to suggest that classical conditioning may in fact occur by purely vicarious means. The child who is not afraid of insects may develop a conditioned emotional response to their pres-ence after seeing his mother leap away from a spider. Of course, the mother has previously learned to fear the spider, which presumably was a neutral stimulus for her at some point. Importantly, the child-observer may vicariously experience an emotional response similar to that of its mother *in the presence of the spider* (CS), and thus avoid spiders and possibly other insects in the future to the extent that an independent observer would say that the child is "afraid," or "phobic". Vicarious classical conditioning probably has some protective value for the developing child. Seeing others exhibit emotional responses to fire, acts of aggression, certain signs or cues (e.g., "poison," "danger," "high voltage") may come to evoke classically conditioned responses in the child observer. In the future the child may become equally or similarly anxious when these anxiety-provoking stimuli appear within his life, and thus avoid them.

In the remaining two Kanfer and Phillips paradigms the specific goals of modeling are less clearly defined for the observer and are thus less applicable to the therapeutic situation that emphasizes well-defined instructions to the client.

4. *Identification.* The identification paradigm accounts for the acquisition of idiosyncratic response styles that observers "pick up" from those with whom they interact (models). Within this identification situation an observer might enact aspects of a model's physical stance, verbal intonation, style of speaking, or other incidental behavior through repeated exposure to the model. There is no specific target behavior that the model presents to the observer, and implicitly this process of identification occurs in an unsystematic fashion through repeated exposure of some O to some M. Bandura (1969) has suggested that *identification* is a confusing term and should be replaced by a technical analysis of what specifically happens when observers learn social behaviors from the array of others to whom they are exposed. With regard to treatment, any time that clients pick up the stylistic behaviors that staff members display, possibly in addition to treatment-directed behaviors that are modeled, identification has occurred.

Some theorists argue that one's style within the interpersonal situation is an important component of "personality," and many therapists retreat from making decisions as to the kind of interpersonal style that a client should or should not display, preferring to focus upon specific repertoire behaviors necessary for adequate functioning. Within any therapeutic situation some identification from therapist-model to client-observer may occur, but often the stylistic behaviors modeled within this identification paradigm are not a specific goal of treatment. Of course, if the BCA wishes to increase the frequency of certain stylistic responses on the part of a client, this paradigm suggests that he should expose the client to an array of similar style models in a situation where the client may carefully discriminate their behavior. Few investigators have experimentally evaluated the identification paradigm, and the author knows of no attempts to relate this paradigm systematically to targeted treatment goals.

5. *No-Trial Learning.* In this situation the observer, although vicariously learning some behavior, is not immediately permitted to practice this behavior and is not reinforced for his efforts. Bandura (1962, 1965, 1969) used no-trial learning in referring to the situation where an

observer learns new responses solely by observing a model's behavior *without performing the behavior at the time of presentation and without receiving any extrinsic reinforcement for his efforts.* Importantly, neither the model nor the observer is reinforced within this paradigm (Bandura, 1965). To differentiate this from the identification paradigm, the behavior modeled may in fact be instrumental. Within treatment the BCA most often carefully communicates to the observer precisely those behaviors of the model that are most relevant, perhaps providing immediate opportunities for the observer to practice these vicariously learned responses. Often, immediate reinforcement is provided for successful approximations of the model's behavior.

When the observer is not provided with an immediate opportunity to practice and possibly be reinforced, there is a good chance that he will covertly rehearse and perhaps later practice some inappropriate, undesirable representation of the behavior. In cognitively rehearsing the model's behavior, certain elements might be forgotten, and so his cognitive attempts may actually reinforce unfortunate representations of what the model actually displayed. Certainly, a good bit of our social behavior is learned within this no-trial paradigm, and perhaps that is why so many inappropriate behaviors are learned along with appropriate responses. Also, because no feedback is provided that enables the observers to focus carefully upon and to practice the important elements of the model's behavior, they may learn and practice an array of irrelevant, non-task-related behaviors along with appropriate behaviors. Thus, the no-trial learning paradigm is much less efficient than those paradigms that provide immediate opportunities for practice and reinforcement on the client's part. For these reasons the no-trial paradigm is poorly suited to treatment and is worthy of little further discussion within this context.

FACTORS AFFECTING THE PROBABILITY OF MODELING

Although many factors control the degree to which an observer imitates a model, one underlying principle seems to cut across all such factors as the most important criterion for modeling to occur. Very simply stated, *for modeling to occur, an observer must actively discriminate the behavior of a model.* The degree to which the model has control over reinforcements for the observer, or the extent to which the observer is in some fashion motivated (reinforced) for observation, are of course extremely important variables that affect the degree to which an observer will attend to a model (Bandura, 1965, 1969). Any aspect of the observational situation or characteristics of the model or observer that increase the degree to which the observer actively attends to the model will facilitate modeling. What follows is a presentation of specific factors that may have some bearing on this important attentional variable.

Reinforcement of Model

Investigators have found that modeling is facilitated if the observer views the model being reinforced for his behavior (Bandura, 1965; Bandura, Ross, and Ross, 1963; Stumphauzer, 1972). Given our previous discussion on vicarious emotional responding, when the model is reinforced, there is a good chance that a positive emotional response will be evoked within the observer. Of course, both the model as well as the reinforcement provided for the model must be relevant to the observer. One could differentiate between vicarious reinforcement, in the present sense, as opposed to direct reinforcement, where the observer is in some fashion directly reinforced for observing the model. Berger (1962) would restrict vicarious reinforcement to mean any situation in which reinforcing effects are induced within the observer by watching the model receive direct reinforcement for behavior. If the model's response *per se* is in fact a reinforcement for the observer, Berger would not call it vicarious reinforcement. Mowrer (1960) uses the term *empathic* to describe the observer experiencing reinforcement vicariously as the model receives it directly.

While a good bit of research suggests that modeling is enhanced when the model is directly reinforced, other studies have shown that the reward styles of observers may also be influenced by consequences administered to the model (Bandura and Mischel, 1965). Bandura and Kuypers (1964) found that children will adopt either a stringent or lenient criterion for rewarding themselves, depending upon the manner in which models reward themselves. Children exposed to adult models who adopted a stringent criterion in paying themselves off within a bowling game also adopted a stringent criterion when they played. Models who had a low criterion for reward in the same game provoked similarly low levels among their young observers. For this population of grammar school children, adult models tended to provoke more powerful modeling effects than did peer models.

Reinforcement of Observer

Whenever the observer is specifically reinforced for observing a model's behavior, we term this *direct reinforcement* for the observer (Berger, 1962). Of course, this externally imposed direct reinforcement is in addition to any vicarious reinforcement that might be induced merely by watching the model experience reinforcing consequences. The *matched-dependent* paradigm is the best example of direct reinforcement for the observer, who may be reinforced for merely watching the model, imitating the model, or often for both. Lira (1972) has emphasized that directly administered positive or negative reinforcement for imitative responses influences behavior by providing cues that indicate whether matching or nonmatching behavior is appropriate or inappropriate within a given social context. If cues provided by the model (and others) indicate that imitative responses are appropriate, giving rewards to the observer is unlikely to increase the incidence of imitative responses. If the model's cues and responses of others do not clarify the situational demands, however, rewards to the observer may be essential for imitation to occur. Lira points out that frequently for both children and severely disturbed clients subtle social cues are not sufficient for imitation to occur, and thus some form of direct reinforcement is necessary within the matched-dependent paradigm.

Very simply stated, direct reinforcement for observation or for imitating the behavior of the model provides the BCA with a means of very clearly identifying for the observer those specific aspects of the model's behavior that are most relevant. When such direct reinforcement is differentially applied to certain important model behaviors, the probability that the observer will imitate irrelevant, nontargeted behaviors is decreased. Of course, the means of distribution and nature of reinforcement depends upon an array of variables, including level of intellectual ability, age, previous exposure to reinforcements, and previous experience in observational learning. It would seem that any cueing device (e.g., tone, light source, verbal prompt) that alerts the observer to maximally attend to specific model behaviors would facilitate observer learning. Unfortunately, the author could find no specific research that has evaluated the use of such simple cueing devices within the modeling situation. Such cues would be particularly relevant when the client-observer is exposed to a videotape of some model behaving ("symbolic modeling," Bandura, 1969). Auditory or visual cues or even verbal prompts could be recorded onto the tape immediately preceding the specific model behaviors that the BCA wishes the client to most actively attend to. Simple instructions such as "Pay particular attention whenever you hear the cue (sound, tone, other source)" would seem to be a simple and practical means of providing the kind of feedback that reinforcement ordinarily provides within the modeling situation.

Model Characteristics

Any characteristic of the model that increases the probability that an observer will actively attend to model behavior will facilitate modeling. Most particularly, the degree to which a model may influence subsequent rewards to the observer will strongly influence observer attention (Mischel and Grusec, 1966; Mischel and Liebert, 1967). In an array of excellent studies Mischel and his associates manipulated the degree to which models provided reinforcement and/or exhibited control over the behavior of preschool children. In these studies preschool children typically were asked to interact with adults who provided high degrees of rewards, adults who provided few or no rewards, and adults whose control over the child's future resources was either high or low. Then the "pre-exposure" adult served as a model in a standard format, exhibiting some specific instrumental behavior. The children modeled the behavior of those adults who had previously been in control of reinforcements for them more significantly than the less powerful adults. Importantly, the degree to which a model is seen as being able to provide a reward of importance to the observer seems to have a significant effect upon the degree to which modeling occurs. Thus, in one study (Mischel and Liebert, 1967) the "vice president of a toy company" that produced a game desirable to subjects proved a more potent model than a neutral person. Of course, the "vice president" may have been perceived as displaying more power to provide reinforcement (e.g., a game) to the subjects than the neutral figure. Because most studies of model characteristics have been directed at preschool and elementary populations, the generality of these findings to adolescent and adult populations and differential demographic groups can only be answered by future research specifically directed at these populations.

Status—Most studies show that models who are viewed by observers as competent will be imitated to a greater extent than those judged as less competent (Bandura and Whalen, 1966; Baron, 1970). However, a well-controlled investigation by Meichenbaum (1971) supports just the opposite conclusion. In investigating the degree to which "fearless" models could alter the approach behavior of fearful undergraduate observers (disinhibitory affect), Meichenbaum found that those models who began by displaying fear responses and gradually "coped" through an array of approach responses until reaching final mastery (in this case touching a snake), induced a greater degree of approach behavior for observers than did a model who exhibited mastery by fearlessly walking over and playing with the snake right off. Since the observers were presumably quite fearful of snakes to begin with, they were perhaps able to empathize and relate better to the "coping" model. In addition, models who verbalized during the approach task by talking out their feelings and thoughts as they approached the snake induced a greater degree of behavioral change than did nonverbalizing models. The results of the Meichenbaum investigation are in direct contrast to the results of an investigation by Baron (1970), who also employed undergraduate students. In this investigation competent models provoked significantly greater modeling effects than did neutral models. At present the large body of literature suggests that models viewed as competent by observers provoke more behavioral change than those viewed as less competent. Further research may serve to better define those specific client populations and targeted behaviors that respond most effectively to particular categories of models.

Similarity—While some studies have found that similarity between M and O seems to facilitate modeling effects, many other findings seem to contradict this proposition. A study by Rosekrans (1967) found that adolescent boys aged 11-14 tended to reproduce the behavior of a model who dressed in similar fashion and was similar in terms of background and interests more than they followed a dissimilar model. The findings of Hicks (1965) previously discussed would seem to be in direct opposition to Rosekrans' findings. Hicks found that preschool boys and girls showed the most long-lasting effects of modeling when exposed to a male adult as opposed to a male peer. Although the importance of similarity regarding sex of model and observer has been investigated in many studies, along with a host of other factors, no study has isolated and studied sex as an independent variable.

To determine the effects of model-displayed aggression on aggressive responses in a population of elementary school-age children, Bandura, Ross, and Ross (1963) exposed subjects to either male or female models displaying aggression via film, cartoon, or live presentation. A control group had no exposure to a model. In addition, subject groups were further subdivided so that half of the subjects viewing human models were exposed to same-sexed models and half observed a model of the opposite sex. Following exposure to the aggressive models, aggressive responses made by subects toward toys in a playroom setting were counted. All three modeling conditions produced higher levels of aggressive behavior among subjects than did the control condition. Importantly, boys displayed significantly more total aggression, more imitative aggression, and more nonimitative behavior. Across boys and girls those subjects who observed the male model displayed higher frequencies of aggressive behaviors than subjects exposed to the female model. It is difficult to relate these findings to similarity. Perhaps because males most often engage in aggressive acts within our society, such behavior is viewed as being more appropriate to the male. This finding of a sex effect might only be related to the special condition within which a model displays aggressive behavior.

Because of the paucity of research relating similarity of sex to modeling effects, no specific conclusions can be reached at present. However, it makes sense that the relative importance of similarity, competence, power, status and other model factors depends upon the particular population to which such models are presented. In addition, as suggested by the Bandura, Ross, and Ross (1963) study, the relative importance of any of these model characteristics may also depend upon the specific behavior displayed by the model. One would imagine that if male and female adult models displayed infant care behavior to a population of observers, the female models would instigate greater degrees of behavioral change than would male models, primarily because they are displaying behavior more appropriate to their role (women's liberation might disagree).

It is hoped that future research will further define the important interaction between model characteristics, behaviors modeled, and the specific demographic population that serves as observer. One major finding seems to cut across all the research: observers seems to be more facilitated by models who can in some way affect their reinforcements. Only through careful observation of clients to whom some model will be presented can the BCA decide upon those model characteristics that will be most suitable. Perhaps peers who seem to assume leadership roles might be good models. They could be carefully trained and concomitantly reinforced to engage in the appropriate targeted behavior and thus serve as models for other clients either in a direct training situation (matched-dependent) or in the no-trial or co-learning situation. Staff members who are esteemed by clients might also be trained to display important targeted behaviors and concomitantly reinforce clients for imitative efforts. While observations of staff and peers may be one important source of information to help determine which ones are most highly valued, the BCA may also use questionnaires or perform a sociogram to do the same thing. Those who receive the highest proportion of positive choices might then be trained to serve in a modeling role within one of the paradigms previously mentioned.

Multiple Models

Few studies have compared the efficacy of employing an array of models as opposed to a single model to facilitate the transmission of modeled information to some population of observers. Bandura and Menlove (1968) found that exposing dog-phobic child observers to boys and girls of various ages who fearlessly approached a dog was more successful in reducing avoidance behavior than exposing observers to a single model. While both conditions were more effective than a no-treatment control condition, observers exposed to multiple models showed the greatest increment in approach behavior. Although it is difficult to draw any firm conclusions from a single study, when observers are exposed to an array of models, the probability that they will find a highly valued, attractive individual to attend to is much greater than if they see a single model.

The use of multiple models also ensures that observers are exposed to multiple appropriate behavioral styles. It makes sense that no one model can have a sufficient repertoire to model all the skill situations the client-observer will face. By employing an array of models, there is a greater probability that even low-rate social behaviors will be modeled. Thus, the behaviors presented to the observers are not limited by the specific characteristics and style of any one individual. It is important that multiple models do not display targeted behaviors in contrasting or opposite ways. Obviously, client-observers who are exposed to divergent enactments of a particular skill behavior are not getting a consistent and clear presentation. Thus, the BCA must carefully observe potential models to ensure that they exhibit a representation of targeted behavior that is consonant with treatment goals. When necessary, those clients of staff members who might serve as models should be carefully trained and provided with appropriate reinforcement for their efforts.

Symbolic Versus Live Models

It may be difficult for the BCA to find a client or staff member who displays an important targeted behavior at a sufficient rate to be repeatedly observed by clients. Staff members who are asked to fulfill an array of responsibilities are often not available frequently enough or at those times when client exposure to modeling is deemed necessary by the BCA. While there is some suggestion within the literature that live models are in fact superior to models presented on film or videotape (symbolic models), many investigators have found symbolic models to be very effective in instigating targeted behavioral change across multiple populations (Bandura, Ross, and Ross, 1963; Bandura and Mischel, 1965; Hill, Liebert and Mott, 1968; Nay, 1974). While Bandura, Ross, and Ross (1963) showed that cartoon or film models provoked more imitation of aggressive responses than did live models in the study previously discussed, Bandura and Mischel (1965) found that behavioral change instigated by live models was more lasting in groups of children who were followed up after treatment. In all reported investigations, however, "symbolic" models were significantly superior to control conditions in promoting behavioral change among children. The author (Nay, 1975) is among several investigators who have found symbolic models to be effective in pro-moting behavioral change among a population of adults. In this investigation a videotape of a mother appropriately employing time out with a young child proved to be very successful in promoting questionnaire as well as behavioral changes in analog situations typical of mother-child interaction. No one would argue that television and other media have radically changed the fund of information as well as the very behavior of a large segment of our population. In fact, recent controversies have focused upon the importance of films and television in promoting certain undesirable behaviors, such as aggression. Thus, when live models cannot be employed, or as a means of augmenting the use of live models, symbolic modeling can be an effective alternative tool within treatment.

Symbolic presentation of models permits increased flexibility, since the BCA can schedule modeling presentations at optimal and/or convenient times. Also, the use of videotape or film allows for frequent repetitions of specific targeted behaviors, recorded cueing of certain behaviors of interest, as well as reinforcements to be more directly applied to observer practice of model behavior. As an example of these virtues of the symbolic approach, assume that the BCA asks a group of client-observers to view a videotape depicting appropriate eating skills. The BCA can ensure that the first portion of the modeling videotape zeroes in upon use of the fork, with appropriate camera focus upon the manner in which the model employs a fork in bringing food to the mouth. Following each specific step of fork handling displayed by the symbolic model, the BCA can ask clients to practice that activity with eating utensils supplied for practice, and can provide immediate reinforcement for appropriate efforts. Should certain clients not master skills upon the first modeling presentation, the BCA has only to rewind the tape and re-present the sequence as many times as necessary to achieve errorless client practice. In fact, clients trained to operate the forward and reverse controls of the videotape recorder could present and re-present an important behavioral sequence as many times as necessary, while each individually learns and practices the novel targeted behavior.

Many clinical settings employ professional technicians who can use sophisticated equipment to produce a training film that best displays specific targeted behaviors of interest. Using the zoom lens, split screen, inserts, dissolves, and other techniques, a training tape can be produced in which specific model behaviors of importance clearly stand out for active attention by the observer. In some cases specific cues telling the observer to pay close attention to particular model behavior, as well as the therapist's reinforcing comments, might be incorporated in the taped presentation, thus increasing the clarity of communication to the observer and reducing the amount of time the therapist spends on that treatment. The BCA and other staff members who are freed from training efforts may then expend valuable time in other treatment pursuits, perhaps with clients who demand intensive, individualized therapist contact.

Characteristics of the Observer

Unfortunately, few investigators have attempted to define the specific observer characteristics that best predict some specific kind of modeling presentation. If more investigators employed classification variables such as a careful specification of differential age groups, socioeconomic levels, and specific targeted behaviors in experimental designs employed to evaluate treatment, the BCA would have more information to use in a careful and systematic tailoring of specific treatments to particular populations. While the previous section presented an array of model characteristics that may importantly affect treatment, it makes sense that model characteristics must be carefully tailored to the specific client population of interest. Thus, while elementary-school-age children might alter their behavior most significantly when exposed to an adult model, adolescents may in fact respond most ideally to peer models who display certain characteristics valued by the group.

The few studies of observer characteristics offer only tentative conclusions. It has been repeatedly pointed out that the observer must actively and discriminatively attend to the model's behavior. Any current state of the observer that interferes with this active attention will also interfere with modeling. Thus, the observer who is heavily sedated, as is often found within the institutional setting, would probably not actively attend to a model's behavior, and this would most likely interfere with learning. In contrast, any drug or agent that increases the ability to attend would also seem to facilitate modeling. Most drug investigations, however, have found that both very low and very high states of drug-induced arousal seem to interfere with learning, while some moderate state seems to be most optimal for behavioral change to occur. In fact, Bandura and Rosenthal (1966) found that undergraduate subjects who were injected with epinephrine (increases arousal) imitated the behavior of a model less effectively than did noninjected subjects. These results seem to suggest that there is a relationship between level of arousal and the degree to which modeling will occur within subjects, but the specific relationship for particular client populations has yet to be determined.

As might be expected, those clients who ordinarily do not attend to the external world as well as others (e.g., schizophrenic clients) do not imitate the behavior of a model as well as do other diagnostic populations (Bishop and Beckman, 1971). Possibly, clients who are further removed from reality require the presentation of highly distinctive models displaying abbreviated sequences of behavior over repeated trials. Clients who exhibit such attentional deficits should be presented very distinctive, discrete bits of modeled behavior in an atmosphere that serves to increase the possibility of their paying attention.

Ross (1966) found that nursery school children who are rated as being dependent tend to model a wider array of both relevant and irrelevant behaviors than do children rated as being independent. The author concludes that a highly dependent child has a substantial advantage in the situation where a model exhibits no irrelevant, non-task-oriented behaviors. Of course, in this case the dependent child would imitate everything that the model presents. Because such a situation is rare, the more independent child probably has the advantage, as he tends to be more selective in imitating important behaviors. The specific relationship between personality variables and modeling is poorly explored at this time. To the degree that personality descriptions predict some characteristic way in which an observer views the world and behaves within it, they may well predict modeling effects.

In summary, any common observer characteristic, induced state of arousal, or transitory factor (e.g., level of fatigue, sickness) that interferes with an observer's ability to discriminatively attend to the behavior of some model will interfere with modeling. While some research and common sense suggest that certain client diagnostic groupings will be less responsive to a model than others, it is strongly suggested that the BCA attempt to capitalize upon any strengths clients may exhibit and then design a modeling situation that increases the possibility that the observer will actively attend.

APPLICATION OF MODELING TO TARGETED BEHAVIORS

The following represents an attempt to pull together the important components of modeling into an outline that may be used as the basis for employing modeling in treatment. This outline represents major steps in the order most typically employed. Although for different targeted behaviors specific steps might be omitted or added, this outline is generally applicable to most treatment goals. For illustrative purposes, the case described below will be related to each procedural step of the outline.

As a BCA working with a population of adults within a psychiatric setting, you have noted that five of the twenty clients within your ward setting typically fail to maintain eye contact with you and with others clients while speaking. While these five clients exhibit an array of social skills deficits, you have decided to begin by focusing upon increasing the frequency with which each of them maintains eye contact while conversing. This seems to be a reasonable goal in that maintaining eye contact is currently within the repertoire of all five clients. It is only a matter of increasing its frequency for these clients to be better able to engage in reciprocal, ordinary social interactions. You have already found that other clients get "turned off," angry, and generally resentful when any one of the five targeted clients does not look at them while speaking. Thus, the maintenance of eye contact will underly later attempts at increasing more complex and sophisticated social interactive behavior. The clients range in age from 29 to 41, have been hospitalized for a mean of 4.9 years, perform at the norm on an I.Q. test, and come from lower socioeconomic or impoverished communities. They have poor vocabularies. All of them seem to come from backgrounds where only minimal social skills were necessary for adequate functioning. As BCA, you have decided that merely providing reinforcement whenever any one of the five engages in eye contact will be a laborious and time-consuming method of increasing its frequency. You thus opt for modeling as a means of facilitating this important skill behavior, followed by practice and concomitant reinforcement for "on-target" efforts. You have already found that your attempts at maintaining high rates of eye contact when conversing with these clients has had no appreciable effect on the frequency of such contact, and have decided that someone other than yourself might be more appropriate to serve as a model.

1. Defining Targets

As in all previous examples of treatment techniques, some behavior or behaviors must be initially chosen for acceleration or deceleration. It is assumed that the BCA will define a target that the client has some chance of successfully exhibiting and then gradually build on more basic skills. In our present example the target is to increase the frequency of eye contact clients engage in when talking or listening with another person.

2. Choice of Model

From the previous discussions it would seem that any staff member or client chosen as a model should be valued in some fashion and relevant to the client-observer's future reinforcements. Also, whoever is chosen ought to interact frequently enough with each of the five clients so that sufficient model presentations occur to promote learning. In addition, the BCA should evaluate the self-reports of the clients as well as his observations of clients' interaction with peers and staff members. Those peers and staff members whom our targeted clients choose to interact with more frequently may be more "highly valued." Now, among peers and staff members who meet the criteria of *frequency* and *reinforcement value* there are specific individuals who either currently engage in appropriate levels of eye contact during ordinary conversation or who might be systematically trained to do so. These individuals might be employed as models. Because of the usual time considerations, the BCA would do well to choose those individuals who ordinarily exhibit the appropriated targeted behavior. Certainly, these peers and/or staff members must be willing to serve as models should a systematic approach to modeling be employed (e.g. matched-dependent design). Or individuals might be employed within the co-learning design and serve as an appropriate model "without knowing it" as they work together with the targeted clients in ordinary task activities. In either case the models chosen must display the previously described characteristics of effective models.

Whenever possible, client-peers who might experience some therapeutic gain by serving a a model for other clients should be employed. This is a nice means of "yoking" those clients who exhibit certain important skills with those who are deficient in similar skills, possibly promoting desired gains in both clients. Whether client-peers or staff members (or both) are chosen to serve as models, they should receive specific reinforcement for their efforts so that they will be motivated to exhibit the targeted behaviors.

With elementary-school-age populations the literature suggests that an adult model may be superior to a peer model, a same-sexed model may be superior to an opposite-sexed model (with the exception of aggressive behavior) (Bandura, Ross, and Ross, 1963), and a similar and competent model may be superior to a dissimilar, incompetent model. Little research has been performed with adults, although the work of Meichenbaum presented previously suggests that the model might begin by "coping" and then gradually display mastery. The BCA must be very attentive to those specific model characteristics that his population of client-observers is most likely to respond to best.

3. Model Display Variants

The BCA might choose to have his models present the targeted behavior within an array of specific paradigms and through either live or symbolic means.

Matched-dependent presentation—Within this design the client-observer observes the model maintaining eye contact while conversing with another person. Following this presentation, the client-observer is asked to converse with some participant, and the model systematically reinforces the client's attempts at maintaining eye contact. This might prove to be an excellent means of carefully focusing the client-observer's attention upon eye contact from among the array of behaviors presented within a conversational situation. In addition, the client receives specific reinforcement for his efforts at displaying the targeted behavior. Here the model would serve more directly in a therapeutic role, and the specific goals of the modeling endeavor are clearly presented to the client.

Co-learning paradigm—Within this paradigm the model and client-observer carry on a conversation together on some topic of interest. For example, the BCA might ask the model and client-observer to discuss previous problems in marriage, job, family. With both members participating, the "model" would be certain to exhibit a high proportion of eye contact in both talking and listening to the client-observer. No specific reinforcement would be given during the co-learning experience; however, following the sessions the BCA would want to be sure that staff members systematically reinforced any attempts on the client's part to increase eye contact. Perhaps the greatest problem with employing the co-learning situation here is that the client-observer might find it very difficult to discriminate within this interaction the specific behavior (eye contact) that the model is attempting to increase.

Alternatively, some combination of matched-dependent and co-learning could be employed.

No-trial paradigm—Some increment in eye contact might be gained merely by having clients come into contact with any model who engages in a high level of eye contact. However, it would seem that the no-trial paradigm's poor manner of communicating treatment goals to the client would make it one of the least desirable choices for a treatment situation.

Live versus symbolic presentation—Because of the possible difficulties involved in getting client-peers and/or staff members to model eye contact behavior for clients, this behavior could be recorded on a videotape. Specific training sessions could be set up at the BCA's convenience to present the peer and staff models, with clients permitted to practice systematically and to receive reinforcement for appropriate eye contact efforts. Live modeling presentations could be supplemented by systematic and frequent exposures to the videotapes. For client-observers who fail to respond to live models the videotape presentation makes possible frequent repetition of specific model behaviors, as the tape is replayed until the client-observer masters the use of eye contact. Efforts made within the symbolic situation would be further enhanced as client-peers and staff members also presented appropriate live models of eye contact in ordinary conversations with targeted clients.

Observer Reinforcement

Whenever possible, a specific program of reinforcement should be provided for clients' observation efforts. Of course, in the co-learning paradigm this is often not possible, except when social reinforcements are provided from model to co-participant. Perhaps the BCA could devise a situation where appropriate models are presented to observers within a positive atmosphere or context. In a sense the situation itself can be reinforcing, thus increasing the probability that O will attend to M. Thus observers might better attend to client-peer and/or staff models within a positive game or recreational or hobby activity. The event itself provides a reinforcing medium within which models are presented to client-observers.

Using a symbolic presentation, the client-observers are merely asked to watch the videotape. Depending upon their age, level of intelligence, and previous experience with reinforcements, they can be reinforced on a frequent basis for observing and reinforcements might be presented within the videotape medium. For example, the BCA might include verbal prompts, praise, and other sorts of social reinforcement as recorded messages within the videotape, perhaps following some important sequence of model behavior. A system of tones or other signals might cue the clients that they have received a token or other kind of reinforcement for paying attention to the modeling tape. Also, such cues may serve to increase O's attention to the tape. In fact, the videotape should be structured in such a manner that the observer does not become restless or bored. Thus, the kinds of behavior modeled, the choice of a medium (film versus real life), as well as the length of the taped presentation must be varied depending upon the characteristics of the observer.

It makes sense for the BCA to capitalize upon the specific interests of the client-observer in producing such a taped presentation. Since younger children often spend a great portion of their Saturdays and Sundays observing various cartoon characters in action, the BCA might do well to present models as cartooned characters within some believable story line or plot, to increase the probability that younger or cognitively impaired subjects will pay close attention. With adolescent clients models might display important targeted behaviors within a story or in role-playing situations that deal with important life events, such as dating, sexuality, and interaction with parents. Very simply, the BCA must ensure that a modeling presentation is in some way relevant to the needs (future reinforcements) of observers.

5. Role-Playing and Feedback

Although the next chapter will discuss role-playing in detail, it is important to emphasize that any behavior modeled may best be translated into client behavioral gains when an opportunity for immediate practice is provided. Thus, whether the model presents important targeted behaviors through live or symbolic media, the BCA should provide the opportunity for immediate observer role-playing of model behaviors and for immediate feedback on the observers' role-playing efforts. For example, our five clients might be presented with an appropriate model engaging in high levels of eye contact in a conversational situation. Immediately following the modeling videotape, the observers and a staff member might form dyads to practice conversations similar to the one presented. The BCA then has the opportunity to observe the client-observers displaying the previously modeled behavior and to provide immediate feedback for both appropriate as well as inappropriate role-playing attempts.

One excellent means of providing feedback is to videotape client-observer efforts at role-playing and then immediately allow them to view the tape. In the present example the client-observers might be asked to use a stopwatch to count the number of minutes they see themselves engaging in eye contact on the videotape. In this way they have the opportunity to be, in a sense, models for themselves. When videotape equipment is not available, the BCA may mirror (show the client-observer what he is in fact doing), and perhaps provide some immediate, appropriate live model of eye contact for the client-observer to witness. Following the live presentation the client-observer may be asked to practice eye contact again, with appropriate feedback being provided by the BCA until errorless performance is observed. Whenever possible, these role-playing and feedback sessions should be performed in the same kind of positive atmosphere that has been suggested for the modeling presentation. Also, the client-observer should be provided with immediate positive reinforcement—either material, social, or both—for appropriate role-playing efforts, with appropriate negative feedback provided for inappropriate efforts. Thus, both modeling and role-playing take place in a positive atmosphere, which thus increases the possibility that the client will actively attend to treatments and derive some therapeutic gain from them.

6. Maintenance with Reinforcement

Once appropriate behavior has been instigated through modeling; the BCA should make every attempt to provide consistent, well-labeled material and/or social reinforcement for each client display of an appropriate targeted event. Thus, immediate positive or negative feedback would be presented to each of our five clients contingent upon their use of eye contact in ordinary conversations within the institutional setting. This reinforcement program should be constructed along the lines suggested in the previous chapters.

MODELING PARADIGMS APPLIED TO TREATMENT: CASE EXAMPLES

The following case examples provide the reader with concrete instances of modeling techniques used in a variety of therapeutic situations. The reader may note that these examples include selections from among the modeling paradigms presented, and the actual designs employed each incorporate certain of the *modeling components* discussed in the previous section.

Example I: Increasing Proper Mealtime Behaviors

O'Brien and Azrin (1972) designed an elaborate coding strategy to evaluate and define both appropriate as well as inappropriate mealtime behaviors for a population of retarded children. They attempted to correct inappropriate eating behavior using a combination of instructions and modeling as well as physical prompting of clients. Among the targeted eating behaviors evaluated by the authors were the following:

> Spoon response: moving appropriate food from the container (e.g. pudding, soup) with the spoon held in one hand, by the handle, right side up and without spilling; glass response: moving the glass with one hand and without spilling; fork response: moving appropriate food from the container (e.g., meat, beets) with a fork held in one hand, by the handle, right side up and without spilling, except back into the container from which the food was taken; hand response: moving appropriate food from the container (e.g. bread, cookies) with one hand and without dropping the food or any part of it. (p. 393)

Training sessions were performed within special space provided so that one staff member-trainer and one resident eat together in an environment devoid of extraneous factors that might distract residents. While certain behaviors were prompted by verbal instructions only—e.g., "John, eat some beets, pick up the fork. Hold it by the handle—move your hand further back. . . . Good! Now, get some beets on the fork" (p. 393)—the staff-trainer often demonstrated the particular behavior for the student. The authors report that modeling was performed in the following manner:

> The student was also told to watch the trainer and to do what the trainer was doing. An example of imitation plus instruction to train a meat cutting response would be as follows: "John, cut your meat. Pick up your fork, like this. No, use your other hand and hold it by the handle. See, like this. Good. Now watch. Pick up the knife by the handle, like this. Good. Now, take the fork, and hold it like this over the meat. . . . Good. Now into the meat. Good. Pick up your knife by the handle, like this. Good. Now bring it over to the meat, like this. No, John. Watch me. Bring it over. . . . Good. Now cut like I am. Good!" (p. 393)

In addition, a form of modeling that Ritter (1968, 1969) has called "contact" modeling and that Bandura, Blanchard, and Ritter (1969) have called "live-guided modeling" was also included within the training procedures. The trainer used verbal instruction, and additionally, when the student was unable to master some particular behavior modeled, the trainer held one or both hands of the student and *manually guided the student in making the correct response*. While most behaviors required manual guidance to begin with, these physical prompts were gradually reduced as the student mastered a particular behavior. When any specific behavior was performed correctly by a student, the trainer would immediately remove all the utensils to their appropriate place and ask the student to perform the behavior again. When the student performed the given behavior correctly for three unassisted trials in succession, the authors assumed that the behavior had been learned, and training for that particular behavior ceased. Thus, the authors employed an older, competent model in a *matched-dependent* paradigm. They found that skills learned in the individual training sessions generalized to the group.

Example II: Increasing Usage of Descriptive Adjectives

Modeling has been employed either to instigate or modify the speech patterns of a wide variety of client populations. Lahey (1971) presented one of few applications of the co-learning paradigm in attempting to increase the use of adjectives within a population of four-year-olds enrolled in a Head Start program. Using a training situation that would be quite reinforcing to this population of rather distractible youngsters, he employed a "tape recorder game."

The children were taken individually to an adjoining room by the experimenter. The room contained a tape recorder and a long table on which were placed seven open boxes. Each box contained several brightly colored toys arranged in groups of one, two, or three similar toys of the same color. They were selected so as to be easily identified by the children (cowboys, indians, airplanes, etc.). After each child was allowed to say his name into the tape recorder and play it back, the experimenter gave the following instructions: "Now, I want you to tell me what you see in this box. Tell me all about what you see. Then it will be my turn and I'll tell you what I see in this box. Then it will be your turn again. Okay, tell me what you see in this box." If a child did not name each object with at least a noun, the experimenter said, "Anything else?" This was frequently necessary for the first one or two descriptions. The child made the first description and this was taken as a baseline of adjective frequency. The next description was by the experimenter, followed by the subject, alternatively for a total of three descriptions by the experimenter and three descriptions after baseline for the subject. After each description, the experimenter said, "Now it's your turn," or, "Now it's my turn. (p. 20)

Lahey found that adjective use increased significantly for subjects exposed to this participant trainer-model. Subjects exposed to a trainer who did not employ adjectives did not significantly increase their use of adjectives within the conversation. This case example nicely points out how the co-learning paradigm might be used within the positive atmosphere of some valued, participatory task. Interestingly enough, while no specific reinforcement was employed by the trainer for adjective speech, frequency dramatically increased merely through the trainer's demonstrational efforts within the "game."

In the previous two examples a staff member within an institutional setting was trained to serve as the model within treatment. Often, the BCA will wish to employ modeling not only as a valuable aid to client treatment but also as a means of training the trainers (e.g., staff members, parents), who then work directly with the clients. In the next example modeling is employed in instruct a parent in appropriate child-management procedures.

Example III: Increasing Parental Management Skills

The mother of a six-year-old "overactive," "distractible," "tense," "excitable" child was referred to Johnson and Brown (1969) for training in child-management procedures. The authors describe David as follows:

> The child's mother was interviewed twice prior to observational diagnostic procedures. She indicated that she was very concerned because her son was "emotionally disturbed" and "sick." She was unable, however, to specify many of the behaviors which upset her, other than indicating that her boy would sometimes wave his arms when excited, and that he became overly involved with mechanical gadgets. At times he would withdraw for long periods to engage in this play. When pressed for more specific instances, she reported that David would refuse to get ready for, or go to school, and that he would refuse to do simple assigned household chores. At these times, mother would either "keep after him,'" or do for David what he would not do for himself. (p. 116)

The authors decided to observe mother and child interact in a task situation within a specially constructed playroom. Using a contrived situation the authors asked the mother to play with David for a period of two minutes with a favorite toy, followed by a five-minute period in which the mother assisted the child in performing arithmetic problems. The authors coded the following behaviors: reinforcements the mother employed, critical remarks made by the mother for his failure to do arithmetic, any acts of attending to David when he was not performing arithmetic problems, as well as the proportion of time David actually performed the arithmetic tasks. The authors decided that David's undesired behaviors appeared to be maintained by the mother's compliance to his demands and her rather intense attention to his unusual and manipulative behavior. In line with this formulation the goal of intervention was the cessation of her compliance and attention. While both "directive counseling" and "didactic group discussion" had been employed with limited success for a period of eight months, the authors decided to model or demonstrate appropriate parental behaviors for the mother, employing the clinically contrived situation as a training vehicle. A therapist served as model and interacted with David in both play and arithmetic periods just as the mother had done. The mother observed the interaction between model and child, and was asked to record each of the targeted behaviors in the hope that this would direct her attention to the behavior of child and model. The mother proved to be an accurate observer, agreeing with an independent observer at a level of 82 percent or above for each of the targeted behaviors. The mother was then sent into the room again with her son and "asked to use whatever methods she thought appropriate to get him to do the arithmetic" (p. 118). Similar procedures were employed during a second modeling session. Following exposure to the therapist-model, the mother's attention to off-task behavior reduced dramatically, and her use of appropriate criticism of the child's efforts increased significantly. The present example would fall within the matched-dependent paradigm, with therapists' social feedback serving as the reinforcement for efforts at imitation.

The present author has employed symbolic models (via videotape) to train parents to communicate more effectively, to use reinforcements, as well as to employ control procedures with their children (Nay, 1972, 1975). Results of that research indicated that modeling, particularly when some provision for immediate role-playing was employed, was much more successful in increasing parental information and in promoting behavioral change than written or lecture presentations.

Each of the preceeding examples employed an adult therapist or staff member as model; in the following case peers were employed to effectively increase the frequency of targeted behaviors.

Example IV: Increasing Assertive Behavior

Hersen, Eisler, Miller, Johnson, and Pinkston (1973) employed peer models to increase the frequency of assertive responses within a population of male psychiatric patients. To assess clients' current repertoire of assertive behaviors, clients referred for treatment were asked to role-play each of fourteen interpersonal encounters that required assertive responses (Eisler, Miller, and Hersen, 1973; see case examples in Chapter 7 for a complete description). Clients were asked to portray how they would behave within scenes like the following:

> Narrator: "You have just come home from work, and as you settle down to read the newspaper, you discover that your wife has cut out an important article in order to get a recipe that was on the back of it. You really like to read the whole newspaper." Role model wife: "I just wanted to cut out a recipe before I forgot about it." (p. 296)

An assistant would play the wife and the client would be asked to respond to this situation as he would have if it had occurred outside of the clinical setting. The authors then coded the behavior of clients according to a nine-category system (Eisler, Miller, and Hersen, 1973). Thus, role-playing was employed as a means of diagnosing important behaviors for therapy. The authors produced a videotape of a male psychiatric patient serving as a model who responded to another actress in the role-playing situation. The model was specifically trained to: (1) respond with a lengthy reply; (2) request that the female "assistant" change her behavior; (3) maintain consistent eye contact with her; (4) demonstrate absence of compliance with her request; and (5) respond to her in a fully audible voice while demonstrating appropriate affect. After the "patient" model evidenced sufficient mastery in responding, the five scenes were videotaped and administered to each client six times within a three-day period. Client responses following the last exposure were compared to pretreatment responses to assess behavioral change. The authors found videotape peer modeling to be an effective means of increasing client assertive responses, particularly when a modeling videotape was accompanied by specific instructions to attend to particular targeted behaviors. Again, the paradigm employed is the matched-dependent paradigm, with therapist feedback serving as reinforcement for each imitation trial.

CHAPTER SUMMARY

The term *modeling* describes the special situation where the *probability of some specific behavior on the part of an observer (O) is altered via the observation of some model (M)*.

The classification systems of Bandura and Kanfer and Phillips were employed to define important classes of modeling. For Bandura, *observational learning* defines an observer acquiring some new behavior not previously within his repertoire, following his exposure to a model. A second class, *inhibitory* and *disinhibitory effects,* applies only to behaviors that have been previously learned. When O observers M undergo punishing consequences for some behavior, inhibitory effects are said to have occurred if the observer then inhibits that same behavior as a result of the modeling experience. Regarding disinhibitory effects, O may begin to display some previously punished behavior if he observes M engage in that behavior with no ill effects. Inhibitory and disinhibitory effects are often employed within treatment. Finally, when some previously learned behavior is increased in frequency following an exposure to M, Bandura would say that this response has been *facilitated* by the model.

Within Kanfer and Phillips' *matched-dependent paradigm,* O is directly rewarded for imitating the behavior of M, who is usually serving in a training capacity. *Co-learning* describes two individuals working together on a task. Both participants alternately serve as M and O. It was suggested that clients with diverse skills could be "yoked" together within this co-learning paradigm. *Vicarious classical conditioning* refers to O's emotional responses, elicited by stimuli that provoke emotional responses within M. An observer could be classically conditioned by observing M receive emotionally provocative consequences in the presence of some neutral stimulus. *Identification* refers to O displaying the idiosyncratic response style of M. Within this situation an observer might enact aspects of a model's physical stance, verbal intonation, style of speaking, or other incidental behavior through repeated exposure to M. Lastly, *no-trial learning* describes O's learning of some behavior that M displays without receiving any extrinsic reinforcement and without performing the behavior at the time of presentation. This was described as the least useful paradigm within which treatment might occur.

Numerous factors that might affect the probability of modeling were presented; primarily extending from the work of Bandura and his colleagues. Each of these factors rests upon the assumption that the *the observer must actively discriminate the behavior of some model for modeling to occur.* Regarding reinforcement, modeling seems to be facilitated if the observer views the model as being reinforced for his behavior, or the O receives direct reinforcement for his observation of M. Any M characteristic that increases the probability that an observer will actively attend to model behavior will facilitate modeling. The model will be particularly powerful when he effects potential outcomes or subsequent rewards for the observer. It was pointed out that most research has been conducted with children, and the generality of these findings to adolescent or adult populations remains to be seen.

A large body of research suggests that competent, high-status models provoke more behavioral change in observers than those viewed as less competent. A contrasting finding by Meichenbaum suggests that the model should display coping rather than mastering response.

Research is quite mixed regarding the similarity of M and O, but there is a finding that interaction exists between sex of M and O's specific behavior. It was also predicted that multiple models would seem to ensure that the observer will find some model characteristic that elicits maximal discriminative attention, and the few studies performed suggested that multiple models were superior to single models in provoking behavioral change in children.

While research seems to indicate that live models may be somewhat superior to symbolic models, the symbolic approach has often been successfully employed. It holds advantages, including increased possibility for special cueing effects, increased temporal flexibility, increased client/ therapist control of presentations, and a reduction in therapist time.

Regarding observer effects any variable (e.g., fatigue, medication, cognitive ability, motor ability) that interferes with O's active attention to M would seem to interfere with modeling. Also, certain personality characteristics might be related to modeling, with dependent nursery school children being more unselective in displaying model behaviors than independent children.

Using an example of increasing eye contact in a population of five psychiatric clients, a series of procedural steps were presented for the use of modeling: definition of target; choice of model (based on M and O characteristics); choice of modeling paradigm; provision of reinforcement for O; use of role-playing and feedback following exposure to M; and maintenance of O behavior with reinforcement.

Finally, four case examples were presented.

Chapter 7

Role-play, Feedback, and Cueing Procedures

When a client is asked to practice or rehearse a targeted behavior, this process is variously termed *role-playing, psychodrama* (Moreno, 1958), or *behavioral rehearsal* (Wolpe, 1969). Any overt (externally observable behavior) or covert (private event) client enactment will be defined as role-playing, although this term usually applies to voluntary client efforts within the context of treatment.

In the previous section it was strongly suggested that clients be given the opportunity to practice or role-play the behaviors presented by a model. Role-playing permits the client to "try out" the targeted behavior and to receive feedback from the BCA regarding the strengths and weaknesses of his performance. Role-playing would seem to be most advantageous for modeled behaviors currently not well developed within the client's repertoire. For example, if you are asked to reproduce the behavior of a model who raises his hand, you obviously will be able to do is without practicing, as you have practiced this behavior on many occasions in the past. Most targeted behaviors are typically not as well developed within the client's repertoire, and the client often is unable to reproduce the model's behavior in errorless fashion on the first trial. Client opportunity to practice or role-play modeled behaviors permits the BCA to assess the degree of learning that has taken place, to provide appropriate feedback to the client regarding his performance, and to allow the client to make repeated trials until mastery is accomplished. Thus, role-playing often becomes an important adjunct to modeling, promoting the translation of modeled behaviors into an alteration of client behavior. Of course, role-playing may be used in isolation, but it is most often employed following client exposure to an appropriate model.

Procedures that employ the "role" seem to have much in common, and this chapter will attempt to review three of the major categories of techniques in an attempt to make clear the similarities and differences between procedures. The discussion will begin with the *psychodrama* procedures of Moreno (1958), who might be called the founder of "role" procedures, followed by a presentation of the specific *fixed role* approach of Kelly (1955), and with a final presentation of the more recently coined phrase *behavioral rehearsal* (Wolpe and Lazarus, 1966). Then, a consideration of factors that might determine the utility of role-playing in changing client behavior will be followed by a series of case examples.

CATEGORIES OF ROLE-PLAY

Psychodrama

Moreno (1958) observed that many of the behaviors that actors portray on the stage become part of their repertoire off the stage. In effect, he observed that there seems to be some translation from what happens on the stage to what happens in real life, and it occurred to him that the playing of a role might be a useful treatment procedure. The psychodramatic procedures he developed are perhaps the most formal of the role-play procedures. Kanfer and Phillips (1970) have suggested that there are four basic elements that most psychodramatic procedures include:

1. The patient is encouraged to act out problems in front of a group of fellow patients.

2. Moment-to-moment feedback on the various aspects of the performance is provided by the group, with appropriate discussion following.

3. An atmosphere exists that supports the opportunity to express extremes of affect before an accepting audience.

4. Spontaneity is always encouraged.

Typically, some member of a therapy group is defined as the "protagonist" for a given session, because the primary therapist within the group ("director") has decided that this client might benefit from working out a life situation of importance ("scene"). The protagonist is asked to describe the specific setting where the scene to be portrayed occurred. Often articles of furniture or even other clients within the group may serve as props in the setting. For example, if the real life scene occurred in a living room, the client may employ chairs and tables within the clinical setting to form the "living room." Once the stage is set to the satisfaction of the protagonist, the director of the psychodrama will ask the protagonist to define the specific characters he wishes to include in the scene enactment. For example, if the scene occurred in the living room of his home with his mother-in-law, wife, father-in-law, and two children present, the protagonist would then choose specific members of the client group to play each role. If one assumes that the protagonist chooses certain group members to play specific roles because of some client characteristic that suits the role, this may provide important feedback to those clients chosen. For example, if a male is chosen to play the protagonist's mother-in-law, this may provide important feedback to the chosen client as to how the protagonist views him (e.g., in a feminine role). To the extent that specific clients are consistently chosen to play particular kinds of roles, this provides important diagnostic feedback to those clients. Such feedback may be the basis of specific treatment plans if the client wishes to alter certain behaviors that lead to role choices.

Once each character within the scene has been assigned to a group member, the protagonist is asked to provide information to the clients as to how best to play their roles. Often this information is provided through verbal instruction as well as modeling by the protagonist. For example, the protagonist may model for the client-actor precisely how his mother-in-law behaved within the scene situation. Then the client-actor would be asked to role-play or practice the "mother-in-law" role until he performed it correctly. Often, this is accomplished by the protagonist and actor *reversing roles,* so that the actor has an additional opportunity to see how the protagonist portrays his mother-in-law. Thus, verbal instruction, modeling, and role reversals all provide the client-actors in the psychodrama with instructions as to how to play their assigned roles.

Often, the director provides feedback to both the protagonist as well as the actors as to the quality of their role portrayals, recommending additional role reversals and instruction as necessary to ensure adequate role-playing. Even though the psychodrama is focused upon the protagonist, client-actors forced to behave differently practice new skills. Thus, every actor as well as the protagonist may make behavioral gains as a result of the psychodrama. Once the actors can adequately play their assigned roles, the director asks that the scene be played through as the protagonist originally described it. For example, the client may show how he responded to an angry confrontation with his wife in which her mother supported her. Following the initial enactment of the scene, the director may ask the client to reverse roles with other characters. In this way the client has the opportunity to see the scene as his mother-in-law might have viewed it, as his wife may have viewed it, or as any character within the scene may have responded to it. Role reversals force the protagonist to take the point of view of another, and may assist him in formulating an alternative approach to the situation.

If the protagonist's approach to the scene was not satisfactory, the director may ask him to try a new behavior. Perhaps the director will ask other clients in the group to model for the protagonist how they would have handled the situation. Thus, the protagonist is exposed to other client-models who portray the scene in ways divergent from his own. Following this exposure the protagonist may be asked to "try out" the scene again, this time attempting to include those behaviors modeled that he can most comfortably employ within the scene. Often a scene is reenacted sufficient times for the client to try out an array of new approaches in the same situation. To the extent that the actors involved behave differently within their specific scene roles, they may continue to expand their behavioral repertoires with each reenactment.

In some cases a specific group member chosen by the protagonist will serve as the *double*. According to Sturm (1970) doubling is a procedure in which:

an auxiliary (or several) is directed to play (physically) alongside and parallel to the subject (protagonist) and other characters. . . . The doubles . . . within the context of their roles, begin spontaneously to articulate and act "what the character is really doing" in the light of the cues to which he is responding. Enacted are the relevant unspoken feelings, thoughts, or wishes that the auxiliary senses the character detrimentally avoids, represses, suppresses, or is simply unaware of. (p. 239)

Thus, the double serves to "prod" the protagonist into identifying important behaviors he is not aware of. Doubling can be an extremely valuable technique both within and outside of the formal psychodrama situation, since it forces the client to attend to particular behaviors that may be difficult or impossible to verbalize. Sturm (1970) views psychodrama within a learning framework and points out that it is based upon a number of important assumptions not shared by many other treatment procedures. First, it is important to deal with impromptu problems that arise instead of enacting planned hierarchies of graded scenes. Second, there is the equivalence of director, audience, and subject, instead of a self-assured helper and patient. Third, role-played scenes are closer to reality than are "imagined" reported scenes. Fourth, providing self-reflective sharing or feedback is better than "objective" analysis. And fifth, anxiety, depression, and guilt can best be handled by training toward social and personal competence.

Unfortunately, there has been very little formal research directed at psychodrama, and it is difficult to evaluate how all the elements of a psychodrama affect the behavioral changes that are often noted. The fact that the protagonist is given the opportunity to reenact behavioral exchange from within his life situation in the protected atmosphere of the group would seem to be an important benefit. Diagnostically, the therapist-director has the opportunity to see, from the client's point of view, specifically how the client behaved in a life situation involving others as well as how the client views other members of the therapy group as reflected in his choices for certain roles. Also, psychodrama permits the client to try out new ways of behaving in a situation prior to trying them out in real life. The client has an opportunity to socially interact with and learn from many other clients, who may possibly exhibit strengths and deficits that relate to the client's own targeted behavioral goals. Sturm (1970) concludes that psychodrama seems to have the properties of generating vivid, lifelike behavior and cues that may serve to increase the generalization of psychodramatic behavior to real-life behavior. It also seems to promote change within all important behavioral spheres—physiological, motoric, and ideational, rather than merely verbal. He points out that many of the phenomena associated with learning theory may in fact be operating within the psychodramatic situation, including systematic desensitization, operant conditioning, shaping, and emotive imagery.

Fixed Role Therapy

George Kelly (1955) suggested that an individual asked to play a fixed role consonant with treatment goals would order the manner in which he viewed himself and the world around him to agree with the role portrayed, thus causing him to change his behavior. Kelly viewed man as if he were a scientist. For Kelly each man constantly attempts to predict and control the events of his life. In order to accomplish this, each individual looks at his world through "constructs" that he creates and "then attempts to fit over the realities of which the world is composed" (pp. 8–9). For Kelly, a "construct" is the manner in which an individual cognitively construes the world around him. According to Kelly, each of us uses such constructs as "good versus bad," "moral versus immoral," "healthy versus sick," "cold versus warm," to view an array of events that impinge upon us. Thus, the way that we construe each of these dimensions predicts the manner in which we will behave toward them. Each man develops his own set of unique personal constructs. In Kelly's theory each construct holds a range of convenience within which a construct is applicable. Thus, the construct "warm versus cold" may be employed to evaluate the relative merits of some particular brand of ice cream or the sensations that come with eating a large piece of filet mignon, but this construct would probably not be applicable in evaluating a piece of art or in comparing gradations of wood paneling for a proposed addition to one's home.

In addition, constructs also vary in the degree to which they might admit new elements into range of convenience. A *permeable* construct readily admits new elements, whereas an *impermeable* construct has already been employed to construe all the elements in its range of convenience, and thus is closed to new experiences. Thus, to the extent that one's constructs are permeable, an individual can process novel information and alter his behavior appropriately. Kelly might say that the individual who behaves in an inappropriate manner, rejecting the punishment and negative feedback that his behavior brings upon him, is a person whose constructs are relatively impermeable.

To alter an individual's behavior the therapist must evaluate the constructs that underlie it and must expose the individual to appropriate role behavior which might then be incorporated into his system of constructs. Kelly called this role-playing consonant with therapeutic goals *fixed role therapy*. The therapist asks the client to play the role of a fictitious person whose behavior is consistent with some construct system hypothesized to be more beneficial to the client. The therapist would write a fixed role sketch, and the client would be asked to portray a particular role. Thus, a very passive, dependent, unassertive individual might be asked to play the role of an open, independent-thinking, aggressive salesman, attempting to sell something to a person who did not desire the commodity.

A relevant fixed role might be constructed for any client by evaluating important targeted behaviors and designing a role around them. Often, an individual who ordinarily displays these goal-relevant behaviors is found, and his character forms the basis for the fixed role the client is asked to play. Kanfer and Phillips (1970) described fixed role therapy from a learning point of view:

1. The patient is invited to explore behavioral patterns sharply contrasted to his own.

2. He is encouraged to practice those patterns in everyday life.

3. From practice he gains experience in how the world appears and reacts when he behaves in a different manner.

4. Practice eventuates in increased skills, supplemented by new experiences from feedback.

Mushala (1974) summarized the importance of designing an appropriate fixed role in using Kelly's approach:

It would seem that the critical point in fixed role therapy is developing the proper fixed role sketch. This requires ingenuity so that it will be informative to the patient and adequately cover a wide variety of situations. For therapy sessions to have maximum effect, the therapist has to be able to effectively role play significant people in the patient's life. This enables the patient to practice the fixed role with people he will eventually have to interact with in the real world. (p. 23)

Kelly (1955) has stated that while the clients begin by viewing their role as "just acting," they often are moving toward increased spontaneity, and with repeated portrayals, they are apt to report that somehow the world seems to be a bit different. The following example (Lira, Nay,

McCullough, and Etkin, 1975) illustrates a fixed role devised for clients who showed an intense fear of snakes which often interfered with ordinary outdoors activities such as walking through grass. Clients were required to make a graduated series of approach responses to a harmless snake while portraying the following fixed role:

"You are to play the role of John Harris. John Harris is a person who enjoys outdoor activities. Often during his outdoor experiences he encounters snakes and other small animals. In fact, he seeks out non-poisonous snakes and keeps them as pets. His favorite snake is a boa constrictor which he bought at a pet shop. Over the years he has collected a number of these harmless reptiles. He collects them not only because of his interest in snakes, but also to amaze his friends by showing and handling them. His friends are much impressed with his hobby and the ease with which he handles snakes.

"John has noted several things about his snakes which provide interesting contrasts to what we have normally heard about snakes. He finds their appearance to be pleasing; some boa constrictors are beautifully colored and have vivid patterns on their skins. The old tale that snakes are scarey and slimy just isn't true. John describes his snakes as being soft, smooth, clean and easy to handle. When the snakes are held they display a certain confidence which can best be described by the fact that they immediately begin exploring their environment when perched on the hands and arms of their human companions. Even the largest of John's snakes can hang by its tail and at the same time lift itself to look around and smell the environment with receptors in its tongue. To John, studying snakes is just a pleasurable hobby."

Unfortunately, little research has been performed to evaluate the effectiveness of the fixed role approach. Karst and Trexler (1970) compared fixed role therapy and a more directive traditional approach—rational emotive therapy—in reducing public speaking anxiety. They found that for a population of college student volunteers, neither condition was superior to a no-treatment control condition. Kanfer and Phillips (1970) have stated: "Unfortunately, there is little research that sheds light on the learning process occurring in role rehearsals. Effectiveness of the techniques is also more frequently established by testimonials than by empirical evidence" (p. 235). It would seem that a fixed role approach might be artfully employed within diagnostic or therapeutic approaches. Diagnostically, the BCA might obtain important information as to how a client reacts to and is able to employ a variety of targeted behaviors. Perhaps a fixed role approach could be used as part of a standard diagnostic battery that requires clients to protray roles that include important behavioral elements of assertiveness, warmth and affectional responses, anger, ability to portray happiness, and so on. For each of these fixed roles the BCA could construct a coding system that might evaluate important behaviors such as body and facial expressiveness, posture, maintenance of eye contact while speaking, appropriateness of voice, as well as any unusual or bizarre behaviors the individual manifests. In addition, the BCA would have the opportunity to evaluate the specific content of the client's re-

sponses. For example, a role calling for assertive behavior requires different content responses than a role calling for affectional behaviors. Thus,
the fixed role approach might enable the BCA to design specific treatments for the client, including treatment of targeted behaviors assessed
within the fixed role portrayal. A review of such role-play "analogue"
assessment procedures may be found in Nay (1976).

Regarding treatment, it is apparent that the fixed role approach offers
a highly specific set of behaviors within a role that the client is asked to
practice until mastery is attained. When the fixed role is carefully constructed, important targeted behaviors are required for role enactment,
thus providing a clear specification of the treatment goals to the client.
This approach would seem to be particularly useful when the BCA is able
to formulate a specific set of targeted behaviors and can design a "role"
that includes them.

Behavioral Rehearsal

This approach requires the client to maintain his own role in practicing highly specified targeted behaviors within a variety of situations typically calling for assertive or approach skills (McFall and Marston, 1970;
McFall and Lillesand, 1971; Flowers, 1975). Often, the therapist takes the
role of a person in the client's life and instructs the client to try out some
new responses to that individual. Behavioral rehearsal is a means by
which the therapist and client can reconstruct the real world within the
clinical setting. It is similar to psychodrama; however, the behavioral
rehearsal procedures are rarely applied as formally and systematically as
the psychodrama. The therapist is often more directive in prompting and
cueing the client to emit certain behaviors in response to the role-play
situation. In addition, not as much time is typically spent in setting the
"stage," choosing individuals to play the various parts, or in employing
doubling, role reversals, or other specific procedures, which most readily
fall within the psychodramatic process. Clients are asked to show the
therapist how they behaved in a situation previously, and then through
modeling, prompting, and/or cueing by the therapist, clients are helped to
engage in new responses within the problem situation. Very clearly, the
client is asked to rehearse certain behaviors that are targeted to be of
relevance. Lazarus (1966) presents a case example of a training procedure
designed to increase the probability of assertive responses. In using behavioral rehearsal, he describes the session as follows:

> In this method patient and therapist role-play various scenes which present
> assertive problems for the patient . . . expressing disagreement with a friend's
> social arrangements, asking a favor . . . contradicting a fellow employee, refusing
> to accede to an unreasonable request, complaining to his employer about the
> inferior office fixtures, requesting an increment in salary, criticizing his father's
> attire . . . the therapist usually role-plays the significant persons in the patient's

life according to descriptions provided by the latter. The patient's behavior was shaped by means of constructive criticism as well as modeling procedures in which the therapist assumed the patient's role and demonstrated the desirable responses. A situation was regarded as "satisfactorily covered" when (1) the patient was able to enact it without feeling anxious (if he became tense or anxious while rehearsing a scene, deep relaxation was applied until he felt calm again); (2) when his general demeanor, posture, facial expression, inflection in tone, and the like, lent substance to his words (repeated play-backs from a tape recorder helped to remove a querulous pitch from his voice) and (3) when agreement was reached that his words and actions would seem fair and fitting to an objective onlooker. In order to expedite the transfer from consulting room to actual life, the patient was initially encouraged to apply his newly acquired assertive skills only when negative consequences were highly improbable . . . he soon grew proficient at handling most situations that called for uninhibited and forthright behavior. (pp. 209–210)

Wolpe (1969) compiled the results of some 75 therapeutic cases in a matched-group design to test the relative effectiveness of reflective and interpretative therapy, "advice," and behavioral rehearsal. The specific behavioral gains made by clients following treatment showed that behavioral rehearsal was significantly more effective in resolving social skills deficits and interpersonal problems than either directive or nondirective therapeutic approaches. Wolpe concluded that behavioral rehearsal is an extremely important treatment tool.

The preceding categories of role-playing are not meant to be inclusive; however, the approaches presented seem to include the major features found within any category of treatment employing "role." The reader may have noted the similarities in what the therapist and client *actually do* cross the three divergent approaches. Perhaps the treatment effects elicited by any one of the three may be explained by this commonality: the clients practice behaviors that diverge from their present behavior . While various theorists might explain the behavioral changes that accrue from role-playing differently, it does seem that role-playing holds important treatment properties and may be employed in many different situations. It is interesting that so-called traditional as well as behaviorally oriented therapists share a commonality in their frequently reported use of role-play.

Much of the research on role-playing is focused upon an attempt to relate role-playing to some overall theory of social or cognitive behavior or personality (Greenwald and Albert, 1968; Wolkon, 1970; Festinger and Carlsmith, 1959; Bandura and Walters, 1963; Bandura, 1969).

Unfortunately, few investigators have attempted to define the specific factors that effect the probability of successful role-playing or to relate such factors to specific demographic client populations. As the focus of the present text is upon the application of various techniques to treatment, the remaining discussion will present factors that may affect the outcome of role-play treatments. As in the previous section on modeling, examples from the literature will be used to illustrate important points.

ROLE-PLAY: FACTORS THAT MAY PREDICT OUTCOME

The factors to be presented are based on the author's reading of the rather scant literature as well as on his personal orientation. Unfortunately, many of the factors presented are not buttressed by a large body of research.

Role-Playing Skills

In assuming a "role," the client must be able to get "out of his own head" and into the point of view of another, much as the professional actor does. In fact, the client must be able to think, feel, and generally perceive things in a fashion different from the ordinary. It would seem that to the extent the client can accurately engage in role-playing of some behavior, there is a greater probability that desired behavioral change will occur. In his 1964 review Sarbin evaluated a number of correlates of effective role-playing and concluded that the ability of the client to perform the desired role seems most crucial. Mushala (1974) has stated:

It is common sense that if one lacks the requisite skills to perform a certain role, there is a high probability of inadequate performance. Further, if there is a general aptitude entering into performance adequacy, it would seem to be the capacity for role taking itself. Thus, George Herbert Mead stated that the ability of a person to ascribe meaning and communicate, and thereby take the role of others, was emphasized as one of the central features of human and social interactions. (pp. 8–9)

Very basically, it would seem that the *ability* to role-play depends upon two major classes of factors, pointed up by these questions: Is the client capable of cognitively taking the point of view of another and understanding the instructions provided by the therapist? Has the client acquired the specific skills necessary to play some part divergent from his current repertoire?

It has been the experience of the author that many adults find it very difficult to role-play on the first trial. Often, the instructions provided by the therapist must be very clearly stated and numerous examples provided before clients get the idea of what they are to do. Many clients begin by "describing" what someone else would do, and have difficulty actually "getting into" the thoughts and feelings suggested by the role. Thus, role-playing does seem to constitute a skill that must be learned, and as with any skill behavior, clients vary considerably in training required for role enactment. Among clients who are cognitively capable, those who are currently out of contact with reality, medicated to the point of sedation, or lacking in motivation to engage in therapy might prove to be particularly poor candidates for role-playing treatments.

When training is required, the BCA might begin by asking the client to write an historical summary from the point of view of certain important others. Or the given client might be asked to write a description of himself as it would be written by his wife, son, employer, or others. Thus, in a less threatening way the client begins the rather difficult task of getting out of his "own skin" and attempts to see things from a different perspective.

Perhaps, as in the dramatic situation, the client could be provided with a play script that has been published (available in most bookstores), and required, perhaps along with the other prospective clients, to read the part of some particular character. This fixed role preliminary training could be carefully tailored to the particular needs of the client. Thus, if the client has difficulties in role-playing a female, a female part might be provided. In another alternative the client could be asked to identify with some character displayed on television and to "get into" the role of that character, attempting to "feel what he is feeling" and to understand what the actor is thinking. Following an initial period of several weeks during which the client becomes acquainted with the character, the BCA might then ask the client to role-play that character within the therapeutic situation. Of course, a televised exposure provides the client with a model of the behavior he will be asked to role-play, which promotes the learning of necessary skills.

As another alternative the BCA might begin by asking the client to play him, with the BCA playing the role of client in a role reversal. Within this dyad both parties could make immediate checks as to the truth of the portrayals, with reversals back into ordinary roles providing a focus for feedback and discussion about the role-playing efforts. If the particular role that the client will be asked to play is very threatening and anxiety-provoking, the BCA might do well to structure the preliminary practice scenes to be as neutral as possible, so that the anxiety attendant with role-playing itself is systematically reduced, and important role-play skills can be learned prior to exposing the client to the anxiety-provoking situation.

Client Repertoire

It is obvious that the client must be capable of reproducing the cognitive and motor behaviors that a role calls for. Developmentally, we know that young children cannot engage in certain motor behaviors until the muscles are developed sufficiently. The same limitation applies to any cognitive skill that a client is asked to rehearse.

An individual learning to play golf would most likely begin with the swing, rather than trying to drive the ball 300 yards out to a green. Once the duffer has mastered certain elements of the swing, the instructor might then provide the opportunity to practice actually hitting the ball. Once the student begins hitting the ball appropriately, he might be asked to practice hitting the ball to some certain point, with ultimate attention focused upon control as to where the ball is placed. Thus, each skill practiced rests upon some more basic skill, in hierachical fashion. Obviously, the instructor would not ask an individual whose right arm is paralyzed to engage in golf swinging that required movement of both limbs. Regardless of how many times the person practiced this behavior, his basic physical deficit would confound his efforts at mastery.

Thus, the BCA must carefully assess the current repertoire of the client within the behavioral area of interest. If the client is asked to enact a role calling for certain verbal behaviors, the BCA must be sure that the client's vocabulary is sufficiently developed to include the necessary verbal content. Clients who are asked to portray a role that is beyond their current verbal repertoire are likely to become very frustrated and possibly angry with the therapy situation. Thus, the role-play task must include behavioral elements that the client is capable of emitting.

Activity

It would seem that the more actively the client cognitively and motorly portrays a role, the greater the probability of behavioral change. In fact, several studies that have evaluated the dimension of activity within role-playing seem to support this point of view (e.g., Janis and King, 1954). A study by Greenwald and Albert (1968) found that to the extent a role-player actively improvises various behaviors displayed within his role, as opposed to merely reading an unimprovised script, increased attitudinal and behavioral changes following role-playing will occur. This tendency to recall and evaluate more highly improvised as opposed to unimprovised role-play behavior has been called the "improvisational effect." Zimbardo (1965) proposed that this improvisational effect results from the increased effort that the role-players must put into their performance, thus tending to increase their regard for their own efforts. Festinger and Carlsmith (1959) have shown that when one behaves in a fashion incongruent with his current behavior or expresses opinions incongruent with his current attitudes, this creates a state of "cognitive dissonance." To relieve this dissonance the individual may alter his behavior or attitudes to bring them into consonance with the "incongruent" events. In a sense this might be viewed in terms of investment. The active role-player who is asked to improvise his activities within the role must make an investment in the treatment situation and more specifically in the novel role behavior. The passive participant who merely reads from a script and is not required to engage actively in improvisation makes very little investment, which may not commit him to altering overt and/or covert behaviors to approximate those behaviors portrayed.

To the extent that the client is *able* to direct himself and improvise within the role, it would seem that the BCA should allow him to do so. When structure and direction are required for the client's initial portrayals, the therapist should intervene, gradually fading out directoral efforts as the client becomes better able to elaborate upon the role.

Overt Versus Covert Variants

Another issue that relates to activity is the dimension of *overt or actual behavioral role-playing*, as opposed to *covert or cognitive/imaginal role-playing*. While most investigators require the client to practice the role overtly, many others have employed a cognitive or covert approach to role enactment. The reader should by now be very familiar with covert processes (Chapter 5). As might be imagined, covert role-playing requires the client to enact the role in his imagination—a purely cognitive effort. Wolpe (1958) was perhaps one of the first to extensively employ covert role-playing procedures, in his systematic desensitization approach to reducing client avoidance behaviors. Within desensitization the client is asked to practice certain approach behaviors to a feared object exclusively within the imagination. While the therapist may provide additional opportunities for *in vivo*, or real life exposure to the feared stimulus, Wolpe and many others have found that the purely cognitive role-play approach is successful in decreasing avoidance behavior in a large proportion of clients. Because overt practice is often impossible within the therapy situation, since it may require that the therapist and client move into the community, covert rehearsal offers an alternative that may readily be employed in any setting. Lazarus (1966) used a covert rehearsal procedure to decrease the anxiety generated by horror movies in a population of adolescent clients. He asked the clients to covertly imagine watching a horror movie and to practice an array of defensive reactions to cope with anticipated anxious experience in imagination. The covert rehearsal was successful in reducing significantly clients' fears.

Corbin (1967) found no significant difference between overt and covert rehearsal in instigating performance on a motor task. Neither approach produced effects that were maintained over time. He suggested that actual experience in performing a task might be a prerequisite for covert rehearsal to promote skill development. McFall and Twentyman (1973) also found no difference between overt and covert rehearsal in promoting assertive behaviors in a population of undergraduate students. Both promoted generalization from the laboratory to "real-life" situations.

In contrast, Longin and Rooney (1973) found overt rehearsal significantly superior to the covert approach in increasing assertive responses in a population of 38 female chronic patients in a psychiatric setting. Training was limited to once each week over a four-week period. Nay, Lira, and Etkin (1976) support this finding in comparing overt and covert procedures with fearful subjects.

Unfortunately, at present, the specific targeted client behaviors that respond best to a covert versus overt role-playing approach have yet to be elucidated. However, it would seem that covert rehearsal provides an opportunity for clients to rehearse important targeted behaviors in those situations such as job or home where overt rehearsal may be impossible or impractical. Perhaps the covert approach is most useful when the targeted behavior includes a strong cognitive/self-verbalization component, and overt rehearsal best promotes behavioral change in which speech and motor elements are of primary importance. It is hoped that further research will elucidate those specific targeted behaviors that respond best to one or the other approach. Certainly, the use of covert rehearsal adds an important dimension to treatment approaches available to the BCA, and should be further explored as a modality of treatment.

Feedback and Cueing Systems

If the client is permitted to practice inappropriate, nongoal-directed behaviors, it may interfere with later attempts to master the targeted behavior. The role-playing situation provides an excellent opportunity not only to assess the degree of mastery, but to provide feedback so that additional role-playing attempts may correct performance errors. Just as we wouldn't think of sending the incipient golfer out with a set of golf clubs to role-play on his own the art of golf (he might start by swinging the golf club like a tennis racket), we do not want the client to practice without receiving some form of feedback that leads to more adequate practice attempts. There are many ways of providing feedback to a client who is role-playing some targeted behavior. Most typically, feedback is provided in verbal fashion. For example, after a client practices maintaining eye contact with another person during some standard conversation (targeted behavior), the therapist might terminate the interaction and provide feedback to the client regarding the extent to which eye contact was maintained. In some cases the client is permitted to complete an entire sequence of behavior prior to receiving a verbal review by the BCA. For example, the author (Nay, 1975) asked mothers of behavioral-problem children to role-play time-out procedure following exposure to a videotape that depicted a mother (model) using the procedure appropriately with her child. Mothers were given a role-playing guide (which may be seen below) and asked to practice each of the component steps of time-out procedure in a dyadic situation where one mother role-played parent and the other role-played child.

Note: One of you play the "parent" to practice using time out while the other plays the "child." General instructions for each scene are listed under *A. Scene.* The correct response to practice for each scene is under *B. Practice.*
I. *Practice the Three Steps of Time Out*
   A. Scene. The "parent" asks the "child" to do something, such as "Pick up

your clothes." The "child" does not comply each time "parent" asks.
  B. Practice
    1. Providing information such as "Pick up your clothes right now."
    2. Warning child ("If you don't pick up your clothes right now, you have to go to time out.")
    3. Time out (Send child to time out and state, "Because you didn't pick up when I asked you to, now you have to go to time out.")

II. *"Child" Cries or Calls Out From Time Out*
  A. Scene. Have "child" on the chair; he/she calls out, cries (actor can do this softly).
  B. Practice. The first time the "child" calls out, state the contingency: "Your time does not begin until you stop this calling out." If "child" continues, ignore it.

III. *"Child" Leaves the Time-Out Area (Chair)*
  A. Scene. Have "child" get off chair and come over to "parent."
  B. Practice. "Parent" takes "child" back, gives him two (imaginary) spanks, and states: "Each time you leave time out you will get two spanks."

IV. *"Child" Makes a Mess of the Time-Out Area*
  A. Scene. Make believe that the child has made a mess and is sitting on the chair when the "parent" comes in.
  B. Practice. Parent states: "Your time does not begin until you clean up this mess."

V. *Mealtime/Snacks*
  A. Scene. "Child" calls out: "Can I come out and eat? How about bringing me something—some water. I'm thirsty."
  B. Practice. "Parent" ignores this calling out. Note: Remember, "parent" has already informed the "child" of the consequence for calling out, so "parent" merely ignores and does not count time until it stops.

Now reverse roles, so that whoever just played the "child" now plays the "parent," so that everyone has a chance to practice the "parent" role. Run through all exercises again. (pp. 16–17)

A BCA who observed the role-playing provided immediate feedback to mothers about their performance and when necessary modeled those procedures that parents had not adequately grasped. Whenever verbal feedback is provided, the BCA must be certain that some specific explication of both correct and incorrectly performed behaviors is provided to the client in language that is readily understandable. In addition, *whenever some rather lengthy sequence of behavior is role-played, the BCA should break down the procedure into its sequential steps;* if possible, the clients should role-play each component step individually, with feedback immediately following each practice occasion. Among other procedures employed to provide feedback to role-playing clients are cueing system and videotape. Since both of these are often employed in other kinds of training situations, they will be discussed separately.

Cueing systems—Rather than verbally interrupt each element of a client's role performance, the BCA may choose to establish a cueing system by which he can communicate to the client that behavior is on or off target. If the BCA were to ask a mother to practice some important new skills with her child in the playroom, it might be impractical and rather frustrating to the parent to be interrupted on a frequent basis while interacting with her child. Instead, the BCA might use some system of hand signals (Hawkins, Peterson, and Bijou, 1966) or a light source that signals the parent when behavior is appropriate or inappropriate (e.g., light on = on target; light off = off target). An auditory stimulus (e.g., a tone or a click = off target), or, where finances allow, some means of providing verbal feedback by way of a transmitter-receiver system might also be helpful. Such systems (e.g., "bug in the ear") permit the BCA, who is positioned in another room, and observing through closed circuit television or one-way mirror, to transmit instructions as to the quality of the parent's role-playing efforts to a receiver the client has placed in the ear.

Such "bugs" thus allow the therapist to talk to the client and perhaps even to prompt him as to what might be said to another party within the process of interaction. Such instructions can be immediately incorporated into role-playing behavior without interrupting the role-playing sequence itself. "Bug in the ear" devices may be purchased from any one of a number of companies, or the BCA might employ rather inexpensive walkie-talkies, with the one built for clients' use having an output jack to the ear (Welch, 1966; Morris, 1974).

Videotape feedback (VTF)—Videotape playback of a client's behavior as a means of pointing out appropriate and inappropriate aspects of performance has been increasingly investigated within the literature (Bailey and Sowder, 1970; Eisler, Hersen, and Agras, 1973; Pollack, Nay, and Bailey 1973). While many practitioners allow clients to see their own behavior on videotape, the manner in which playback is employed seems to vary considerably. Most investigators have used VTF as a means of altering certain personality or self-concept measures, often within a traditional group therapy approach (e.g., Danet, 1967; Boyd and Sisney, 1967). Those who have employed videotape to alter targeted overt behaviors have provided feedback in such a variety of ways that an evaluation of the effectiveness of this approach does not seem warranted at this time (Bailey and Sowder, 1970). Often clients are asked merely to watch a videotape of themselves without being instructed to focus upon specific targeted behaviors (Paredes, Gottheil, Tausig and Cornelision, 1969). Geersma and Revich (1969) concluded: "If the video component is to be engaging to the subject, some type of coaching, structuring, or interactional processes involving a therapist seems to be required, or at least invited" (p. 221).

In evaluating the essential components of VTF, a few investigators have focused upon the importance of instructions. That is, will clients change if they are merely provided with verbal instructions to attend to some specific behavior in a future portrayal, or is the videotape feedback a vital adjunct to such instructions? Eisler, Hersen, and Agras (1973) conducted a series of analog studies on the utility of employing VTF in altering two targeted behaviors—looking and smiling—in a population of 12 married couples. They found that while VTF with instructions to focus on looking and smiling was significantly superior to presenting clients with irrelevant television, it was not superior to focused instructions alone in evoking behavioral change. The authors conclude:

> The independent use of videotape feedback as a therapeutic agent of behavioral change still remains questionable. . . . It does not seem likely from the results of this investigation that videotape feedback alone will produce sufficient cues for specific behavioral changes. (p. 557)

Pollock, Nay, and Bailey (1973) found VTF with instructions to be more effective in altering a physical behavior—hand gestures—than instructions alone. However, for a verbal targeted behavior (references to past experiences), VTF was not superior to the instructions condition. In addition, five nontargeted behaviors (no instructions to change) did not change for subjects in either condition, suggesting that focused instruction is an important prerequisite for VTF to be effective. In discussing the significant behavioral change promoted by VTF in nonverbal as opposed to verbal behavior, the authors hypothesized that playback provides a natural repetition of feedback we ordinarily receive when we talk. However, with physical behavior VTF provides a novel feedback, in that we do not have the opportunity of seeing ourselves and only receive feedback via proprioceptive (internal sensations) mechanisms. The authors conclude, "Thus we might expect subjects to profit more from VTF when a physical behavior is focused upon, then when verbal behavior is of interest" (p. 26).

It is not within the purview of the present text to fully elaborate the research that has been performed to evaluate VTF; however, those studies that focus on specific targeted behaviors seem to conclude that VTF is *maximally effective when subjects are specifically instructed to focus on certain aspects of their behavior.*

Certainly, in employing VTF to provide feedback as to a client's role performance, the BCA would want to carefully specify those behaviors that the client should attend to in viewing the videotape. When clients are asked to observe a videotape of themselves, with no instructions provided, it seems apparent that they may focus upon any one of an array of behaviors, or in the group situation they may focus upon the behavior of the other persons. Alternatively (or in addition), the client may be asked to self-observe and code targeted behaviors. If clients are asked to code their own behavior, they are forced to attend to specific behaviors and will probably not be distracted by some of the other behaviors occurring within the playback sequence. In addition, one could imagine using a cueing system (e.g., tone or light) to further focus the client's attention on specific elements of the behaviors that are presented. Thus, when the mother fails to provide reinforcement for some appropriate child behavior, or when the husband makes a very indirect communication to this wife, or when any appropriate or inappropriate behavior is engaged in, the BCA might use one of these cueing mechanisms to alert the client. We might term the situation where the client self-codes certain behaviors from the videotape *intrinsically directed feedback;* when the BCA cues the client as to important elements (verbally or via cueing system), it is *extrinsically directed feedback.*

Thus, VTF may provide the client with highly specific feedback as to precisely which appropriate and inappropriate behaviors were engaged in during a role-playing sequence. It would seem to be particularly important to employ VTF when the targeted behavior is a complex, particularly nonverbal behavior that the client may ordinarily be unable to observe—or in the special case where the client does not understand why specific verbal feedback is provided by the BCA. The provision of a videotape playback ensures that the client can see those behaviors, rather than listening to a verbal account that may not clearly identify specific elements for which behavioral change is desirable. Kanfer and Phillips (1970) consider VTF an important means of developing self-regulation within behavior. They state: "Conceptually these approaches provide the patient with objective information about his behavior that can become the cue for the self regulation action" (p. 438). They also point out:

A number of studies seem to indicate that fully adequate self-observation is rarely encountered in people, but the opportunity to observe one's own behavior objectively results in changes of relatively large magnitude in contrast to the minimal effects due to information about one's self that is verbal, abstract, and based on the observations of others. (p. 442)

In addition, VTF might allow clients to self-monitor the causal relationships that seem to predict their behavior. Thus, the client observes himself within the group situation becoming angry whenever another group member questions his opinion. The mother who can see herself providing reinforcement in the form of attention whenever her child whines and cries and the married couple who witness themselves consistently referring back to past behavior ("You've done it, too!") to avoid dealing with present behavior are examples of clients who might receive important diagnostic information from a VTF.

When clients are provided with specific instructions that do not alter targeted behaviors, VTF can serve as an important means of focusing client attention upon specific aspects of performance—and unlike therapist verbal feedback, VTF cannot be denied or misinterpreted. It is the opinion of the author that VTF may be most efficacious within this diagnostic process; however, *unless the client's current behavioral repertoire contains those elements required for desired behavioral change, such change is not likely to occur from a VTF exposure alone.* Following a VTF, the many therapeutic procedures already presented may be employed to expand the client's repertoire. Importantly, VTF may provide the client with the motivation to carry out treatments and with the means for assessing therapeutic change as it is repeatedly employed to record client progress.

Number of Trials

As with any learning situation, it would seem that the number of trials in which the client role-plays specific targeted behaviors would be an important predictor of the degree of learning that takes place. If a targeted behavior is complex, and particularly if it consists of an array of novel, nonrepertoire behaviors, the BCA should provide sufficient opportunities for role-playing beyond the first trial. The BCA and client should agree upon a carefully specified criterion of mastery when working on any new behavior. If the behavior is complex, criteria of mastery should be set up for each of the elements that make up the particular behavior. For example, in parent training perhaps the first criterion skill is a mother's use of direct communication with her child. She could be asked to role-play situations calling for direct communication, with the therapist (or another client) playing "child." The criterion for mastering this role-play sequence might be a certain number of direct communications used within a 20-minute role-play period, as observed by an independent observer.

The next step might include training the parent to use reinforcing comments, most notably those that are direct in nature, carefully identifying the specific behaviors the parent likes or dislikes. A certain number of direct reinforcements emitted/total reinforcements emitted could serve as the criterion of mastery. Once the mother reaches the criterion proportion of direct rewards/total rewards, the BCA may well direct the mother's role-playing efforts toward more sophisticated child interactive behaviors. Obviously, the number of trials necessary to achieve a given level of mastery depends upon the characteristics of the behavior as well as the client. In addition, if what we know about human verbal learning is accurate (see, for example, Underwood, 1954) it would seem desirable to instruct the client to *overlearn* certain important behaviors—that is, *to practice them beyond the level at which some criterion of mastery is achieved.* Because clients often forget what they are supposed to do in a situation within the "real world," it would seem that the provision of overlearning might decrease the possibility of forgetting and certainly would promote a well-learned, smooth execution of these important targeted events.

Practice in Natural Environment

Once a targeted behavior is mastered within the clinical setting, it would seem important that clients be encouraged to practice or role-play in their natural environment. Such practice, combined with careful client self-monitoring and record keeping, ensures that clients will be forced to engage in the behavior within the natural environment. In addition, it would seem that such practice will promote the possibility of generalization from the clinical to the natural environment. Perhaps such practice could occur covertly, with the client imaginally rehearsing the targeted behavior prior to an overt attempt at employing the skill in ordinary interaction.

Additionally, it may be valuable to actually *train the client within the natural setting*. For example, it may be useful to train the parent at home rather than have her role-play within the clinical setting. To the extent that important classes of stimuli within the environment come to control behavior, it would seem important to associate these newly learned behaviors with those stimuli present. To the extent that the client is encouraged to practice the behavior in the natural environment, or optimally to learn the behavior in the everyday situation, the potential of role-playing to promote permanent behavioral change would seem to be enhanced.

Provision of Reinforcement

Because role-playing is an activity that many clients have not engaged in prior to the therapeutic situation (not everyone played "Sy Crowell" in "Our Town" in high school), it would seem desirable that the BCA provide a good deal of reinforcement for the client's practice efforts. Not only should specific, appropriate targeted behaviors be reinforced within the role-playing situation, but the entire situation should be a positive one, with frequent encouragement offered by the BCA for the client's efforts. In addition, any practice efforts made by the client through "homework assignments" in the natural environment should also be reinforced by the BCA.

Contracting

As an example of how role-play procedures might be effectively communicated to a client, a contract to employ covert/overt rehearsal for a targeted assertive behavior is described in Fig. 7.1.

CASE EXAMPLES

Three case examples illustrate the manner in which role-playing has been employed within treatment. The first of these examples shows the use of role-playing as a diagnostic as well as treatment medium.

I, *Henry Addams* agree to perform the following homework at the designated times each and every day: 1) to imaginally rehearse asking my boss for a raise for at least five minutes of each hour of the day from when I get up until 6:00 p.m. in the evening. I agree that I will particularly rehearse maintaining eye contact, using a loud and firm voice, standing full in front/face-to-face, using the facial cues suggested in therapy on each and every imaginal rehearsal.

2) I also agree to overtly practice asking my boss for a raise at least once each evening, with my wife playing the role of "boss." Again I will attempt to act the scene as suggested in Number 1.

Also, I will write down a summary of each time I practice which will include the following: time, time begun, time terminated, and a written evaluation of the role play efforts. I will write down this information in the spiral notebook provided by Mr. Edwards. I realize that Mr. Edwards will look at my notebook at the beginning of my therapy session each week, and will not continue the therapy session if I have not completed my homework.

Signed: *Henry Addams*
Henry Addams

Witness: *John Edwards*
John Edwards
Psychologist Technician

Fig. 7.1
A "homework" contract for covert and overt rehearsal.

Example I: Increasing Assertive Responses

Eisler, Miller, and Hersen (1973) developed a "Behavioral Assertiveness Test" that includes a series of role-play situations designed to simulate real-life encounters. Each of these situations involves a male psychiatric patient and a female role model who plays the role of a wife, a sales clerk, waitress, etc., to "promote subject's responses." The 14 standard role-play situations employed are as follows:

1. *Narrator:* "You have just come home from work, and as you settle down to read the newspaper you discover that your wife has cut out an important article in order to get a recipe that is on the back of it. You really like to read the whole newspaper." *Role Model Wife:* "I just wanted to cut out a recipe before I forgot about it."
2. *Narrator:* "You have just punished your son for his inconsiderate behavior and told him that he must stay in his room for the rest of the afternoon. Your wife feels sorry for him and tells him that he can go out to play." *Role Model Wife:* "It's so nice outside; it's a shame to make him stay in his room."

3. *Narrator:* "You come home late one night, and your wife demands an explanation of why you are so late. As soon as you begin to explain she interrupts you and starts screaming about how inconsiderate you are." *Role Model Wife:* "I don't care what happened. You are the most inconsiderate person in the world for making me worry about you."

4. *Narrator:* "You have just bought a new shotgun, the one you've always wanted." *Role Model Wife:* "You didn't need another shotgun. You have too many now."

5. *Narrator:* "You have just come home from a hard day's work hoping to have a nice home-cooked meal. Instead you find that your wife has another frozen TV dinner in the oven." *Role Model Wife:* "I didn't have time to cook again today. I hope you don't mind having a frozen dinner."

6. *Narrator:* "Your wife has just told you that she just has to have another chair for the living room. You know that you can't afford it." *Role Model Wife:* "Please let's order the chair now. You promised we could have it."

7. *Narrator:* "You're in the middle of an exciting football game. Your wife walks in and changes the TV channel as she does every time you're watching a good game." *Role Model Wife:* "Let's watch the movie instead; it's supposed to be real good."

8. *Narrator:* "You've just put up a new shelf in the kitchen which has taken you some time to put together. Your wife comes in and makes some critical comments to the effect that you're not a very good carpenter." *Role Model Wife:* "Would you mind taking that awful-looking shelf down."

9. *Narrator:* "Your wife proudly presents you with a shirt she has bought you for your birthday. You don't like the color and would like to exchange it for another, but you don't want to hurt her feelings." *Role Model Wife:* "Here's your birthday present. I hope you like it."

10. *Narrator:* "You have just come home from a hard day's work dead tired. Your wife informs you that she has accepted an invitation for you both to visit some friends that evening. You are definitely not in the mood to go out." *Role Model Wife:* "I just knew that you'd like to visit tonight; let's go right after dinner."

11. *Narrator:* "You're in a crowded grocery store and are in a hurry. You've picked up one small item and get in line to pay for it when a woman with a shopping cart full of groceries cuts in line right in front of you." *Role Model Woman:* "You won't mind if I cut in here, will you? I'm late for an appointment."

12. *Narrator:* "You're in a drug store, and you buy something that costs 75 cents. You go to the cashier to pay for it and hand her a five-dollar bill. She rings up the sale and hands you 25 cents, change for only a dollar." *Role Model Cashier:* "Here's your change, sir."

13. *Narrator:* "You have just bought a new shirt and upon putting it on for the first time notice that several buttons are missing. You return to the sales clerk who sold it to you." *Role Model Clerk:* "May I help you, sir?"

14. *Narrator:* "You're in a restaurant with some friends. You order a very rare steak. The waitress brings a steak to the table which is so well done it looks burned." *Role Model Waitress:* "I hope you enjoy your dinner, sir." (p. 296)

The authors have developed a coding system that describes behaviors in three categories: (1) nonverbal behavior: duration of looking and smiles; (2) speech characteristics: duration of reply, latency of response, loudness of speech; fluency of speech; content and affect: (3) compliance content (e.g., does client resist or not resist a role model?), content requesting new behavior, affect. Thus, the authors can assess specific targeted behaviors as well as the overall degree of assertiveness displayed by the client as he role-plays each of the scenes. These same situations are then employed in treatment, with clients exposed to appropriate models and then asked to practice the behavior displayed by the model within the role-play situations. Thus, the "clinically contrived" role-play situations are employed both as an assessment procedure (Nay, 1976) and as a medium for treatment. One could imagine coming up with role-play situations that could be employed to diagnose how a client would behave in any number of important situations.

Example 2: Increasing Social Interaction

Investigators have employed role-playing procedures as a means of fostering social skill behaviors in a variety of client populations (Goldstein and Simonson, 1971; McFall and Marston, 1970; Goldstein, Martens, Hubben, Van Belle, Schaaf, Wiersma, and Goodhart, 1973). Gutride, Goldstein, and Hunter (1973) randomly assigned 30 "acute" and 57 "chronic" psychiatric clients diagnosed as having "social interaction difficulties" to either "structured learning therapy" or "no treatment conditions." Clients receiving "structured learning therapy" were assigned to a small group of five to eight clients that met three times each week over a four-week period. Four modeling tapes depicted several variants upon a basic social-interaction theme: tape 1 modeled appropriate interaction when another person approached the model; tape 2 showed the model initiating interaction with another person; tape 3 showed the model initiating interaction with a group of persons; tape 4 showed the model engaged in more complex interactions with relatives, friends, and business associates. Multiple models employed were similar to clients along an array of dimensions. Following exposure to the modeling tapes, clients were required to role-play important targeted behaviors suggested by the tapes:

Each of the four modeling tapes served as stimulus materials for three consecutive group meetings. Each session began with the modeling tape display, during which the group leaders actively drew attention to those model behaviors representative of effective social interaction. At frequent intervals the sound was turned off and the importance of nonverbal aspects of social interaction was highlighted, for example, forward leaning, eye contact, smiling, etc. Each tape was immediately followed by an "idiosyncratizing" group discussion in which the behaviors and circumstances depicted were related to each patient's personal experiences and environmental demands. The remainder of each session was devoted to role-playing both the depicted and personalized social interaction sequences. The role-playing enactments were themselves videotaped and played back to the group for comment and corrective feedback. Both the group leaders and, frequently, other group members provided the role-play enactor with frequent social reinforcement as his depiction more and more approximated that of the videotaped models. (p. 410)

Paper-and-pencil scales given pre- and posttraining as well as changes in independent observations of the following social skill behaviors were employed to evaluate the "structured learning therapy" approach.

Eight raters were trained in the use of a social interaction checklist developed by the present authors for this investigation, by means of which they could rate the following interactional patient behaviors: (a) eye contact, (b) forward leaning, (c) physical contact, (d) smiling, (e) initiates conversation, (f) responds to conversation, (g) talks 10 or more consecutive seconds, (h) seated alone, and (i) seated with others. Interrater reliability for these ratings, determined during three training sessions, yielded an overall percentage of agreement (taking raters two at a time in all possible pairings) of 85%. Patients were observed by these raters during mealtime for the two-week period immediately following the posttesting described above. Each rater was randomly assigned to rate 10 or 11 patients; each patient was observed for one 10-minute period. In addition, each rater completed social behavior ratings (using a semantic differential format) on each patient whom they had observed. These ratings were on the dimensions (a) general social skill, (b) interactions with others, and (c) social impact on others. (p. 411)

On all measures of client behavior the "structured learning therapy" approach promoted significantly greater client behavioral change than was observed for "no-treatment" controls or for clients receiving "psychotherapy."

In line with previous recommendations in the chapter regarding the importance of a hierarchy in employing role-play techniques, these authors concluded:

We noted earlier that our modeling displays were presented in a sequence we conceptualized as hierarchical, from the more simple, less threatening, and less demanding type of social interaction to that representing greater complexity, potential threat, and demanding more social skill. Inspection of our findings contains at least a suggestion that across treatments and type of patients, the simpler and perhaps less threatening skills were learned better than the more complex types of social interaction behaviors. To the extent that our inferences here regarding the simplicity and complexity of given behaviors are correct, it may be appropriate to consider the desirability in future implementations and evaluations of structured learning therapy of (a) a more extended series of sessions, (b) proportionately greater time and materials devoted to the more complex behaviors representative of the given skill, and/or (c) the augmentation of structured learning therapy with other intervention procedures. (p. 414)

Example 3: Increasing Verbal Self-Instructions

Meichenbaum (1973) has found that the overt behavior of a variety of clients is positively altered when they instruct themselves regarding task requirements. Meichenbaum and Cameron (1973) attempted to train a group of five clients diagnosed as "schizophrenic" to covertly rehearse and self-instruct themselves in performing tasks calling for careful attention to auditory and visual information. These "experimental" clients were compared to control clients not receiving this training (pseudotherapy and no-treatment controls). Treatments were performed as follows:

The cognitive self-guidance training technique proceeded as follows: first the experimenter modeled a task talking aloud while the subject observed; then the subject performed the same task while the experimenter instructed the subject aloud; next the subject was asked to perform the task again while instructing himself aloud; then the subject performed the task while whispering to himself (lip movements); and finally the subject performed the task covertly (without lip movements). The verbalizations which the experimenter modeled and the subject subsequently used included: (a) questions about the nature and demands of the task which were intended to encourage a general orienting preparatory set; (b) answers in the form of cognitive rehearsal and planning, designed to focus the schizophrenic's attention on relevant task requirements; (c) self-instructions in the form of self-guidance while performing the task to facilitate the maintenance of task-relevant attention and the inhibition of the schizophrenic's response to any internally or externally generated task irrelevancies; (d) coping self-statements to handle failure and frustration; and (e) self-reinforcement to maintain task perseverance, feedback and reward.

Two tasks were used during training. The first was the digit symbol task. Six forms which were not being used for assessment were employed for training. The following is an example of the experimenter's modeled verbalizations which the subject subsequently used (initially overtly, then covertly):

"What is it I have to do? I'm supposed to fill in these numbered boxes with symbols. Now look up at the top code of symbols and numbers. Good. The first symbol I have to look for goes with number 94. It's three lines. That's it. Now quickly to the next one, number 24 has a circle with a dot in it. Just continue this way until I finish the line. I'm getting it. Let me see how many I can get. Remember, I must go quickly, but also carefully."

Thus, the experimenter modeled thinking aloud by producing a set of task-relevant self-statements which acted both as a goad and a guide for performance. Over the course of each of the six parallel forms of the digit symbols test, the experimenter behaviorally and cognitively modeled for one line of 20 digits; then the subject tried doing a line with the experimenter instructing him; and eventually the subject self-instructed while completing a line. As the training session progressed, the schizophrenic's overt self-statements were faded to the covert level. (pp. 518–520)

The following is an example of the coping verbalizations that a client employed, first overtly, then covertly, on a digit symbol test:

"That tape recorder is trying to distract me. Just pay attention to what I have to do. Number 56 gets a circle. Good. Number 12, two lines. I can disregard the distraction. Number 15, a triangle. No that's wrong. That is okay, even if I make an error I can go on carefully and quickly. Good, I'm getting it. If I make up my mind distractions won't bother me." (p. 520)

As in the Gutride, Goldstein, and Hunter (1973) example, Meichenbaum and Cameron (1973) demanded increasingly more difficult behaviors as clients were moved from overt to covert practice in hierarchical fashion. The authors found experimental subjects to be significantly superior to controls in performing each of the tasks, particularly under conditions where they were distracted. Meichenbaum and his associates have successfully employed self-instructional procedures with a wide variety of populations (see Meichenbaum, 1975, for a review).

CHAPTER SUMMARY

Following the broad definition of role-playing as any overt or covert behavioral enactment, specific categories of role-play were presented. Within psychodrama, a client (protagonist) role-plays some life situation from his immediate past (scene), using members of the psychodramatic group to portray important characters. Following enactment of the scene, other members may model more appropriate ways of behaving for the client, and he then has the opportunity to try these out within the scene proper. Psychodrama seems to generate vivid, lifelike responses that may provoke generalization to real-life behavior. In Kelly's fixed role therapy a highly specific, fixed role is devised, and the client is asked to play this role within treatment. This is based upon Kelly's role construct theory, which suggests that by playing a fixed role, a client may alter the constructs that control his behavior. Finally, behavioral rehearsal encourages the client to role-play highly structured roles by receiving extensive modeling, cueing, and prompting from the therapist. It was pointed out that the three categories of role-playing are not mutually exclusive, and their major commonality seems to be that the client practices behavior divergent from his present behavior. There are many factors that might predict the outcome of role-playing efforts. Because the client is asked to "act," it would seem that there are specific array of skills necessary to get into the role of another. Suggestions for training in role-playing were offered. Also, the client must have the cognitive and motor ability to display behavior within the role-play situation to avoid practice of inappropriate behaviors that may be contrary to treatment goals. Many studies suggest that the probability of behavioral change is enhanced when a client is more active cognitively and motorily within the role-play effort. The client might be given freedom to portray his part to the extent that he is able to operate without structure.

Differences between overt or actual behavioral role-playing and covert or cognitive/imaginal role-playing were presented. In covert role-playing the client imagines himself engaging in the targeted behavior exclusively within his imagination, and no overt behavior is produced. At present the research findings regarding the differential effectiveness of overt and covert role-playing are quite mixed. The specific target behavior will be an important determinant of the utility of each.

Clients should receive explicit feedback as to the worth of their role-play efforts. Verbal feedback is most typically employed, but the BCA might use some system of tones, lights, or a "bug in the ear" approach to cueing as an alternative. Also, a videotape playback of client behavior may be employed. When videotape feedback is employed, clients should be instructed to focus on specific aspects of their behavior or to self-observe and perhaps code the videotape. It was hypothesized that videotape feedback will not alter a client's behavior unless the client's current repertoire contains those behavioral elements required for desired behavioral change.

It was suggested that the BCA and client carefully construct criteria of mastery for each step within a role-play hierarchy and that the client be encouraged to perhaps overlearn important behaviors. Also, it was hypothesized that the number of training trials is an important predictor of client behavioral change and maintenance of that change. Finally, clients should be encouraged to practice within the natural setting those behaviors mastered via role-playing in the clinical setting. As with any client efforts, a systematic program of reinforcement should encourage behavioral change made within the role-play situation, and be employed to maintain behavioral gains. Finally, case examples were presented, including an important class of self-instructional procedures taught using role-playing.

Chapter 8

Self-Control

Much of the material presented within the previous chapters has delineated attempts by the BCA to employ extrinsic control of client-targeted behaviors. The reader may recall that many of these treatment formats presented options for gradually transferring control from some external agent to the client. Perhaps Chapter 5 is the best example of a treatment approach that strongly emphasizes *client* control of reinforcement contingencies through covert processes. Treatment mechanisms that rely exclusively upon some external agent to control client behavior do not promote the kind of independent, self-directed approach to dealing with problem situations that we often include within our definition of "adjusted." Also, certain problems are not readily controllable by extrinsic agents or mechanisms. Among these Kanfer (1975) has defined the following: (1) behaviors such as sexual fantasies or acts or one's thoughts about some event may not be sufficiently observable by a extrinsic agent; (2) incidental or infrequent behaviors may be difficult or impossible for an extrinsic agent to monitor; (3) certain verbal targeted behaviors (e.g., a person's self-reactions or self-evaluation) may remain hidden from an observer, while the client's other productive activities mask the problem; (4) the client must ultimately assume responsibility for his behavior, particularly when the extrinsic sources of feedback are no longer present.

In reviewing the personality theories that have been presented from many orientations over the last half-century or so, it becomes apparent that most writers have attempted to deal with the idea of "self" in some fashion. Self is viewed as "ego" (Freud, 1933), an individual's phenomenal view of the environment (Rogers, 1951), the array of cognitions that make up a person's "construction" of his surroundings (Kelly, 1958), or the sum total of a person's learning experiences (Ullman and Krasner, 1969). In fact, the term *self* has been specifically employed by such divergent writers as Jung (1928), Sullivan (1947), and Rogers (1951). While the language varies a good deal, the term *self* often defines that conscious, aware aspect of a person's overall behavior that is involved in making choices and generally regulating the manner in which one moves about his world.

While the early writings of experimentalists attempting to apply the procedures of the laboratory to human behavior may have tended to ignore self in favor of more peripheral stimulus-response explanations of behavior, this certainly has not been true of the literature within the past decade. While certain critics have attempted to classify behaviorally oriented therapists as employing a limited peripheral and simplistic view of the individual (e.g., Breger and McGaugh, 1965), the vast majority of behaviorally oriented researchers are attempting to employ procedures that strongly emphasize the *individual's* "self-control" of the assessment and treatment process and thus function within the phenomenal-behavioral model presented in Chapter 1.

DEFINITIONS

When extrinsic controls are employed a systematic move from extrinsic to self-control is often incorporated into treatment planning. While the terms *self-control* (Kanfer and Phillips, 1970), *self-management* (Mahoney, 1972, 1974), *self-monitoring* (McFall, 1970), *self-directed* (Harris, 1969), as well as the general term *self-regulation* have been employed by a variety of investigators, these various labels most typically refer to the possible means by which a client gains control of important targeted behaviors. Behaviorists would not often employ such terms as *consciousness, ego,* or *ideal self,* and most typically would not posit *self* as a structure, process, or part of one's personality, but they have employed the term *self* to define behaviors that the individual may be aware of that are employed to direct and manage ongoing behavior. Skinner (1953) has summarized this succinctly:

When a man controls himself, chooses a course of action, thinks out the solution to a problem, or strives toward an increase in self-knowledge, he is *behaving*. He controls himself precisely as he would control the behavior of anyone else— through the manipulation of variables of which behavior is a function. (p. 228)

The behaviors employed by the individual to manage his own behavior thus have become the focus of attempts to explain and define treatment strategies regarding self-control (Thoreson and Mahoney, 1974; Kanfer, 1975).

Ferster (1965) has defined specific classes of self-control. According to his model efforts at self-control are typically directed toward those behaviors that ultimately lead to aversive consequences for an individual, while they might provide immediate gratification. For example, cigarette smoking, overeating, avoidance of required task behaviors (e.g., studying, writing a term paper) may all lead to immediately gratifying consequences for the individual, but in the long run such behavior may lead to dire consequences. Self-control may then be directed toward controlling the frequency with which such behaviors are displayed by the individual, thus decreasing the probability of ultimate aversive consequences. For Ferster,

the existence of the self-control performances depends upon contingencies in the milieu, just as with any other performance in the individual's repertoire. The existence of behaviors by which an individual may control his own eating depends upon the ultimate aversive consequences in the individual's milieu of being overweight. If, in fact, there are no aversive consequences for the individual as the consequence of being overweight, then no contingency exists by which the self-controlled behaviors may be maintained. (p. 21)

Another class of self-controlling behaviors has to do with the individual's performance of behaviors that may not be immediately gratifying but may ultimately increase the individual's effectiveness (and reinforcements?). Thus, when individuals practice the guitar or piano, attend a rather boring psychology course, read a textbook in behavioral intervention or engage in other behaviors that may not be immediately gratifying, we might say that they are engaging in relatively less reinforcing behaviors so that the probability of reinforcement is increased at some future time.

The academic behaviors that many individuals quite ordinarily engage in are often important components of the self-control strategies to be described in this chapter. The student who sets up a study schedule; monitors study time; outlines material to increase its comprehension; self-instructs himself to study or complete a required paper; reinforces himself with a "night out on the town" following the successful completion of an exam; feels good and thinks positive thoughts about himself following the compliment of an instructor; and finds that studying is optimal when performed in the same location under low-interference conditions—is employing many of the procedures that form the foundation of a self-control program.

Another form of self-control suggested by Ferster involves the procedures by which an *individual alters his physical environment to achieve control over some important behavior*. He gives the example of the worker who moves to a new community to obtain a job that better employs his particular skills. Other examples are the student who studies in the same location each evening so that the stimuli present become associated with studying via stimulus-control mechanisms (thus facilitating studying) and the obese person who limits eating to the kitchen table to avoid stimuli about the house that have become associated with eating (e.g., watching television, reading, talking on the telephone).

A comprehensive working definition of self-control has been put forth by Goldfried and Merbaum (1973), who have defined this process along the following lines:

1. An important prerequisite for self-control is that a *goal or outcome of one's behavior is defined by the individual himself* and not by some extrinsic agent. While the individual may in fact be influenced by some other factor, the choice of goal remains an individual decision.

2. The specific behaviors and strategies employed to exert self-control must be systematically and consciously arranged by the individual either to increase or to decrease the frequency of some targeted behavior. Along the lines suggested by Ferster (1965), the individual may attempt self-regulation or alteration of the physical environment to enhance self-controlling attempts. Importantly, the individual should be able to verbalize the goal and to specify each of the procedural steps employed to achieve it.

3. The authors define self-control in a functional fashion—that is, by the consequences of a client's behavior, not by the procedures employed. Thus, we would say that self-control is achieved when the individual engages in some targeted goal behavior that is the result of a systematic series of steps directed toward that goal.

4. As is stated by many other writers (Skinner, 1953; Kanfer and Phillips, 1970; Bandura, 1969), self-control refers to a specific response or class of responses relevant to the achievement of some present goal; it may not be regarded as a structure or a process of one's personality.

5. In opposition to the various existential writers who emphasize the self-directed choices that we each make in achieving certain goals (e.g., Fromm, 1941) the authors assume that self-control does not emerge from some innate potentiality or hierarchy of needs within the individual, but is acquired through experience which occurs either by trial and error or more systematically.

Following a discussion of client motivational variables, this chapter will present an outline of component steps that the BCA might entertain in constructing a self-control program.

CLIENT MOTIVATION

The reader may wonder why an individual who is failing to exert control over some important behavior will seek out the BCA in the first place. It has already been mentioned that many people fail to exert self-control over behaviors that result in immediate and frequently potent reinforcement, often failing to take heed of possible aversive consequences. To take a contemporary example, many professionals regard obesity as one of the important problems of our present society (U.S. Public Health Service, 1970). It has been estimated that there are from 40 to 80 million obese Americans. Recent medical findings indicate that overweight may result in an array of serious conditons such as hypertension, diabetes, kidney dysfunction, heart failure, and increased susceptibility to infectious disease. Crisp, Douglas, Ross, and Stonehill (1970) found that obese children suffer more health-related problems such as tonsillectomies, while Tracey and Harper (1971) found more respiratory problems among overweight youngsters than among children of normal weight. If the data are at all accurate, it is apparent that we are not successfully reducing the proportion of our citizenry that is overweight. While a small number of obese individuals may blame metabolic and other physical/disease factors for their excess weight, the vast majority simply consume more calories than they burn (Mayer, 1968).

We might say that most obese individuals have not learned to self-regulate their eating behaviors and /or to adjust their activity levels (Mahoney, 1975) to match consumption. Because of the immediate gratification associated with eating (or smoking or high rate ingestion of alcohol), it may be difficult for an extrinsic agent (e.g., physician, BCA, "disgusted spouse") to motivate the individual to alter this behavior and exert self-control.

In fact, one might wonder about the success of intervention when it is applied to an individual who is not motivated to change (e.g., our prison populations), and one can readily see the potential ethical as well as practical problems involved. It is the author's opinion that the motivation to exert self-control must come from the individual himself. Typically, a prospective client is motivated to engage in a self-control program by many and varied contingencies that operate upon him in the natural environment. For the obese individual, motivation to reduce may come from certain punitive consequences of overweight. Thus, the individual may be motivated to decrease socially mediated punishment in the form of such comments as "Look how fat ____ is becoming" and "You mean you can fit into a size __?" Or significant information regarding possible aversive consequences (finding out one has diabetes, heart disease, or hypertension), or the threat of dire social consequences (a spouse who says, "If you don't reduce, I'm leaving you") may motivate the individual. Obviously, it is impossible to catalog the array of such natural consequences that might motivate a client.

In some cases the client engages in behavior that violates some societal code and is directed by a legal body to alter behavior related to the ingestion of alcohol or drugs, to stealing, or to other socially "undesirable" acts such as exposing oneself and rape. The BCA may very well question the extent to which such extrinsically directed clients are willing to participate in any program of behavioral change.

Alternatively, the increasing inefficiency that a client observes in his task- or goal-related activities may generate sufficient anxiety regarding future performance to motivate him to control his behavior. Thus, the student who finds it difficult to study, the bookkeeper who finds it increasingly difficult to concentrate on computational tasks, or the salesman who finds the completion of his daily calls to require greater amounts of time than in the past might become candidates for a self-control program.

Perhaps it is the relative balance of positive reinforcement for one's uncontrolled behavior to punitive feedback for engaging in that behavior that determines the probability of an individual's submitting to treatment voluntarily. Kanfer and Phillips (1970) have made the plight of this category of clients very definite: "The vacillations encountered when a person initiates a program that may eventually require changes in the distribution of available reinforcers and the postponement of some, can often be observed in the behavior of making voluntary contact with the therapist" (p. 417). They emphasize the importance of the client's making a commitment in the form of an agreement with a spouse or friend as well as an appointment for therapy. In fact, the use of verbal and written contracts with self-controlling clients is frequently reported as a means of maintaining motivation both initially and throughout the treatment program.

The presentation to follow will provide an *outline of procedures* that are typically included within a self-control program. Many of the procedures presented within previous chapters will be specifically related to self-control strategies, and the order of presentation will reflect the manner in which successive steps might optimally be entertained.

ASSESSMENT AND DEFINITION OF GOALS

The client may report an inability to control certain behaviors in an imprecise and global fashion. For example, the obese client may report that he "eats all the time, eats everything, and just can't seem to control his eating." The BCA may wish independently to observe the client's eating behavior—if that is possible. For example, if the client is functioning within some controlled setting such as a ward or cottage, it may be possible to ask staff members who interact with the client during the day to keep a record of the frequency with which the client ingests certain foods, and more specifically to monitor the client's eating during mealtime. As an example of the extensiveness that should characterize data collection, staff members may be asked to record the amount of food consumed; some measure of the number of bites per mouthful of food; the speed with which the client ingests food; the types of food the client ingests (e.g., high-protein versus high-carbohydrate foods); the amounts and types of fluids ingested. If some fixed amount of food is available to the client, a measure could be taken of the amount of food left after the client has finished eating. If the client is seen on an outpatient basis, certain family members might be asked to provide the same kind of information.

The use of independent observational methods is often impossible with many of the behaviors that a client may wish to control. The opportunity for independent observers to be present on those occasions when a client engages in the targeted behavior may be limited, particularly if a client moves rather freely about an institutional setting or is seen on an outpatient basis. However, independent observation is a means of collecting information that may be a good deal more reliable than client self-reports or record-keeping.

Self-monitoring

Regardless of the possibilities for independent assessment, the BCA will typically require the adolescent or adult client to self-gather information necessary for treatment planning. In addition, one or more behaviors (targets) related to the client's "control" problem will be self-monitored by the client. Simple frequencies counts are readily collected with a wrist (golf) counter, check-marks on a card, or by employing any method of noting occurrence (e.g., transferring coins from one pocket to another, making one tear/occasion on a 3x5 card, etc.). Optionally, written diarylike records collected in a notebook permit more extensive data collection.

For example, Mahoney, Moura, and Wade (1973) asked subjects to record their weight on a chart and to maintain a behavioral diary in which they were asked to record the frequency of "fat thoughts" (discouraging self-verbalizations); thins thoughts (encouraging self-verbalizations); instances of indulgence (eating of fattening foods or overeating); and instances of restraint (refusing fattening food or reducing food intake). In attempting to reduce smoking, Chapman, Smith, and Layden (1971) required clients to register on a wrist counter each cigarette lighted, and then recorded the total number of cigarettes smoked daily on a graph. Others have asked clients to save cigarette butts as a measure of cigarettes smoked.

Many investigators have found that self-monitoring alone may reduce the targeted client behavior (McNamara, 1972; McFall, 1970; McFall and Hammen, 1971). McFall and his associates have evaluated such "reactivity," focusing on the manner in which instructions are provided to the clients. In two studies (McFall, 1970; Gottman and McFall, 1972) it was found that when clients were asked to monitor the urge to engage in some behavior, the behavior decreased as a result of self-monitoring; however, when clients were asked to self-monitor the targeted behavior itself, the behavior paradoxically increased in frequency. In opposition to these findings McFall and Hammen (1971) found no significant difference when clients were asked to monitor either a resistance to smoking a cigarette or their inability to resist. It would seem that additional research is necessary to further specify how the specific target of one's self-monitoring efforts (e.g., urge versus overt behavior) differentially affects the frequency of the overt targeted behavior.

Frequently stated reasons for instigating client self-monitoring include the following:

1. A sufficiently extensive sample will be provided so that a baseline as to the frequency of the behavior or some important parameter of it (e.g., amount of food consumed by food category) can be obtained prior to treatment. Of course, such baseline data is the necessary preliminary step to careful evaluation of the effectiveness of treatment.

2. Important information regarding those specific variables that control the targeted behavior will be obtained. Whenever possible, some form of client-written records should be employed so that the client notes the *times, places,* and *specific conditions* within which the targeted behavior occurs. This information as to controlling variables will provide the foundation upon which treatment planning can be based. Are there certain times at which eating occurs at high rates? Are there certain places where the client frequently eats that may be associated with eating? Are there specific conditions within which eating occurs (e.g., while reading, watching TV, studying)? In addition, the BCA may well ask clients to record those *cognitive/physical covert behaviors* that seem to be a part of the "urge" to eat. It may be important to know what that "urge" feels like to clients in terms of specific behavioral referents, so that they may identify the "urge" in the future and thus perhaps apply some procedure to avoid it. A diary description made at certain times during the day when the targeted behavior is at a high rate or a low rate provides a complete record of client activities and places the targeted behavior within the context of time, situation, and conditions. In addition, important information as to high-rate activities (which may serve as reinforcers within a Premack paradigm) as well as possibilities for negative consequences may also be identified.

3. The client is trained to self-observe systematically and carefully those important covert and overt behaviors associated with the "control" problem. Within the theoretical models of Kanfer (e.g., Kanfer, 1970, 1975) as well as Mahoney and Thoreson (1974), self-monitoring is a necessary prerequisite for self-controlling responses. Self-monitoring permits the individual to identify ongoing behavior and to self-evaluate it in terms of standards or criteria previously learned. These self-evaluations would of course be placed on a continuum from very negative (e.g., very

dissatisfied with performance) to very positive and would serve as the basis for self-directed feedback. The reader may recall Kanfer's paradigm for self-reinforcement/self-punishment presented in some detail in Chapter 5. Thus, the obese client might identify the piece of cake just eaten (self-monitoring) as being too calorie-laden for her diet (self-evaluation) and proceed to self-punish herself with negative self-statements (e.g., "only a pig would eat that much," "terrible!") or some self-imposed consequence (e.g., skipping dinner). Regardless of theoretical orientation, variants of monitoring, evaluation, and differential self-rewards/punishments figure heavily within most self-control programs, perhaps attesting to the utility of Kanfer's model.

It has been the experience of the author that many clients fail to complete self-monitoring assignments, often because they are required to perform elaborate and time-consuming record-keeping tasks. Given that such clients have already demonstrated their inability to assert control over important classes of behavior, it makes sense that the often nonreinforcing, mundane activities of self-monitoring may prove to be a set of behaviors that they will avoid.

To increase the probability of client self-monitoring, procedures should be systematically geared to clients and their ordinary life situations. It is strongly suggested that the BCA initially require only minimal record-keeping (for obese clients perhaps weight recorded each day at the same time). By making minimal initial demands on clients, the BCA increases the probability that they will perform the recording assignment. If a client fails to perform even a minimal record-keeping task, it is most important that the BCA and client sit down together and talk over the specific problems that hindered the client's efforts. In addition, the specific requirements for monitoring should be carefully written out so that the client clearly knows what is asked and can refer to it as necessary between treatment sessions. Often with less motivated clients, this written explication of "homework" is developed into a contract wherein the client agrees to perform certain self-monitoring activities. This initial contract provides a nice model for structuring client and therapist responsibilities within treatment, and may be modified on a continuous basis as the client is increasingly able to entertain additional responsibilities. An example of an initial self-monitoring contract is provided in Fig. 8.1.

The reader may notice that the self-monitoring contract includes (1) data specifying when the contract begins; (2) a highly specific explication of those behaviors the client is asked to engage in; (3) the specific times, situations, and conditions during which the client is to engage in self-monitoring; (4) the positive consequences that will accrue from adequate completion; (5) the punitive consequences that will accrue if self-monitoring is not carried out (the client must be able to exert control over this behavior as in, say, TV watching); and (6) the signatures of both the client and the therapist (often the signatures of witnesses such as spouses, other family members, and friends are also included). The steps listed make up the primary components of any written contract.

The initial step of self-monitoring represents an extremely important component of any self-control program, and it may provide important prognostic data as to the degree to which the client will participate in later, more demanding self-mediated efforts.

I, _____*Fanny Mae*_____, *agree to self-record my*

ingestion of <u>any</u> *solid food or liquid in the following manner, beginning*

on ___*12-26-75*___ *, and continuing until* ___*1-16-76*___ :

(a) *I will record the* <u>category</u> *of food eaten; the* <u>amount</u>

(*in ounces*); *the* <u>time</u> *of ingestion; and the*

<u>activity</u> *that I was engaged in.*

(b) *I will carry out my recordings* <u>throughout the day</u>.

(c) *I am permitted to stay up after 11:00 PM if I complete*

(a) and (b).

(d) *If I do not complete (a) and (b) I must retire to*

bed with all lights out by 11:00 PM.

SIGNED: _____*Fanny Mae*_____

WITNESS: _____*James Mae*_____

WITNESS: _____*Marie Sage*_____

Fig. 8.1
A contract for self-monitoring of food ingestion.

Pinpointing goals

Following this initial period of assessment the BCA is ready to define with the client the specific goals of a self-control program. If assessment has been properly carried out, client and therapist will now have sufficient information to define the following:

1. *The frequency of the targeted behavior* (e.g., studying, eating, smoking) *within and across days.*

2. Those *times* when the behavior occurs at a high rate or at a low rate.

3. The *specific locations* within the client's environment where the behavior occurs at a high rate or at a low rate.

4. The *conditions* within which the behavior occurs at a high rate or at a low rate (e.g., while watching television, listening to records, reading, working on a manuscript).

5. Any *persons* who seem to be consistently present when the behavior occurs and might hold cue value for the client.

6. The *reinforcements* that motivate the client to engage in the behavior. As an example, for an obese client the important reinforcements may be in terms of smell, specific tastes, a certain feeling within the abdomen, and so on. The BCA ascertains the specific foods (or cigarette brands, kinds of alcohol) that hold greatest reinforcement value for the client.

7. The *cognitive and physiological events* that define the "urge" to engage in the behavior.

8. Some notion of *successful and unsuccessful procedures* the client has employed to deal with the behavior in the past.

9. From *case history information,* some notion of the course of the targeted behavior over time, as well as specific life situations that may have facilitated or inhibited this behavior in the past. Any medical history data of relevance would of course be included here (this might be particularly important with an obese client or a smoker).

While these data categories are certainly not all-inclusive, sufficient data within each would place the BCA and client in an informed position to decide: What are the goals of a potential program of self-control? It has already been emphasized that specific methods of treatment will not be readily suggested from inexplicit or globally defined goals. Thus, while "weight loss" is certainly the ultimate desirable goal for an obese client, the strategies of treatment will be defined by the specific categories of behavior pinpointed for change (that presumably will lead to the ultimate goal of reducing the client's girth). This pinpointing process may require a careful consideration of potential targets from among a multiplicity of options, and must be undertaken with careful analysis of the assessment data and within the context of the client's resources. To illustrate the heterogeny of possibilities for targets, our obese client will be employed as an example.

Let us assume that the client's diary entries include a high proportion of foods that are rich in carbohydrates (which most experts say are fattening). One goal might be to train him to make a discrimination between those foods rich in carbohydrates and those that hold proportionately greater protein. Some mechanism of feedback and reinforcement could thus alter his eating habits in the direction of a high-protein diet. Here the goal is not a reduction in overall food consumption but merely a change in the category of foods consumed. A similar goal might be merely to reduce the client's consumption of certain snack/junk foods, while substituting more appropriate, low-caloric/carbohydrate foods as snacks. Thus, the client might be instructed to substitute celery, tomatoes, carrots, diet beverages, and other nonfattening foods for cake, candies, ice cream, and sodas. Within this limited goal the client could be asked to monitor the specific snack items eaten between meals.

The client might report that it is easier for him to avoid eating when he works in his darkroom, on handicrafts, or engages in any task that requires careful attention to hand movements. Realizing that such activities seem to be *incompatible with* eating, another goal might be to schedule the client's free time so that these kinds of activities supplant the television watching, reading, and other activities that seem to be associated with consumption of junk foods. Other goals might focus on the specific stimulus characteristics that seem to trigger an "urge" to eat. Perhaps because he has previously consumed snack foods while watching television, the client reports that he is literally unable to get through the evening news without breaking out a bag of popcorn or a gigantic carton of pretzels. In fact, many locations and activities within the house (lying in bed, talking on the telephone, reading in the study) seem to trigger an urge to eat. (He reports that he has even taken to hiding a bag of licorice in the glove compartment of his car, which he consumes on the way to and from his job.) One goal might be to narrow stimulus control by requiring that the client eat only at the kitchen table in his home. Regardless of the degree to which his eating at the table interrupts television, reading, or a phone conversation, he may consume foods *only* in that location, so that the other locations soon lose their cue value for eating.

Another set of goals might require the client to control the *amount* of food intake systematically by altering his eating habits (e.g., "chew each bite *x* number of times," "pause between mouthfuls"). In a similar fashion a number of investigators have suggested that it might be more practical to train alcoholics to consume alcohol more appropriately—in small sips and without gulping, since many alcoholics are forced by their job and social obligations to drink "socially"—than to require abstention. Of course, this same kind of a goal could apply to any kind of behavior to be controlled.

Another goal might be to alter the specific cognitive referent of the urge to eat by way of covert sensitization procedures, as described in a previous chapter. Each time the client experiences the cognition associated with an "urge," he might be asked to imagine an array of aversive images (e.g., he is 250 pounds, in a white bathing suit at the beach, surrounded by a pointing, laughing audience). The goal here is not to alter specific behaviors associated with eating, to alter the environment, or even to substitute incompatible food or behaviors, but to alter the "urge" itself, so that it will not occur for specific food categories or as frequently. Presumably, if the urge to eat is reduced, the specific occasions of eating might also be reduced, again leading to our goal of weight reduction. As a last example, a program might concentrate exclusively on increasing our client's level of activity so that more calories are metabolized.

Each of these delimited goals (and potential others) seems very readily to predict a course of treatment. It thus is important that BCA and client carefully state the *specific* goals of treatment rather than letting such goals be rather loosely couched as the client engages in a "grab bag" of self-control procedures. Most frequently, self-control programs include multiple goals and an array of procedures designed to move the client toward these goals.

While many options are available, it is obvious that goals defined for the client must be practical, within the client's capability to implement, and certainly in consonance with the client's wishes. The BCA *and the client* should sit down together, review the assessment data collected, and together define some realistic and practical goals for the self-control program. It is particularly important for the BCA to remember that goal attainment within treatment is often very reinforcing for clients, and not being able to carry out some treatment may be experienced as a punishment. Perhaps goals could be placed within a hierarchy, so that those goals that the client may address more easily will come before goals that call for skills the client has not yet attained. Such a program ensures that the client will be initially reinforced for efforts at exerting self-control. In our example of the obese client an initial goal might require him to cut down on only one category of foods, rather than attempting to cut out all snack foods at once. Even if the client is systematically asked to move toward total abolition of certain snack items over a period of a week or two, this is preferable to requiring complete abolition on a given day. The BCA is able to monitor client success in meeting short-term goals and can thus offer additional challenges as the client is capable of meeting them.

METHODOLOGICAL OPTIONS

Once targets have been pinpointed, a variety of method variants are available for program inclusion.

Stimulus Manipulations

It has already been mentioned that certain stimuli within the client's environment may serve to maintain the client's inappropriate behavior through previous association. Approaches to altering such stimulus factors involve either physically altering the environment or altering the individual's access to the environment (narrowing stimulus control).

Altering the environment—In certain cases the environment may be constructed so that the probability of inappropriate behavior is high. For example, an obese client who worked in a bakery would certainly be exposed to inappropriate foods on a frequent basis. The smoker who works in an office where his co-workers constantly smoke cigarettes, or who lives in a house that is filled with ashtrays and packages of cigarettes, would be another example. Often it is impractical to restrict the client from functioning within certain environments, and so some alteration of the environment is the only approach possible.

The obese client whose cupboards are filled with every conceivable kind of snack food might be asked to remove all of these inappropriate snacks from his home and to refrain from purchasing such items in the future. The availability of these items, which may increase the probability of undesired eating behavior, is thus dramatically reduced. While this doesn't train the client to more appropriately consume such items when they are available, it does provide an initial environment within which the client may realistically avoid consumption.

Smoking clients may be asked to reduce the frequency with which they attend parties or engage in other social behaviors where they are apt to be exposed to other individuals consuming large quantities of cigarettes. The reader will recall the notion of social facilitation presented in Chapter 6 (Bandura, 1969). By watching a model engage in a certain behavior, the observer may be faciliated to engage in that behavior. Anyone who has watched a television actor consume a glass of beer or munch on the latest snack food, and has immediately retreated into the kitchen to consume a similar product, has been socially facilitated by the "symbolic" model on television. In altering the environment the client may be asked to turn off the television set or change to another station when some highly appealing presentation related to the target behavior occurs.

It may occur to the reader that removing all of the "temptations" does not help the client to exert controls when those ordinary elements are present. However, by providing the client with the opportunity to begin exerting self-control over certain aspects of his behavior (e.g., his eating during mealtime) without the constant interference of an array of instigating cues, the BCA increases the likelihood of initial client successes. In addition, all the behaviors that have become associated with such items (e.g., searching the house for food, smoking a cigarette while watching television, raiding the cookie jar) should become less dominant within the client's repertoire of behaviors. Once the client is capable of exerting self-control, certain of these items might be reintroduced (e.g., our "smoking" client may attend a small party with friends who smoke) so that self-controlling responses can be practiced. In similar fashion, by constructing the environment to favor appropriate alternative behaviors, such as having only high protein foods available for the obese person, the probability of these behaviors is enhanced.

Whenever possible, the BCA should systematically evaluate the environment within which the client functions, rather than relying upon the client's self-report of that environment. Perhaps the BCA and client can physically move about the setting and alter it together or make plans to do so. Setting alterations might be specified in the form of a verbal or written contract.

Limiting access to the environment—One approach employed by a number of investigators (Ferster, Nurnberger, and Levitt, 1962; Goldiamond, 1965; Stuart, 1967) is to limit client access to certain locations within the environment when the client engages in the targeted behavior. Ferster et al. (1962) termed this "narrowing stimulus control"; very simply, clients are asked to restrict their eating, smoking, studying, to one specified location. Thus, the client who is used to eating while listening to records, watching television, lying in bed, or riding in an automobile may be asked to limit eating exclusively to the kitchen table. An excellent example of this approach was reported by Goldiamond (1965), where the procedure of narrowing stimulus control was applied to a young man who wished to reduce overeating:

The initial strategy for slimming the young man was to bring his eating behavior under the control of food alone, since food is normally not available as a stimulus. He was instructed to eat to his heart's content and not to repress the desire. He was, however, to treat food with the dignity it deserved. Rather than eating while he watched television or while he studied, he must devote himself to eating when he ate. If he wished to eat a sandwich, he was to put it on a plate and sit down and devote himself to it. Thus, reinforcing consequences such as watching television or reading would be withdrawn when he engaged in the behaviors of preparing the food, eating, and cleaning up. Responding to the refrigerator in between meals resulted in withdrawal of such consequences, as did going to the refrigerator while watching television. Television, studying, and other stimuli would lose their control of initiating the chain of conditions that terminated in eating. Within one week, the young man cut out all eating between meals. "You've taken the fun out of it," he said to me. We then worked on the contents of the meals as well, and he stopped attending sessions. I met him about three months later; he was considerably slimmer and remarked that he needed neither me nor the clinical psychologist to solve his problems. He could handle them himself. (p. 855)

Goldiamond (1965) also reports upon a young woman who was asked to restrict her studying to a single desk within her home. Writing letters, reading a comic book, daydreaming, or other activities were not permitted at this desk—only studying. She was informed that it was desirable that studying come under the control of her desk, and she reported that she was able to spend increasingly longer periods studying under this program of stimulus control.

The specific conditions to which stimulus control is limited should maximize the probability that optimal behavior will occur. Thus, in the studying example the therapist would want to carefully evaluate the specific conditions of the desk and the room where it was placed. Sufficient lighting should be available, distracting noises should be absent, and a time schedule should be agreed upon that ensures that the client is alert and willing to study when she sits at the desk. For example, if the client began her study efforts late at night and consistently fell asleep at the desk, the desk might become associated with drowsiness.

In some cases the area to which stimulus control is limited is made as uncomfortable as possible, to preclude the possibility of reinforcement occurring within the situation. In applying a program of limiting stimulus control to reducing the frequency of his parents' cigarette smoking, the author restricted all smoking to a rather small bathroom within the home. The "clients" reported that it was most uncomfortable and unpleasant to interrupt television programs, reading, or ordinary conversation to "race back to the bathroom" to smoke a cigarette. Within about two weeks the mean frequency of cigarettes consumed dropped from about 50 to 20 per day, and was maintained at that rate for a number of months. Thus, limiting stimulus control succeeded in drastically reducing the targeted behavior but not eliminating it, as there was apparently still sufficient reinforcement for smoking the 20 cigarettes to maintain that behavior.

Attempts at limiting access to the environment will be maximally successful when the client receives a rationale for his efforts, is well motivated, and receives a good deal of reinforcement within the therapy situation for his efforts (which may be mediated by some contract). Family members or others in the natural environment may quite beneficially provide such encouragement for client efforts.

Incentive Systems

To maintain client motivation it would seem desirable to include a systematic means of providing incentives for client efforts as well as an approach to negative feedback for client failures at using program mechanisms. While the relationship between client and therapist may well be reinforcing and supportive of client efforts, often, particularly with self-control clients, an additional, explicitly stated system of reinforcement (usually defined within a contract) is desirable. Most investigators have reported employing such an incentive system within their self-control approaches (Mahoney, Moura, and Wade, 1973; Morganstern, 1974; Mahoney, 1974a, Kanfer, 1975). Readers may wish to refer back to Chapters 3 and 4 to remind themselves as to those incentive systems available to the treatment agent. The following options are available.

Within an *extrinsic positive* approach material or social reinforcement is made contingent upon client efforts at achieving certain targeted goals.

Material incentives provided by the therapist have often been employed—typically, monetary rewards. In some cases the client is asked to "deposit" some fixed amount (e.g., $25, $50), which will be repaid to the client for pounds lost, decrements in cigarette smoking, or upon termination of the program proper. Hall (1972) told obese clients to choose a reinforcer that symbolized weight loss that would cost no more than $20. After each client was given $5 and told to put the item on layaway, she was instructed that if she reached her weight reduction at the end of five weeks of treatment, the therapist would pay her the remaining $15 as a prize. Thus, "*S* sampled the reinforcer in the sense that she was exposed to the visual and tactile cues associated with it" (p. 63). The client was frequently reminded of the weight she had left to lose, the time left to lose it, and the reinforcement that would be provided if she met her goal. The author found that this approach was superior to a self-mediated program of reinforcement. Certainly, these results must be qualified by the small number of subjects employed (14) and the case study nature of the experiment.

Tokens within some institutional system can be employed to reinforce efforts at self-control. Clients working at controlling aggressive behavior, at certain self-care behaviors, as well as other classes of events (such as time on task) could be paid off by the experimenter with tokens, accompanied by social reinforcement. Certainly, any sort of verbal or nonverbal social feedback by the BCA for a client's efforts would apply within this category, and should be used regardless of what other system of reinforcement is employed. In some cases the positive reinforcement that results from a program of self-control is defined by the environment. For example, exerting control might mean that the undergraduate student earns a grade in a particular course or gets a degree, or that an employee earns a promotion/pay raise or maintains his job. Often, equal and opposite negative consequences operate along with the positive consequences. That is, if the client fails to exert self-control, he might fail the course or not graduate, fail to gain the promotion or be fired. Thus, it is often difficult to see how extrinsic positive reinforcement can operate in isolation. When an individual is *not reinforced,* this may serve as a response cost. In fact, most investigators have employed some combination of positive and negative consequences.

Within an *extrinsic negative* approach, aversive stimuli applied by the therapist are employed to reduce the frequency of certain targeted behaviors. Smoking (Whitman, 1969; Ober, 1968), obesity (Stollak, 1967; Harris, 1969), as well as some sexual behaviors have most often been the focus for aversive approaches to self-control.

Often, a form of response cost mediated by the therapist is made contingent upon the client's efforts. Thus, loss of therapeutic time, monetary loss, spouse-mediated loss of conversational time, and other costs could be employed as extrinsic options. Jeffrey and Christensen (1972) as well as Manno and Marston (1972) have employed monetary reinforcements as well as fines for failure to attend weight-loss meetings and for not losing a specified amount of weight. Many investigators require clients to deposit money at the onset of treatment, and then fine the client some portion or even the entire deposit when the client misses meetings or drops out. Often, this agreement is stated within a contract that client and therapist sign at the outset. Both Jeffrey and Christensen (1972) and Mahoney (1973) fined clients portions of a deposit for failure to achieve weight loss. Certainly, within a token approach to reinforcing self-control a response cost in tokens could be assessed for client failure to complete agreed-upon homework assignments, failure to reduce smoking or weight, or failure to increase studying.

Unfortunately, few investigators have evaluated the differential effectiveness of extrinsic positive as opposed to extrinsic negative procedures within self-control programs.

A recent review provided by Hall and Hall (1974) makes the following points:

One consistent finding of studies employing EM (experimenter-managed) procedures has been the relatively rapid weight loss obtained when these techniques were successful. The findings are particularly encouraging with respect to methods which do not use aversive stimuli. The status of EM aversive stimuli, particularly electric shock and noxious odors, is unclear. (p. 360)

It has already been mentioned that the primary focus of most recent approaches to self-control has been upon self-mediated procedures, which will be discussed in the next two sections.

While the preceding approaches required the extrinsic agent (therapist) to differentially apply either reinforcement or punishment contingent upon the client's efforts at self-control, *self-mediated procedures* require the client to control his own consequences. Regarding *self-mediated, positive* procedures, clients may be asked to reward themselves from a list of previously agreed-upon reinforcers such as a shopping trip, night out on the town, meal at a restaurant, watching television, reading a desired novel, purchasing a desired article of clothing, and so on, contingent upon certain self-controlling behaviors. These approaches are often preceded by a careful survey of reinforcers in the clients' lives that might be self-applied contingent upon their behavior. Typically, a contract defines precisely those behaviors the clients must engage in, such as not drinking or not eating, to earn specified reinforcements.

Mahoney and his colleagues (Mahoney, Moura, and Wade, 1973; Mahoney, 1974) have attempted to systematically evaluate the effectiveness of self-imposed monetary rewards for weight loss in comparison with self-monitoring, self-imposed punishment, and other treatment procedures. Obese clients who undertook this treatment program were required to leave a refundable deposit of $35 with the experimenter for the duration of the program. Clients were told that a fine of $5 would be levied for each absence from a treatment meeting. They were assigned to one of four groups: self-reward for weight loss (SR-weight), self-reward for habit improvement (SR-habit), self-monitoring, or a no-treatment control group.

All treatment subjects began their participation by reading basic material describing the manner in which stimulus control might affect eating habits (Stuart and Davis, 1972). Also, subjects were provided with weight charts and booklets on eating habits to help them monitor their weight and eating habits on a daily basis (Mahoney, 1972). Habits were described according to quality and quantity of food eaten as well as situational determinants. Over a two-week period all subjects recorded their daily weight and eating habits and were weighed by the experimenter on a weekly basis. Following this baseline period subjects in the self-monitoring condition were asked to continue their self-recording and continued to be weighed on a weekly basis. Subjects in the two self-reward conditions continued their self-monitoring over the subsequent six-week period; in addition, they were instructed to reward themselves with portions of their own deposit as reinforcement for meeting a series of goals defined by the experimenter in pounds lost. Subjects in the SR-weight condition were asked to reward attainment of a weekly goal of weight loss; the SR-habit subjects were asked to self-reward changes in their habits as defined by goals laid down by the experimenter. Using the "reduction quotient" as a measure of weight loss (number of pounds lost divided by number of pounds overweight), the authors found both of the self-reward conditions to be superior to self-monitoring; subjects who rewarded themselves for habit changes showed the best degree of weight reduction. At a one-year follow-up 70 percent of the SR-habit subjects maintained or improved their weight losses, as compared with 40, 37.5, and 40 percent on the part of SR-weight, self-monitoring, and untreated control subjects. These results reemphasize the importance of the specific goal chosen for treatment. In this case, when the goal was defined as improving eating habits, the results of weight loss were superior than when the goal was merely to reduce weight.

The success of self-managed approaches would certainly seem to be borne out by this study, and Hall and Hall (1974) have pointed out that in every reported case that they could find the self-management paradigms directed toward weight reduction have produced greater weight losses than those obtained under no-treatment conditions. While the present discussion has emphasized self-reward as it is directed toward obesity, these procedures could be applied to virtually any targeted behavior contingent upon particular self-controlling responses.

The covert positive reinforcement procedures of Cautela, the self-reinforcement procedures discussed by Kanfer and others, as well as the Premackian approach discussed by Homme, could optionally be employed as self-mediated reinforcers for achieving self-control of a variety of targeted behaviors. The reader is referred to each of these covert approaches as possible adjuncts to a self-control program (see Chapter 5). It is difficult to decide whether the covert procedures should be listed in a chapter on self-control or in separate chapter, and the bias of the author is obvious. However, it should be noted that self-control is merely a rubric within which many of the procedures previously discussed may be included in an overall self-control program. In reviewing covert approaches that have been employed within self-control formats, Mahoney (1972) has stated that this area must be viewed with "cautious optimism" because of the difficulties in assessing the reliability of covert phenomena.

Within *self-mediated, negative* strategies a client may be asked to "avert" himself, using electrical, chemical, or other means, whenever some targeted behavior occurs within the natural environment. As much of this research have been directed at reducing smoking behavior, some examples from that area of approach will be discussed. In a well-controlled investigation Ober (1967) asked clients to shock themselves with a pocket-sized aversive stimulator whenever they "craved a cigarette." Thus, clients self-delivered a shock in the natural environment contingent upon an "urge" to smoke. He found that this technique, as well as other techniques involving operant self-control, were superior to no treatment. The drop-out rate was not high (many have suggested that aversion may cause clients to leave treatment) nor did the effects of aversive control diminish more rapidly than those of operant self-control.

Another technique that has been employed with "smoking" clients is the breath-holding procedure first suggested by Mees (1966). Within this approach the client is asked to hold his breath (aversive stimulus) contingent upon the urge to smoke a cigarette. Rutner (1967) found this procedure to be as successful as covert sensitization (Cautela, 1966), Homme's coverant control procedure (Homme, 1965), and contract management (Pratt and Tooley, 1967) in significantly reducing smoking. Unfortunately, no follow-up data was reported, which seems to be frequently the case in the smoking literature (Keutzer, Lichtenstein, and Mees, 1968).

Using a "negative practice" procedure (Yates, 1958) clients were asked to smoke three cigarettes in succession without extinguishing them (a "drag" every 12 seconds) while remaining in a relatively small room with no ventilation (presumably an aversive control procedure). Clients were then informed that they should practice this procedure between the experimental sessions. These subjects showed significantly greater smoking decrements than did nontreated controls, but showed no significant differences when compared with clients receiving Homme's coverant control procedure and Mees' breath-holding technique. The manner in which this negative practice procedure works is not understood, and additional research might clarify the specific elements involved. Whitman (1972) used aversive tastes to significantly decrease smoking in a population of 146 subjects. Clients were asked to suck on a pill that produced a burning sensation and bitter taste whenever they had the desire to smoke a cigarette.

Perhaps any form of aversion that subjects can apply to themselves in the natural environment could be used as a self-mediated, negative consequence. Many of these procedures seem to "work" when weekly and/or one-month followup is evaluated; however, few investigations follow up subjects for sufficiently long periods of time to evaluate the maintenance of effects.

The following case (Morganstern, 1974) falls within a self-mediated, negative paradigm and offers a very nice presentation of the array of options that the therapist has in setting up a program of self-control, while also illustrating the creativity and the pragmatism employed in devising procedures that meet a client's needs.

Miss C was a 24 year old, attractive but extremely obese graduate student when she presented herself for treatment. In addition to eating three regular meals a day, the client reported that she ate candy and junk all day long, completely unable to control herself despite callous attempts at dieting and medically prescribed appetite suppressants. Miss C was seen once a week for a total of 18 treatment sessions. At the start of each week the client was weighed and a record made (starting with week 2) of her eating behavior. In addition, she was contacted by telephone after weeks 21 and 24 to report follow-up data on her food consumption and her weight. At the beginning of the fourth week the rationale of covert sensitization was explained and the covert procedure briefly attempted. When it soon became apparent that Miss C could not consistently maintain a clear image, the intended treatment was abandoned and other possibilities explored. Electric shock was mentioned in passing, only as an example, but the prospect so frightened the client that no serious consideration could be given to its clinical implementation. During previous discussion, Miss C had reported that a few experiences with smoking had produced extremely unpleasant sensations for her, which included nausea and dizziness; therefore, the possible utilization of smoking as UCS was suggested to the client. Although skeptical, Miss C agreed to try the technique. A cigarette was lit and Miss C was asked to hold it in her hand as she took a bite of candy (the food which showed the highest consumption rate during baseline) and chewed it for a few seconds. Before swallowing the candy she was told to take one long "drag" on the cigarette and then to immediately spit out the food, exclaiming at the same time, "eating this junk makes me sick." This procedure was repeated ten times in each session and the client was also asked to practice it on her own twice a day. During weeks 5–10, different types of candy were used as targeted stimuli for aversion treatment. Employing an additive multiple baseline design, cookies were included as target stimuli during week 11 of treatment and doughnuts were added at week 15. In this manner, after an initial baseline of these problematic eating behaviors (consumption of candy, cookies, and doughnuts), each response was sequentially targeted in the aversion procedures. In addition to her daily practice assignments at home, Miss C employed the technique *in vivo* in a variety of problematical situations. (pp. 256–257)

The results showed a significant reduction in the consumption of candy, cookies, and doughnuts over a period of 18 weeks, with these items being consumed at zero leval at a 21- and 24-week follow-up. Thus, the authors tried a variety of self-control approaches only to arrive at employing an aversive stimulus suggested by careful observation of the client. The multiple-baseline design showed that targeted behaviors did not change until treatment was directed at each in succession. It would seem that procedures that allow the client to present an aversive stimulus in the natural environment on those occasions when the targeted behavior occurs are vastly superior to procedures that employ aversive consequences exclusively within the clinical setting.

Another procedure that falls within this category is covert sensitization, described by Cautela (1966) and discussed in Chapter 5. The specific manner in which this procedure might be applied to self-control was extensively covered in that chapter, and the reader is referred there for a review. Often, these covert "negative" procedures are employed along with other treatment components to deal with the cognitive/physiological referent (e.g., "urge") that may be associated with the client's problem behavior at the overt level. Thus, such procedures may readily be applied toward *decreasing the "urge"* rather than toward punishing the behavior itself. Once the behavior occurs (e.g., the client lights up a cigarette, puts food in the mouth), the reinforcement attendant to that behavior is experienced by the client, which may in fact be incompatible with the goals of decreasing its frequency. By intervening at the level of the urge and thus reducing its frequency, the overt manifestation and its subsequent reinforcement for the client does not occur. It would seem that intervention early in the chain of events that produces the problem behavior would be optimal.

Self-instructions

As an alternative or complementary covert procedure, the BCA might encourage the client to self-instruct himself regarding the targeted event, along the lines suggested by Meichenbaum and his colleagues (Meichenbaum, 1973, 1974, 1975; Meichenbaum and Cameron, 1974). For example, each time the client self-monitors an "urge" to eat, he might be instructed to employ certain standard self-instructions, like: "I really should eat some celery" (substitution behavior); "I think I'll go work out in the garage" (incompatible event, removes client from food-eliciting cues); or "I'll go for a jog" (metabolizes calories, incompatible event, removes client from cues). The reader may recall that self-instructional statements have been found to be an important class of events that often precede and direct a person's behavior. Meichenbaum gives an excellent example of how self-statements might alter the responses of high- and low-anxious persons to the standard condition of giving a speech before an audience.

During each speaker's presentation some members of the audience walk out of the room. This elicits quite different self-statements or appraisals from the high and low speech anxiety individuals. The high speech anxiety individual is likely to say to himself: "I must be boring. How much longer do I have to speak? I knew I never could give a speech," and so forth. These self-statements produce anxiety and result in the very speech anxiety behavior that the person fears (i.e., they become self-fulfilling prophecies). On the other hand, the low speech anxiety individual is more likely to view the audience's departure as a sign of their rudeness or to attribute their leaving to external causes. He might say something like: "They must have a class to catch. Too bad they have to leave; they will miss a good talk. (p. 358)

Thus, what is self-stated in response to the environment may determine the covert and overt behaviors the individual displays. Obviously, the task for the BCA is to encourage clients to self-monitor their adaptive as well as maladaptive self-verbalizations so that they may be differentially rewarded/punished (perhaps using one of the covert variants presented in Chapter 5). In addition, more appropriate nonrepertoire instructional statements can be modeled for a client, with avenues of first overt (verbal), then covert, rehearsal available for client practice. Chapter 6 provides an extensive example of how appropriate instructional statements might be modeled for a client, while Chapter 9 discusses the role of coping versus mastery self-statements when modeling is employed to reduce avoidant behavior.

Contingency contracting

While most investigators define the various self-control procedures for the client within a contractual agreement, many others have evaluated the utility of contracts as the sole means by which a client can assert control over important targets (Mann, 1972; Hall, 1972; Pratt and Tooley, 1964; Tooley and Pratt, 1967; Watson and Tharp, 1972). Although any agreement made between therapist and client might be considered a contract, the present discussion will emphasize those contracts made explicit in writing. Also, it should be noted that contracts could be employed to specify client/therapist responsibilities within any of the treatment strategies presented in previous chapters.

The example that follows illustrates each of the major components of a contract. In this case the contract defines a "homework assignment" for a parent attempting to increase positive feedback to her son.

1. The *date* at which the contract goes into effect.

2. Some *statement as to the goals* of the contract. For example, "In order to increase the frequency and kind of positive statements that I make to my son Billy, I, (name), agree to practice each of the following . . ."

3. *Specification of the behavioral tasks* that the contract calls for. For

example, "I agree to: (a) spend ten minutes each evening between the hours of 7 and 9 P.M. playing with Billy. I will play any game that he desires. During this play period I agree to (b) play with Billy by attending to what he is doing as frequently as I can; (c) tell Billy as clearly as possible what I like about his efforts, using the labeled rewards discussed in treatment; (d) touch Billy in a positive way, using the pats, hug, kiss from the list I have; and (e) try to use smiles and other facial expressions discussed in therapy to make play positive for Billy." Usually, the elements specified here refer to specific procedures that have been discussed *at length* within the therapeutic situation (e.g., use touch in a positive way), and have been practiced within the clinical setting using such mechanisms as modeling, role-playing, and feedback by the BCA. The contract specifies that these agreed-upon procedures will be employed within the natural setting.

4. Delineation of the *specific times and/or schedule* that the behaviors listed under paragraph 3 will be engaged in. For example, "I understand that I must play with Billy for the period of ten minutes each evening of the week between the hours of 7 and 9 P.M. during week nights and for the period of twenty minutes on Saturday and Sunday between the hours of 9 A.M. and 9 P.M." Often within this portion of the contract the overall time frame that the contract defines will be stated: "I agree to continue playing with Billy for the period of one month, commencing on (date) and ending on (date)."

5. Next, *positive and negative consequences for compliance/noncompliance* with the contract are clearly specified. For example, "I understand that if I meet the terms of this contract, my husband and I may go out to a restaurant of our choice on the Friday or Saturday after a week (seven days) of successful completion of the terms. I understand that theater, bowling, or some other positive activity may be substituted for the restaurant. I understand also that failure to meet the terms of this contract on one or more evenings will result in loss of our night out the following Friday or Saturday evening." Within the institutional setting these consequences are often defined in terms of tokens; however, any category of consequences could be applied.

6. Finally, the client, relevant staff members/therapist, as well as optionally witnesses all *sign the contract*, and it is put into effect at the date specified. Often, the BCA may wish to ask important persons in the client's life to serve as witnesses, thus increasing the investment of husbands, wives, friends, or others in the client's efforts at completion, and setting up a situation where the client has committed himself to those who hold reinforcement value for him.

Fig. 8.2 shows how those components were incorporated into a contract to increase studying for a 22-year-old university student.

In order to increase the amount of time that I study each evening to a <u>minimum</u> of 1 hour, I, <u> John Davis </u>, agree to perform the following:

(1). I will study only at my desk and provide my complete attention to the material, thus no TV, radio or other noise will interfere.

(2). I will set my timer for 30 minutes and study until signalled. Following a 10 minute break I will reset my timer for another 30 minutes.

I understand that I must complete the above <u>each</u> evening between <u>6:00 p.m. and 8:00 p.m.</u> to earn the right to watch the 9:00-11:00 movie on TV. If I do not, I understand that I may <u>not</u> watch TV on that evening.

For every 5 minutes that I study beyond 60 minutes, I earn 15 minutes of additional TV time which may be applied towards the 11:30-1:00 late movie.

This contract commences on <u>March 7 at 6:00 p.m.   </u>, and extends until <u> March 31 at 1:00 a.m.   </u>.

I agree to faithfully execute the terms described above.

Signed _____ 3/6/75
       John W. Davis   date

Witnessed _____ 3/6/75
       Mrs. Ann Davis   date

_____ 3/6/75
       Mr. B. Technician   date

Fig. 8.2
A contract directed at increasing self-control of study behavior.

Fig. 8.3 shows a contract directed at assisting a 43-year-old male to gain control of critical statements directed toward his wife.

In order to *increase* the *positive* statements that I make to my
wife, and *decrease* *negative*, critical remarks, *~~George King~~*
agree to perform the following:

(1) I will keep a record of each positive statement that
     I make (as defined by a list of suggested positive
     statements that I have with me) in the notebook.

(2) To smoke a cigarette (high-rate behavior), I must first
     make one positive statement (low-rate behavior) to my wife;
     or if she is *not* present, record it in my notebook.

I understand that I must follow this program each morning (from 8:00AM
to 9:00AM) and each evening from 6:00PM to bedtime, beginning on
10-04-75 and extending until *10-31-75*   .

                    SIGNED: *George King*

                    WITNESS: *Nancy Howard*

                    WITNESS: *Sylvia Nance*

Fig. 8.3
A contract directed at increasing self-control of positive and
negative statements.

The BCA should carefully evaluate contracts to be sure that each
component is dealt with in some fashion. Kanfer and Karoly (1972) and
Kanfer (1975) have emphasized the importance of the contract and have
stated that the probability of the client "initiating" behavior that leads to
fulfillment of a contract can be viewed as a "complex function" of many

variables. A discussion of some of these variables may assist the BCA in defining the manner in which a contract should be constructed (from Kanfer and Karoly, 1972).

1. The authors emphasize the importance of the *explicitness or clarity* of the contract as an important predictor of contractual fulfillment. They state that it may be important that the desired *outcome* derived through the contract *be specified* clearly in some detail, to provide the client with a perspective as to how the behavior described leads toward therapeutic goals.

2. Also, a careful delineation of the *specific methods* that the client must use as well as of the consequences that accrue to that performance should be carefully specified for the client within the contract. Bandura (1969) and Watson and Tharp (1972) are among the designers of behavioral treatment programs who have emphasized the importance of explicit definition of behaviors, reinforcers, and timing schedules.

3. A clear specification of the *therapist's end* of the contract (what is required of the therapist) as well as of the client part may facilitate a relationship that is more "mutual," and clients can clearly see how the behavior of themselves and the therapist comes together to achieve the ultimate goals of treatment.

4. The individual's *skill and experience* in engaging in the specific behaviors required within the contract are posited as another important predictor of success. It has already been emphasized that any therapeutic task assigned to the client must be based upon behaviors currently within the client's repertoire, and practically emitted. If clients do not have the skill to fulfill their end of the contract, then their efforts may lead to the aversive consequences of failure and perhaps decrease the probability of their making future attempts. Thus, contracts that are agreed to by client and therapist must systematically build upon the client's behavioral repertoire, becoming more demanding as the repertoire is expanded and the client is increasingly capable of exerting self-control.

5. *Self-monitoring* is an important component within any contractual agreement. The authors posit that self-monitoring permits behavioral gains or losses to have maximal motivational impact, thus permitting the client to see very clearly the results of his efforts at exerting control.

6. Finally, the *past experiences* of the client are predictors of success. Obviously, to the extent that the client has experienced difficulty in exerting self-control and perhaps has failed to honor agreements, the probability of successful contractual completion is diminished. The BCA must integrate case history information obtained, observational data collected, and reports of important others within the client's natural environment, and then make a decision as to the likelihood of a client's meeting a particular demand. To the extent that these characteristics can be related to the kind of demands made within the contract, the probability of successful execution would seem to be enhanced.

CHAPTER SUMMARY

While many of the previous chapters emphasized extrinsic control, this chapter presented a variety of approaches toward establishing client self-control of important targeted events. Following a historical review of the notion of "self" within the literature, self-control was defined as follows. The client self-determines the goals for his behavior, and should be able to verbalize and devise a systematic and consciously arranged set of procedures to attain self-control. Self-control is defined by its function. It is not a personality construct or structure, but a specific class of responses. Self-control results from experience, not from some innate potentiality within the individual. Finally, self-control procedures do not rest upon any one theoretical foundation, but seem to be based upon pragmatic criteria.

Factors that should be included or considered in a self-control program include:

Client Motivation to Assert Self-Control. Given the positively reinforcing consequences of many inappropriate behaviors, it is difficult to assist a client in achieving self-control unless the client is motivated. Possible sources of motivation were discussed.

Self-Monitoring Skills. It was concluded that the client must reliably identify the occurrence of the targeted behavior in order to impose a control procedure.

Stimulus Control. Because clients have engaged in the uncontrolled targeted behavior in the presence of certain stimuli within their environment, these stimuli may come to elicit the behavior. Often, clients are asked to "narrow" stimulus control by limiting certain behaviors such as eating, studying, and smoking to highly specific locations within the environment. In addition, the environment itself may interfere with the goals of self-control and may be restructured as part of treatment.

Incentive Systems. Most investigators employ some system of extrinsic or self-mediated reinforcement to maintain the client's self-controlling efforts. These techniques may be divided into two major categories: SR (self-reward) and SP (self-punishment). Within the SR paradigm the self-presentation of positive consequences would be termed $SR+$, and the removal of negative consequences would be termed $SR-$. Regarding approaches to SP, the self-presentation of negative consequences would be termed $SP-$, with the removal of positive consequences called $SP+$. Often SR or SP procedures are employed as the sole means of altering a client's behavior; however, most investigators employ these procedures as part of an overall treatment program.

Self-Instructions. Because client self-statements may predict subsequent covert and overt behavior, clients should be trained to carefully self-monitor the incidence of adaptive/maladaptive self-verbilizations. Procedures incorporating modeling and role-playing may be useful in instigating alternative, nonrepertoire self-instructional stratagies.

Contractual Agreement. Often, the obligations of client as well as therapist will be carefully delineated in a verbal or written contract; examples were provided.

Each of the factors described above was then integrated into an outline of components that might be included in a self-control program. The following were presented: self-monitoring; pinpointing goals; alteration of stimulus factors; incentive systems; and the use of contracts to integrate self-control procedures.

Chapter 9

Reducing Avoidant
Behavior:

PROCEDURAL VARIANTS

At some time during our lives most of us have experienced anxiety when exposed to some particular situation or object. The mother who yells at her children who are about to jump into the water, play with matches, or run into the nearest roadway may provoke them to experience cognitive and physical phenomena we might call anxiety. As Chapter 6 pointed out, the anxiety that we experience may stem from the models we have been exposed to, and it may be transmitted vicariously. For example, the young child who sees his mother leap away from a roach or some other "dread" insect may very likely experience anxiety and attempt to avoid insects following this very potent parental model. When an individual *systematically avoids some specific stimulus situation, we often speak of a "fear" or "phobia."* Certainly, many of the anxieties experienced in childhood are protective of the developing child's well-being. It is probably most important that the child, in the absence of the parent, experience anxiety when about to cross a busy street, approach a fireplace or pan on the stove, or disturb a large unknown animal. While parents don't like to think of themselves as inducing "fears" in their children, the emotional responses to verbal admonitions, punishment, and fearful models often promotes anxiety and ultimate avoidant behavior.

In time most of us learn ways of appropriately approaching previously feared situations, and often such approach behavior is evidence of being "brave" and generally masterful when viewed by peers who share similar fears. Particularly in boys, approach responses to feared objects or situations become a test of one's ability and prowess in the social situation. The young boy who is afraid of the water and jumps in at the urging of friends may perhaps succeed in thwarting his "fear," and no doubt will find it somewhat easier to engage in similar approaches in the future. Thus, many fears are probably adaptive; a good many fears are shared by large numbers of persons, particularly at certain times within their development; and most fears seem to be overcome as the developing individual begins to assert himself.

As adults, most of us experience some level of anxiety when peering down from a great height, driving rapidly in an automobile, or when exposed to certain animals. While we might experience (perhaps adaptive) anxiety, we are still able to tolerate those situations. In fact, the avoidance of many feared stimuli does not interrupt our lives sufficiently to create inefficiency and/or discomfort for us. Avoidant behaviors that radically disrupt a client's life or cause extreme degrees of subjective discomfort are often the subject of programs of intervention by the BCA. Height may provoke some degree of anxiety within all of us, but the client who reports that his fear of heights causes him to drive 15 extra miles each day to avoid crossing a bridge, or the individual who avoids any job that calls for entering an elevator or walking up stairs, may well seek to alter this pattern of avoidant behavior. Concomitantly, the teenage girl who will not enter her backyard, walk through a wooded region, or view any picture that portrays a reptile may also seek to reduce the inefficiency that her avoidant behavior causes. The author has often worked with clients whose fears—of public speaking, of males/females, of test taking, or of open spaces—have caused great disruption to their life situations. One particular client became so restricted by his fear of open places that, over the period of one year, he found himself increasingly confined to his house. This fear not only caused a great deal of subjective discomfort, but caused him to lose a very good position that obviously required him to show up each day. Ultimately, he found himself uncomfortable even within his house, and could only reduce his subjective anxiety by moving into his basement, where he lived with his wife for a two-month period prior to seeking treatment. The cost for this individual in terms of job, finances, and the obvious strain on his marital relationship were not enough to outweigh his desire to reduce anxiety by avoiding these life situations. Many traditional therapists have talked about the "neurotic paradox," that is, the cost a given client will incur to engage in certain inappropriate behaviors often described within the "neurosis" classification. It may seem "stupid" for an individual to incur such costs to avoid a situation that most of us find neutral, but for the individual who has learned a pattern of avoidance, such costs are often willingly paid as a means of reducing anxiety.

In recent years a variety of procedures has been developed to successfully reduce the subjective anxiety, physiological responses and subsequent avoidant behavior that define "fear." While procedures to reduce avoidant behavior, often called "desensitization," were reported in unsystematic fashion early within the literature (e.g., Jones, 1924), the "systematic desensitization" procedure (Wolpe, 1958) serves as the base upon which an array of alternative desensitization formats have been developed. Beginning with a brief presentation of Wolpe's systematic desensitization format, this chapter will discuss the major options the BCA has for designing a program to reduce avoidant behavior. Following a specification of major factors that appear to operate within the desensitization process, other alternatives to reducing avoidant behavior will be offered, with case examples of important variants of desensitization serving as illustrations.

SYSTEMATIC DESENSITIZATION

Wolpe (1958) first worked with rats in the laboratory, exposing them to analogs of potential fear-arousing situations in the "real world." Wolpe found that after classically conditioning anxiety to a buzzer by employing an unconditioned stimulus of electric shock, this anxiety response could be desensitized by systematically (gradually) reintroducing the animal to the learning situation and by provoking the incompatible responses associated with the ingestion of food. Wolpe felt that the responses associated with eating actively inhibited the anxiety engendered by the training situation, and termed this process reciprocal inhibition, following an earlier idea of Sherrington (1906). Others have called this process *counterconditioning* (e.g., Davison, 1968).

In first employing the systematic desensitization approach with human clients, Wolpe used assertive responses as the counterconditioning agent, training clients to assert themselves in situations that originally provoked anxiety. Because an assertive response would not be a plausible counterconditioning agent for fears of inanimate objects, animals, and other situations (Wolpe, 1969), Wolpe decided to extend some of the earlier work of Jacobson (1939) and employ relaxation as the counterconditioning agent. In addition, the graded exposure initially employed with infrahuman subjects was also included in the package.

The procedure involves four steps:

1. *The client is trained to carefully relax the various muscles of his body* by systematically contracting each muscle group; in this way the difference between a state of tension and relaxation can be experienced. Although investigators have modified this tension-relaxation procedure, many still

employ some variant of the original Jacobsonian format (Jacobson, 1939).

2. Next, the *therapist and client together construct a hierarchy of the various situations or objects that provoked anxiety.* Typically, the hierarchy focuses on one specific fear, with each scene depicting some element of the client's avoidance. For example, the client who reported that he was afraid of heights might construct scenes involving looking up a staircase, climbing stairs, getting into an elevator, looking out of a window, looking down from some height, flying in an airplane, and so on. The hierarchy might contain ten or more scenes, with scene 1 representing some situation or object that promoted relatively low degrees of subjective discomfort, and scene 10 describing a maximally fearful situation or object involving height. Client toleration of the last scene on the hierarchy without experiencing anxiety would be considered the optimal goal of treatment.

3. Next, the *client is trained to carefully imagine situations or objects described by the therapist,* with practice trials calling for the client to imagine an array of neutral stimuli (e.g. moving clouds against a background of hills, the various aspects of a tree, a sunset).

4. A client who is able to adequately visualize upon therapist request, the client is then asked to *visualize the first hierarchy scene while in a state of complete relaxation.* Whenever the client experiences any degree of subjective discomfort, he is instructed to signal the therapist via the movement of a finger or some such cue, and the therapist immediately orders him to "stop" imagining the fearful scene. Again, the client is asked to relax completely, and the scene is presented again until he is able to tolerate it in imagination without experiencing anxiety for some specified period of time.

When scene 1 is mastered as described, the therapist then relaxes the client and presents the second scene, followed by the third and succeeding scenes, until the client is able to visualize the last scene on the hierarchy without experiencing subjective discomfort.

Systematic desensitization or one of its variants has successfully reduced avoidant behaviors in hundreds of cases and experimental studies within the literature; at present it is doubtful that any investigator would question its efficacy (Rimm and Masters, 1974). Wolpe (1973) reports that most clients can be successfully desensitized in from 16 to 18 hours. Because the procedures of systematic desensitization are so easy to use and because its effects can be readily measured (e.g., a client either can or cannot approach a feared object or situation following treatment), it has been subject to more careful and systematic evaluation than any previous treatment approach. Within this investigative process every aspect of the original Wolpian procedure has been scrutinized regarding its importance as a live elment within the desensitization package. In fact, the role of "reciprocal inhibition" and the importance of the hierarchy, two major components of the procedure, have been questioned, and alternative explanations for desensitization have been formulated (Borkovec, 1972, 1973; Wilkins, 1971).

Rather than present a detailed example of Wolpe's systematic desensitization approach in isolation, the procedures of desensitization will be presented within the context of a series of choice points or alternatives that the BCA is faced with in reducing avoidant behavior. These alternative approaches have been gleaned from the recent literature, and as in other chapters, the outline of steps represents a "suggested" outline. Each of the possibilities calls for the BCA to make a choice as to inclusion within the desensitization package, and the order of presentation of procedural variants suggests the possible order in which such choices might typically be made.

OVERVIEW OF PROCEDURAL VARIANTS

Viewing across desensitization formats, certain major commonalities that are perhaps intrinsic to any process of desensitization seem to emerge. The process of defining the specific fear or fears exhibited by the client is a typical first step. Following the elicitation of a verbal report from the client regarding the specific situations and objects that promote anxiety, an assessment is made of the degree of avoidance each elicits. The client's "fear" is often operationally defined in terms of the client's written responses to a questionnaire, a verbal report and rating of subjective discomfort, or the degree to which the client can behaviorally tolerate the feared object (e.g., the nearest point to which a client could approach a feared snake). Once the specific feared objects/situations, as well as the degree of subjective discomfort/approach/avoidance, have been ascertained, most intervention strategies then expose the client to the feared stimuli in some fashion. This may be direct exposure, where the client himself is exposed, or vicarious exposure, where a client observes some model engaged in exposure to the feared stimuli. Finally, the client is assessed throughout as well as following treatment using the operationally defined indices of "fear" employed prior to treatment.

It should become obvious to the reader from this very general overview that many possibilities exist for alternative procedures, both within the assessment process as well as treatment proper.

MEASURES OF AVOIDANT BEHAVIOR

Measures of avoidant behavior seem to fall within four major categories: *verbal self-ratings; written self-assessments; observations of behavior* when the client is exposed to the feared stimulus; and *physiological indices* of arousal. Because many investigators have developed their own idiosyncratic measuring devices, a comprehensive inclusion of all such devices is beyond the scope of this presentation. Each category of assessment procedure will be defined by popular measures that might suggest alternative approaches to the BCA who decides to design a special instrument for a population of interest.

Verbal Self-Ratings

The BCA will typically wish to obtain a complete *case history* of the client's fear, from the time the client remembers experiencing anxiety/ avoidance to the present. Often, the client is asked to verbally rate the severity of the fear at various periods during its development to ascertain any changes in the avoidant behavior over time and possibly to relate them to life situation events. If the client's avoidant behavior is more extreme in certain situations, the BCA may want to focus treatment upon those specific situational areas. Conversely, if the client is better able to approach the feared stimulus in certain other situations, the BCA may set up a treatment program that allows the client to maximize the probability of successfully exposing himself to the feared stimuli. Thus, as in all treatment situations, a thorough job of assessment is called for.

Typically, some *rating system* is agreed upon between the BCA and client as to how the client will rate the intensity of certain covert and overt responses associated with avoidance. For example, if the BCA wished to assess the degree of anxiety associated with heights (e.g. stepping on the first rung of a ladder), the first task would be to define very carefully what the client labels "anxiety" or "discomfort." For a particular client anxiety may be experienced as a burning, flushed feeling upon his face, coupled with a tight, burning sensation in the region of his stomach. Cognitively, the client may report that he experiences an image of "falling and hitting the ground" as part of this experience. Thus, the terminology the client uses to describe the discomfort experience must be translated into some operationally defined covert and overt behaviors that can then be the focus of treatment efforts. While the BCA cannot treat "anxiety" as a construct, it is possible to work at altering the client's cognitions of "falling" and to reduce the tenseness in the stomach or wherever. In fact, these specific elements that make up "anxiety" for the client may then become the targeted behaviors for change within the desensitization format.

The rating system employed to assess the intensity of some particular response on the client's part is often rather informal, though it is applied in a systematic fashion. Thus, the BCA might ask the client to rate the degree of "tenseness" in his stomach according to a scale from 1 to 7. The client and BCA should agree as to what a rating of 1 operationally means in terms of the client's behavior, as well as what the extreme opposite rating of 7 indicates. Often, an item at the center of the scale will also be defined, so that certain points are anchored in terms of specific referents. An example of this kind of rating system is provided below:

1. Stomach muscles feel loose, sensation of coolness, stomach smoothly moves in and out while breathing.

2.

3.

4. Stomach muscles feel moderately tight; a slight burning is noticed, particularly when exhaling; stomach movements in and out somewhat limited; when press stomach with hand, experience moderate degree of pain.

5.

6.

7. Stomach muscles extremely tight; movement during breathing produces extreme degree of pain; even touch of stomach muscles produces pain; movement severely limited.

While this rating system is rather simplistic and could be agreed upon within the course of a therapeutic session, it provides a standard and systematic way for the client to verbalize the intensity of discomfort associated with his stomach throughout the course of treatment.

Bandura, Blanchard, and Ritter (1969) assessed the degree of fear arousal accompanying responses made toward a snake within a population of snake-phobic clients. Clients were asked to make increasingly closer approaches to a snake and were required to rate on a scale from 1 to 10 the intensity of the fear they experienced when each snake approach response was described to them and again while they were performing the corresponding behavior. The authors then averaged the clients' ratings across approach responses as a measure of "fear arousal."

It would seem to be important that a rating system be clearly and explicitly communicated to the client, with operationally defined anchors providing the client sufficient information to make a reliable rating. While the findings at present are not altogether clear, many studies report a good correspondence between verbal self-ratings and client behavior in approaching a feared stimulus (Bandura, Blanchard, and Ritter, 1969; Lira, Nay, McCullough, and Etkin, 1975).

Written Measures

The Fear Survey Schedule (FSS) originally constructed by Wolpe and Lang (1964) describes 122 objects and/or situations and calls for the respondent to rate the degree of fear aroused by each item on a scale ranging from 1 to 5 (5 is the highest level of fear). Rubin, Lawlis, Tasto, and Namenek (1969) factor-analyzed the 122 items within the FSS and identified five factors that seem to be conceptually pure—that is, around which the various items cluster. The five factors included: (1) fears related to small animals; (2) fears of the precipitators and manifestations of hostility; (3) primitive, moralistically related fears and sexual fears; (4) fears of isolation and loneliness; and (5) fears of anatomical destruction and physical pain. The authors found that only 40 items were necessary to tap each of these five factors optimally, and thus severely modified the original FSS. Tasto, Hickson, and Rubin (1971) have presented a format within which each of the five factors can be profiled for an individual client as a means of designing and evaluating the success of treatment.

In research the FSS is typically used as a screening device. In treatment it provides a quantitative means assessing the degree of client's fear across multiple categories of potentially feared items.

The degree of relationship between the FSS and behavioral and physiological changes has not been clearly defined within the literature, although some degree of relationship is often reported (Bandura, Blanchard, and Ritter, 1969). In summary, the FSS or one of its variants provides the BCA with an efficient and relatively inexpensive means of profiling a client's fears.

The Fear Thermometer (Walk, 1956) is frequently employed, although its use varies somewhat within the literature. Very simply, the client is asked to rate a specific feared stimulus on a scale from 1 to 10 or, in some cases, from 0 to 100. This kind of measurement is very similar to the verbal self-ratings discussed above, and provides a measure of the client's subjective view of the feared stimulus. Perhaps this instrument is most useful as a means of defining the intensity of this fear response along some dimension of interest, once the client's verbal report and the FSS have demonstrated specific feared areas.

Some investigators have employed attitude and/or personality measures as an indicant of anxiety or fear (e.g., *Semantic Differential Scales;* Osgood, Suci, and Tannenbaum, 1957). In using the Semantic Differential the respondent is asked to rate a feared object (e.g., dogs, closed-in spaces, heights) on each of eight bipolar adjective rating scales. Each scale consists of the following pairs of contrasting adjectives: good–bad, clean–dirty, ugly–beautiful, belligerent–peaceful, interesting–dull, worthless–valuable, nice–awful, and pleasant–unpleasant. A rating scale from −3 to +3 defines the respondent's attitude for each of the adjective pairs. Often, the ratings obtained from these scales are averaged (Bandura, Blanchard, and Ritter, 1969; Lira, Nay, McCullough, and Etkin, 1975).

Other attitude scales are often idiosyncratically developed to assess clients' attitudes toward certain phobic stimuli of interest. For example, in evaluating attitudes toward snakes, Bandura, Blanchard, and Ritter (1969) developed six attitude scales to assess clients' attitudes toward various encounters with snakes (e.g., visiting a reptile exhibit, being unexpectedly shown a documentary film on the habits of snakes, and others) upon a seven-point scale (7 = strong enjoyment, 1 = strong dislike).

Another measure often employed is the state anxiety scale (Spielberger, Gorsuch, and Lushene, 1970) that assesses the subject's current degree of experienced anxiety.

In summary the written approach provides a quantitative means of assessing a client's fear and might be employed prior to, during, and following treatment as a measure of self-reported change.

Behavioral Approach Tests (BATs)

The BCA may wish to set up an "analog" situation within the laboratory to permit behavioral observations of the client's ability to approach or tolerate some feared stimulus. Because of the observed poor correspondence between self-ratings, verbal reports, and overt behavior (Lang, 1969), the BCA may well wish to systematically look at the client's behavior in situations related to the feared stimulus.

In an early report (Lang and Lazovik, 1963) individuals who reported fears of snakes were asked to enter a room that contained a live harmless snake within a cage. The experimenter then asked the client to approach, touch, and hold the snake, with each invitation repeated once if immediate compliance was not observed. The client's behavior was then rated using a three-point scale to evaluate the subject's ability to look at, touch, and hold the snake. While many such tests are idiosyncratically designed, a number have gained widespread prominence within the literature. Using the distance/rating approach to behavioral testing, Bandura, Grusec, and Menlove (1965) exposed potentially dog-phobic children to a standardized performance test as a screening procedure prior to treatment. Each child was asked to perform 14 tasks requiring increasingly closer interactions with a brown cocker spaniel confined in a modified playpen. The child was asked to walk up to the playpen, look at the dog, touch the dog's fur, and pet the animal. Following these performances each child was asked to perform tasks that included opening the hinged door of the playpen to let the animal out; walking the dog on a leash; remaining alone in the room with the animal; feeding the animal; climbing into the playpen; and petting and scratching the dog's stomach. The authors used a behavioral coding format and measured the "strength of the children's avoidant tendencies" by the number of items successfully completed and the degree of vacillation, reluctance, and fearfulness that accompanied each response. Children were credited two points for executing a given task willingly or spontaneously and one point when they carried out the task minimally after considerable hesitancy. Thus, within the 14 items a possible total score of 28 served as the perfect approach criterion; scores below that number indicated various degrees of avoidance. Using this numerical format, the authors were able to quantitatively screen out those children who did not meet certain predefined criteria. A similar test (29 items) was employed by Bandura, Blanchard, and Ritter (1969) and Lira, Nay, McCullough, and Etkin (1975) in assessing degree of approach behavior toward snakes.

Gilner, Lipsitz, and Davenport (1973) constructed a behavioral approach test to be applied to individuals fearful of heights. Subjects were given verbal instructions to complete each of the following tasks:

1. 3 ft. away from 2nd floor stairwell looking straight ahead for 10 seconds. (1 pt.)
2. 2nd floor landing looking over rail for 10 seconds. (1 pt.)
3. 3rd floor landing looking over rail for 10 seconds. (1 pt.)
4. 4th floor landing looking over rail for 10 seconds. (1 pt.)
5. Climb up to 3rd rung of the ladder and look down for 10 seconds. (1 pt.)
6. Climb up to 6th rung of the ladder and look down for 10 seconds. (2 pts.)
7. Climb up to 8th rung of the ladder and look down for 10 seconds. (3 pts.)
8. Climb up to 10th rung of the ladder and look straight ahead for 10 seconds. (4 pts.)
9. Stand on 10th rung of the ladder and look down for 10 seconds. (5 pts.)
10. Climb up to the 11th rung of the ladder and look straight ahead for 10 seconds. (6 pts.)
11. Stand on 11th rung of the ladder and look down for 10 seconds. (10 pts.)
12. Stand on 11th rung of the ladder and look down for 30 seconds. (15 pts.) (p. 22)

The authors said to each subject, "I have a series of tasks related to heights and I would like you to do as many as you can within the time available. You may refuse to do any task you feel you cannot perform. Please try to do as many as you feel you can" (p. 5). The reader may note that a certain point value was assigned to each task completed, and the experimenter recorded the point at which the subject could go no further. Each subject was given three minutes to accomplish each task, with the score being the total points accumulated at the last successfully completed task. The Fear Thermometer assessed the subject's ratings of the height completed immediately following the behavioral approach test.

Many designers of behavioral approach tests attempt to quantify each level of performance by using a numerical scaling system to make comparisons between approach test scores suitable for statistical analysis. An excellent example is the timed behavioral checklist for performance anxiety (Paul, 1966). Employing 30-second observation periods, observers record the presence or absence of each of the following categories: Paces, Sways, Shuffles Feet, Knees Tremble, Extraneous Arm and Hand Movements, Arms Rigid, Hands Restrained, Hand Tremors, No Eye Contact, Face Muscles Tense (tics, grimaces), Face "Deadpan," Face Pale, Face Flushed, Moistens Lips, Swallows, Clears Throat, Breathes Heavily, Perspires, Voice Quivers, Speech Blocks or Stammers. Observations could be taken while the client completes each step of a BAT or as a measure of anxiety within any assessment medium.

A behavioral approach test employing time as the dependent variable measure was used to assess the degree of claustrophobia exhibited by a 51-year-old female client by Leitenberg, Agras, Thompson, and Wright (1968). The client reported that she could not stay at home by herself in any room with a closed door, a cinema, a church, or even drive her car alone for more than three or four miles. In designing a clinical analog to measure her fear behaviorally, the authors designated a room four feet wide and six feet long illuminated by a 100-watt shaded bulb as the testing situation. The client was asked to sit in a chair within the room and was not allowed to read or engage in other activities. The total number of minutes and seconds that the client was able to remain within the room until feeling discomfort was used as a measure of her fear. Thus, Leitenberg et al. (1968) constructed a very inexpensive, easily interpretable means of observing the client's targeted behavior; one that could be employed as a measure of behavioral change.

If the BCA is creative and has carefully specifyied the stimuli that a client avoids, it seems reasonable that an analog situation could be devised within the clinical setting to assess client behavior. Particularly when a client's fear involves the interpersonal situation, role-playing might be employed, with other clients or staff members portraying important others related to the client's avoidant behavior. Thus, for the male client who is afraid of interacting with females, the BCA could construct a series of role-playings in which the client might be asked to telephone a female, begin a conversation, or ask a female for a date. Observational methods used to assess the client's behavior within the role-play would need to be directed at those specific behaviors provoked by the client's enactment.

While it may be impossible to observe a "burning sensation" and "tightness" within the client's stomach, independent observers might very well be able to assess the degree of color within the client's face, his voice characteristics, or his motor activity as a measure of anxiety within the situation. Also, assessment of self-report might enable the client to rate the degree of discomfort experienced within the role-play, and perhaps he might best be asked to terminate the situation at that point where targeted "anxiety" behaviors (e.g., tightness in stomach, flushed face) occur. Thus, a measure of the latency from onset of the role-play to client-reported discomfort might be useful in determining the client's ability to tolerate the particular situation. The BCA should be able to set up an analog of virtually any kind of situation that might be difficult to directly measure within the natural environment.

More recent research (Bernstein and Nietzel, 1973) has found that behavioral approach performance may be "biased" by the manner in which the BCA sets a high or low demand for performance. This may be particularly true for the mildly phobic undergraduate subjects often employed within investigations. Bernstein and Paul (1971) have employed a "high demand" BAT that seems to discriminate the mildly phobic from clients who show intense and reliable avoidant responses in the natural environment. The instructions actively provoked snake-phobic subjects to engage in the terminal responses of actually picking up the snake within a contrived situation that legitimized such behavior (e.g., "It's necessary to assess your physiological responses"). While all subjects initially reported intense fears of reptiles, fully 25 percent were able to engage in those terminal responses under demand conditions, and were thus dropped from the study. Evans (1975) has suggested an alternative set of demand conditions, which are cast in a "diagnosis/treatment" context rather than experimental format.

It would seem that the behavioral approach test, in its many variations, provides important information to be added to the verbal reports and the written profiles obtained for the fearful client. Behavioral ratings enable the BCA to ascertain that the client not only "feels better" about his fear as treatment progresses, but can actually tolerate situations that were previously impossible for him.

Physiological Indices

Increasingly, a variety of physiological indices have been employed to accompany self-report and overt behavioral data collection as a means of obtaining a more complete perspective on a client's avoidant behavior. Lang (1969) has suggested that the BCA should assess as many components of the client's fear as possible. Mathews (1971), in an excellent review of physiological measures employed within desensitization, has stated:

> Current opinion based on what evidence is available appears to be converging on the view that fear, normal or abnormal, may most usefully be viewed as a label referring to the simultaneous occurrence of responses, physiological and psychological, in a series of imperfectly coupled systems, for instance the verbal/ cognitive, behavior/motor, and physiological/autonomic systems. (p. 73)

Physiological measurement has most often included an assessment of some component of *heart rate* (Craig, 1968; Lang, Melamed, and Hart, 1970; Lehrer, 1972), measures of *skin resistance* (Geer, 1966; Wilson, 1967; Barlow, Leitenberg, Agras, and Winzse, 1969; Lehrer, 1972), of *respiration rate* (Paul, 1969; Mathews and Gelder, 1969; Lehrer, 1972), or of *muscle activity* as measured by the electromyogram or *EMG* (Mathews and Gelder, 1969; Grossberg and Wilson, 1968; Paul, 1969; Lehrer, 1972).

In some cases physiological measures determine whether or not the client is fully relaxed (Lehrer, 1972), and desensitization does not proceed until some criterion response on a physiological measure is reached. In most cases physiological indices are combined with self-report and behavioral indicants to obtain an overall assessment of client "fear" prior to, during, and immediately following treatment. While most investigations have indicated that desensitization procedures are most effective in reducing autonomic responses that indicate anxiety, the degree of relationship between physiological, behavioral, and self-report measures is often poor (Moore, 1965; Paul, 1966; Lang, 1969). Mathews (1971) has stated: "It seems extremely unlikely that no causal relationship exists between autonomic responding during desensitization and subsequent behavioral change" (p. 88). While no established relationships seem to exist between the various measures of fear, particular investigators have found that each of these measures changes in a somewhat systematic fashion (Hoenig and Reed, 1966; Barlow et al., 1969; Bandura, Blanchard, and Ritter, 1969; Lira et al., 1975). Mathews (1971) has postulated the following "most common order of change" resulting from desensitization: (1) a progressive reduction in autonomic responses to phobic imagery; (2) associated, or immediately following, reports of diminished subjective anxiety (self-reports); (3) increased behavioral approaches to the feared object, followed by autonomic response reductions to the real-life stimulus. In a sense, then, this author postulates that the degree of correlation between self-reports, behavioral indices, and physiological measures will be greater over time, following the desensitization process, although such postulated relationships have yet to be completely clarified within the literature.

With regard to a choice between the various measures available, it should be noted that the most consistently significant changes following treatment have been observed using skin resistance (galvanic skin response, GSR) or cardiovascular responses, particularly heart rate (Mathews, 1971). Both GSR and heart rate responses seem to be related to the vividness of the phobic image within the desensitization process (Grossberg and Wilson, 1968; Lang, Melamed, and Hart, 1970); and the phobic scenes within a part of a desensitization hierarchy do seem to evoke larger autonomic responses than neutral scenes when presented imaginally (Lang et al., 1970) or in the real-world situation (Barlow et al., 1969)

The increasingly sophisticated technology of physiological measurement makes it possible for the BCA to employ physiological assessment of a client's fear most economically. The author would suggest that such measurement, when combined with self-reports and behavioral ratings, provides the BCA with a more total picture of response modalities involved. Physiological measurement is particularly useful when a client reports intense physiological responses to the phobic stimulus. Certainly one could imagine that a desensitized, socially phobic client could now behaviorally interact with others within the group situation (a real change in approach behavior) but still experience intensely discomforting physiological responses. Careful assessment of the physiological mode, in combination with the other measures discussed, ensures that all modalities of a client's fear may be assessed and perhaps brought into consonance as desensitization treatments provoke behavioral change.

RELAXATION

In the Wolpian (1958) model of systematic desensitization the client is asked to imagine each scene of the hierarchy while in a state of deep muscle relaxation. According to this model the state of relaxation "reciprocally inhibits" anxiety originally generated by the scene presentation. In fact, many investigators have obtained successful desensitization of client fears without using a counterconditioning agent such as relaxation (Rachman, 1968; Cooke, 1968), and the importance of relaxation seems to be called into question by many findings. In contrast, a mass of evidence attests to the successfulness of Wolpe's "systematic" approach which employs relaxation (Lomont and Edwards, 1967; Hyman, 1971; McReynolds and Tori, 1972). The author could find no study that found relaxation to interfere with or inhibit the desensitization process, but the question remains, is relaxation necessary?

While relaxation is typically employed in combination with the presentation of phobic scenes, it is often used in isolation, too, as the treatment of choice. In many cases the individual who reports "free-floating anxiety," "tension," or other unpleasant physiological sensations in the absence of some specific feared stimulus can be trained in relaxation procedures.

For example, Sherman (1976) reports two-year follow-up data for subjects trained to use relaxation as a self-management skill. Subjects reported continued success in using the procedures to reduce anxiety in a variety of situations such as taking exams, being interviewed, and speaking in public and found them useful in "general relaxation" and in "reducing fatigue." Thus, once given the skills, subjects were able to "self-apply" them to a variety of situations. As another example, a number of investigators have successfully employed relaxation to reduce insomnia (e.g., Borkovec, Kaloupek, and Slama, 1975). Thus, whether the BCA employs relaxation within the desensitization process or as a separate treatment, relaxation training would seem to be an important treatment tool.

The early work of Jacobson (1938) presented the first systematic approach to training a client to relax the various muscle groups of the body. Jacobson would ask the client to first tense and then relax each muscle group, so that the difference between a state of tension and a state of relaxation could be learned. The idea here is that only when clients can discriminate relaxation from tension can they assess the muscle groups of the body and bring those groups into a state of complete relaxation. While many relaxation formats are based upon the original Jacobsonian procedures of tension/relaxation, they also include additional components such as hypnotic suggestion or the adjunctive use of drugs (mostly briefly acting barbiturates such as Brevital) to facilitate relaxation (Munjack, 1975).

Relaxation Procedures

The client is first asked to sit in a cushioned chair that adequately supports the neck, back, and limbs in a firm and comfortable fashion. Often, relaxation training takes place in a setting free of noise distractions so that the client may carefully attend to the relaxation instructions which are administered either verbally or by audiotape. The tape approach allows the client to self-administer the instructions and return to the beginning as necessary while practicing. Most typically, the instructions proper are preceded by an introduction which defines the goals and rationale of the relaxation exercises. An introduction often employed by this author proceeds as follows:

Many of us go about our daily activities in a state of tension . . . the muscles of our body are very tight, almost to the point of pain and yet often we don't recognize that this state of tension exists. A good many of the physical complaints that we experience might be directly related to this state of tension. The idea of the present exercise is to train you to be able to do two things: first, to be able to tell when the muscles of your body are tense, and to experience the sensation of relaxation within each muscle group. Secondly, the goal is to train you to be able to produce that state of relaxation in a brief period of time.

You will be asked to systematically tense and then relax each of the major muscle groups within your body, beginning with the hands, arms, the upper area of your body including your neck and facial region, the trunk of your body, and then your legs and feet. As I give you instructions to tense certain muscles, be sure to tense them just as tightly as you can, until you are given the instruction to relax, at which time you should allow those muscles to be as free and loose as possible. As we proceed, you should focus your full attention upon each muscle group and *say the instructions to yourself* as I say them to you. Of course the goal is to train you to *self-instruct* those muscles to relax. Focus upon what it feels like within the muscle group. As we proceed, I will first instruct you to tense and then relax a particular muscle group, then ask you to *perform the same tension and relaxation at your own instruction.* I will then move on to the next muscle group; I will again give instructions, then turn over the control to you so that you may then relax that muscle group as suggested.

Now before we begin, make sure that you are seated very comfortably and well supported by the chair so that you don't have to use your muscles to support your body. If you wish to close your eyes, please do so. Many clients find that in closing their eyes they are better able to attend to the instructions, as well as the specific sensations produced within their muscles as we proceed. If you have any questions at any point, please feel free to interrupt me, and I'll try to answer you as best I can. Do you have any questions now? Okay, let's begin. . . .

The deep muscle relaxation procedure of Paul (1966), while meant to be self-presented (read) by the client, is presented below as an outline that might assist the BCA is verbally presenting instructions. The BCA is likely to develop a verbal style that most successfully relaxes the client with repeated practice. The BCA should enunciate very clearly as the instructions are provided and attempt to present the material in a relaxed, almost monotonic voice to assist the client in feeling relaxed within the situation. The male BCA may find that females wearing a skirt or dress and facing the BCA are somewhat uncomfortable due to the possibility of exposing certain body areas. In this case the client's chair might be turned so that the BCA faces its side. This permits the BCA to view the client's activities without being in a position that might promote some anxiety on the part of the client.

1. Make a fist with your dominant hand (usually right). Make a fist and tense the muscles of your (right) hand and forearm; tense it until it trembles. Feel the muscles pull across your fingers and the lower part of your forearm . . . relax . . . just let your hand go. Pay attention to the muscles of your (right) hand and forearm as they relax. Now how those muscles feel as relaxation flows through them (20 to 30 seconds).

Again, tense the muscles of your (right) hand and forearm. Pay attention to the muscles involved (5 to 7 seconds) . . . Relax; attend only to those muscles, and note how they feel as relaxation takes place, becoming more and more relaxed, until your arm and hand are completely relaxed with no tension at all, warm and relaxed.

Continue this procedure until your "hand and forearm are completely relaxed with no tension (usually 2 to 4 times is sufficient)."

2. . . . Tense your right biceps, leaving (your) hand and forearm on the chair. Proceed in the same amnner as above . . . using the right hand as a reference point, that is, move on when . . . (your) biceps feel as completely relaxed as (your) hand and forearm.

Now all the other muscle groups, one at a time.

Proceed to other gross muscle groups (listed below) in the same manner. (Be sure to continue to note how each set of muscles feels as it relaxes.) Feel the relaxation and warmth flow through these muscles; pay attention to these muscles so that later you can relax them again. Always use the preceding group as a reference for moving on.

3. Nondominant (left) hand and forearm—feel muscles over knuckles and on lower part of arm.

4. Nondominant (left) biceps.

5. Frown hard, tensing muscles of forehead and top of head (these muscles often "tingle" as they relax).

6. Wrinkle nose, feeling muscles across top of cheeks and upper lip.

7. Draw corners of mouth back, feeling jaw muscles and cheeks. . . .

8. Tighten chin and throat muscles, feeling two muscles in front of throat.

9. Tighten chest muscles and muscles across back—feel muscles pull between shoulder blades.

10. Tighten abdominal muscles—make abdomen hard.

11. Tighten muscles of right upper leg—feel one muscle on top and two on bottom of the upper leg.

12. Tighten right calf—feel muscles on bottom of right calf.

13. Push down with toes and arch right foot—feel pressure as if something were pushing up from under arch.

14. Left upper leg.

15. Left calf.

16. Left foot (pp. 118–119)

When you are finished with this procedure, all muscle groups will be relaxed. In some cases this procedure is followed by a relaxation of the whole body, where the client is asked to tense all the muscles of his body (or as many as possible) at once, and then completely relax. The BCA should check with the client to see if tension is experienced within any particular muscle group, and if so, to go back and repeat the tension/relaxation instructions for that particular muscle group. The author has found that asking the client to take a deep breath and to exhale it slowly "while pushing the tension out" of a particular muscle group is often a useful adjunct to the procedure. We know that when we take a deep breath and exhale a couple of times, this promotes a state of "lightness" and often assists in reducing the tension that resides within the chest cavity area. Should the client be susceptible to cramps from the muscular tension, reduce the tension period from about 10 seconds to 2 or 3 seconds, and ask the client not to tense the muscles so firmly in future trials. Many agencies require a complete medical examination of the client prior to initiating relaxation to ensure that the muscular activities involved are not contraindicated. In terminating relaxation, the client should be asked to countbackward from 10 to 1 while sequentially moving the various muscle groups of the body.

Most therapists ask clients to practice the relaxation on their own by providing a written handout that reviews the procedures that have been presented verbally, or by providing the client with an audiotape of instructions that may be played in the natural situation. Most often, a client is asked to practice the relaxation exercises two to four times each day, often keeping records of the particular muscles that have been successfully/unsuccessfully relaxed, and this information may structure additional relaxation training sessions within the clinical setting. In addition, the BCA may wish to construct a rating scale with the client (e.g., 1–10), with operationally defined anchors at each end that will allow the client to rate the degree to which a muscle group is relaxed. In this way quantitative data with regard to the course of relaxation can be obtained. A useful manual (Bernstein & Borkovec, 1974) has been directed exclusively toward the procedures of relaxation.

Client practice of the procedures within the natural environment is most important. To ensure practice, the BCA may wish to write out a *contract* that carefully specifies the times and characteristics of the relaxation practice sessions the client should complete each day. Client record-keeping allows the BCA to evaluate the client's efforts and also provides information with regard to the course of relaxation. Of course, the goal of any relaxation enterprise is to gradually and systematically turn over control of relaxation to the clients so that they may self-direct relaxation efforts. The following case example, which illustrates the application of self-relaxation to the treatment of insomnia in an 11-year-old female, provides a good example of the sequence by which relaxation training may be transferred from the BCA to the client (Weil and Goldfried, 1973).

> After two assessment interviews with Susan and her parents and a home observation, relaxation procedures were instituted. The therapist went to Susan's home in the evening and while the client was lying in bed gave her instructions for relaxation. The relaxation procedure consisted of alternate tensing and relaxing of various muscle groups. Susan responded favorably to relaxation and fell asleep one hour afterwards. A thirty minute tape recording was made of the therapist's relaxation instructions, which Susan used by herself for the next two weeks. During this time, she fell asleep either halfway through or immediately after the instructions were completed. According to the mother's report, Susan appeared to be more rested and relaxed during the day. An independent observation made by Susan's piano teacher indicated that there was a noticeable improvement in her performance during the lessons. After the two week period, a new recording was made, eliminating the tension phase and providing instructions only for relaxation. Susan typically fell asleep during or immediately after the tape, and after one week was provided with a fifteen minute version. This shortened version was used each night for another two weeks; as in the case of the previous recordings, she was usually asleep by the end of the instructions. Susan was provided with a final recording only five minutes in duration, consisting of instructions for self-relaxation. She used this version for approximately one week, and had no difficulty in falling asleep shortly after the completion of the tape. At this point, the use of external instructions for relaxation were completely eliminated, and Susan was instructed that, as soon as she was in bed and ready to go to sleep, she was to shut out all external noises and ruminations, and concentrate only on self-relaxation. She did so for the following few weeks, and reported that the use of self-relaxation helped her to get to sleep almost immediately (p. 283)

Follow-up at three months and six months indicated that the effects of the relaxation exercises had been maintained. Very little contact with the therapist was required due to the audiotape presentation of instructions. Although the client had approximately 40 relaxation "sessions" over a two-month period, the therapist met with the client and her parents on only seven occasions, thus suggesting the efficiency of this approach.

The early work of Jacobson (1938) and Paul (1969) indicated that muscle relaxation procedures induce physiological changes in such measures as heart rate, respiration rate, skin resistance, and EMG, although the particular physiological modalities affected by relaxation may vary with the individual client. Mathews (1971) states that it is most difficult to summarize the available knowledge regarding the effects of brief relaxation training, and the results indicate the operation of certain factors that are as yet not understood.

IMAGINAL VERSUS "IN VIVO" PRESENTATION

Numerous studies have found that changes that clients report imaginally within the therapeutic situation do generalize to the client's behavior in the natural setting. While the Wolpian procedure of systematic desensitization previously presented requires the client to vividly imagine each phobic scene, many investigators expose the client to the phobic stimulus in the natural setting or in some clinically contrived situation that approximates the natural environment. Thus the BCA is faced with a choice of presenting the phobic stimuli to the client in *imagination* or *in vivo*. The variable of imagery as it might be employed within a "systematic" desensitization program will be discussed, followed by a presentation of approaches to *in vivo* presentation. In addition, a comparison of the relative effectiveness of both procedures will be made.

Imaginal Presentation

While most studies have found that the imagination of phobic scenes as used in desensitization evokes greater autonomic responsivity than neutral scenes (Mathews, 1971), many investigators question the importance of the vividness of imagery as related to therapeutic success. In a review of studies employing imagery Richardson (1969) concluded that the controllability of imagery as well as its vividness are positively related to therapeutic gain. Subsequent investigators have contradicted this point of view, with Davis, McLemore, and London (1970), McLemore (1972), and Jones (1972) finding no relationship between the vividness of imagery or its controllability and the success of desensitization. In contrast, Wilkins (1971) found that neither relaxation, a hierarchy, nor even some process of reciprocal inhibition are necessary for desensitization to take place. The only necessary condition "appears to be (instructed) imaginations of fear-relevant scenes not necessarily arranged into a hierarchy and not necessarily concomitant to muscular relaxation" (p. 311). As is natural, others have questioned Wilkins' premise (Davison and Wilson, 1972), and the issue is not yet resolved. Another important problem in evaluating the role of imagery in any treatment procedure (e.g., covert processes) is the difficulty in determining precisely what the client is experiencing. Because the BCA cannot see the client's imaginings, their vividness and other important factors must be self-reported and are open to questions of reliability.

It is important to know that many clients experience difficulty in imagining objects vividly, and for that reason certain clients may not be ideal candidates for an imaginal desensitization approach. Most often, the BCA will attempt to assess the client's ability to vividly imagine by attempting to invoke a neutral imaginal scene prior to desensitization proper. Wolpe (1969) begins by presenting a "control" scene that is neutral in the sense that the client is not expected to experience an anxiety reaction to it. Wolpe carefully explores this scene with the client prior to its presentation to ensure its neutrality. Scenes employed by Wolpe include having the client imagine lying back on the grass on a summer's day while watching the clouds move overhead, seeing an intense bright spot at some standard distance in front of the client, or watching a leaf move erratically in the water along a riverbank. Almost any kind of neutral image could be employed, such as having the client imagine holding a penny between two fingers and looking at the various characteristics of Lincoln's profile—or the presentation of any fixed scene relating to a calm, neutral location out of doors. These exercises allow the client to report to the BCA the degree to which vivid imagination is possible, and provide a medium for practice with those clients who have difficulty. Thus, imaginal exercises are often employed not only as an assessment device (e.g., can the client vividly imagine?), but also as a training procedure. Typically, the client is asked to sit back and first completely relax, using the procedures described previously. Then the BCA asks the client to listen very carefully to the sound of his voice, and might present a neutral scene as follows:

I want you to imagine now that you are standing in a park and facing a rather large oak tree. Try to imagine that you are now about 50 yards away from the tree, and imagine first the shape of the tree . . . the colors that it reflects toward you, the green of the leaves contrasted with the rich color of its trunk. Try to visualize the blueness of the sky in the background of the tree, and its contrast with the green leaves of the tree. Picture as best you can this rather large oak tree standing against the background of blue. Now imagine that you're walking toward the tree and try to imagine as vividly as possible the sensations of your legs moving, and the rest of the bodily feelings associated with walking. Imagine as you walk toward the tree now that its form becomes even larger, and its colors become ever more vivid and pronounced. Imagine the green becoming more and more intense as you look at the leaves of the tree with its trunk becoming richer and richer in hue. Imagine now that you are ten yards away from the tree, and that you're looking up through its branches and leaves to see bits of the blue sky reflecting through. Imagine the intense greens, in contrast to the rich hues of the limbs of the tree. Now, I want you to stand there for a couple of minutes and just look about, and try to imagine each part of that tree as vividly as possible. . . . Now imagine that you are looking down at its trunk. Imagine the rich colors of brown and black which make up the bark of the tree. I want you to move toward the tree now and reach over and touch the tree with the tips of the fingers of your right hand. Imagine now the irregular contour of the bark on the tree as it touches the tips of your fingers. Try to feel that bark as best you can. . . . Now imagine that you are walking away from the tree moving out into the open space again, and into the bright intense sunlight, and feel the warmth of the sun now on your cheek, as it produces tingling sensations of warmth. Imagine the warmth on the entire left side of your body as you look over your left shoulder and up at the very bright sun. Imagine squinting your eyes now as you look in the direction of the sun, and try to picture again the blueness of the sky in contrast with the whiteness of the sun. Imagine that you hear a dog barking in the background, as you walk away from the tree into the open spaces of the park. Imagine the sound of the dog's bark, and try to distinguish each barking sound, from the rustling of the grass as you walk through it. Off to the right now you hear the sounds of traffic, which for some reason you haven't been able to hear until now. Try to imagine the sounds of engines moving off; horns; and the general combined sound that automobiles make as they move toward a destination. Try to contrast this sound with the dog barking in the background, and concentrate as vividly as possible on the differences between the two sounds. Now imagine as you walk across this open field that you become a bit hungry, that you remove a stick of your favorite gum or candy from your pocket, and place it in your mouth. Try to imagine what it feels like when the object is placed within your mouth; focus as intensely as possible on the flavor, taste and the consistency as you chew or suck on the object. As vividly as possible taste that object, and imagine the sensations it provokes within your mouth and throat. Try to imagine the smell that the object promotes as you move it about your mouth, and try to contrast this smell with the previous smell of the open air, and the wooded surroundings. When you've sufficiently consumed the object, you may then open your eyes, and we will talk about the things you just did in your imagination.

In the above example the BCA directs the client to carefully and vividly imagine an array of stimuli within each of the major sensory modalities: sight; hearing; touch; taste; and smell. Following the client's attempt in imagination the BCA should carefully question the client to assess the *rapidity* with which the client initially was able to "get into" the imaginal scene; those stimuli that were most easy for the client to imagine; those that were most difficult; the sensory modalities that provoked the most vivid image; the sensory modalities that provoked the least vivid image; and any specific thoughts or physical sensations that competed with or interfered with the client's imagination. If the client has difficulty in some specific aspect of imagination, this can become the focus of additional practice sessions that are specially tailored to focus upon the problem object or within problem sense modality. In addition, the BCA may ask the client to rate the vividness of imagery on some previously agreed-upon scale. The client may be rated after each training session so that the BCA can gain information as to the changes in client imaginal ability over training sessions.

If imaginal training is a preliminary to desensitization, it is important for the client to be able to obtain a mental image very quickly and to maintain it at a level of vividness that might feasibly produce anxiety similar to the object in the natural environment. Although the importance of the client's imagination provoking a physiological response is open to question, it would seem that if the client can readily tolerate the various phobic scenes presented in imagination, then the imagination is not really simulating the client's phobic experiences in the natural environment. If such scenes are presented in imagination within a hierarchy, the BCA might very well question the effectiveness of imagination if the client is able to tolerate each of the hierarchy scenes on the first trial, moving through the hierarchy in one session. The process of systematic desensitization (Wolpe, 1958) requires that relaxation reciprocally inhibit the client's fear of each of the phobic stimuli within the hierarchy. If the imaginal presentation of the phobic stimulus induces no fear, it would seem that the procedure would not be effective. Unfortunately, at present, this hypothesis cannot be supported or rejected, due to the wealth of incompatible findings.

Perhaps the imaginal training procedures described above might also be useful as a preliminary to the covert approaches described in Chapter 5. Obviously, if a client is asked to systematically employ some positive or aversive image, the BCA would want to carefully assess the degree to which the client could successfully employ imaginal processes.

In Vivo Approaches

Often, the BCA may wish to expose the client to the actual stimuli that provoke fear *in the natural environment,* or in contrived *"analog" situations* that approximate the natural environment. Thus, instead of having the height-phobic client imagine that he is looking up a stairwell, the *in vivo* approach would require that the client actually look up a stairwell, either in the clinical or natural environment. Many investigators have compared an *in vivo* presentation of phobic stimuli to the imaginal approach (Barlow, Leitenberg, Agras, and Wincze, 1969; Cooke, 1966; O'Neil and Howell, 1969) and typically find no significant difference when phobic clients are randomly assigned to an *in vivo* versus imaginal treatment approach. As an exception Barlow et al. (1969) found that the *in vivo* approach was superior to an imaginal approach for a population of snake-fearful subjects. Importantly, the subjects in this study could not be described as phobic, and are typical of the university student, "snake-fearful" clients employed in many analog studies (Bernstein and Paul, 1971). This is not to take away from this study, only to suggest that these "fearful" clients may have been better able to tolerate an *in vivo* exposure than truly "phobic" clients, who may be unable even to enter a room that contains a snake. In fact, Cooke (1966) found that in imaginal desensitization clients who are relatively more anxious tend to show a greater decrease in fear than do slightly anxious subjects. However, highly anxious clients may not be willing to expose themselves to the feared stimulus in the real-life setting, and for these clients an imaginal presentation will at least permit treatment to begin. It is the experience of the author that an imaginal approach is the only procedure that many clients will tolerate.

While the *in vivo* approach may be used as the sole treatment, it is often used as an adjunct to an imaginal approach. Clients are asked to expose themselves to a feared stimulus in the real world, following imaginal desensitization of that stimulus. Thus, after the dog-phobic client imagines herself in a small room that contains a dog without experiencing anxiety, she might then be asked to expose herself to the same situation in real life before proceeding to the next scene on the hierarchy. This adjunctive use of *in vivo* exposure permits the BCA to assess the degree of generalization from imaginal to real-life experiences as the client moves through each successive phase of desensitization. If the client is unable to tolerate the real-life situation without experiencing unacceptable levels of anxiety, the BCA may then reexpose the client to the imaginal approach or employ a straightforward *in vivo* approach if the imaginal procedure seems to be ineffective. Wolpe (1973) has stated that *in vivo* approaches are the treatment of choice for 10 to 15 percent of patients in whom imaginal stimuli do not produce emotional responses similar to those produced by the corresponding real situations. It has already been suggested that certain clients may not be able to visualize adequately or to imagine the phobic stimulus with sufficient vividness to provoke anxiety, and certainly for this population some form of *in vivo* approach might be the treatment of choice.

Often, *in vivo* desensitization proceeds in much the same fashion as the imaginal approach. The *client may be asked to relax while being exposed to the real-life situation/object* to increase the probability that some sort of counter-conditioning will occur. *Or the BCA may wish merely to expose the client to the situation without relaxation* so that the fear provoked by the stimulus will extinguish over a period of time. Also, the client may be exposed to the phobic stimuli in a systematic fashion using a hierarchy or rather unsystematically exposed across stimulus items. Most often, the client exposes himself to some graded series of stimuli in hierarchical fashion, with the therapist present. The therapist may assist clients in relaxing themselves within the situation if relaxation is employed, provide support for them and reinforcement for their efforts at approaching the feared stimulus, and provide immediate feedback as to the qualitative characteristics of their responses. Also, particularly if clients are to expose themselves to any situation that could provoke bodily harm (e.g., a car-phobic client driving an automobile; a height-phobic client climbing a ladder), the BCA will certainly wish to be present for both pragmatic as well as ethical reasons. It is important to note that *an in vivo approach should never be employed in any situation in which the client's approach efforts may lead to physical harm.*

A case example from the author's experience illustrates both the manner in which an *in vivo* approach to desensitization was employed with an intensely phobic individual as well as some of the important considerations regarding client welfare that should underlie any such approach:

A 28-year-old male reported that over the previous six-month period he had experienced increased anxiety whenever he exposed himself to the out-of-doors, or viewed a picture which described an out-of-doors scene. Most particularly, the situation of driving an automobile provoked such intense discomfort that the client was often forced to pull his automobile off to the side of the road. This behavior had almost resulted in a severe accident on a number of occasions over the immediate two-month period prior to treatment. The client's fear of open spaces became so intense during the month prior to treatment that the client was "confined" to his house, unable to go to work, or even move about his own property out-of-doors. The client reported that any exposure to open spaces caused him to think that he was going to "fall down," and he became very dizzy and sometimes nauseated. Physical examination had indicated no physical factors that might explain the client's behavior. At his wife's urgent request, the client was admitted to a psychiatry ward setting. The client showed a good deal of insight, and was able to trace his "problem" to an earlier episode in his life, and knew that he must attempt to expose himself to out-of-doors situations to overcome his fear. Unfortunately, on his own he was unable to tolerate the phobic situation long enough in the rather erratic way he had attempted to reduce his "fear." After a complete behavioral analysis was obtained, the client was trained in the procedures of relaxation, and responded well within five or six training sessions. Asked to practice the relaxation on his own during the day, an attempt was then made to structure a hierarchy of those situations relating to open spaces which provoked an anxiety response. The following are representative scenes from this hierarchy:

Scene 1: Moving outside the client's room on the ward for the period of 1 minute.

Scene 2: Moving outside of his room for the period of 5 minutes.

Scene 3: Seated in a chair at the end of the patients' lounge area (a congregating place for clients on the ward situation), for the period of 5 minutes.

Scene 12: Moving halfway down the hall toward the elevator for the period of 1 minute.

Scene 13: Moving down the hall to the halfway point for a period of 5 minutes.

Scene 14: Moving down the hall to the halfway point for the period of 10 minutes.

Scene 20: Moving out of the elevator and standing on the first floor adjacent to the elevator for the period of 1 minute.

Scene 21: Standing on the first floor adjacent to the elevator for the period of 5 minutes.

Scene 32: Standing at the glass doors and looking outside for the period of 10 minutes.

Scene 33: Standing at the glass doors and looking outside for the period of 20 minutes or more.

Scene 34: Opening the doors and stepping immediately outside for 1 minute.

The hierarchy described above was traversed by client and therapist in the following fashion. The client was asked to completely relax himself and then to expose himself to Scene 1 of the hierarchy. At any point when the client became anxious, the therapist (who was standing in proximity to the client) would assist the client in achieving relaxation again. Once the client was able to tolerate a given scene with no anxiety, the next scene was entertained in similar fashion. Over the period of about three weeks, the client was able to complete the hierarchy described above, moving from his room (where he had been "confined" due to his anxiety prior to treatment) to just outside the glass doors. Additional hierarchies were constructed to systematically expose the client to graded and increasingly more difficult "outside" situations, until finally the client was able to leave the hospital setting and resume the ordinary life situation. It should be noted that when the client exposed himself to similar situations in the natural environment, he initially did experience moderate degrees of anxiety but continued to tolerate the situations until ultimate desensitization occurred.

This case example illustrates how client movement through a graded and systematic hierarchy of *in vivo* situations can often be a time-consuming process. Due to this client's intense fear an array of "small steps" was necessary to achieve mastery over the previously feared situations. In addition, it is obvious that the BCA would not want to send such a client "out on his own" because of the possible harm that might come from an intense anxiety experience. In the present case the client often became dizzy and would fall to the ground when exposing himself to phobic stimuli. One can only imagine the possible harm that could have occurred if such an "attack" took place on a stairwell, while walking across a street, or while driving an automobile. Thus, the therapist's careful monitoring of the client at each step of the hierarchy was both practical and of course necessary to insure the client's safety.

In summary, the *in vivo* approach seems to be as effective as the imaginal approach to desensitization. It may be particularly useful for clients who have difficulty imagining the phobic stimuli or for those less fearful clients who may be able to expose themselves to real-life situations right away, perhaps decreasing the time of treatment. The example cited points up the extreme care and orderly approach that must be employed when clients are exposed to situations within the natural environment, particularly when a potential for injury to the client is evident. For those clients that cannot tolerate a real-life exposure, the imaginal approach offers the ideal compromise—possibly used as a first step, with *in vivo* exposures following each mastery of an imaginal scene. Such an approach ensures that the client will not be asked to tolerate a real-life situation that may provoke such intense levels of anxiety as to confound all therapeutic efforts up to that point.

Automated Presentation

While relaxation instructions are often presented on audiotape, virtually any aspect of the desensitization procedure could be presented through visual and/or auditory presentations controlled by automated mechanisms. In fact, investigators have recorded the hierarchy on videotape or slides and permitted the client to self-present the scenes in a fashion similar to the usual systematic approach, as well as recording both the hierarchy and all therapist instructions on audiotape to effect a completely automated desensitization (Paul and Trimble, 1970; Donner and Guerney, 1969; Lang, Melamed, and Hart, 1971). Interestingly, Lang and his colleagues found that the automated means of presenting desensitization without the therapist present was as effective as desensitization with the therapist present, thus stimulating an array of research investigations into the role of the interpersonal relationship in desensitization.

Because clients presenting complaints (e.g., a specific fear) often do not adequately describe important problem behaviors and potential controlling variables within the natural environment, the development of a therapeutic relationship that fosters a comprehensive gathering of "assessment" information should *precede* any assignment of a client to automated procedures. The author often finds great discrepancies between initial client self-reports of the "problem" and data gathered in a comprehensive fashion. When the client's needs are assessed within a warm and positive relationship between client and BCA, there is a feeling of trust and expectation of success when treatments are applied.

SYSTEMATIC VERSUS TERMINAL PRESENTATION

Another major choice for the BCA is whether to present the phobic stimuli in some systematic, graded hierarchy from least to most anxiety provoked, or to present only those scenes that are maximally anxiety provoking. When the "systematic" procedure is employed, the goal is to expose the client only to those stimuli he can tolerate with relatively low degrees of evoked anxiety, and in systematic fashion proceed to expose the client to stimuli that evoke ever-increasing degrees of anxiety. Implicitly, once the client is able to successfully tolerate a scene earlier in the hierarchy without becoming anxious, it would seem that the next scene would be more easily tolerated, thus allowing the client to proceed at each step without extremely intense degrees of anxiety being evoked. In the "terminal" presentation approach, which includes procedures such as "flooding" (e.g. Rachman, 1966) and "implosion" (Stampfl and Levis, 1967), the therapist exposes the client exclusively to those stimuli that evoke maximally intense anxiety responses. Thus, the flooding and implosive procedures incorporate the highest items on a standard stimulus hierarchy. The two approaches just described vary a good deal both in the procedures employed as well as in their theoretical underpinnings, and so they will be discussed separately. Following a presentation of the important issues relating to the "systematic," or hierarchical approach, there will be a discussion of procedures and issues related to the "terminal" flooding and implosive procedures. In addition, a comparison between the systematic and terminal approaches will enable the reader to evaluate the relative efficacy of these two divergent approaches.

Systematic Presentation

In the classical systematic desensitization approach of Wolpe (1958) carefully constructed, individualized hierarchies are constructed from the client's verbal report of those stimuli that provoke avoidant behaviors. Whether the items of the hierarchy are to be presented in imagination or *in vivo*, the BCA carefully interviews the client to generate a list of anxiety-provoking experiences ranging from least to most anxiety-provoking experiences ranging from least to most anxiety-provoking. The BCA might ask the client:

I know that you've told me that you're afraid of height, but now I would like to ask you about those specific situations which either in real life or in your imagination are a part of your fear. For example, it may be that looking down a flight of stairs, looking out a window, or even looking at a photograph of a mountainous region promotes the anxiety responses that we've already talked about. Some of the situations or objects that made you feel anxious may seem silly to you, and you may think that I'm not interested in hearing about them, but I am. I want to know about as many of the situations involving height that make you anxious as you can tell me about.

Often, the BCA will provide the client with 5 x 7 cards and, after presenting the task very carefully, ask the client to write down each of these situations or objects on a separate card as part of a homework assignment. The BCA might state:

On these 5 × 7 cards, I'd like you to write down each and every separate situation or object involving height that makes you feel anxious. Try to write down this information in as much detail as you can, including information not only about what you *think about,* but what you *physically feel* when exposed to the situation or object. Be sure to write down each situation or object on a separate card, and please bring them to our next meeting.

By requiring the client to write down each separate item on individual cards or pieces of paper, the BCA may now flexibly put each scene in its proper order in the hierarchy. Once the scenes and situations are developed, the goal of constructing the hierarchy becomes threefold: (1) to ensure that each scene evokes some degree of anxiety on the client's part; (2) with the client's assistance, to order the scenes from least to most anxiety-provoking; and (3) to ensure that the degree of distance between scenes regarding anxiety provoked is approximately the same.

Scene-provoked anxiety—In order to assess the degree to which a given scene provokes anxiety within the client, the BCA must decide upon a system of measurement. The BCA might employ some form of client self-rating system, as previously suggested (e.g., rate each card on a scale from 1 to 100), or items may be evaluated by the degree of physiological responses provoked (e.g., BCA asks client to imagine each scene for a standard time period and measures the client's heart rate, GSR, or other physiological index throughout the presentation). If the BCA has decided to employ an *in vivo* approach to scene presentation, the client may be exposed to each of the scenes in real life, with self-report, physiological measures (via telemetry), or even distance of approach providing information as to the anxiety evoked by the scene.

Those scenes that do not provoke even a low degree of anxiety may then be discarded, and it is now the task of the BCA to construct a hierarchy from the scenes that remain.

Ordering scenes—Now that the BCA has some kind of quantitative information as to the degree of anxiety provoked by each scene, an initial ordering of the scenes may be performed. The number of scenes within the hierarchy at this point could range from a few to very many. It is the task of the BCA to make the order correct. Scenes that greatly overlap (e.g., are no different in the anxiety that they provoke) may be discarded. When clients themselves rate the degree of anxiety, the initial order of scenes that the client devises may be numerically written *on the back* of the cards. The cards are then shuffled and given the client again, in a *face-up* position, for another go-round. When the client has completed this task, the BCA can compare the numbers on the back of the cards with the new order to determine whether the initial ordering agrees with the client's current ordering of the cards. Often, there is a divergence in order of one or two points, and this can be corrected with additional presentations to the client for ordering. When the client is satisfied that the order does indeed display least to most anxiety, the next task of the BCA is to ensure that the distance between each of the scene-cards is as comparable as possible.

Distance between scenes—Once the scenes have been ordered and scenes that seem to be very similar in amount of anxiety provoked are discarded, the task is to require the client to rate the degree to which Scene 1 is different from Scene 2, Scene 2 is different from Scene 3, and so on, as to the degree of anxiety provoked. We might call this the "perceived distance" between cards. Obviously, if there is a great difference between the anxiety provoked by Scene 1 and that by Scene 2, a hierarchy will not be systematic at all. The goal of a hierarchy is to expose the client to a graduated series of presentations of the phobic stimuli, so that each scene is a systematic increment from the preceding scene. Thus, the importance of distancing becomes obvious.

The client's self-ratings of anxiety provoked by each scene (previously obtained) may assist in this distancing procedure. As a check, the author often employs a physical scaling procedure which is easy to set up in virtually any clinical situation.

Using the longest portion of a desktop, a series of gradations marking points 1 through 10 are applied using marking tape. So that the subject may not only rate but *physically* show the distance between each pair of cards within the hierarchy, the following procedure is employed, using the cards for Scene 1 and Scene 2 as examples.

1. Scene 1 is placed at the end of the desk closest to the client (the client stands at one end of a desktop); the client is then given the card representing Scene 2 and asked to push it "away" as far along the desktop as it should be from card 1, based on the 1–10 rating system. Thus, the client rates the distance by moving card 2 to a certain point (e.g., 3 units) away from card 1. The client actually sees the space between items, too, and many clients have reported that this assists them in making this determination.

2. After the BCA notes the rating for the distance between cards 1 and 2, card 2 replaces card 1 at the "bottom" of the scale. Then the

client is given card 3 and asked to move it the appropriate distance from card 2, using the established rating system.

3. All additional ascending pairs of the hierarchy are treated in similar fashion, and the distance ratings (1–10) between each pair (e.g. 1–2, 2–3, etc.) may now be compared.

4. As the client was asked to rate the distance, with a rating of 5 being the midpoint, those card-items that vary more than one or two points from the 5 rating (e.g., ratings of 1, 2, or 3; 8, 9, or 10) must now be modified or replaced, so that the distance between cards is as similar as possible.

If the distance between a pair of hierarchy items is very low (one or two points), it may be that one of them can be dropped, as they are seemingly duplicative. For example, if the distance between card 1 and card 2 is only a point, perhaps card 2 could be removed, with card 3 taking its place. The BCA then asks the client to rate the distance between card 1 and card 3, and if it falls within the criterion distance, the third card now becomes the second scene within the hierarchy. When the distance between two cards is very great (e.g., eight or nine), the BCA may wish to add a scene between these two. For example, if the distance between Scenes 6 and 7 is ten points, perhaps a new scene, which the client rates as being "between" these two in terms of anxiety that is provoked, could be interpolated between the two scenes. Once all of these determinations are made, the BCA will have removed some of the original scenes within the hierarchy, added others, and may now place a hierarchy number (position) on the scenes that remain.

Paul (1969) has distinguished between two major categories of hierarchy, *thematic* and *spatial-temporal*. In the thematic hierarchy items are related to the same basic theme but are not necessarily related in time and space. Thus, any items that involve the theme (e.g., height, open spaces, social situations, animals) would be included in the hierarchy, based upon the client's ordering of anxiety provoked. A good example of such a hierarchy is presented by Bruno and McCullough (1973), which was constructed for a 24-year-old female experiencing a fear of tests. Regarding the material she was to study (English literature), she was required to order each of the authors to be studied in terms of the anxiety that they evoked in her (see Table 9.1).

Within a thematic hierarchy ordering of the items does not have to "make any sense" regarding time—that is, studying the material prior to an examination might be Scene 1, with Scene 10 being the professor announcing the exam three weeks prior. One would think, on the face of it, that studying the night before would be more anxiety-provoking than the professor's merely announcing the exam, but this may not be the case. In terms of the client's subjective report the professor's announcement may indeed provoke more anxiety than her studies immediately prior to the examination.

Table 9.1

A Thematic Hierarchy

Author hierarchy

1. Pope (most anxiety provoking)
2. Wordsworth
3. Gray
4. Bunyan
5. Johnson
6. Burns
7. Sheridan
8. Blake
9. Swift
10. Whycherley
11. Richardson
12. Fielding
13. Sterne
14. Defoe (least anxiety provoking)

The spatial-temporal hierarchy includes items that are graded with respect to their closeness in space (e.g., 20 feet away from phobic stimulus, 10 feet, 5 feet, 1 foot), or time prior to some targeted event (e.g., two weeks, one week, one day, one hour). In most cases a hierarchy will include spatial-temporal as well as thematic features. An excellent example of a mixed thematic/spatial-temporal hierarchy has been presented by Kanfer and Phillips (1970). This was employed with clients fearful of an impending examination. While the theme (taking an examination) is consistent, certain items are obviously ordered in time and space.

1. Beginning a new course
2. Hearing an instructor announce a small quiz two weeks hence
3. Having a professor urge you personally to do well on an exam
4. Trying to decide how to study for an exam
5. Reviewing the material I know should be studied—listing study to do
6. Hearing an instructor remind the class of a quiz one week hence
7. Hearing an instructor announce a major exam in three weeks and its importance
8. Hearing an instructor announce a major exam in one week
9. Standing alone in the hall before an exam
10. Getting a graded exam back in class
11. Anticipating getting back a graded exam later that day
12. Talking to several students about an exam right before taking it
13. Thinking about being scared and anxious regarding a specific exam
14. Studying with fellow students several days before an exam

15. Hearing some "pearls" from another student that you doubt you'll remember, while studying in a group
16. Cramming while alone in the library right before an exam
17. Thinking about not keeping up in other subjects while preparing for an exam
18. Thinking about being anxious over schoolwork in general
19. Talking with several students about an exam immediately after
20. Thinking about being generally inadequately prepared
21. Thinking about not being adequately prepared for a particular exam
22. Studying the night before a big exam (p. 151)

When a systematic approach to imaginal or *in vivo* desensitization is employed, it becomes extremely important that the BCA construct the hierarchy carefully and with as much client input as possible. Should scenes be out of order or consistent distancing not carefully adhered to, the client may be faced with too great a jump in anxiety provoked. Certain scenes may actually interfere with the desensitization process. Of course, if the scenes do not optimally tap the targeted elements of the client's fear, the BCA will be attempting to desensitize irrelevant material.

Research aimed at evaluating the hierarchy within the desensitization process has found overwhelmingly that standardized hierarchies (pretailored hierarchy used across large groups of similarly phobic clients) are as effective as individually tailored hierarchies in reducing phobic behavior (Emery and Krumboltz, 1967; McGlynn, 1971). Thus, the BCA may employ, with some probability of success, a standard hierarchy across clients who exhibit similar fears. If an individual's fears are quite divergent from a standardized hierarchy, it makes sense to construct an individually tailored series of items using the procedures outlined above. Certainly, standardized hierarchies reduce the amount of time directed toward preparation for desensitization, and when appropriate to a client's reported fears, they may well be usefully employed.

Another important finding has been the highly significant relationship between the number of fear scenes completed within the hierarchy and reduction of avoidant behavior (Lang and Lazovik, 1963; Lang, Lazovik, and Reynolds, 1965; Davison, 1968). Clients who complete a greater proportion of items within the hierarchy show greater fear reduction in terms of a number of indices than clients who do not come near completion, with the number of sessions held constant (Wilkins, 1971). Thus, it would seem that movement up the hierarchy is in some fashion related to ultimate success of the desensitization process; however, many investigators disagree as to what factors underlie this relationship (Wilkins, 1971). Wilkins has made the point that the hierarchy is important because it provides feedback to the client regarding improvement. Self-perceived improvement within the hierarchy may thus alter the client's cognitive view of himself in relation to the phobic stimulus, and this cognitive change may be responsible for the desensitization that is observed. The role of client expectancy, cognitive variables, and demand characteristics will be discussed in a later section.

"Terminal" Presentation

A number of investigators have suggested that for desensitization to proceed at the most rapid rate, maximally fearful scenes should be the sole focus of presentation. Treatment begins by presenting to the client items that generate high degrees of anxiety in the hope that, in the absence of any harm coming to the client, this will cause the client's anxiety to extinguish. Very simply, in terms of a classical conditioning process the CS (phobic stimulus) is presented with no additional pairings of the UCS (presumably the aversive stimulus that may have originally caused the client's fear). As the reader will remember, when the CS is presented in isolation without additional pairings of the UCS, conditioned responses to the CS will gradually extinguish over time (see Chapter 2). While these procedures are often variously labeled *implosion, flooding* or *extinction,* these different labels do in fact often apply to procedures that vary a good deal operationally. A review by McNamara (1972) has attempted to evaluate these terminal presentation procedures within three major categories:

Type 1. Following the construction of a graded hierarchy, the client is repeatedly exposed to those items within the hierarchy that received the highest anxiety ratings. In presenting the aversive stimuli, the therapist does not intensify them in any way, and the presentation occurs within a neutral context. Often, the client is trained in relaxation and is required to maintain a state of relaxation during scene presentation. Typically, these procedures would be approached within the systematic framework, as a hierarchy is constructed; the only main difference is the degree of severity of the scenes that are presented within the hierarchy.

Type 2. This approach, which is most often described as flooding, has the characteristics of Type 1 with the exception of the possibility of relaxation. Most typically, clients are presented scenes that elicit great degrees of anxiety for long durations of time until extinction occurs. Presentations may run as long as one hour. Importantly, the client is not usually exposed to scenes within which he is subjected to aversive consequences.

Type 3. This procedure, most often called implosion (Stampfl and Levis, 1967), forces the client to imagine maximally fearful scenes in which he is the victim of extremely negative consequences. Often, the therapist attempts to build upon the scene to increase the vividness of the aversive stimuli. This procedure is based upon a rather well defined set of procedures first put forward by Stampfl and Levis (1967).

Morganstern (1973) agrees with McNamara's distinction between

Type 2 (flooding) and Type 3 (implosive) approaches. While these terms are often used interchangeably and inappropriately (Kirsch, Wolpin and Knutson, 1975) within the literature, Morganstern contends that there are considerable differences. Perhaps the major difference is that flooding presents the scene in imagination in a fashion that attempts to duplicate the client's real-life exposure to it, whereas implosion presents the scene in an unrealistic and terrifyingly vivid fashion in which the goal is to promote extreme anxiety within the client. Each of these procedures will be presented, but the major emphasis will be upon "implosion," because of the array of very specific procedures and issues associated with that approach.

Flooding—Flooding may be best thought of as a straight and simple extinction procedure that may be performed either imaginally or *in vivo*. Wolpe (1973) presents an earlier account of what he calls the first successful use of flooding, in which an adolescent girl with a phobia of automobiles was forced to remain in the back of a car in which she was driven continuously for four hours. After her fear reached panic proportions, a gradual extinction began to take place, and at the end of the automobile ride she reported that she was quite comfortable. This is similar to the life experience where a child who has fallen off a horse is forced to immediately get back on and ride, or where a child who has a bad experience in the water is forced to return to the pool. Parents often employ such procedures without calling them by name to successfully reduce incipient fears on the part of their offspring. Of course, these procedures usually work, since the child is forced to expose himself immediately to the stimulus situation (CS) in the absence (hopefully) of any additional aversive consequences (UCS). There are two important issues here: Will clients reexpose themselves to a feared situation voluntarily? Will clients be able to tolerate the feared situation for sufficient time so that extinction may occur? Obviously, if clients expose themselves to some feared situation, become anxious, and leave prior to extinction, this exposure may succeed in augmenting their fear, rather than reducing it.

Marks and his colleagues at the Maudsley Hospital in London report upon the extensive use of flooding procedures to deal with a variety of phobic situations (Watson, Gaind and Marks, 1971; Marks, 1972). The client who is afraid of the motion picture theater may be assigned to a therapist who will immediately take him to the movies and sit with him for some long period of time until extinction occurs. The client who is afraid of riding on the subway system may spend his therapy sessions riding the London tubes with his therapist, thus employing an *in vivo* flooding procedure. Marks has reported that clients rarely refuse to expose themselves to these fearful stimuli when the therapist urges them to do so. Presumably, an imaginal presentation or more straightforward systematic presentation could be employed for clients who are initially unable to expose them-

selves to flooding. The following case example (Boudywns, 1973) illustrates the use of an imaginal flooding procedure with a 25-year-old male
who reported a fear of dentists' offices:

> After Mr. N entered our program . . . the author discovered that he had a
> circumscribed phobia for dentists and dental offices. He complained that even
> though his teeth were in a severe state of decay, his fears had made him unable to
> consult a dentist since he was a child. Further, if he even attempted to enter a
> dental office, he would become sick to his stomach, gag, and sometimes vomit. It
> seemed obvious that such avoidance behavior kept this patient's conditioned emo-
> tional response to dentists from extinguishing. The phobia seemed to stem from a
> frightening childhood experience (age 7) when Mr. N had a tooth pulled by what
> he described as "a mean and ugly dentist." He seemed highly motivated to over-
> come his fears, and after a short explanation of the flooding procedure, agreed to
> try therapy. Not counting the initial clinical interviews, therapy included three 45
> minute sessions, each spaced one day apart. All three sessions consisted of two
> basic themes. In the first, the patient was asked to imagine a visit to the dental
> service of the hospital to have a tooth pulled. The second consisted of a scene in
> which he imagined, in complete detail, the original traumatic dental visit. This
> included a detailed account of the trip to the office, the actual visit, and his
> behavior after the visit. Mr. N manifested his disturbance in both scenes by
> profuse sweating, crying and gagging. At one point he vomited. At the end of the
> first session the patient was assigned homework tasks of reviewing both scenes on
> his own. By the third and final office session, the patient was able to review the
> scenes with considerable reduction in emotionality. To test the effects of therapy,
> the patient was instructed to go to the hospital's dental service, sit in the outer
> office, and observe his response. He was able to do this with only mild discomfort.
> About a week later, Mr. N successfully endured his first visit to the dentist in 18
> years, and was able to make numerous return visits for dental work (pp. 5–6)

Another example of the flooding approach provides imaginal presentation within the session (45 minutes) followed by a 45-minute *in vivo* presentation of the same intensive stimuli (Everaerd, Rijken, and Emmelkamp, 1973) with a population of clients experiencing fear of open places
(agoraphobia).

The first flooding session was spent making a list of the phobic situations and
their cues which were relevant for the client. At the same time the client was
trained in imagining both neutral situations (e.g. his own sitting-room) and
phobic situations as vividly as possible.
The next five sessions consisted of 45 min. of flooding in the imagination,
immediately followed by 45 min. of flooding *in vivo*. With the flooding in the
imagination the client was instructed to sit as relaxed and comfortably as possible
and to close his eyes. Then the therapist asked the client to try to imagine the
situations which the therapist was going to describe as vividly as possible and not
to avoid these images in any way. Those situations which the client found the most
frightening were then described to him—for example sitting in a hall full of people,
travelling by bus, train or car, or walking alone in the streets. Here is an example
of one of these scenes, described to one particular client.
"Imagine that you are going out of the front door of this house. You walk
through the front garden and then you are in the street. You turn left and walk in

the direction of the shopping centre where you have to go and buy something. Imagine it as well as you can: the houses you walk past, the cars that rush past you. You are walking there alone and you are going in the direction of the railway crossing. The bars are down and you have to wait. A group of people is standing there waiting and they look at you. You find it very disturbing, this waiting, and you hop a bit from one leg to the other. At last the bars are going up, you walk on and arrive in the shopping centre. it is fuller there, there are more and more people. You begin to feel rather bad now. You become dizzy. You feel it in your legs. But you nevertheless walk on, because there is nowhere you can go there on the street, you cannot flee inside anywhere. Now you have to cross the street. There is a string of cars and you run between them. On the other side of the street there are still more people. Now you are feeling completely dizzy. Your legs are heavy. But there you are walking in the middle of the pavement and there is nowhere you can go. You begin to panic and you think, I want to go away, I want to go home, but you cannot go home. You hold onto a gate for a while, but you can't manage anymore. You are sweating terribly, you take another couple of steps and then you fall. You fall there in the middle of the street. People come and stand all around you and are wondering what has happened. And there you lie, in the middle of the street."

The duration of these scenes varied from 3 to 8 min. About 3 to 6 different phobic scenes were presented during each session. Variations were introduced into the scenes if certain scenes proved on inquiry to have lost their frightening quality. Stampfl and Levis (1967) and Hogan and Kirchner (1967) used psychodynamic cues in their implosive therapy. As flooding is also effective without psychodynamic cues (Barrett, 1969), we did not include them in the scenes.

The 45 min. of flooding in the imagination were immediately followed by 45 min. of flooding *in vivo*. The client was instructed to enter the anxiety-arousing situation. The therapist and the client agreed upon a route through the city, for example, which the client had to follow alone. The therapist and the client met again after 45 min. and the therapist then asked how it had gone, but did not give explicit verbal reinforcement. It is not, however, possible to determine the reinforcement value of the very presence of the therapist, of his attitude and his facial expressions.

If it proved to be impossible to persuade the client to go into the street alone, the therapist helped him by accompanying him for the first few minutes. This was necessary in only a few cases. When walking in the streets alone no longer presented any problems, other anxiety-arousing situations connected with for example the bus, the train or the cinema were dealt with. (pp. 107–108)

While originally expressing reservations, Wolpe has recently stated his conviction of the efficacy of these procedures (Wolpe, 1973), but advocates a cautious attitude for "little is really known of the ingredients for success, and prolonged *in vivo* exposure does exacerbate some neurosis" (p. 195). Perhaps because of the failure of many investigators to distinguish between flooding and implosion, the specific procedures of flooding seem to vary a good deal across experimental investigations. The following are procedural characteristics of flooding procedures reported across an array of investigators:

1. The client is willing and able to undergo a "terminal" presentation.
2. Scenes provoking maximal anxiety are presented to the client either

in imagination (e.g., Boudywns, 1973), *in vivo,* or in some combination (e.g., Everaerd et al., 1973).

3. Most usually, the client is required to remain within the stimulus situation until self-report assessments, observable behaviors, or physiological indices reveal that anxiety has sufficiently extinguished. Additional presentations (three to ten) are usually required to further extinguish the client's anxiety response and to further assess treatment effects.

4. Often, the client is asked to practice scene presentations on his own (e.g., Boudywns, 1973). Importantly, such practice *in vivo* should *not* be suggested until the BCA is assured that the client has sufficiently mastered the scene within treatment.

Implosion—Reviews of the literature (Ayer, 1972; Morganstern, 1973; Smith, Dixon, and Sheppard, 1973) have extensively evaluated the findings regarding implosive therapeutic techniques. The results of these reviews indicate that the specific procedures employed, the effectiveness of treatments, as well as the theoretical foundations of implosion are still in need of considerable experimental evaluation. Most investigators have employed some variant of the procedure originally formulated by Stampfl (1964) and elaborated by Stampfl and Levis (1967, 1968). This procedure will be presented in terms of its components.

1. Standard clinical diagnostic interviews. Two or three *standard clinical diagnostic interviews* are employed to gain information as to the situations that provoke anxiety for the fearful client. These initial sessions aid the therapist in hypothesizing the specific anxiety-provoking stimuli that may be related to the client's fears.

2. *Training in imagination,* employing neutral imagery, is conducted as described in the prior section.

3. The *Avoidance Serial Cue Hierarchy (ASCH)* is constructed. This is a hierarchy of the specific stimuli that the client is avoiding, from least to most anxiety provoking. The authors emphasize an array of cues within multiple sense modalities (auditory, tactile, etc.), which may be a part of the client's fear. The cues that are highest on the ASCH are those capable of eliciting the most intense degree of anxiety, and they are thought to be most closely related to the original aversive stimulus. Often, cues high on the ASCH cannot be identified by the client and must be hypothesized by the therapist. The client avoids thinking about such information because of the aversive response it produces. Cues low on the ASCH are typically more assessable and may be more readily identified by the client. These cues are typically divided into two major categories: *symptom-contingent cues* and *hypothesized sequential cues.*

Symptom-contingent cues are typically lower on the ASCH, often highly correlated with the occurrence of the client's fear, and can be identified quite easily. The height-phobic individual may be able to identify such cues as "the sight of a tall building," "looking down a stairwell," and "looking off a bridge." The major task of the therapist is to identify as many as possible of these symptom-contingent cues that are a part of the phobic stimulus "complex," so that they may be employed within therapy.

The *hypothesized sequential cues* are higher on the ASCH than symptom-contingent cues. In employing a somewhat psychodynamic orientation, Stampfl and Levis attempt to evaluate the degree to which each of the following areas (important to psychoanalysis) may be involved in the fear experience for the client, yet are currently unidentified. By presenting scenes relating to each of these areas, the therapist attempts to hypothesize which areas may be involved in the client's fear.

a. Aggression. Scenes center around the client expressing anger, aggression, and hostility toward important figures within his life, such as parents, siblings, or spouse. Often, body injury and mutilation is described as well as death.

b. Punishment. Clients are asked to picture themselves the victims of anger or aggression that is inflicted upon them by someone else important within their lives.

c. Oral material. Scenes involve eating, biting, spitting, sucking, and cannibalism.

d. Anal material. Scenes relate to excretion.

e. Sexual material. A wide variety of cues relating to the sexual act are presented, including scenes of fellatio, castration, and homosexuality.

f. Rejection. Scenes are introduced where the client is rejected, deprived, shamed, or left helpless.

g. Bodily injury. Descriptions of mutilation and death of the patient are most typically used when the client reports a fear of injury *(symptom-contingent cue)*.

h. Loss of control. Clients are asked to imagine themselves losing impulse control and acting out aggressive or sexual impulses. They may be asked to imagine themselves hospitalized in the back ward of a mental hospital for the rest of their lives because of their loss of control. This is mainly employed with clients who indicate a fear of becoming "insane" or have an attitude that they are incurable.

i. Acceptance of conscience. Scenes are presented in which clients confess their wrongdoings and are convicted, sentenced, and executed.

j. ANS and CNS reactivity. Sensations caused by the autonomic and central nervous systems, such as heart pounding, increasing muscular tension, and involuntary release of bladder or bowels are presented to the clients.

The ASCH hierarchy is thus the base upon which an individual client's implosive therapy rests. While the *symptom-contingent cues,* which the client can identify, often define the major theme to be presented, the *hypothesized cues* are presented within each of the ten theme areas described above so that the therapist may increasingly determine those specific stimulus areas that may be involved in the client's fear.

4. *Presentation of scenes proper.* Initially, the client is asked to imagine a scene that is low on the ASCH, and some of the hypothesized cues may be included as the therapist begins to generate hypotheses regarding the client's fear. The therapist becomes actively involved in presenting the scene, requiring the client to imagine the material as vividly as possibly and leading the client in imagining the sights, sounds, smells, and sensations that the scene produces. Often, the client is asked to talk to the people being visualized. Emotional responses are intensified by the use of technical gimmicks, and therapist creativity is stressed. The therapist might imitate growls or hisses of animals, or might touch the client lightly, as the client is asked to imagine a spider crawling up his arm. Often, auditory presentations (e.g., sounds of traffic) might accompany the client's imagination of driving in his automobile. Typically, the client is asked to undertake implosion in an untranquilized state, as tranquilizing medication may interfere with the elicitation of anxiety. Therefore, the authors recommend that any medication be removed or at least reduced prior to treatment. Once the therapist observes that a high level of anxiety has been reached, the therapist continues presenting the scene until there appears to be a reduction in anxiety. As anxiety is reduced, new variations are introduced into the scene in an attempt to elicit more anxiety, and the procedure is repeated until the scene appears to be incapable of eliciting further anxiety on the client's part. A client may then be asked to imagine the scene on his own in self-presented trials as part of a homework assignment.

Sessions may be one hour or more in duration, and there seems to be little specific advice offered regarding the manner of terminating a session.

5. *Progression up the hierarchy.* Once the client masters the initial scene on the ASCH, scenes higher on the hierarchy are presented sequentially; again, *hypothesized cues* from the list of ten thematic situations are built into the scene, as the therapist additionally attempts to determine those areas of fear and to elaborate them fully within the therapeutic session until extinction occurs.

According to Stampfl and Levis (1968) the goal of implosive therapy is to reproduce in the absence of physical pain a very close approximation of the sights, sounds, and touch experiences of the actual experience that presumably underlies a client's fear. The *hypothesized-sequential cues* are presented within the scene so that the therapist may ensure that possibly unknown but anxiety-provoking stimuli are also extinguished within the treatment procedure. The example that follows, shows an initial scene presentation with a snake phobic client (Stampfl and Levis, 1968).

Close your eyes again. Picture the snake out in front of you, now make yourself pick it up. Reach down, pick it up, but it in your lap, feel it wiggling around in your lap, leave your hand on it, put your hand out and feel it wiggling around. Kind of explore its body with your fingers and hand. You don't like to do it, make yourself do it. Really grab onto the snake. Squeeze it a little bit, feel it. Feel it kind of start to wind around your hand. Let it. Leave your hand there, feel it touching your hand and winding around it, curling around your wrist. (p. 426)

In this second excerpt the level of anxiety is raised and the tempo of the presentation is increased.

Okay, now put your finger out towards the snake and feel his head coming up. No, it is in your lap, and it is coming up. It's head [is] towards your finger and it is starting to bite at your finger. Let it, let it bite at your finger. Put your finger out, let it bite, let it bite at your finger, feel its fangs go right down into your finger. Oooch, feel the pain going right up your arm and into your shoulder. You want to pull your hand away, but leave it there. Let the snake kind of gnaw at your finger. Feel it gnawing, look at the blood dripping off your finger. Feel it in your stomach and the pain going up your arm. Try to picture your bleeding finger. And the teeth of the snake are stuck right in your finger, right down to the bone. And it is crunching like on your finger there. Let it. Feel it biting, it is biting at your hand, feel it. Now squeeze the snake with your hand. Make it bite you harder. Squeeze it. Make it bite you. Squeeze it hard, squeeze it. Let it bite you, squeeze it hard, squeeze it hard. Okay, slowly put the snake out in front of you. Now pick him up again. Put it in your lap. Let it wiggle around uh—leave your hand on him. Let him wiggle around your hand and touch it; snap at it.

In the third section the level of anxiety is increased as the animal begins to attack the person's face or vital organs and this material is thought to be closer to the real fears of such clients (Stamfl and Levis, 1968).

Stampfl and Levis (1967) have stated that the implosive approach has been successful in dealing with a variety of behavioral problems, including anxiety, fears, obsessive-compulsive behaviors, and depression; it has also been effective when applied to client's diagnosed as psychotic, including affective, schizophrenic, and paranoid reactions. They also have contended that their preliminary work suggests the possibility of successful application of implosive treatment to altering homosexuality, alcoholism, and other problem areas. The authors claim considerable improvement in 100 percent (London, 1964) of cases treated, usually in from one to 15 one-hour sessions, with the total treatment time rarely in excess of 30 hours. Reports of case studies have been overwhelmingly encouraging (Hogan, 1966; Hogan and Kirchner, 1967, 1968; Kirchner and Hogan, 1966; Levis and Carrera, 1967).

Reviews (Morganstern, 1973; Smith, Dixon, and Sheppard, 1973) have pointed out methodological problems that seem to mark a good deal of the research on implosive therapy. In many studies no control groups were employed, as the presentations were of a case nature exclusively. In two of the studies (Hogan and Kirchner, 1967, 1968) posttreatment observations were conducted by the same experimenter who had administered treatment, opening the findings to the possibility of experimenter bias. In many cases personality tests have been used as the only measure of change.

In *comparing the terminal approaches with each other and with systematic desensitization,* an array of investigations have produced somewhat conflicting results (Boulougouris, Marks, and Marset, 1971; Willis and Edwards, 1969; Barrett, 1969; Kirsch et al., 1975). The findings of Barrett, who employed a long-term follow-up of clients, are interesting. This author found no significant difference between the implosive and the systematic approaches at the end of treatment, with implosive therapy requiring only 45 percent of the time required for systematic desensitization. However, clients treated with the systematic approach maintained the behavioral gains made in treatment more consistently and over a longer period of time than clients treated with the implosive approach who showed more variable followup data.

Kirsch et al. (1975) report upon the first "direct comparison" of flooding and implosion. Employing a population of 72 speech phobic subjects (as defined by Paul's 1966 Behavior Checklist), abbreviated exposure to these two treatments (four-minute sessions) in a speech class was compared to a "successive approximation" procedure (similar to *in vivo* desensitization) and control conditions (class discussions of speech anxiety). While all treatments were superior to the control condition, flooding was significantly superior to the other two treatments. It should be noted that the implosive presentations were very unlike the procedures outlined by Stampfl and Levis (1968), thus making these results difficult to interpret.

Both flooding and implosion have exhibited a good deal of success in altering the behavior of fearful clients; however, due to the lack of sufficient well-controlled, methodologically sound investigations regarding the both approaches, any firm statements regarding a comparison between implosive, flooding and systematic approaches must wait for future research.

Perhaps a more important issue is the possibility of the implosive technique increasing anxiety in phobic clients, because of the manner in which extremely aversive material is presented in massed fashion. Barrett (1969) and Fazio (1970) are among a number of researchers who have proposed that the implosive technique may result in an increase in anxiety if improperly employed. Fazio reports upon several subjects considered nonphobic who became phobic after implosive sessions. Similarly, Barrett reported that a college student subject being imploded for a snake phobia became so obsessed with "visions" of snakes when she closed her eyes that her sleep was interrupted and she could not attend lectures; she refused a second implosive session.

Many investigators have pointed out that the essential variable in determining the effectiveness of implosion is the length of stimulus presentation (Staub, 1968). If the client is exposed for a sufficient period of time to the phobic stimulus, the chances that implosive therapy will be success-ful are of course improved. One questions the possibility that a very fearful client might terminate the implosive session prior to extinction occurring because of the generation of intolerable degrees of anxiety. Of course, such a client might very well become more fearful following the session, and it would seem that the primary issue is one of *careful client selection.* Implosion should be undertaken only when the BCA is assured that the client is willing to tolerate the unpleasantness of an implosive presentation and is likely to continue on until extinction occurs.

Systematic Versus Terminal Approaches: An Evaluation.

In comparing the systematic desensitization approach, flooding pro-cedures, and implosion, there are a number of important considerations that the BCA must address. The literature seems to indicate that the "terminal" flooding and implosive procedures are less costly in therapist time than is the "systematic" approach. If a client can commit only a limited number of hours to treatment, perhaps the flooding and implosive alternatives should be considered. One cannot think of many examples where this time factor should outweigh other potentially more important concerns.

The level of pretreatment fear and avoidance that the client exhibits might be another variable. It has been the experience of the author that the intensely phobic individual just will not tolerate the kind of scene presentation that flooding and implosion require. This sort of client, in line with the concerns voiced by Barrett (1969) and Fazio (1970), may very well terminate therapy prematurely if required to tolerate extremely aversive scene presentations. It would seem that the systematic approach would be the treatment of choice for the intensely phobic client. At the present time no well-controlled research has attempted to relate the de-gree of client fear across dependent variable measures to the success of "terminal" versus "systematic" approaches. Unfortunately, a clear majority of experimental reports of desensitization procedures has been performed with "fearful" university students (often "snake phobics"), and such findings may not be relevant to the "clinically phobic" behaviors seen by the BCA (Cooper, Furst, and Bridger, 1969; Bernstein and Paul, 1971).

It would seem that the BCA is ethically bound to *review the nature of such procedures* with the client, including the potential for success and specifi-cally the kinds of phenomena that the client might experience during the treatments proper, prior to providing the client with some choice regard-ing treatment. The BCA should be careful to *present alternatives* in a manner that reduces "demand" characteristics on the therapist's part. Verbal and nonverbal communications that might lead the client to believe that the BCA will be "pleased" if a certain treatment is chosen, given the client's typical desire to satisfy the therapist, may place the client in a difficult dilemma: "Do I choose a procedure which will promote unpleasantness for me but will please my therapist?"

Certainly, *if the client is being treated for some medical disorder that could be aggravated by intensive stress, a "systematic" approach would be called for.* The array of client factors that are presented to the BCA prior to treatment must all be considered prior to selecting a treatment that best meets the pragmatic concerns of efficiency and the ethical concerns of protecting one's client.

TEMPORAL PARAMETERS

Given that the BCA has decided to employ some variant of desensitization, the question arises: How will clients be exposed to the phobic stimulus over time? Such temporal factors as the duration of scene presentation, usual length of desensitization session, range of scenes presented within sessions, expectations regarding the total length of therapeutic contact, and other considerations will be addressed within the present section; however, it should be pointed out that many investigators proceed in an idiosyncratic fashion without carefully reporting the specific parameters of presentation. The systematic desensitization procedure of Wolpe, considering the frequency with which it has been employed within the literature, will provide the focus for defining temporal parameters and the information presented here should be considered as primarily relevant to that approach.

[Note: Specific temporal parameters of the "terminal" procedures have already been presented. In the main, temporal parameters within flooding/implosive treatments vary with the course of extinction and would be individually related to each specific client.]

Duration of Scene Presentation

Wolpe (1958, 1973) has stated that the usual duration of scene presentation is five to seven seconds, "but it may be varied according to several circumstances" (p. 126). Of course, using the systematic approach, the scene would be immediately terminated if the client reports anxiety. In addition, if the BCA suspects that the scene may evoke a strong reaction within the client, an initial brief presentation of one to two seconds may precede longer presentations as the desensitization process continues. Beyond this, Wolpe has indicated that many clients require a longer period of time to obtain a clear image of the scene, and that certain scenes require more time for complete elaboration than do others, so the therapist must carefully tailor the duration of scene presentation to the client's individual needs or to the characteristics of the scene.

The latency between the onset of scene presentation and the client report of anxiety is a useful measure of the course of desensitization. As this latency increases, it is obvious that the client's anxiety response to the stimulus has been altered as the desensitization process continues. One problem that the author has experienced in using a brief scene presentation is that the client just gets "into" the scene as the therapist is terminating it. With clients who experience difficulty in obtaining a vivid image or whose typical pattern of anxiety response is rather "slow and building, " a criterion of seven seconds of presentation without client-signaled anxiety may be misleading. For these clients desensitization has not occurred, and moving on to the next scene within therapy would be inappropriate. In fact, using a very brief scene presentation, the "slow-to-build" or poor imaginal client might, on the face of it, successfully complete all the scenes on the hierarchy without any desensitization having occurred, as indicated by an array of measurement procedures. The author often employs scene presentations of one minute or longer to ensure that the client has sufficient time to get into the scene and report any anxiety that might accrue. Also, during these rather lengthy presentations any unreported anxiety to the scene thoroughly extinguishes. Proctor (1969) and Ross and Proctor (1973) found that longer presentations (30 sec.) were significantly superior to briefer durations (3, 12 sec.) in altering both behavioral and self-report of fear in an "analog" investigation (undergraduate snake phobics), thus supporting the present suggestion. It is hoped that further research will examine this finding across phobic stimulus categories.

Careful records should be kept of the latency between onset of presentation and client report of anxiety. When the client is able to tolerate the scene for the "criterion" period of time (e.g., 7 sec., 30 sec., 1 minute), this should also be noted as a successful completion.

Length of Desensitization Session

Wolpe (1969, 1973) has suggested that the typical desensitization session lasts 15 to 30 minutes; however, considerable variability has been reported within the literature. Wolpin and Pearsall (1965) reported the successful elimination of a phobic response within a single, continuous 90-minute session. Marquis and Morgan (1969) have suggested that most individuals would rather not tolerate a total duration of scene presentations much more than 20 minutes and Rimm and Masters (1974) have stated that "in most instances, twenty or thirty minutes might be thought of as a reasonable upper limit" (p. 64). Within the ordinary therapeutic session (50–60 minutes), 20 or 30 minutes of scene presentation can be augmented with therapist-client discussions of the course of therapy, client reports of exposures to phobic stimuli in the natural environment, and any other pertinent information that therapist or client wish to bring to the therapeutic relationship. Should the BCA wish to accelerate the course of therapy, multiple desensitization sessions might be held within a given day.

Assignment of sessions to days—It has already been mentioned that more than one desensitization session may be performed within a given day; however, most investigators, once beginning the desensitization process, meet with the client for as many days out of the week as are feasible for the brief 20–30 minute presentation. Wolpe has stated that the "spacing" of sessions does not seem to matter very greatly, with sessions typically occurring once or twice per week. Wolpe (1973) maintains that sessions may be separated by many weeks or take place daily. He also reports that some clients can successfully receive as many as four desensitization sessions within a day.

Clients who are frequently exposed to the phobic stimulus in the natural environment should perhaps be treated with a massed approach rather than spreading treatments out over a longer period of time, as repeated and frequent reexposure to the phobic stimulus in the natural environment can lead to a relearning of avoidance patterns that will compete with the desensitization process. By massing of sessions within days, the BCA may ensure that the client's fear is as completely desensitized as possible prior to client reexposure to the phobic stimulus in the natural environment.

Careful records should be maintained regarding the specific dates and times of sessions. Following sessions the BCA should ask the client how the session went, employing such questions as, "Were you really able to get into the scene today?" or "What was the anxiety like for you when you reported in today?" Careful questioning may enable the BCA to find specific times during the day when the client is better able to relax, imagine, or generally get into the therapeutic process. The author has found that for some clients a presentation of scenes early in the morning, when the client reports that he is "fresh" and "relaxed," is superior to scene presentation later in the day. In contrast, a "socially phobic" undergraduate student referred to the author experienced so much difficulty staying awake during early-morning presentations that desensitization was changed to an afternoon time block. Obviously, the client had no difficulty relaxing in the morning; however, it is most difficult to present hierarchical scenes to a client who is in the process of snoring and making other interesting sounds. Only by carefully questioning clients can information as to the optimal time for scene presentation be ascertained. The careful assignment of scene presentation to optimal times is perhaps most important with a client who, to begin with, has difficulty in relaxing, imagining, or in some other aspect of the procedure. Careful ongoing assessment of the therapeutic process maximizes the possibility of optimal application of treatments to times.

Number of Desensitization Sessions

Wolpe (1973) has emphasized the difficulty in designating any set number of scene presentations prior to successful desensitization. The number of scene presentations necessary, and thus the number of sessions proper, depend upon the nature and degree of the client's avoidance behaviors, upon the number of related phobias (perhaps requiring individual hierarchies), and upon the ability of the client to participate actively in relaxation and imaginal processes. Wolpe has said that while "one patient may recover in half a dozen sessions, another may require a hundred or more" (pp. 126–127). He also reports that in desensitizing a death phobia, a total of about 2,000 sessions were required for a particular client. Of course, by computing the number of desensitization sessions completed over time, the BCA obtains an initial idea of the course of treatment, and some projection as to the ultimate amount of time necessary will probably be suggested.

It is obvious that no clear statement of temporal factors can be offered at present. It is hoped that the above considerations provide information to the BCA as to the kinds of considerations necessary to define temporal parameters when the variants of desensitization are employed. Certainly, careful observation of the manner in which the client participates within the sessions and the degree of behavioral change that occurs across time allows the BCA to artfully adjust temporal parameters to the client's individual needs. The author has emphasized that the BCA should compile careful records regarding the temporal parameters of each desensitization session as well as any relevant comments regarding the client's behavior within the session proper. The "Desensitization Data Sheet" in Fig. 9. offers a format the BCA may wish to consider for record-keeping.

DESENSITIZATION DATA SHEET

Client's Name: _____

Therapist: _____

Presentation

Date	Scene Number	Trial Number	Time Begun	Time Terminated	Latency	Comments
8/20	1	1	9:32:00	9:32:15	15 SEC	T. signalled anxiety-became quite anxious (eg flushed)
"	1	2	9:35:00	9:35:20	20 SEC	T. signalled again - a bit less flushing
"	1	3	9:38:00	9:38:30	30 SEC	MET CRITERION
"	1	4	9:41:00	9:41:30	30 SEC	MET CRITERION
"	2	1	9:44:00	9:44:10	10 SEC	T. signalled -very anxious at mention of "open" - FLUSHED AGAIN

Fig. 9.1
Desensitization data sheet.

When a standard record-keeping system is employed on preprinted sheets, the probability of noting all relevant material may be enhanced, ensuring that record-keeping takes place in a systematic and comprehensive fashion.

IMPORTANT ISSUES IN DESENSITIZATION

The previous sections have forcefully suggested that successful desensitization of client fears may be approached in a variety of ways, and the literature would show support for any of the variants of desensitization that have been presented. One of the primary theoretical speculations on "what happens" in desensitization has been posited by Wolpe (1958). The notion of counterconditioning, or "reciprocal inhibition," states that desensitization requires that some ongoing client process compete with the client's anxiety responses in the presence of the phobic stimuli. While many investigators have conducted research that seems to strongly support a counterconditioning explanation of desensitization (Davison, 1968), many alternative explanations for desensitization have been stated in recent years. Perhaps the greatest commonality across these explanations is their emphasis upon the manner in which the relationship between therapist and client alters the client's cognitions regarding his behavior or the possible effectiveness of treatment. In addition, the role of therapist reinforcement for client progress within desensitization has also been evaluated. As early as 1971 Wilkins stated, "It appears that the cognitive and social aspects of the therapeutic situation, which are common both to desensitization as well as more traditional forms of psychotherapy, are critical variables for successful therapeutic outcome" (p. 316). Among factors that have been proposed to predict outcome in desensitization are the importance of client *expectancy* for therapeutic gain (McGlynn, Reynolds, and Lindner, 1971; Borkovec, 1973; Wilkins, 1973); the role of *feedback* to the client regarding progress or changes in physiological state (Leitenberg, Agras, Thompson, and Wright, 1968; Wilkins, 1971; Wilson, 1973; Valins and Ray, 1967; Guapp, Stern, and Galbraith, 1972); therapist *reinforcement* for client improvement (Leitenberg, Agras, Barlow, and Oliveau, 1969; Oliveau, Agras, Leitenberg, Moore, and Wright, 1969; Murray and Jacobson, 1971; Wilkins 1971, 1972) as well as a variety of other variables defining the *relationship* between therapist and client (Klein, Dittman, Parloff, and Gill, 1969; Ryan and Gizynski, 1971; Donner and Gurney, 1969).

The literature has been ripe with theoretical papers expounding one or another "live element" to explain the desensitization process, and in recent years a good deal of research has been generated at supporting these hypotheses. Excellent reviews of this research have been conducted (Borkovec, 1973; Wilkins, 1973), and it is certainly beyond the scope of the present text to deal with these issues in a comprehensive fashion. However, to alert the BCA as to some of the possible alternative explanations for the desensitization process, the major issues and findings within three of these areas will be presented. The role of *expectancy, feedback,* as well as *therapist reinforcement* as alternative and somewhat overlapping explanations of desensitization will provide a focus for this discussion.

Expectancy Of Therapeutic Gain

The reader may be familiar with the notion of the "placebo effect" in medicine. Very simply, a client may improve upon the administration of one or another therapeutic agent because he expects that the drug will promote desired changes in his physical state. This expectancy that the drug will be effective may come about in a variety of ways. The treatment agent (physician) may well lead clients to expect that the drug will be effective or bring the clients to believe, in some subtle fashion, that the physician will be "disappointed" if the drug does not promote the expected changes. The client may indeed bring into the treatment situation some perception that the drug will be effective, and will cognitively believe this regardless of what the therapist states. This again leads to an expectancy of therapeutic gain. Or, the client may hear other "like" individuals (peers) report favorably regarding the treatment agent, and come to gain a positive expectancy through such social ineractions. Regardless of the manner in which this expectancy is generated, a tremendous body of research suggests that the expectancy effect alone may promote or enhance changes in the direction expected by the treatment agent (e.g., drug). Thus, someone evaluating the effects of the treatment agent might think that physical or behavioral changes are due to the agent itself, when in fact the client's expectancy may be the sole "live element" of change. In studies evaluating drugs certain subjects typically receive the drug of interest, while others are given a placebo (inactive agent). Since both subject conditions are lead to believe that they are receiving the treatment agent, expectancy is held constant across the experimental and placebo control groups. Any differences in physical or behavioral measure that result from these "treatments" should then be due to the specific drug employed, not to differences in expectancy.

The role of such placebo effects within behavioral treatment paradigms has been increasingly discussed (Wilkins, 1973), and the current research directed toward "expectancy" may be traced back to earlier formulations within medical research. To evaluate the importance of expectancy in a procedure such as the systematic desensitization approach, investigators have often assigned "phobic" subjects to conditions that increase their expectancy of therapeutic gain, that decrease the client's expectancy of therapeutic gain, or that attempt to provide neutral instructions that would not generate a client expectancy (McGlynn et al., 1971;

Leitenberg et al., 1969). In reviewing some 20 studies directed at evaluating clients' response to desensitization within treatments such as those just mentioned, Borkovec (1973) found that in roughly half of the investigations expectancy of therapeutic gain promoted greater changes in avoidant behavior than when clients were not provided with an expectancy (Borkovec, 1972; Oliveau et al., 1969). Roughly half of these investigations, in contrast, found that systematic desensitization is effective regardless of the manner in which therapeutic expectancies are manipulated (Lomont and Brock, 1971; McGlynn et al., 1971). In evaluating specific characteristics of these rather divergent studies, Borkovec (1972) has hypothesized the following: external demand characteristics for improved overt behavior seem to have a greater effect on low-fearful subjects than upon high-fearful subjects within the analog phobic populations typically studied within the literature. The implication of his findings, given that most investigations are directed at low-fearful, "analog" populations, indicates that many of the "analog" results reported may be strongly influenced by such expectancy effects.

Although previously supporting an expectancy explanation of desensitization, Wilkins (1971, 1973) has noted that studies dealing with expectancy either define it as a *trait* characteristic, which the subject brings with him into the therapy session, or as a *state* characteristic, which is induced by therapeutic instructions. None of six studies reviewed by Wilkins successfully relates expectancy *trait* to fear reduction. The majority of studies would fall into the *state* expectancy category, and here Wilkins found no clear pattern of differences between expectancy and nonexpectancy conditions, high versus low expectancy instructions, or expectancy versus nontherapy instructions (Krause, Fitzsimmons, and Wolf, 1969; McGlynn et al., 1971; Lietenberg et al., 1969). In addition, he reports that when an expectancy effect has been found, the therapists were not experimentally blind to the goals of treatment (e.g., therapist knew that "expectancy" was being evaluated). Wilkins concludes that "instructions that the subject receives may lead to both an increase in expectancy and an increase in therapeutic outcomes; however, it is not valid to conclude that expectancy of gain causes improvement" (p. 75).

It seems probable that the degree to which a client believes that the therapeutic procedure will be successful does contribute to the client's motivation and perhaps willingness to engage in therapist-directed behaviors, but the specific manner in which this phenomena operates must be further evaluated. The author cannot imagine that in any application a BCA would foster an expectation of therapeutic failure, so perhaps, other than being of theoretical importance, the present issue is not of practical interest. In most practical therapeutic situations the therapist does everything possible to promote a positive expectancy on the client's part that change will occur. Importantly, however, if change is found to be based primarily upon expectancy manipulations, this certainly may have implications for the specific procedures employed.

Feedback

A second major area of investigation has been directed at the manner in which client feedback as to progress within desensitization may affect outcome. Interest in the role of feedback perhaps extends from an early study by Valins and Ray (1967). These authors found that when snake-phobic subjects were provided with false feedback (via earphones) that led them to the conclusion that their heart rate did not change with presentation of a snake, they altered their approach behavior toward the snake to come into concordance with the feedback. Thus, merely by altering the subjects' cognitive set regarding heart rate response to snakes, they showed dramatic improvements in approach behavior. This finding suggested that cognitive variables—more specifically, feedback regarding one's behavior—may be important predictors of success in desensitization. While attempts at replicating their findings were unsuccessful (Sushinsky and Bootzin, 1970; Guapp, Stern, and Galbraith, 1972), this early finding stimulated a growing body of research regarding the role of feedback and cognitive variables within the treatment process. Others have criticized the conclusions of Valins and Ray (Davison and Wilson, 1973; Borkovec, 1973), suggesting that false feedback may modify fear behavior only in low-fearful subjects if "the pretest experience does not mitigate the effects of the feedback stimulus and if post-testing is done under conditions high in demand for improved overt behavior" (Borkovec, 1973, p. 497). Again, the hypothesis that low-fearful subjects respond more significantly to variables of expectancy, feedback, and cognitive manipulation is offered. Perhaps an intensely phobic client would not be able to alter long-standing patterns of avoidant behavior based merely upon "false feedback" or "the expectancy of therapeutic gain." Such intensely phobic clients, even if they might desire to please the experimenter or justify experimental outcomes ,would probably not be able to alter such long-standing patterns of behavior without undergoing a systematic and comprehensive approach to behavioral change.

The investigator must proceed cautiously in considering feedback and expectancy as separate variables. In any desensitization situation, regardless of instructions relating to expectancy, the client receives feedback regarding his progress. Wilkins (1971) has stated that perhaps the major benefit of the hierarchy is that it provides a systematic medium within which the client can evaluate change in the desired direction. Because any client within desensitization may be aware of overt and covert ongoing behaviors and their progressive change or alteration, it would seem difficult to separate the effects of feedback from those of any other independent variable of interest (e.g., expectancy).

Other investigators have found that encouraging clients to self-monitor behavior within desensitization may be related to the successful outcome (Rutner, 1973; Koenig, 1973). The reader may recall that video and audiotapes are often employed as a means of providing feedback to clients regarding their behavior, and these classes of feedback have been shown, rather variably, to alter an array of self-report as well as overt behaviors (Nay, Pollock, and Bailey, 1975; Nay, Gottlieb, and Bailey, 1974).

Perhaps feedback should best be thought of as an assessment tool that allows the client to obtain a more distinctive view of ongoing processes and perhaps motivates him to self-modify his behavior in a more desirable direction. However, since many clients who are referred to treatment do not have behavioral repertoires sufficient to engage in such self-modifications at the outset of treatment, feedback for them may lead to increased information and awareness, but not to desirable behavioral change. It is hoped that future investigations can further explicate the relationship of cognitive variables and specific behavioral characteristics (e.g., low versus high fearful) as predictors of behavioral change.

Reinforcement

Leitenberg et al. (1969) found that approach behavior following treatment was significantly greater for a group of snake-phobic subjects who received therapist reinforcement for performance than it was for a no-treatment control group. Unfortunately, "experimental" subjects were exposed to other desensitization components (e.g., graded hierarchy, relaxation). In a later investigation Oliveau et al. (1969) exposed clients to well-controlled conditions that manipulated and parceled out the role of reinforcement. The authors found that praise for improvement seemed to have no significant effect upon the outcome of treatment. It is difficult to surmise how a therapist could "praise" a client without providing feedback, and certainly reinforcement might be viewed within the domain of feedback. Most clinical applications of desensitization are probably marked by extensive therapist reinforcement of the client for attending therapeutic sessions, performing homework assignments, and for performance within desensitization proper. It has been the experience of the author that the relationship between BCA and client is most important and that this is particularly true for highly phobic clients, who must tolerate a good deal of aversion within procedures. Thus, any reinforcement that the therapist can provide for these clients' efforts might go a long way toward maintaining and extending their motivation to continue. It is hoped that further research will more fully explicate the role of reinforcement within desensitization.

While desensitization does not seem to depend upon any of these factors for success, and can be successfully performed using automated equipment in the absence of the therapist (Lang, Melamed, and Hart, 1971), it is obvious that such variables may have an effect upon the outcome of treatment. The author does not think it possible to prove that any one cognitive or relationship variable is "the" predictor of success within desensitization. There is no doubt that in the individualized client-therapist relationship within which desensitization is applied, any one of these variables as well as the specific aspects of the treatment may make a relatively greater or lesser contribution. Importantly, however, the present research points out the important role of such variables and suggests that the client is not a passive recipient of treatment. One could imagine a variety of variables that might predict whether or not the "relationship" would be important within desensitization. The degree to which the client displays very dependent behaviors, the degree to which the client seeks out directions from others (locus of control), the degree of client motivation to complete treatment, and a host of other variables may predict the manner in which client-therapist variables interact with treatment procedures to produce behavioral change.

CHAPTER SUMMARY

Wolpe developed the procedure of systematic desensitization as a means of reducing avoidant behavior. Using this approach, clients engage in some behavior (e.g., relaxation) that is incompatible with the anxiety and discomfort provoked by a fearful stimulus. According to Wolpe, relaxation comes to reciprocally inhibit or countercondition the emotional responses associated with the stimulus. This approach has been found to be most successful in altering client avoidant behavior across both of case and experimental studies.

Many variants of desensitization have been developed, and this chapter has attempted to outline the procedural options available to the BCA in "desensitizing" a client.

First, a client's fear is assessed using one of an array of measures: verbal self-ratings; responses to surveys (e.g., Fear Survey Schedule); behavioral approach test scores; and physiological measurement.

If relaxation is employed within treatment, the client is often trained to relax, using a muscular tension/relaxation procedure. An example of relaxation exercises was presented, and it was emphasized that any program of relaxation should encourage the client to develop self-control over muscular responding.

While Wolpe originally presented the fearful stimulus in imagination, other investigators have exposed the client to the fearful stimulus in reality *(in vivo)*. The imagination of phobic scenes does seem to evoke greater autonomic responses than imagination of neutral scenes, although contradictory evidence exists as to the importance of vividness of imagery in promoting behavioral change. Regarding *in vivo* approaches, the therapist often goes with the client into the natural environment or exposes the client to analog situations constructed in the laboratory. The client is asked to approach the feared object systematically, with the therapist present, and in some cases relaxation is employed as a counterconditioning agent. Most investigators have found the *in vivo* approach to be as effective as imaginal presentation in inducing client behavioral change.

Virtually any aspect of the desensitization procedure can be successfully presented through visual and/or auditory means that are controlled by automated mechanisms, and phobic scenes recorded on film or videotape provide an alternative to the *in vivo* or imaginal approaches.

Stimuli may be presented in a systematic (hierarchical) or terminal fashion. Using a systematic approach, careful construction of the hierarchy ensures that scenes are ordered systematically from least to most anxiety evoked, and the distance between scenes in terms of anxiety provoked is constant. In using a thematic heirarchy, items are related to the same basic theme but are not necessarily related in time and space. In a spatial-temporal hierarchy items are graded with respect to their closeness in space to some phobic stimulus, or in time prior to some targeted event. Most hierarchies include spatial-temporal as well as thematic features. Research has indicated that standardized hierarchies seem to be as effective as individually tailored hierarchies in promoting behavioral change, and there seems to be a highly significant relationship between the number of fear scenes completed and reduction of avoidant behavior. Also, it may be that the hierarchy is important because it provides feedback to the client regarding improvement.

McNamara has differentiated three major classes of terminal approaches. Type 1 involves a presentation of scenes high on a client's hierarchy, and often relaxation is employed as a counterconditioning agent. This approach is rarely used. Type 2, called flooding, presents maximally fearful scenes, and no counterconditioning agent is employed. Scenes may be presented either imaginally or *in vivo*, and the client is permitted to remain in the scene until discomfort is reduced, presumably through avenues of extinction. Type 3, called implosion, forces the client to imagine maximally fearful scenes in which he is the victim of extremely negative consequences. Flooding and implosion were heavily emphasized as terminal approaches, and specific procedures were presented. In comparing the implosive approach with systematic desensitization conflicting results have been found. A number of authors have emphasized the possibility that implosion can promote an increase in anxiety if it is improperly employed, and careful selection of clients was strongly suggested. Temporal parameters of desensitization include the usual duration of scene presentation (5 seconds to about a minute); typical length of desensitization session (15 to 30 minutes); and number of desensitization sessions (very variable).

Investigators have recently questioned the counterconditioning model to explain desensitization, and the following areas have most often been emphasized in these investigations.

Expectancy of therapeutic gain. Behavioral change may occur because of placebo or expectation effects of therapeutic gain, not because of other elements in the treatment package. Most studies have found that manipulations of expectancy with undergraduate, "analog" populations do alter effects in the desired direction; however, the effects of expectancy upon clinically phobic individuals remain to be seen.

Feedback. Many investigators have emphasized the importance of feedback to clients with regard to progress, and one major investigation found that clients provided with false heart rate feedback desensitized in line with their expectations of change. Other investigators failed to replicate this finding; however, many have hypothesized that client self-monitoring of progress may be important in allowing the clients to obtain a more distinctive view of ongoing processes and in thus motivating them to apply self-modifications to alter their behavior.

Reinforcement. The role of reinforcement from the therapist for client performance has been evaluated with mixed results, although it is difficult to imagine a clinical situation within which a client is not reinforced for his efforts.

Thus, a host of cognitive as well as therapeutic variables may enter into and affect the degree of behavioral change found within various desensitization formats.

CHAPTER 10

Training

From the foregoing chapters it may have become apparent to the reader that a reading of any textbook is not sufficient to promote those skills necessary for contact with clients. It would thus seem that this text or any written presentation is limited as a training medium, providing only an information base that must then be translated into behavior with clients via mechanisms of practice. Certainly, the availability of competent models who might display these and other procedures within a context where the BCA might immediately practice and receive feedback would be a necessary adjunct to any written presentation. The author is strongly opposed to suggestions that merely by reading certain materials, listening to audiotapes or videotapes, or attending a "weekend workshop," sufficient skills may be learned to function competently within a therapeutic role. Unfortunately, an explication of training procedures often takes a second place within the literature to careful and comprehensive presentations of methodologies, results obtained, and discussions of findings. For the BCA faced with the task of training unsophisticated persons to employ specific procedures with clients, the issue of training becomes most important, and the manner of training becomes critical to the outcome of such endeavors. It is perplexing to the author that no systematic, well-controlled body of research has attempted to define and carefully evaluate the procedures that are often rather arbitrarily included within training programs.

A great many procedures have been directed at training a a variety of persons to function as behavioral change agents. For that reason a sufficient array of options is presented so that the trainer might selectively conduct a program of training based upon the specific needs of a particular intervention. The term "staff member" will be used to define *any* indigenous person trained to carry out intervention with a client, although most of the issues and procedures presented are focused upon the institutional setting.

The reader must fully conversant with the procedures presented in the previous chapters, as they form integral parts of the training suggestions offered. Training might best be thought of as a "treatment" applied to staff members or others only after careful assessment and with much forethought. If training procedures were designed with as much care as are treatment procedures typically directed at clients, the problems often associated with the introduction of novel treatments might be obviated. Staff members who are asked to serve in a variety of roles and whose duties are often "endless," may rapidly become dissatisfied with a lengthy training presentation that is disorganized and poorly presented, and thus fail to learn designated procedures. When staff members lack a firm understanding of the rationale and specifics of procedures they are asked to employ, the obvious result is an increase in ordinary staff resistance to change and a level of dissatisfaction that can very quickly impede any effort at treatment. Thus, it is not merely "optimal" that a systematic and thoroughgoing approach to training be adopted, but practical and necessary. The author has seen treatment programs fail because the program was hastily implemented without appropriate attention to designing training for staff members that met their needs.

PROCEDURAL OPTIONS

While the procedural options that follow are not meant to be inclusive of all possibilities, they would seem to present the major categories of approach most often employed within the literature.

Written Approaches

Most investigators employ some written means of communicating procedural information to staff members. Written materials take many forms, ranging from brief handouts describing a specific procedure such as "time out" or "how to reinforce," to elaborate and comprehensive manuals describing the basic principles of behavior and behavior management.

In many cases the trainee is provided with a textbook of some sort that covers "operant principles" (Pizzat, 1973), social learning theory (Davison, 1965), or some other formal presentation of the fundamentals of learning. When highly specific manuals describe how to use a certain set of procedures or deal with some particular category of client, they are often accompanied by visual illustrations and/or written examples, presented at a level commensurate with staff vocabulary level and ability (Nay, 1974). Many authors have employed the programmed learning approach, in which the reader tests himself and is provided with immediate feedback as to correctness of response on an ongoing basis (e.g., Becker, 1971; Patterson and Guillion, 1968). Programmed presentations may maintain the reader's motivation to the extent that immediate feedback holds reinforcing properties. Often, the basic textbook approach precedes highly specific presentations of techniques, so that the learning of treatment strategies rests upon some basic rationale.

A written "staff training manual" may be an excellent means of providing staff members with the information they will need to employ assessment and treatment techniques. Much of what we do with clients depends upon a certain fund of information: what a "labeled reinforcement" is; what "time out procedure" is; what the rules and regulations of the institution are; and so on. Nay (1975) found that when the goal of training is to provide procedural information on a topic, a written presentation of material is as effective in promoting high scores on paper-and-pencil tests as are procedures that incorporate modeling and role-playing. Obviously, a written approach reduces staff training time and is certainly less costly. Many have systematically tested trainees over written material prior to "admitting" them to more elaborate training procedures that require a basic fund of information (e.g., Patterson, Cobb, and Ray, 1973; Nay, 1974, 1975). Often, investigators report that trainees' do not learn sufficient information from an initial reading of written materials, and additional reading trials are necessary. A paper-and-pencil assessment administered to staff members within the group situation is an effective means of assessing mastery of materials as it would seem to be inefficient to involve trainees in more elaborate training procedures—perhaps involving discussions, modeling, and role-playing—when they have not yet mastered basic information.

Because trainees may balk at having to read lengthy and exhaustive materials, it would seem important that the BCA construct such materials to be brief, explicit, simply stated, and directed at the reading level of the audience. It has been the experience of the author that very brief presentations employing extensive visual illustrations are the most effective means of presenting written information, particularly to staff members of modest intellectual abilities. When the author presented a comprehensive 35-page manual of procedures to houseparents and other "line" staff within a "training school" setting virtually no one read the complete manual. On reflection, it was obvious that the construction of the manual was more appropriate for university students than for houseparents, night matrons, and other staff members who often had achieved fewer than 12 years of education. When a brief, well-illustrated, multicolored pamphlet was constructed that reviewed each of the basic components of the treatment program, students and staff members not only read the material, but seemed to enjoy and understand it (Nay, 1974). Material should be presented in nontechnical language, with examples from the institutional setting to illustrate important points. Fig. 10.1 shows a sample page from this manual.

POSITIVE BEHAVIORS

<u>Appearance</u>: The first behavior you can earn points for is appearance.

1. In you cottage will be posted a list of the things(such as taking a shower and brushing your teeth) that you must do to earn one point   for appearance.

2. The staff member will <u>check you over</u> about 5-10 minutes before you leave for <u>breakfast. Present her your card</u>!

3. If you have done <u>all</u> of the things on the list, you will be awarded <u>one point.</u> ♥

4. So to be certain of earning one point for appearance, remember to:

    A. Read the list carefully. Be sure you know exactly what you must do and how you should be dressed, etc.
    B. Get up and do everything on the list. Check yourself or have a friend check you over.
        ---Have you missed anything?---
    C. <u>If you don't earn a point</u>, listen carefully as to why! <u>Your night matron will</u> tell you why you didn't earn **one point for your appearance.**

Fig. 10.1
A sample page from a training manual directed at an adolescent "delinquent" population.

Unfortunately, program administrators often use the written approach to the exclusion of other training procedures. Nothing could be a surer way of promoting failure within a treatment program. In training 77 mothers in child-management procedures, Nay (1975) compared a written procedure with a lecture approach, a modeling of information, and modeling coupled with role-playing. While the written approach was sufficient to promote an understanding of procedures, it did not produce a significant change in behavior when mothers were asked to interact with a child in analog situations calling for an immediate response. Procedures employing modeling and role-playing were significantly superior to the written or the lecture approach in promoting appropriate responding. While written procedures may be useful in promoting the learning of procedural information, they must be accompanied by opportunities for trainees to practice appropriate behavior when behavioral change is the goal of training.

Another approach that is widely employed, yet is as limited as the written approach, is the lecture or discussion.

Lecture/Discussion Approaches

Discussion periods, lectures, or question-and-answer interactions are often employed as a major component in training staff members (Lee and Znachko, 1968; Haffey, 1970; Gripp and Magaro, 1971; Gardner, 1972; Glickman, Plutchick, and Landau, 1973; Allen, 1973). Often, these verbal presentations are similar to classroom procedures in that basic principles of learning are offered (Gripp and Magaro, 1971; Gardner, 1972; O'Brien, Raynes and Patch, 1971; Allen, 1973). It would seem that when the lecture is employed as the exclusive approach to treatment, it is even more limited than the written approach. When staff members are presented with procedural materials or even basic principles within a lecture format, they must be prepared to take notes in a sufficiently organized fashion to ensure adequate understanding. Many staff members, particularly those who are not used to note-taking and "lecture listening," have a difficult time comprehending information presented within the verbal format. In contrast, the written approach, which provides standard and (we hope) well-organized reference materials, would allow the trainee to read and review at his own pace.

A lecture might usefully *augment* the written approach in presenting procedural information, in that trainees would have the opportunity to ask questions and to discuss the advantages and limitations of proposed intervention. Perhaps the major advantage of the lecture/discussion is that it provides trainees with input into the training process and permits a mutual sharing of the problems in asking staff members to take on new responsibilities in treatment (time limitations, "resistances," and so on). A discussion provides trainees with the opportunity to vent feelings of anger, anxiety, or fear related to doing something "different." When employed as a vehicle for program planning, the discussion approach permits staff members the opportunity to present their ideas about a particular client's needs, or the needs of a grouping of clients, *prior* to having a program "laid" on them. To the extent that staff members who are called upon to work with clients have the opportunity to invest themselves in designing a treatment plan, it would seem that the possibility of their active participation would be enhanced.

A potential lecturer/discussant should be someone that staff members can relate to; most optimally, a person similar to the trainees in characteristics and interests, who has been previously trained in program procedures. The presentation should be well organized, perhaps following a written outline passed out to the listeners, and should proceed at a level of vocabulary and at a pace in line with the ability of the trainees. It has been the experience of the author that any trainer who is viewed as being "from the outside" or "not really aware of our problems" will often be rejected rather readily by the listening audience. A parent, aide, or teacher who presents procedural information to client-peers has an investment in the everyday problems of trainees, and is able to couch the presentation in a language and with examples appropriate to their needs. Training staff members to serve as trainers of their peers is important for another reason. The trainer is present within the setting on an everyday basis to answer the questions that staff members have about the program and to serve as an immediate source of information. Trainers from the outside cannot perform this service, and their usefulness is limited by the number of times they can be present within the setting.

Modeling

Either live or symbolic models could be employed to demonstrate treatment procedures for trainees. As suggested in Chapter 6, a model should have some relevance to the population of observers, and might ideally be a peer who has been trained to appropriately display program procedures.

Videotaped models of important program procedures may be particularly beneficial when an institution suffers from frequent staff turnover. A videotape can thus be replayed as new staff members come in, and may be reviewed as many times as necessary until the trainee has mastered important behaviors. When the resources of the institution permit it, sophisticated training films may be produced that employ split-screen presentations, inserts, cues, and other options that the technology of video recording has developed. Thus, using a corner insert, a trainer-model can be describing some bit of behavior that is occurring within the larger portion of the visual field and verbally cue staff members as to "what's important" within the visual array. Using split-screen procedures, the reviewer can see ·a full face view of both staff member and client as some particular treatment procedure is modeled.

Film media may be quite costly, and often $300 to $500 is expended to produce a film of ten minutes or less. It would seem that the use of videotape offers an ideal means of employing symbolic models and provides a permanent, economically produced training vehicle that may be used as often as necessary for training.

Role-Playing

Any modeling of targeted behaviors should be followed by the opportunity for staff members to role-play procedures presented. Staff members may be separated into dyads, with one playing "staff" and the other playing "client." This procedure not only allows trainees to practice important procedures in their role of BCA, but to experience what the procedures are like from the viewpoint of the client. This may assist trainees understanding how to best present themselves to clients. Role-playing experiences should be followed by feedback from trainers regarding the enactment. Feedback should be as specific as possible; perhaps the trainer could model an alternative, more appropriate means of dealing with the "client." The value of role-playing as an adjunct to modeling within staff training cannot be overemphasized; any comprehensive training program should encourage trainees to systematically practice those procedures that have been presented within other training formats.

Planning Training: A Synthesis

It is perhaps artificial to present the four previous "options" as separates. Most training programs employ them in some combination to efficiently provide staff members with procedural information and behavioral practice. It would seem that training might best begin with a written presentation of procedural information that staff members must learn by rote (e.g., "aggressive physical behavior results in an immediate time out"; "when Mr. Jones attends morning group he earns 5 points"). Following the written presentation, staff members might complete paper-and-pencil tests to demonstrate that they have reached some predetermined criterion level necessary for adequate understanding of procedures. Then a lecture might review important procedural points, with a discussion focusing on questions and issues. Trainers who have difficulty in mastering the material in the written format might be dealt with on an individual basis, with training procedures tailored to overcome specific learning deficits. For staff members who have difficulty in reading, material might be presented via audiotape or individualized instruction.

Once trainees know "what to do," trainee-relevant models could then be employed to demonstrate each important procedure within a live or symbolic modeling format. When the "model" will not be available on a continuous basis, the symbolic approach, which permits a "replay" as often as necessary, would seem to be the optimal choice. Trainees might then be required to behaviorally rehearse procedures in dyads or other configurations, using the role-playing procedures. Then group members or trainers might provide the "actors" with immediate feedback as to performance so that inappropriate behaviors can be immediately defined and not rehearsed. Thus, it would seem that some combination of the four training options presented would maximize the possibility of learning.

The Apprentice Model

An alternative to group-oriented procedures is the "apprenticeship" approach, such as that employed by Poser (1972). Just as prospective craftsmen have for centuries been "apprenticed" to a senior artisan who could comprehensively and systematically show the newcomer the "ropes," this model typically involves "yoking" experienced, well-trained role-models to inexperienced staff members. Poser (1972) assigned "non-professionals" to experienced behavior therapists in the teaching unit at a psychiatric hospital. Apprentices began by role-playing important skills with their experienced trainers, and then were permitted to apply what they had learned to clients. It also helps to have senior staff members make some investment in the training of newcomers. By serving as trainers, the senior people must review and redefine their own skills.

Certainly, this "apprenticeship model" could follow a formal series of training sessions along the lines suggested above. Following formal training each trainee could be "yoked" to a person who would serve as a resource to the trainee in answering questions, providing immediate feedback, and as a source of reinforcement (and criticism). In addition, data collected by the trainers as to the progress of the trainees could be more comprehensively gathered within this one-to-one relationship, as each senior staff member could have a role in monitoring the performance of the apprentice. This would seem to be an excellent model for training as well as followup assessment of trainee performance.

MONITORING AND INCENTIVE SYSTEMS

Followup

There are a number of options available to the BCA in assessing how well staff members employ program mechanisms over time. Many investigators have reported that staff members meet once per month, week, or day to review program procedures and evaluate client change (Brierton,

Garms, and Metzger, 1969; Pizzat, 1973). Others do not specifically mention a systematic series of followup meetings with staff members, but it is supposed that many settings do employ this mechanism. While the global group meeting may provide a forum for staff members to receive additional training, ask questions, or raise important issues, it fails to provide any system of monitoring individual staff members over time. It may be thought of as a further training vehicle rather than an assessment vehicle.

There are several approaches that might be employed to assess individual staff performance. The "yoking" procedure described above would ensure that the "apprentice" is monitored by a senior staff member who might be required to maintain records of the novice's effectiveness in dealing with clients. And if all senior staff members were used as trainer/monitors, no one of them would be picked out as "informing" on junior members. Thus, this approach might be readily accepted by institutional staff. In addition, such an approach increases the probability that the personnel asked to monitor the performance of others may become more aware of their own behavior in interacting with clients.

In combination with the above a system of charting could be employed to monitor client progress. When specific staff members are assigned to particular clients, charts of client progress may be employed as indicators of staff effectiveness (e.g., Panyon, Boozer, and Morris, 1970). Often, charts that are self-maintained by staff members can be supplemented by charts depicting the progress of some setting at large in terms of discharges, number of clients attending treatment sessions, and other factors. Charts of individual and/or group behaviors may be posted to provide visual feedback to all staff members as to their individual efforts with clients as well as to the progress of clients within particular settings (e.g., across wards, cottages, classrooms). Staff members could be asked to keep and post in a public place records of important program-related behaviors, such as number of interactions with clients, number of reinforcements used, charts indicating client behavioral change, and other activities, so that each staff member may compare his performance with that of others. Panyon et al. (1970) found that such posting served as an important incentive and seemed to motivate staff members to alter their inappropriate behavior in the desired direction. In addition, staff members within one setting could visually compare their performance with the performance of staff in other settings, which might instigate social pressure to achieve among the different staff groups. To the extent that this kind of feedback is employed with much praise from supervisory personnel directed at achieving staff members, it may serve as an important motivational tool, especially to indicate that program administrators are interested in each individual staff member's efforts.

Chapter 7 discussed the use of videotape feedback as a means of altering client behavior. Perhaps videotapes of individual staff members interacting with clients could be employed as a means of defining staff performance and client progress. These tapes might be displayed for the individual staff member in private, with the provision of additional modeling and role-playing to improve upon inappropriate behaviors. They might also be shown within the group situation where the progress of clients is discussed among staff members. It would seem that with video feedback the staff member has the opportunity to clearly define his performance in carrying out treatment goals. Feedback directed at an individual staff member might also prove to be of benefit to other staff who are experiencing similar problems in dealing with clients.

Last, some method of obtaining self-ratings from staff members as to their own performance, their supervisor's performance, and the overall performance of the treatment program would seem to be an important adjunct to any program of monitoring. Whether or not program administrators deem self-reports an accurate reflection of setting problems, it is important to realize that the way staff members view themselves and their functioning within a program may importantly predict the success of therapeutic efforts. Even if a treatment program is successfully altering client behaviors, it may be important to know that staff members do not view the program as being successful, "resent" the amount of time the program requires, or are dissatisfied with some other aspect of their working situation.

Thus, some combination of these different methods—direct observation; charting of targeted staff and client behaviors; videotape feedback to display important staff and/or client behaviors; and the collection of staff self-reports—might collectively be employed in a comprehensive way to monitor staff and program performance.

The results of such monitoring can be employed to direct further "in-service" training efforts and provide the basis for designing training programs to deal with specific staff members. Thus, monitoring efforts continuously suggest the frequency and characteristics of followup necessary to achieve program goals. Staff members who require further or regular training can then be dealt with on a flexible basis, using the individual or group-oriented approaches previously described.

Incentive Systems

The extent to which staff members actively participate in treatment activities may well depend upon specific incentives provided for performance (O'Leary and Drabman, 1971; Kazdin and Bootzin, 1972). Although most program designers provide explicitly communicated incentives to the client for progress, the importance of incentives which might serve to increase staff motivation is frequently ignored. In reviewing scores of reports of both case study and ward-wide behavioral change programs in a variety of institutional settings, the author found that most investigators do not report upon staff incentives (e.g., Zimmerman, Zimmerman, and Russell, 1969; Boren and Coleman, 1970; McLaughlin and Malaby, 1972; Ferritor, Buckholdt, Hamblin, and Smith, 1972; Bolstad and Johnson, 1972). In their review of institutional token programs, Kazdin and Bootzin state that "even when staff are trained adequately, positive consequences must be associated with desirable performance" (p., 345). Yet these authors report upon only three investigations that employed any staff incentive system, indicating the lack of such efforts by program administrators. Perhaps one reason for this is that many administrators believe client "progress" is sufficient reinforcement to maintain staff behavior. Loeber (1971) compared the effects of client improvement with monetary rewards as incentives for increasing staff effectiveness. Staff effectiveness increased significantly when a monetary reward was provided; however, staff performance did not improve when client improvement was the only incentive. Katz, Johnson, and Gelfand (1972) also supported the superiority of monetary incentives over client improvement as a means of maintaining staff behavior. Panyon, Boozer, and Morris (1970) emphasize the importance of incentives other than client improvement or job satisfaction, particularly with staff attempting to manipulate behaviors that may show no immediate improvement (e.g., training retarded clients in self-help skills).

Another reason has to do with the limitations placed upon institutional administrators in providing differential incentives. State and federal institutions and some local agencies provide salary and benefits according to a staff member's "grade level." This level is typically determined by years of service and may be affected by performance only at specified times during a given year when supervisors rate staff. Thus, flexibility in altering staff salaries, benefits, working hours, or even "bonus" payments to outstanding staff members may be significantly limited by rules and regulations beyond the administrator's control (Nay, 1976). In many cases it is impossible to promote an outstanding staff member or remove an incompetent and disinterested employee because of legal requirements. Differential treatment of staff based upon performance may lead to "grievance meetings" and litigation as less competent staff begin to feel the effects of such endeavors. Thus material incentives will be relatively deemphasized in the presentation of incentive categories that follows.

Material Incentives

Performance-related monetary rewards have been used with success by a number of investigators (e.g., Kaufman and O'Leary, 1972; Katz, Johnson, and Gelfand, 1972; Pomerleau, Bobrove, and Harris, 1972). For example, Katz et al. found that merely providing instructions for psychiatric aides to reinforce client task-oriented behavior did not alter the aide's use of reinforcers (e.g., praise, tokens, cigarettes). When the aides were prompted to reinforce clients by independent observers, a slight increment in aide use of reinforcers was noted. Only when the aides were informed that they could earn a $15 bonus for increasing their use of reinforcers to a certain level was a significant increase observed. Martin (1972) attempted to use group monetary contingencies to increase staff performance by placing varying amounts of money in a staff party fund if certain percentages of staff met work criteria posted by program administrators. If less than 50 percent of the staff met these criteria, money was removed from the fund. Although this approach has highly successful, the author reports that rewards were terminated when he ran out of funds to reinforce staff. Hollander and Plutchick (1972) provided trading stamps to staff members based upon their performance. While these trading stamps could then be exchanged for desirable material items of their choice, their cost would be beyond the scope of most programs. An intriguing but perhaps not practical option is offered by McNamara (1971). He reinforced groups of teachers with beer at the end of the day as a means of providing incentive for staff activities within a classroom token program.

In summary, because of the financial limitations within most institutional settings, any kind of material items that are purchased and employed as rewards may be too dependent on the whims of the economy and probably should not serve as a primary source of staff reinforcement.

Institutional Prequisites

Institutional settings often seem to vary considerably regarding those privileges and activities that may be viewed in a positive way by staff members. There are a number of special privileges or perquisites that may be employed in differentially reinforcing staff members for their efforts, and the present list should be thought of as suggestive and certainly not comprehensive.

Among such "perks" are the following: time off; choice of working schedule; choice of vacation times; length of vacation time; choice of space within the setting (e.g., office space); quality/decoration of space; choice of institutional tasks; access to staff lounge; access to desirable staff parking; choice of lunchtimes; early daily dismissal (e.g., a half-hour); choice of clients; choice of working partners; and choice of uniform.

Social Incentives

Program administrators or other overseers may provide verbal feedback tied differentially to staff performance. In addition, options include the public posting of the names of "outstanding" staff members; posting of charts depicting staff and/or client behavior; citation of achieving staff members in institutional magazines, newspapers, or other media; laudatory letters placed in a staff member's permanent folder; letters of commendation for outstanding efforts at achieving program goals, possibly countersigned by public officials and recognized during special award presentations each year (the BCA can be very creative in designing an array of citations or awards that staff members may very well strive to achieve). The posting of pictures of outstanding staff members, and dinners, get-togethers, parties, or other social activities might be further options for providing staff reinforcement.

Promotion/Responsibility Incentives

To the extent that rating and promotional systems permit, staff members might be advanced in grade, job description, title, level, and so on, depending upon their performance. Even within specific grade levels the BCA may be able to create a series of "levels" that define staff members at various positions of responsibility as a means of providing differential feedback. Such levels systems might be designed much like those directed at client populations, with novice staff members beginning at lower levels of responsibility and gradually working their way up through various teams, color-coded levels, or other recognized groupings. Increasing a staff member's responsibility for supervising other staff members or increasing responsibility in designing treatment plans to evaluate client performance are among other ways of using responsibility within the setting as an incentive class.

Whenever possible, the BCA might provide course credit by agreement with a local college or university for staff efforts at learning program skills. Such efforts might be designed into a course that would include the basic principles in behavior management and practical experiences in which staff members employ procedures with clients, with concomitant feedback from the "instructor." Because successful completion of courses is often a prerequisite for promotions within many personnel systems, grades obtained might combine social feedback with the salary/promotion advantages of staff efforts at "continuous" education. Whenever possible, such courses should be offered within the institutional setting. It has been the experience of the author that many staff members will not attend a college or university "lecture-oriented" course, viewing such academic enterprises as being "useless" and not meeting the needs of their setting. They are often correct in this surmise. Whenever possible, a consultant, educator, or other competent professional within the institution or community should conduct such a course.

While BCA's or administrators may maintain that they have "nothing" that may be employed to reinforce staff members, it is obvious from the preceding presentation that many options are in fact available, limited only by the creativity of the reinforcing agent. The author realizes that many of the foregoing suggestions are impractical or unfeasible in certain institutional settings due to institutional policy, legal restrictions, or other regulations. In addition, the employment of such incentive systems often seems to fly in the face of the tradition of many institutions, and the BCA must be careful to educate institutional personnel gradually and systematically as to the notion of differential reinforcement for their behavior. In addition, the BCA must be very careful to obtain clear permission from institutional authorities prior to announcing such a program of reinforcement. There seems to be a prevailing point of view within many settings that "everyone should be treated the same," and differential reward/ punishment of certain persons is "unfair." The author submits that lack of differential patterns of reinforcement in many federal, state, and local agencies (as well as academic institutions) often results in an atmosphere where mediocrity is sanctioned and creative efforts are punished. Often, when we think of an institution, we are tempted to throw up our hands and say "Nothing can change it." In fact, the institution may offer remarkable opportunities for staff development as direct agents of treatment.

When training programs are artfully designed, when opportunities for continuous feedback and training provided, and when staff members are permitted to realize that they do have a place within treatment, an atmosphere conducive to reaching therapeutic goals may be achieved within any setting.

The author can only conclude that the careful and systematic construction of assessment and training paradigms for altering staff behavior should certainly be viewed in the same light as paradigms for altering client behavior, and treated with as much consideration.

CHAPTER SUMMARY

Because most published reports do not provide explicit information regarding training methods, this chapter attempted to discuss the procedural options available to the BCA in training staff and client members to serve in assessment and therapeutic roles. Most investigators seem to employ some written means of communicating procedural information, ranging from brief handouts describing specific approaches to elaborate and comprehensive manuals describing the basic principles of behavior. A written approach may be very useful in providing trainees with the fund of information that underlies important therapeutic procedures, and the effectiveness of this approach should be assessed via paper-and-pencil tests or other means. Unfortunately, the written approach provides little more than information to staff, and other approaches incorporating modeling and role-playing seem to be necessary to translate information to behavioral change.

It would seem that the lecture/discussion approach is most relevant as a means of answering questions that staff members have about written materials or as a vehicle for providing programmatic input from staff members or clients. Also, it was suggested that such sessions be conducted by a person similar in interests to the trainees. In employing modeling as a training approach, some relevant, competent model (ideally, a peer) displays appropriate programmed behaviors by staff members or clients. It was suggested that the "symbolic," or videotape, model should be employed whenever possible to augment "live" models, as the symoblic medium offers much more flexibility to the trainer and may be more amenable to special effects, inserted cues and reinforcers, and an array of other audio/visual learning aids that may promote attention to the material. Trainees should be provided with some opportunity to role-play or behaviorally rehearse information presented by models or through written or lecture/discussion means. Role-playing permits the trainee to rehearse important procedures, receive feedback from the trainer, and perhaps redirect his efforts in a more appropriate fashion.

It was suggested that a combination of all four of these training approaches is optimal.

Using an "apprentice" model of training, a less knowledgeable staff member or client is systematically yoked to a person possessing more well-developed skills. Within such a model the trainer is responsible for the trainee's learning, and may be systematically reinforced for his efforts at training. It was strongly suggested that staff members or clients be carefully and systematically followed up after initial training. The provision of a continuous, in-service approach to training ensures that appropriate behaviors are maintained over time. While many programs have emphasized material incentives for staff, it is often difficult to alter salary, promotions, or other material items, which may be controlled by local and/or state regulations. In addition, material incentives are often impractical due to their cost. An array of other options (institutional perquisites, social incentives, and "responsibility" systems) that the BCA may use were discussed.

CHAPTER 11

Behavioral Intervention Strategies

CONTEMPORARY ETHICAL AND LEGAL ISSUES

A number of ethical and legal issues suggested by a behavioral approach to assessment and treatment have been raised by a wide variety of professionals (London, 1964, 1969; Krasner, 1969; Golann, 1969) as well as by members of the news media and interested lay persons. While much of the earlier criticism of a behavioral approach (e.g., behavior modification as "peripheral," "S-R," "simplistic") was raised by more traditionally minded therapists (e.g., Breger and McGaugh, 1965), recent criticism has often culminated in court action. The potential for "control" being exerted over the behavior of institutionalized clients against their will (Wexler, 1973; Ennis, 1971); the notion that behavioral approaches rob the client of his individuality and treat him in a "mechanistic" and/or "artificial" fashion (Carrera and Adams, 1970; Shoben, 1963); as well as the nature of clients' rights within institutional treatment programs (Wexler, 1973; Braun, 1975; Martin, 1975) have been among the most frequently considered issues.

It is not surprising that procedures that bear the term *behavior* should be the subject of so much criticism. A debate between behaviorally and humanistically oriented professionals has been going on perhaps since the time of John B. Watson, but in recent years the discussion has become more intensive (Yates, 1970)—and often rhetoric has been the communication style of choice. It is well beyond the scope of the present discussion to present all the important philosophical issues that underlie this debate. The reader's belief that man's behavior is free and uncontrolled or that it is predetermined; the view that "humanistic" is somehow different from "behavioral" (even though it is difficult to define "humanistic" without reference to client behavior); or the basic manner in which one views intrapsychic versus behavioral models of man—may very well predict the manner in which the reader will address himself to these issues.

Unfortunately, we often do not agree among ourselves as to what such dichotomous continua (e.g., "free will" versus "determinism") actually mean. It is the thesis of the author that any modality of asssessment of treatment should be subjected to comprehensive scrutiny so that the client's requirements are met in an ethical and professional fashion.

The Issue of Control

The issue of "control" within therapeutic regimens seems to arise as a therapist clearly defines methods, carefully evaluates the results of those methods upon a client's behavior, and begins to develop a systematic body of research that permits increasingly successful predictions of outcome. Perhaps because many behavioral regimens have demonstrated their efficiency and success, and because these methods may be replicated and employed by relatively unsophisticated therapists, the relationship becomes redefined as "therapist controlling client." Behaviorally oriented therapists would probably not be accused of "controlling" or "overcontrolling" a client's behavior if their efforts were not successful. According to Skinner (1971), we are all controlled by a myriad of variables within society; the goal of society's supervisory agents is to exert more systematic control so that man's plight might be bettered over time.

Perhaps the important issue is not the fact that a therapist exerts some "control" over a client's behavior, but the manner in which control is exerted. It would certainly be difficult for any therapist to suggest that he did not exert some implicit or explicit control over client behavior. Even the therapist who avoids making directive statements (e.g., Rogers, 1951) may differentially influence the client by the manner in which he nods, inflects his voice, or reflects upon specific statements that the client makes from among those emitted. One might say that the kind of transference-parental relationship that many therapists encourage is controlling to the extent that the client seeks it out and becomes dependent upon it.

London (1969) has made the point that most therapeutic problems seem to involve some aspect of the client's behavior that is *out* of control, either from the client's point or from the viewpoint of those who interact with him, and that the goal of therapy is to restore client control by exerting "a complex series" of controls over him. Obviously, the nature of a controlling process varies a good bit across various modalities of therapy, but is implicit in the very nature of a therapeutic relationship. One might ask why a negative view is taken of precise controls over specific behaviors within the client's repertoire and a more positive view is taken of imprecise controls exerted upon client behaviors that may be ill defined (e.g., "unconscious," "ego," "self") and not available within the client's immediate experience. Within most adult behavioral paradigms the "targeted" behaviors are decided upon by the client and therapist, and often become the focus of a contractual agreement that clearly defines the responsibilities of both. A discussion of recent legal decisions defining guidelines for "informed consent" will serve to clarify this issue.

"Consent" to be treated—Because institutionalized clients have frequently been required or implicitly coerced into participating in behavioral and other kinds of treatment programs, a variety of client lawsuits against agencies (as well as staff members) have resulted in clear-cut requirements that client participation be voluntary (e.g., Kaimowitz vs. Michigan Department of Mental Health, 1973; Knecht vs. Gilman, 1973).

While the issues involved are rather complex, the following guidelines summarize the major components of consent.

1. Whenever a client has the capacity of consenting, as defined by "a sound mind and sufficient age to be able to act on one's own behalf" (Martin, 1975, pp. 27-28), it is necessary for the BCA to obtain the client's permission to perform any assessment activity (e.g., testing, systematic observations, videotaping) or institute any therapeutic regimen *prior to undertaking such activities*. Importantly, consent must be completely voluntary and not obtained under duress.

a. The BCA must ensure that the client has sufficient information to make a reasoned decision and can understand the various alternatives offered. Specifically, the client must understand that he has the right to refuse the proposed procedures and may voluntarily withdraw from participation at any time. The specific benefits, possibility of success (e.g., for a proposed treatment in terms of the literature), as well as any risks (e.g., possibilities for physical or psychological problems; possibility of client's problem becoming worse as a result of treatment) must be disclosed. This information should be presented in written and oral fashion in the client's native language and vocabulary level (Martin, 1975).

2. If the proposed procedures are experimental in any fashion (outside of the approaches that a majority of reasonable practitioners would employ with the client) or employed in some novel way, the requirements for consent should be more stringent. In summarizing the results of court decisions, Martin (1975) states:

So as you select a strategy, determine if you are using something so novel, or applying it in such a novel way, that you are in effect conducting an experiment. If so, your clients should be volunteers, you must be able to clearly detail risks and benefits, the benefit:risk ratio must be substantial, there must be a general public interest in undertaking the experiment, the information should not be obtainable in any other way, and the results must be carefully gathered through a well-planned research design. If you are not prepared to meet each of these criteria then you must leave experimental techniques to others. (p. 38)

While it is obvious that these requirements make the task of the applied researcher more difficult, they ensure that only qualified, responsible BCAs are permitted access to clients, thus reducing the possibility that incompetents and charlatans will behave unethically and unprofessionally while calling what they do "behavioral" therapy or research.

3. The status of juveniles and other clients who may not have the capacity to consent (e.g., certain psychotic individuals, certain mentally retarded persons) is somewhat clouded at present. While court decisions require that juveniles (Morales vs. Turman, 1974), the retarded (Pennsylvania Association for Retarded Children vs. Commonwealth of Pennsylvania, 1971), and legally insane (Rouse vs. Cameron, 1966) be either provided with an *individualized* treatment program or released, the extent that institutions can force such clients to *participate* in treatment is still being defined in the courts.

Given that such clients may be unable to define such things for themselves, BCAs are often called in to alter or gain control of clients' behaviors in line with staff, institutional, or parental goals. While very few of us would question the parents' role in modeling behaviors consonant with a certain set of values for their children, or in exerting control over a child's behavior using punishment and rewards, many question the role of a behavioral change agent in performing similar acts for populations of clients who may be unable to help themselves. In a sense, is it ethical for a parent to exert controls upon a child's behavior within the home situation and unethical for institutional personnel to exert similar controls upon clients incapable of defining goals within the institutional setting? This is not an easy question to answer.

It may be that we are justifiably more concerned about those institutionalized clients whose behavior is more readily controlled by others than about the verbal, intelligent, motivated adolescents and adults who seek out (and perhaps pay for) a therapeutic relationship. These latter individuals might be better able to protect themselves from abuses than the former. If this premise is at all true, it suggests that this issue is more focused upon behaviorally oriented modalities of treatment, because these approaches have been frequently and often successfully employed with such unskilled/unsophisticated populations; while one-to-one, verbally oriented therapeutic approaches have generally been unsuccessful, are too costly, and generally impractical.

It might be very easy for us to tolerate therapist controls if the BCA is called in to alter the head banging, face scratching, or other injurious behavior of a five-year-old child (against his will?). The depressed, actively suicidal adult whose current goal is to take her own life would similarly not present much of an ethical dilemma for the BCA. The clear goal here would be to restrict opportunities of committing suicide (control) and to attempt to define some aspect of the client's life situation that is reinforcing as a place to begin treatment. Although this is an extreme example, one could ask: Doesn't a client have the right to take his own life? In point of fact, the BCA in that situation has to take a stand—the immediate threat of client injury does not permit a philosophical discussion. Even though control in the present example would seem to be justified and perhaps encouraged, the idea of control is often unjustly associated with inhumanity and callousness, while autonomy and free will are associated with kindness and consideration (Saslow, 1964).

If the targeted behaviors the BCA defines for a client do not involve potentially destructive outcomes, does this make the issue of control a different one? For example, if a teacher and principal wish to control the behavior of a classroom of young adolescents so that the teacher may more easily present material to them, would a behavioral change program directed at increasing cooperative interactions and attending be an example of unethical control? Certainly, the students' goals within the class might not be the same as the teacher's, and in fact they might very possibly resist such a program of change. An important question arises: Might it be unethical not to control? For example, would it be unethical for the BCA to hold back those skills that might enable the teacher to gain control of these problem social behaviors, particularly if the goals of the educational process focus heavily upon the development of certain consensually validated social skills? Perhaps this question would be easier to answer if these students were engaged in destructive behavior of some sort. Thus, a case could be made that it is often unethical to *avoid* taking a stand and exerting control, particularly when the BCA possesses a compendium of procedures that might assist the parent, teacher, staff member, or others in decreasing the discomfort and inefficiency of a client's behavior. Both Baer (1968) and Skinner (1971) have presented an argument in favor of systematic control, rather than leaving control to other parts of the social and nonsocial environment in haphazard fashion.

While it is obvious that the issue of control is far from being resolved within the professional literature, the reader should keep in mind that those guidelines for informed consent constitute the law as it is currently being expressed. Failure to comply with these guidelines could make a BCA liable to prosecution or a lawsuit.

The "Man as Machine" Issue

Perhaps because behaviorally oriented BCAs employ an extensive variety of assessment procedures to carefully pinpoint highly specific, operationally defined "targets" for change, many writers have accused them of viewing man as a complex machine (Shoben, 1963; LeShan and LeShan, 1968) or of lacking in humanistic and/or client-centered values (Carrera and Adams, 1970). While early efforts in applying a technology of behavior were derived largely from the animal literature and were focused primarily upon rather simplistic overt behaviors that could be seen, touched, and counted, it is an exercise in flailing "strawmen" to characterize contemporary behavioral BCAs in this manner (Weist, 1967). The vast amount of research concerned with training clients to exert self-control, the emphasis upon a wide array of covert phenomena within treatment programs, as well as recent research emphasizing the role of relationship variables within a host of treatment modalities (e.g., systematic desensitization) suggests that a behavioral approach views all aspects of man's behavior as relevant foci for assessment or therapeutic efforts. Chapter 1 emphasized the "phenomenal" nature of many behavioral approaches. In fact, while more traditional therapeutic approaches have emphasized man's verbal behavior as a primary focus for intervention, a phenomenal-behavioral approach emphasizes the broad-based assessment of covert phenomena, overt behavior, verbal self-reports, as well as physiological measures. This approach offers the real possibility of dealing more systematically with phenomena that have been successively emphasized and ignored, yet never adequately defined from the earliest of times. To call this phenomenal-behavioral approach peripheral, "simple stimulus and response," or simplistic is to ignore the contemporary literature, and is analogous to discussing computers in terms of vacuum tubes in this age of transistors and microcircuitry.

Krasner (1969) has emphasized that an investigation of processes that underlie human behavior is an attempt to humanize rather than robotize. The present author often has difficulty in defining *humanism* for and with the assistance of his students. Often, *humanistic* is linked with an emphasis upon "self," "values," or "actualization," and yet it becomes very difficult to define any of these phenomena without using examples of behavior. In simple language, how does one learn about the "value system" another person holds, if not through behavioral interactions? Skinner (1953) has emphasized the difficulty of discussing attitudes, instincts, and many other frequently employed labels without reference to behavior of some kind. He points out that when we speak of person A holding a certain "attitude," we really mean that he exhibits certain kinds of verbal and nonverbal behaviors at a high frequency. A person who is prejudiced will be defined by the verbal and nonverbal communications that he emits to certain ethnic minorities, while the client who holds a "poor self-concept" will no doubt be defined by the negative verbalizations that he directs toward himself.

Goodall (1972) has pointed out the respective language and jargon of different therapeutic approaches tends to isolate them and make them appear much more different than they are. Perhaps any approach that attempts to define carefully and operationally rather abstract concepts such as an *attitude, value system,* or *self-concept* will be viewed as mechanistic, although it is difficult to see how we can effectively communicate about such processes if they are wrapped in mysticism and if there is no common agreement as to what such terms mean. This author's premise is that any therapist who does a competent and thorough job of understanding and assessing his client, who includes the client in the decision-making process as much as is feasible, and who focuses his best efforts (based upon the prevailing body of literature) toward achieving the client's goals is behaving in a humanistic fashion. It would seem that if humanistic defines an approach that emphasizes the dignity of man, then nonhumanistic therapists who do not deal with clients in a professional and ethical manner are certainly not limited to any one therapeutic modality.

The Issue of Clients' Rights

Because institutional treatment programs often make privileges and activities that clients currently possess contingent upon certain desirable "targeted" behaviors, many institutionalized clients, civil libertarians, as well as BCAs have questioned such procedures as a violation of clients' basic human rights. The issue may be stated very simply: Is it ethical to contingently withhold any privilege, activity, or item that holds reinforcing properties for a client? Often, items that are very basic to most of us have been employed as reinforcers. One of the earliest token economy programs (Ayllon and Azrin, 1965, 1968) employed room dividers, visits with professional staff, locked cabinet privileges, ground privileges, supervised walks, and religious services as reinforcements contingent upon certain self-care and task targets. Following this model, Atthowe and Krasner (1968) used participation in group activities, recreational therapy, movies, wake-up times, passes, clothing, clothing maintenance, dances, reading materials, and even release from the institution as consequences made contingent upon certain targeted behaviors. While Ayllon and Azrin recommended that food or a bed space be employed as reinforcements when other items do not hold motivating properties for clients, Schaefer (1966) was perhaps the first to report their use. Using a system of levels in which clients could earn their way (with points) from basic to more sophisticated privileges and activities, Narrol (1967) made room and board, clothing maintenance, canteen purchases, Alcoholics Anonymous meetings, short leaves of absence, different kinds of psychotherapy, certain drug treatments, and special instruction contingent upon point earnings within the hospital labor force. He reports that patients considered the program to be "aversive," and a weekly group meeting became a "grievance session" centering around project rules. Token economies generally vary a good deal regarding the kinds of items that are employed as reinforcers; however, most institutional programs include at least some of the items mentioned in the preceding examples. Thus, basic rights of the individual have been made contingent upon certain behaviors deemed desirable by program designers and/or institutional administrators. Such motivational programs may be viewed as punitive by clients, and targeted behaviors have often included work within the institution that may not have therapeutic benefit.

Until very recently the courts maintained a "hands-off" attitude toward the limits of administrative discretion in operating mental institutions, prisons, and similar settings (Martin, 1975). In effect, such establishments were free to devise and conduct therapeutic programs more or less as they saw fit. The courts have recently shown an increasing interest in the rights of clients, and already decisions have been rendered that may hold far-reaching implications for treatment within the institution (e.g., Covington vs. Harris, 1969; Wyatt vs. Stickney, 1972). In reviewing this legal trend, Wexler (1973) maintains that the encouragement of targeted responses such as proper personal hygiene and self-care "surely seems beyond legal question" (p. 91). The focus of legal precedents to date has been to clearly define the kinds of institutional work assignments that token administrators may make contingent upon reinforcements, as well as the kinds of privileges, activities, and other items that may be withheld from an individual without violating any legal rights.

Many program administrators would argue that participation in custodial, food-handling, and other institutional tasks holds "therapeutic" value for clients by requiring them to become active and to meet the requirements of a job, perhaps generally reducing the apathy, boredom, and "institutionalization" that many clients exhibit over time. Critics (e.g., Ennis, 1971) would argue that many of these tasks merely exploit clients as an inexpensive source of labor. Within this context such tasks are viewed as menial, often unsuitable for employment in the natural environment, and generally benefiting the institution economically, as clients take the place of salaried personnel. Certainly, client performance of such activities does save the institution money and often increases the efficiency of a ward or cottage operation (Ayllon and Azrin, 1968). In fact, Ayllon and Azrin report that the hours of paid employees almost doubled when they were required to carry out such tasks during client vacations, suggesting the financial advantages to the institution of client labor. According to Wexler (1973), court decisions seem to indicate that the law will not tolerate forced patient labor that is devoid of therapeutic purpose and that is solely devised to save the institution labor costs (e.g., Jobson vs. Henne, 1966). In a more recent decision (Wyatt vs. Stickney, 1972) all involuntary patient labor involving the maintenance and/or operation of the institution was barred. Patients were permitted to engage in voluntary institutional work of either a therapeutic or nontherapeutic nature so long as they were compensated at a fair wage level (e.g., minimum wage). In

addition, payments to patients were not to be applied to offset hospitalization costs.

This decision thus drastically reduces the possibilities for patient vocational participation within most settings. Regarding the issues of
therapeutic versus nontherapeutic activities, Ennis (1971) has suggested
that therapeutic labor be defined as the kinds of activities that patients in
private facilities would be expected to perform. Those tasks that are performed by the employees of private facilities would be viewed as nontherapeutic activities. It is obvious that the Wyatt decision, in combination
with the suggestion made by Ennis, would require the administrators of
public institutions to generate a much more comprehensive array of vocational choices that might hold "therapeutic" value for the patients.
Wexler (1973) has maintained that the Ennis formula does not take into
account the important differences between clients in public settings compared with private settings. According to Wexler, private hospital patients
often possess adequate vocational skills, remain in the hospital for a short
stay, and might often be seen as having a better prognosis than patients in
public settings. The chronic, psychotic patients within many state institutions, on the other hand, are often persons who have been hospitalized
and unemployed for long periods of time. They are overwhelmingly poor,
unskilled, of advanced age, and likely to be negatively labeled by others
upon their release from the setting. Given these important differences
between private and public clients, combined with the apathy, dependency, and institutionalization that many public clients display, Wexler
maintains that ambitious employment activities for such clients are often
severely limited upon release from the institution. In fact, housekeeping,
maintenance, food handling, and other basic vocational tasks are perhaps
more in line with the kind of job possibilities available to them.

Many "chronic" clients who are released from institutional programs
fail to make an adequate adjustment within the community and return
after brief periods of time. One of the few reported programs that dramatically increased the frequency of successful community adjustment was
constructed by George Fairweather (1965). Patients released from the
institution were required to live and work together in a community lodge.
While it was originally planned that these clients would open a restaurant,
the men eventually settled into janitorial and gardening positions, which
would seem to be very consistent with the kinds of housekeeping/
maintenance activities that have been targeted within many institutional
treatment programs. Wexler (1973) concludes: "It should be apparent
that many forms of institutional labor, even though concededly cost sav-
ing, prevent apathy and prepare the patients for life, however marginal,
on the outside" (p. 99). He suggests certain safeguards. To ensure that no
patient is ever kept in a task for the benefit of the institution, patients
might be periodically rotated to different positions, with no client required
to perform some activity for which he alone was qualified. Thus, the

chance that a program administrator would hold the client in a position for institutional gain would be decreased.

In summary, it is incumbent upon the institutional administrator to provide a variety of vocational options for clients and to be sure that each employment option holds therapeutic possibilities in terms of each client's current level of ability and the range of job possibilities available to him. Thus, while a food-handling or housekeeping job might be viewed as therapeutic for a client whose job possibilities are drastically limited, such menial tasks would be nontherapeutic for clients whose level of abilities might permit them to engage in some more complex activity within the community. Perhaps institutions will be provided with the necessary funds to greatly expand their vocational-training facilities. This would certainly provide clients with increased options for voluntary participation. It does make sense, however, that no matter how much funding is available for sophisticated vocational training, many of these public clients will be best suited for training in rather fundamental activities such as the maintenance and operations activities employed in some of the programs previously discussed.

The legal decisions of recent years increasingly require that program designers more flexibly tailor targeted behaviors to a client's individual needs, and not apply the same "involuntary" requirements for all (e.g., "Wyatt"; Morales vs. Turman, 1974). To the extent that these decisions force institutions to acquire additional staff members capable of devising such individually tailored programs for clients, these decisions may have very positive benefits in the long run.

The Wyatt and other decisions have also further defined items that might be used as reinforcers and those that should be provided noncontingently. Under the Wyatt decision a comfortable living space—including a good bed, a closet or locker for personal belongings, a chair, and a bedside table—are all required, in addition to nutritionally adequate meals. Patients also have a basic right to receive visitors, to attend religious services, to wear their own clothing, and to have clothing laundered. In addition, Wyatt speaks of the right to exercise physically on multiple occasions each week and to be outdoors on a regular basis. Other rights include a television set in the dayroom and ground privileges, if clinically acceptable. Borrowing from the Covington vs. Harris decision (1969), Wyatt also recognized that "patients have a right to the least restrictive conditions necessary to achieve the purposes of commitment" (Wyatt vs. Stickney, 344 F.Supp.373, 379 M.D. Ala. 1972).

Obviously, the "least restrictive conditions" require that patients receive on a noncontingent basis many of the privileges, activities, and other items often employed as reinforcers. Of course, it is difficult to define what "least restrictive" means, and Wexler (1973) and Martin (1975) have emphasized that program administrators must now explore creatively for reinforcers that are beyond the basic rights enumerated in the Wyatt decision. Thus, while every client must be provided with a bed and basic furniture, pictures, choice of color scheme, and other decorations might be used contingently, as these certainly go beyond the "least restrictive conditions." While clients must be provided with nutritional meals, choice of entrees, desserts, provision of table settings, candles, and other decorative materials might be used contingently, while patients are still receiving their basic right to a meal. While every client is required to have ground privileges if clinically possible, the choice of a staff member to walk with, the locations visited, or choice of time of day for a walk are among the elements that might be made contingent upon client targets.

Thus, recent court decisions would seem to make the task of defining incentives for clients a bit more difficult for program administrators, in that a more elaborate assessment of idiosyncratic client preferences and a careful scrutiny of the ways that basic rights can be satisfied must now be considered. The author has found that such carefully defined, individually tailored reinforcers are much superior to those that are generally applied across large groupings, suggesting that the end result of court decisions might be to increase the precision with which treatments are assigned to individual clients.

In summary, each individual is entitled to certain basic rights, although the manner in which these rights are provided could perhaps hold incentive value. When targeted behaviors include vocational tasks, program administrators must ensure that such activities hold therapeutic benefit to the clients in terms of their abilities and vocational potential. In addition, administrators must be more creative in increasing the attractiveness of such jobs so that clients will voluntarily choose them. Patients who decide to undertake certain "institutional" tasks must be paid the minimum wage, and they cannot generally be "exploited" in performing activities that by all rights should be performed by salaried personnel. To the extent that this results in a more creative approach to individualized treatment planning, the recent controversy will promote behavioral change regimens that rest on firmer ethical grounds and that may in fact be more successful in achieving desired goals because of their careful and systematic construction.

The "Abuses" Issue

Because many behaviorally oriented procedures have been described in paperback books, articles, films, and other media in recent years, many staff members within institutional settings have assumed that such procedures are simplistic or could be used by anyone. Unfortunately, the nature of such procedures is often distorted. While the author would think it unlikely that a psychologist ward administrator would ask a treatment aide to engage in "psychoanalysis" or some other form of individual, one-to-one verbal therapy with a client, the same supervisor may ask a relatively unsophisticated and untrained person to design a token economy or write a contract for a client using "behavior modification." In the author's experience many institutional staff members who know very little about the important theoretical and technological issues that underlie a phenomenal-behavioral approach reach for a reading list, technical manual, or some other easy way to learn about "behavior modification techniques." The manner in which behavioral procedures are employed in many settings makes it very difficult to define precisely what procedure is used to what end. For example, the author has witnessed long-term isolation of eight hours or more being employed as a "time out procedure." Obviously, this violates the nature of a time out and is illegal (e.g., Morales vs. Turman, 1974), yet this potential abuse might be labeled "behavior modification" by the staff member who employs it.

Because the unsophisticated often think of "behavioral" in terms of a rather simplistic use of material (usually food) reinforcers, many school systems and other institutional settings have witnessed the use of candy, gum, and trinket rewards applied to alter an array of child behaviors, referring to such programs as "behavior modification." While use of a material reinforcement might be included within a systematically developed behavioral program, many of these unsophisticated "practitioners" are not at all aware of the array of procedures developed in recent years to assess a client's needs thoroughly, to deal with covert as well as overt events, and to move the client in the direction of self-control rather than extrinsic control.

In describing a behavioral approach to members of the community within workshops and/or lectures, the author often meets with a shocked reaction from his audience when behavioral treatment is described as a systematic and comprehensive approach to instigating client self-control of important problem behaviors, whenever feasible. Often, when the abuses that have been perpetrated in the name of "behaviorism" are brought up at such meetings, the audience quickly learns that the lecturer is more appalled than they are, and that such practices are most typically perpetuated by persons who have not been sufficiently trained and who use a behavioral approach in *name* only. Miron (1970) has stated that many programs labeled as "operant conditioning" truly are not. Often, physical restraints and prolonged seclusions are "desperate measures" employed when an overwhelmed staff who cannot control the behavior of patients by more effective and humane measures (p. 335). Miron points out that such practices are antithetical to an operant conditioning approach, and yet such abuses, and the ill will engendered by the surveillant community that results, are linked with a "behavioral approach" (p. 335). In fact, behavioral approaches have been categorized with psychosurgery, drug treatment, and electro-convulsive shock procedures in recent years, perhaps indicating the depth of ignorance that exists as to their nature.

Aversive procedures: The role of "due process." —The major problem in employing a procedure of *aversive control*, even if it is defensible on logical and ethical grounds (e.g., brief mild electric shocks to terminate self-mutilation), is the real possibility of its abuse by punitive or poorly trained staff members. Chapter 3 discussed specific safeguards and recommendations for careful monitoring of such interventions when they are employed, as well as more ethically defensible alternatives to drug and shock approaches. It was strongly emphasized that even uncomplicated, rather benign procedures like response cost or brief (in minutes) time out can be employed in an extraordinarily punitive fashion, suggesting that other alternatives be explored before any aversive procedure is instigated. However, when such procedures are employed for defensible reasons, the BCA should keep in mind the following procedures relating to due process, as defined by the Fifth Amendment to the U.S. Constitution.

1. Any procedure that might be construed as "cruel and unusual punishment" (prohibited by the Eighth Amendment) should be carefully reviewed by an independent and unbiased panel of experts. In recent years the courts have ruled that merely calling an aversive procedure "treatment" does not preclude Eighth Amendment scrutiny (Knecht vs. Gilman, 1973) and has raised serious questions about aversive drugs (Mackey vs. Procunier, 1973).

2. All court rulings have required that clients be provided with due process prior to moving them from a less to a more restricted environment (e.g., Williams vs. Robinson, 1970), involuntarily subjecting them to "special" treatment programs such as a behavior modification ward or classroom that is segregated from the ordinary institutional environment (e.g., Clonce vs. Richardson, 1974), or prior to any administration of severe punishment procedures (e.g., Wyatt vs. Stickney, 1972).

It should be noted that the kinds of negative consequences that would require due process remain somewhat vague; perhaps future court decisions will better define them. For example, while stating that some treatment techniques are sufficient deprivations of liberty to require due process, Morales vs. Truman (1974) excluded certain less aversive procedures (e.g., "time out" for less than one hour) from the due process mandate. The BCA should carefully review proposed punishments and might best employ due process whenever there is a question among staff as to the severity of deprivation involved. The present author's experience with enforcement of due process procedures has been quite positive. In one institution for adolescent "delinquents" the procedures dramatically reduced staff use of isolation (e.g., for over one hour) and even extreme loss of privileges, as staff were forced to be explicitly accountable for their efforts at punishment.

Due process requires the following:

1. Punishable offenses must be specified to clients in writing, so that

they have sufficient information to know the results of their behavior.

2. The client must be informed that the punishment is to be applied and provided sufficient opportunity to plan a defense, if desired.

3. The client must be provided with a hearing so that a defense might be presented. Martin (1975) points out that courts are increasingly requiring that the hearing be made before an impartial entity (e.g., someone from outside the institution), although it is obvious that this would place a great burden upon agencies. Also, the client must be provided with counsel, can call witnesses, and may appeal any decision rendered.

A Case for Quality Control?

Perhaps in the not too distant future some sort of qualifying procedures or standards will be devised by professional groups such as the Association for the Advancement of Behavior Therapy, the American Psychological Association, or state/local governing bodies to further define the nature of behavior therapy and the manner in which individuals must be qualified to employ such procedures. Braun (1975) presents an array of arguments for and against a "code of ethics" for behavior therapy approaches. He suggests that such a "code" might be based upon certain existing prototypical models. Among these he includes:

1. The Nuremberg Code (U.S. Adjutant General's Department, 1947).

2. The Declaration of Helsinki adopted by the World Medical Association (1964).

3. The Bill of Rights of the United States Constitution, notably: First Amendment rights to communication, visitation, and access to media; Fifth Amendment rights to due process in disciplinary procedures; Sixth Amendment rights to legal counsel; Eighth Amendment rights relating to experimental treatments and inhumane living conditions; and Thirteenth Amendment rights pertaining to fair labor standards and practices.

4. The Patient's Bill of Rights defined by the American Hospital Association (cf. Lee and Jacobs, 1973).

5. The "bill of rights" proposed by the Mental Patients' Liberation Project.

6. The codes of ethics written by the American Psychological Association (cf. Lazo, 1973) and the American Psychiatric Association (cf. Judicial Council, A.M.A., 1969).

These documents as well as the emerging body of law defining the relationship between BCA, institution, and client may provide a beginning point for such a code. While the courts provide a necessary "watchdog" role, perhaps the best protection against ethical violations comes from the careful scrutiny of the BCAs in monitoring their own activities and those of their colleagues. Such accountability within the profession must ensure the rights of clients to ethical and humane treatment while not punishing the creativity of the practitioner or researcher in devising more effective treatments.

CHAPTER SUMMARY

Contemporary ethical issues suggested by a behavioral approach were discussed within three topic areas—control, man-as-machine, and abuses of behavioral intervention.

It is difficult to define "control," and discussions of free will versus determinism are often useless in providing a contemporary focus for behavior. It was suggested that "control" was associated with a behavioral approach because of the clear explication of methods within this model, the fact that behavioral treatments have been directed at institutional populations (when other therapeutic approaches have failed to treat such persons), and perhaps because of the predictable success of certain treatment methods as reported within the literature. An important focus was upon the institutionalized person who is often "controlled" against his will, and legal guidelines for obtaining a client's informed consent were presented. The point was made that it may in fact be unethical not to control, particularly when the alternative to control is institutionalization of the client, apathy, dependence, or nonproductivity.

In viewing "man as machine," a number of writers have suggested that a behavioral point of view emphasizes simplistic, overt behavior to the exclusion of intrinsic phenomena (e.g., thought, feelings, emotions). The contemporary interest in covert phenomena, self-mediated control, self-instructions, and the relationship within treatment was reviewed as suggesting that this issue is no longer relevant and that a "machine view" of man might best be relegated to the past.

Many institutional treatment programs require clients to participate in treatment where they earn tokens for engaging in custodial task-related behaviors, and very basic or primary items (e.g., bed, food, shelter) have been employed as incentives. The issue of clients' rights was placed in the perspective of recent court decisions, which have strongly suggested that clients must be accorded the "least restrictive condtions," a choice of targeted goals (and perhaps even a choice of treatments), and must be provided with individualized treatment programs that focus upon "therapeutic" targeted behaviors. In addition, if clients are asked to perform "nontherapeutic" roles, they must be paid minimum wage according to various court decisions. The problems in defining a "therapeutic" activity were presented, and it was suggested that the BCA carefully evaluate a proposed targeted task behavior to ensure that it relates to client resources and potential for vocational placement upon leaving the institutional setting. In addition, the implications of limiting items that might be employed as reinforcers were discussed, and options for creativity devising options within a client's basic rights were suggested. To the extent that these decisions result in a more creative approach to individualized treatment planning, it was suggested that the recent controversy may promote treatments that rest on firmer ethical foundations; however, practical limitations may restrict institutional settings from reaching these goals.

Finally, the issue of "abuse" of behavioral intervention procedures was discussed. It was suggested that such procedures have been employed by untrained, incompetent persons because they are so clearly and operationally defined within the literature and because they are often viewed as being "simplistic," particularly by those who do not understand them. Examples of such abuses (e.g., long-term isolation being called "time out") were discussed, and it was suggested that if such abuses are not dealt with, an elaborate program of legal and/or professional restrictions may result. Suggested models for a code of ethics were presented.

Appendix A

This survey has been compiled from the information gathered from individual interviews conducted with some of the 7th Floor residents. Hopefully, this information will be helpful in trying to get you more of the activities and privileges you find meaningful. Thank you for your cooperation!

NAME: _____

AGE: _____

SEX: _____

The following is a list of *foods* which you may or may not like. The foods have been divided into groups like meats, desserts, etc. In each group, please choose any five (5) that you like and circle them. After you have done that, please indicate which one of the five you like the most by putting a number one (1) beside your first choice, a number two (2) beside your second choice and so forth through your fifth choice. Under each group three spaces have been provided for items which are your favorites but have not been listed. If you decide to use one or all of these spaces, please indicate your order of choice as instructed above.

MEATS

steak	hamburger with the works	lobster
pork chops	liver	roast beef
fish	veal	shrimp
sausage	chicken	eggs
bacon	turkey	
hot dogs with the works	ham	

OTHER:
1) _____
2) _____
3) _____

DESSERTS OR SNACKS

potato chips	ice cream	donuts
fritos	graham crackers	lifesavers
cheetos	doritos	chewing gum
pies	cookies	sweet rolls
cakes	candy bars	
pudding	sunflower seeds	

OTHER:
1)_____
2) _____
3) _____

VEGETABLES

corn	cucumbers	tossed salad
peas	radishes	french fries
carrots	turnips	soup
potatoes	onions	baked beans
string beans	broccolli	potato salad
lima beans	asparagus	

OTHER:
1) _____
2) _____
3) _____

DRINKS

pepsi	mountain dew	iced tea
coke	ginger ale	hot cocoa
7-up	milk	fresca
Dr. Pepper	chocolate milk	teem
orange	milkshake	diet drinks
limeade	coffee	
lemonade	hot tea	

OTHER:
1) _____
2) _____
3) _____

SPECIALTY FOODS

lasagna	Chinese food
spaghetti	Kosher food
garlic bread	subs
pizza	

OTHER:
1) _____
2) _____
3) _____

This next list includes *outdoor activities* which you might enjoy participating in while in the hospital. Again, please circle any five (5) that you like or write in others not mentioned in the space provided. Also, indicate your order of preference as you did in the previous section.

SPORTS

football	basketball	handball
baseball	hockey	croquet
softball	golf	darts
tennis	jogging	pool
badminton	soccer	foos ball
swimming	frisbee	

OTHER:
1) _____
2) _____
3) _____

OTHER ACTIVITIES

hunting	going to the movies
fishing	riding a bicycle
going on picnics	sightseeing
going on trips	going to games
taking hikes	going to a park
taking walks	going to a farm
going to a museum	going shopping
going to a party	going out to dinner
going to a concert	visiting relatives
camping	going home for a weekend
playing some kind of sports	

OTHER
1) _____
2) _____
3) _____

This list contains *indoor activities* you might like to participate in while in the hospital. Please follow the same directions as before and circle five (5) choices and number them.

MAGAZINES

Glamour	Hot Rod	Needlecraft
Brides	Handyman	Popular Mechanics
Psychology Today	TV Stars	Good Housekeeping
Scientific American	True Story	Newsweek
Dog Fancy	Reader's Digest	Time
People	Family Circle	Seventeen
National Geographic	Ladies Home Journal	Essence
Sports Illustrated	Cosmopolitan	Vogue
Tennis	McCalls	Cat Fancy

OTHER:
1) _____
2) _____
3) _____

BOOKS

autobiographies	religious	adventure
fiction	mysteries	occult
plays	biographies	history
poetry	love stories	
textbooks	science fiction	

OTHER:
1) _____
2) _____
3) _____

MUSIC FAVORITES
1) _____
2) _____
3) _____

OTHER ACTIVITIES

listening to music	sleeping
watching television	getting together with some friends
listening to the radio	talking on the telephone

taking a warm bath or shower crocheting
playing cards or games knitting
spending time alone embroidery
dancing sewing
playing an instrument building models
singing ceramics
writing tinkering with electronics

OTHER:
1) _____
2) _____
3) _____

Finally, make your own list of your five favorite people (staff members you have met here, family or friends). These can be anyone that you like well or just like to talk to.

1) _____
2) _____
3) _____
4) _____
5) _____

Thanks!

(Developed by Cathy Crandell, Virginia Commonwealth University)

References

CHAPTER 1

Bandura, A. *Principles of behavior modification*. New York: Holt, 1969.

Breger, L., and McGaugh, J. L. Critique and reformulation of "learning theory" approaches to psychotherapy and neurosis. *Psychological Bulletin*, 1965, *63*, 338–358.

Freud, S. Beyond the pleasure principle. In J. Strachey (Ed.), *The standard edition of the complete psychological works of Sigmund Freud*, vol. 18, 1955, pp. 7–64.

Goldfried, M., and Merbaum, M. *Behavior change through self-control*. New York: Holt, 1973.

Heath, R. A biochemical hypothesis on the etiology of schizophrenia. In D. D. Jackson (Ed.), *The etiology of schizophrenia*. New York: Basic Books, 1960.

Kanfer, F., and Phillips, J. *Learning foundations of behavior therapy*. New York: Wiley, 1970.

Karoly, P., and Kanfer, F. Situational and historical determinants of self-reinforcement. *Behavior Therapy*, 1974, *5*, 381–390.

Kazdin, A. E. Self-monitoring and behavior change. In M. J. Mahoney and C. E. Thoreson (Eds.), *Self-control: Power to the person*. Monterey, Calif.: Brooks/Cole, 1974.

Kazdin, A., and Bootzin, R. The token economy: An evaluative review. *Journal of Applied Behavior Analysis*, 1972, *5*, 343–372.

Kiesler, D., and Bernstein, A. A communications critique of behavior therapies.

Unpublished manuscript, Virginia Commonwealth University, Richmond, Va., 1974.

Lipinski, D., and Nelson, R. Problems in the use of naturalistic observation as a means of behavioral assessment. *Behavior Therapy,* 1974, *5,* 341–351.

Mahoney, M. Research issues in self-management. *Behavior Therapy,* 1972, *3,* 45–63.

Mahoney, M. Self-reward and self-monitoring techniques for weight control. *Behavior Therapy,* 1974, *5,* 48–57.

Maslow, A. *Toward a psychology of being.* Princeton: Van Nostrand, 1962.

Meichenbaum, D. The nature and modification of impulsive children: Training impulsive children to talk to themselves. Research Report No. 23, Department of Psychology, University of Waterloo, Ontario, Canada, 1971.

Mischel, W. *Personality and assessment.* New York: Wiley, 1968.

Pavlov, I. *Conditioned reflexes: An investigation of the physiological activity of the cerebral cortex* (trans. G. V. Anrep). London and New York: Oxford University Press, 1927.

Rimm, D., and Masters, J. *Behavior therapy.* New York: Academic Press, 1974.

Rogers, C. *Client-centered therapy.* Boston: Houghton Mifflin, 1951.

Shoben, E. J. The therapeutic object: Men or machines. *Journal of Counseling Psychology,* 1963, *10,* 264–268.

Skinner, B. *Walden two.* New York: Macmillan, 1948.

Skinner, B. *Science and human behavior.* New York: Macmillan, 1953.

Skinner, B. *Verbal behavior.* New York: Appleton-Century-Crofts, 1957.

Skinner, B. *Beyond freedom and dignity.* New York: Knopf, 1971.

Szasz, T. *The myth of mental illness: Foundations of a theory of personal conduct.* New York: Harper, 1961.

Watson, J. Psychology as the behaviorist views it. *Psychological Review,* 1913, *20,* 158–177.

Wolpe, J. *Psychotherapy by reciprocal inhibition.* Stanford, Calif.: Stanford University Press, 1958.

Woolley, D. *The biochemical basis of psychoses.* New York: Wiley, 1962.

CHAPTER 2

Ashem, B., and Donner, L. Covert sensitization with alcoholics: A controlled replication. *Behaviour Research and Therapy,* 1966, *6,* 7–12.

Bandura, A. *Principles of behavior modification.* New York: Holt, 1969.

Bandura, A., and Kupers, C. Transmission of patterns of self-reinforcement through modeling. *Journal of Abnormal and Social Psychology,* 1964, *69,* 1–9.

Bandura, A., and Perloff, B. The efficacy of self-monitoring reinforcement systems. *Journal of Personality and Social Psychology,* 1967, *7,* 111–116.

Berger, S. M. Vicarious aspects of matched-dependent behavior. In E. C. Simmel, R. A. Hoppe, and G. A. Milton (Eds.), *Social facilitation and imitative behavior.* Boston: Allyn and Bacon, 1968.

Borkovec, T. D. The role of expectancy and physiological feedback in fear research: A review with special reference to subject characteristics. *Behavior Therapy,* 1973, *4,* 491–505.

Davison, G. Elimination of a sadistic fantasy by a client-controlled counterconditioning technique: A case study. *Journal of Abnormal and Social Psychology,* 1968(a), *73,* 84–90.

Davison, G. Systematic desensitization as a counterconditioning process. *Journal of Abnormal Psychology,* 1968(b), *73,* 91–99.

Ferster, C., Nurnberger, J., and Levitt, E. The control of eating. *Journal of Mathematics,* 1962, *1,* 87–109.

Goldfried, M., and Merbaum, M. *Behavior change through self control.* New York: Holt, 1973.

Kanfer, F. Issues and ethics in behavior modification. *Psychological Reports,* 1965, *16,* 187–196.

Kanfer, F., and Marston, A. Conditioning of self-reinforcing responses: An analogue to self-confidence training. *Psychological Reports,* 1963, *13,* 63–70.

Kanfer, J., and Phillips, J. *Learning foundations of behavior therapy.* New York: Wiley, 1970.

Kanfer, F., and Saslow, G. Behavior analysis: An alternative to diagnostic classification. *Archives of General Psychiatry,* 1965, *12,* 529–538.

Kazdin, A., and Bootzin, R. The token economy: An evaluative review. *Journal of Applied Behavior Analysis,* 1972, *5,* 343–372.

Kiesler, D., and Bernstein, A. A communications critique of behavior therapies. Unpublished manuscript, Virginia Commonwealth University, Richmond, Va., 1974.

Krasnogorski, N. I. The conditioned reflexes and children's neurosis. *American Journal of Diseases of Children,* 1925, *30,* 753–768.

Lichtenstein, F. E. Studies in anxiety. I. The production of feeding inhibition in dogs. *Journal of Comparative and Physiological Psychology,* 1950, *43,* 16–29.

Liebert, R., and Allen, M. The effects of rule structure and reward magnitude on the acquisition and adoption of self-reward criteria. *Psychological Reports,* 1967, *21,* 445–452.

Mahoney, M. J. *Cognition and behavior modification.* Cambridge, Mass.: Ballinger, 1974.

Mischel, W., and Liebert, R. Effects of discrepancies between observed and imposed reward criteria on their acquisition and transmission. *Journal of Personality and Social Psychology,* 1966, *3,* 45–53.

Pavlov, I. *Conditioned reflexes: An investigation of the physiological activity of the cerebral cortex* (trans. G. V. Anrep). London and New York: Oxford University Press, 1927.

Pavlov, I. *Lectures on conditioned reflexes,* Vol. 1 (trans. W. H. Gantt). London: Lawrence and Wishart, 1928.

Rachman, S. Studies in desensitization II: Flooding. *Behavior Research and Therapy,* 1966(a), *4,* 1–6.

Rachman, S. Studies in desensitization III: Speed of generalization. *Behavior Research and Therapy,* 1966(b), *4,* 7–15.

Rachman, S., and Hodgson, R. Experimentally-induced "sexual fetishism": Replication and development. *Psychological Record,* 1968, *18,* 25–27.

Schachter, S. The interaction of cognitive and physiological determinants of emotional state. In L. Berkowitz (Ed.), *Advances in Experimental Social Psychology.* Vol. I. New York: Academic Press, 1964.

Schacter, S., and Singer, J. Cognitive, social and physiological determinants of emotional state. *Psychological Review,* 1962, *69,* 379–399.

Skinner, B. *Science and human behavior.* New York: Macmillan, 1953.

Skinner, B. *Verbal behavior.* New York: Appleton-Century-Crofts, 1957.

Stuart, R., and Davis, B. *Slim chance in a fat world.* Champaign: Ill.: Research Press, 1972.

Valins, S., and Ray, A. Effects of cognitive desensitization on avoidance behavior. *Journal of Personality and Social Psychology,* 1967, *7,* 345–350.

Watson, J., and Raynor, R. Conditioned emotional reactions. *Journal of Experimental Psychology,* 1920, *3,* 1–14.

CHAPTER 3

Allen, E., Hart, B., Buell, J., Harris, F., and Wolf, M. Effects of social reinforcement on the isolate behavior of a nursery school child. *Child Development,* 1964, *35,* 511–518.

Ayllon, T., and Michael, J. The psychiatric nurse as a behavioral engineer. *Journal of the Experimental Analysis of Behavior,* 1959, *2,* 323–334.

Ayllon, T., and Haughton, E. Control of the behavior of schizophrenic patients by food. *Journal of Experimental Analysis of Behavior,* 1962, *5,* 343–352.

Azrin, N. Some effects of two intermittent schedules of immediate and non-immediate punishment. *Journal of Psychology,* 1956, *42,* 3–21.

Azrin, N., and Holz, W. Punishment. In W. K. Honig (Ed.), *Operant behavior: Areas of research and application.* New York: Appleton, 1966.

Bancroft, J. Aversion therapy. Unpublished DPM dissertation, University of London, 1966.

Bancroft, J. *Deviant sexual behavior.* Bungay, Suffolk: Richard Clay Ltd., 1974.

Bandura, A. *Principles of behavior modification.* New York: Holt, 1969.

Barlow, D., Becker, R., Leitenberg, H., and Agras, W. A mechanical strain gauge for recording penile circumference change. *Journal of Applied Behavior Analysis, 3,* 1970.

Barlow, D. Increasing heterosexual responsiveness in the treatment of sexual deviation: A review of the clinical and experimental evidence. *Behavior Therapy,* 1973, *4,* 655–671.

Barton, E., Guess, D., Garcia, E., and Baer, D. Improvement of retardates' mealtime behaviors by timeout procedures using multiple baseline techniques. *Journal of Applied Behavior Analysis,* 1970, *3,* 77–84.

Becker, W., Madsen, C., Jr., Arnold, C., and Thomas, D. The contingent use of teacher attention and praise in reducing classroom behavior problems. *Journal of Special Education,* 1967, *1,* 287–307.

Becker, W., Thomas, D., and Carnine, D. Reducing behavior problems: An operant conditioning guide for teachers. In W. Becker (Ed.), *An empirical basis for change in education.* Chicago: Science Research Associates, 1971, pp. 129–165.

Berecz, J. Aversion by fiat: The problem of "face validity" in behavior therapy. *Behavior Therapy,* 1973, *4,* 110–116.

Birnbrauer, J. Generalization of punishment effects—A case study. *Journal of Applied Behavior Analysis,* 1968, *1,* 201–211.

Blake, B. The application of behavior therapy to the treatment of alcoholism. *Behavior Research and Therapy,* 1965, 165, *3,* 75–85.

Bostow, D., and Bailey, J. Modification of severe, disruptive and aggressive behavior using brief timeout and reinforcement. *Journal of Applied Behavior Analysis,* 1969, *2,* 31–37.

Brooks, R., and Snow, D. Two case illustrations of the use of behavior-modification techniques in the school setting. *Behavior Therapy,* 1972, *3,* 100–103.

Brown, P., and Elliott, R. Control of aggression in a nursery school class. *Journal of Experimental Child Psychology,* 1965, *2,* 103–107.

Buell, J., Stoddard, P., Harris, F., and Baer, D. Collateral social development accompanying reinforcement of outdoor play in a preschool child. *Journal of Applied Behavior Analysis,* 1968, *1,* 167–173.

Burchard, J., and Barrera, F. An analysis of time-out and response cost in a programmed environment. *Journal of Applied Behavior Analysis*, 1972, *5*, 271–282.

Butterfield, W. H. Electric shock safety factors when used for the aversive conditioning of humans. *Behavior Therapy*, 1975, *6*, 98–110.

Cautela, J. Treatment of compulsive behavior by covert sensitization. *Psychological Record*, 1966(a), *16*, 33–41.

Cautela, J. A behavior therapy approach to pervasive anxiety. *Behavior Research and Therapy*, 1966(b), *4*, 99–109.

Cautela, J. Covert sensitization. *Psychological Reports*, 1967, *74*, 459–468.

Church, R. The varied effects of punishment on behavior. *Psychological Review*, 1963, *70*, 369–402.

Danaher, B. G. Theoretical foundations and clinical applications of the Premack principle: Review and critique. *Behavior Therapy*, 1974, *5*, 306–324.

Danaher, B., and Lichtenstein, E. Aversion therapy issues: A note of clarification. *Behavior Therapy*, 1974, *5*, 112–116.

Davison, G., and Wilson, G. Attitudes of behavior therapists toward homosexuality. *Behavior Therapy*, 1973, *4*, 686–696.

Estes, W. An experimental study of punishment. *Psychological Monographs*, 1944, *57* (Whole No. 263).

Eysenck, H. *Behavior therapy and the neuroses.* Oxford: Pergamon Press, 1970.

Fantino, E. Aversive control. In J. A. Nevin (Ed.), *The study of behavior.* Glenview, Ill.: Scott, Foresman, 1973, pp. 239–279.

Farrar, C., Powell, B., and Martin, L. Punishment of alcohol consumption by apneic paralysis. *Behavior Research and Therapy*, 1968, *6*, 13–16.

Feldman, M., and MacCulloch, M. The application of anticipatory avoidance learning to the treatment of homosexuality. I. Theory, technique and preliminary results. *Behavior Research and Therapy*, 1965 *2*, 165–183.

Foreyt, J., and Kennedy, W. Treatment of overweight by aversion therapy. *Behavior Research and Therapy*, 1971, *9*, 29–34.

Freund, K. A laboratory method for diagnosing predominance of homo-heteroerotic interest in the male. *Behavior Research and Therapy*, 1963, 1, 85–93.

Gantt, W. Experimental basis for neurotic behavior; origin and development of artificially produced disturbances of behavior in dogs. *Sychosomatic Medical Monographs*, 1944, *3 & 4*, pp. xv, 211.

Greene, R., Hoats, D., and Hornick, A. Music distortion: A new technique for behavior modification. *Psychological Record*, 1970, *20*, 107–109.

Hamilton, J., Stephens, L., and Allen, P. Controlling aggressive and destructive behavior in severely retarded institutionalized residents. *American Journal of Mental Deficiency*, 1967, *71*, 852–856.

Hanf, C. A two-stage program for modifying material controlling during mother-child (m-c) interaction. Paper read at Western Psychological Association Meetings, Vancouver, 1969.

Hawkins, R., and Hayes, J. The school adjustment program: A model program for treatment of severely maladjusted children in the public schools. In R. Ulrich, T. Stachnik, and J. Mabry (Eds.), *Control of human behavior.* Glenview, Ill.: Scott, Foresman, 1974.

Hunt, W., and Matarazzo, J. Three years later: Recent developments in the experimental modification of smoking behavior. *Journal of Abnormal Psychology*, 1973, *81*, 107–114.

Kanfer, F., and Marston, A. Determinants of self-reinforcement in human learning. *Journal of Experimental Psychology*, 1963, *66*, 245–254.

Kanfer, F., and Phillips, J. *Learning foundations of behavior therapy.* New York: Wiley, 1970.

Kazdin, A. The effect of response cost in suppressing behavior in a pre-psychotic retardate. *Journal of Behavior Therapy and Experimental Psychiatry*, 1971, *2*, 137–140.

Kazdin, A., and Bootzin, R. The token economy: An evaluative review. *Journal of Applied Behavior Analysis*, 1972, *5*, 343–372.

Kendall, P., Nay, W. R., and Jeffers, J. Timeout duration and contrast effects: A systematic evaluation of a successive treatments design. *Behavior Therapy*, 1975,*6*, 609—615.

Kenny, F., Solyom, L., and Solyom, C. Faradic description of obsessive ideation in the treatment of obsessive neurosis. *Behavior Therapy*, 1973, *4*, 448–457.

Kleinknecht, R. A., McCormick, C. E., and Thorndike, R. M. Stability of stated reinforcers as measured by the Reinforcement Survey Schedule. *Behavior Therapy*, 1973, *4*, 407–413.

Kushner, M., and Sandler, J. Aversion therapy and the concept of punishment. *Behavior Research and Therapy*, 1966, *4*, 179–186.

LeBlanc, J., Busby, K., and Thompson, C. The functions of time-out for changing aggressive behaviors of a preschool child: A multiple-baseline analysis. In R. Ulrich, T. Stachnik, and J. Mabry (Eds.), *Control of human behavior.* Glenview, Ill.: Scott, Foresman, 1974.

Legum, L., and Nay, W. A color coded discriminative stimulus in a successive stage token economy program for retardates. Paper presented at the Southeastern Psychological Association meeting, New Orleans, 1973.

Lemere, F., and Voegtlin, W. An evaluation of the aversion treatment of alcoholism. *Quarterly Journal for the Study of Alcoholism*, 1950,*11*, 199—204.

Lichtenstein, P. Studies of anxiety: I. The production of a feeding inhibition in dogs. *Journal of Comparative Physiological Psychology*, 1950, *43*, 16–29.

Lovaas, O., Freitag, G., Gold, V., and Kassorla, I. Experimental studies in childhood schizophrenia: Analysis of self-destructive behavior. *Journal of Experimental Child Psychology*, 1965, *2*, 67–84.

Lovaas, O., Freitag, L., Nelson, K., and Whalen, C. The establishment of imitation and its use for the development of complex behavior in schizophrenic children. *Behavior Research and Therapy*, 1967, *5*, 171–181.

Lovaas, O., and Simmons, J. Manipulation of self-destruction in three retarded children. *Journal of Applied Behavior Analysis*, 1969, *2*, 143–157.

Madsen, H., Jr., Becker, C., and Thomas, R. Rules, praise, and ignoring: Elements of elementary classroom control. *Journal of Applied Behavior Analysis*, 1968, *1*, 139–150.

Malmo, R. Anxiety and behavioral arousal. *Psychological Review*, 1957,*64*, 276–287.

Marks, I., and Gelder, M. Transvestism and fetishism: Clinical and psychological changes during faradic aversion. *British Journal of Psychiatry*, 1967, *113*, 711–729.

Marks, I., and Gelder, M. Controlled trials in behaviour therapy. In R. Porter (Ed.), *The role of learning in psychotherapy.* Churchill, London: Ciba Foundation Symposium, 1968.

Marks, I., Gelder, M., and Bancroft, J. Sexual deviants two years after electric aversion therapy. *British Journal of Psychiatry*, 1970, *117*, 173–185.

Masserman, J. *Behavior and Neurosis.* Chicago: University of Chicago Press, 1943.

McGuire, R., and Vallance, M. Aversion therapy by electric shock, a simple technique. *British Medical Journal*, 1964, *1*, 151–152.

McReynolds, L. Application of timeout from positive reinforcement for increasing the efficiency of speech training. *Journal of Applied Behavior Analysis*, 1969, *2*, 199–205.

Meichenbaum, D., and Goodman, J. Training impulsive children to talk to themselves: A means of developing self-control. *Journal of Abnormal Psychology*, 1971, *77*, 115–126.

Merbaum, M. The modification of self-destructive behavior by a mother-therapist using aversive stimulation. *Behavior Therapy*, 1973, *4*, 442–447.

Nay, W. A small group program for training parents in child management procedures. Paper presented at Southeastern Psychological Association, Atlanta, April, 1972.

Nay, W. Comprehensive behavioral treatment in a training school for delinquents. In K. Calhoun, H. Adams, and K. Mitchell (Eds.), *Innovative treatment methods in psychopathology*. New York: Wiley, 1974, pp. 203–243.

Nay, W. R. A systematic comparison of instructional techniques for parents. *Behavior Therapy*, 1975, *6*, 14–21.

Nay, W. R., Schulman, J., Bailey, K. G., and Huntsinger, G. Territoriality in the classroom: An exploratory case study. *Behavior Therapy*, 1976,*7*, 240—246.

O'Leary, K., Becker, W., Evans, N., and Saudargas, R. A token reinforcement program in public school: A replication and systematic analysis. *Journal of Applied Behavior Analysis*, 1969, *2*, 3–13.

Parke, R., and Walters, R. Some factors influencing the efficacy of punishment training for inducing response inhibition. *Monographs of the Society for Research in Child Development*, 1967, *32*, (1, Serial No. 109).

Patterson, G., and Gullion, M. *Living with Children: New methods for parents and teachers*. Champaign, Ill.: Research Press, 1968.

Patterson, G., Cobb, J., and Ray, R. A social engineering technology for retraining aggressive boys. In H. E. Adams and I. O. Unikel (Eds.), *Issues and trends in behavior therapy*. Springfield, Ill.: Thomas, 1973, pp. 193–210.

Pavlov, I. *Lectures on conditioned reflexes* Vol. 1 (trans. W. H. Gantt). London: Lawrence and Wishart, 1928.

Pendergrass, V. Effects of length of timeout from positive reinforcement and schedule of application in suppression of aggressive behavior. *Psychological Record*, 1971, *21*, 75–80.

Powell, J., and Azrin, N. The effects of shock as a punisher for cigarette smoking. *Journal of Applied Behavior Analysis*, 1968, *1*, 63–71.

Premack, D. Reinforcement theory. In D. Levine (Ed.), *Nebraska symposium on motivation*. Lincoln: University of Nebraska Press, 1965, pp. 123–180.

Rachman, S., and Teasdale, J. *Aversion therapy and behavior disorders: An analysis*. Coral Gables, Florida: University of Miami Press, 1969.

Ramp, E., Ulrich, R., and Dulaney, S. Delayed timeout as a procedure for reducing disruptive classroom behavior: A case study. *Journal of Applied Behavior Analysis*, 1971, *4*, 235–239.

Raymond, M. Case of fetishism treated by aversion therapy. *British Medical Journal*, 1956, *2*, 854–857.

Rimm, D., and Masters, J. *Behavior therapy*. New York: Academic Press, 1974.

Risley, T. The effects and side effects of punishing the autistic behaviors of a deviant child. *Journal of Applied Behavior Analysis*, 1968, *1*, 21–34.

Sanderson, R. E., Campbell, D., and Laverty, S. G. An investigation of a new aversive conditioning treatment for alcoholism. *Quarterly Journal of Studies on Alcoholism*, 1963, *24*, 261–275.

Schmahl, D., Lichtenstein, E., and Harris, D. Successful treatment of habitual smokers with warm, smoky air and rapid smoking. *Journal of Consulting and Clinical Psychology*, 1972, *38*, 105–111.

Sherman, J., and Baer, D. Appraisal of operant therapy techniques with children and adults. In C. M. Franks (Ed.), *Behavior therapy: Appraisal and status.* New York: McGraw Hill, 1967, pp. 192–219.

Siddall, J. W., Vargas, J. M., and Adesso, V. J. Standards of safety for electrical apparatus used in aversion therapy. *Behavior Therapy,* 1975, *6,* 274–275.

Skinner, B. *The behavior of organisms.* New York: Appleton, 1938.

Skinner, B. *Science and human behavior.* New York: Macmillan, 1953.

Soloman, R. Punishment. *American Psychologist,* 1964, *19,* 239–253.

Solyom, L. Variables in the aversion relief therapy of phobics. *Behavior Therapy,* 1972, *3,* 21–28.

Tate, B., and Baroff, G. Aversive control of self-injurious behavior in a psychotic boy. *Behavior Research and Therapy,* 1966, *4,* 281–287.

Thorndike, E. *The psychology of learning* (Educational Psychology, II). New York: Columbia University Press, 1913.

Thorndike, R. M., and Kleinknecht, R. A. Reliability of homogenous scales of reinforcers: A cluster analysis of the Reinforcement Survey Schedule. *Behavior Therapy,* 1974, *5,* 58–63.

Tondo, T. R., and Gill, K. A. Technique for the assessment of the effects of electrical aversion on human operant behavior: An exploratory study. *Behavior Therapy,* 1975, *6,* 43–50.

Twardosz, S., and Sajwaj, T. Multiple effects of a procedure to increase sitting in a hyperactive, retarded boy. *Journal of Applied Behavior Analysis,* 1972, *5,* 73–78.

Tyler, V., and Brown, G. Token reinforcement of academic performance with institutionalized delinquent boys. *Journal of Educational Psychology,* 1968, *59,* 164–168.

Ulrich, R., Stachnik, T., and Mabry, J. *Control of human behavior.* Glenview, Ill.: Scott, Foresman, 1970.

Ward, M., and Baker, B. Reinforcement therapy in the classroom. *Journal of Applied Behavior Analysis,* 1968, *1,* 323–328.

Watson, J., and Rayner, R. Conditioned emotional reactions. *Journal of Experimental Psychology,* 1920, *3,* 1–14.

Weiner, H. Some effects of response cost upon human operant behavior. *Journal of Experimental Analysis of Behavior,* 1962, *5,* 201–208.

White, G., Neilson, G., and Johnson, S. Time-out duration and the suppression of deviant behavior in children. *Journal of Applied Behavior Analysis,* 1972, *5,* 111–120.

Whitman, T. Aversive control of smoking behavior in a group context. *Behavior Research and Therapy,* 1972, *10,* 97–104.

Wilson, G., and Davison, G. Aversion techniques in behavior therapy: Some theoretical and metatheoretical considerations. *Journal of Consulting and Clinical Psychology,* 1969, *33,* 327–329.

Wilson, H., and Williams, R. *Before the geraniums die: A primer for classroom management.* New York: M.S.S. Information Corp., 1973.

Wilson, G., and Davison, G. Behavior therapy and homosexuality: A critical perspective. *Behavior Therapy,* 1974, *5,* 16–28.

Winkler, R. Management of chronic psychiatric patients by a token reinforcement system. *Journal of Applied Behavior Analysis,* 1970, *3,* 47–55.

Wolpe, J. *Psychotherapy by reciprocal inhibition.* Stanford: Stanford University Press, 1958.

Yates, A. *Behavior therapy.* New York: Wiley, 1970.

Zeilberger, J., Sampen, S., and Sloan, H. Modification of a child's problem behaviors in the home with the mother as therapist. *Journal of Applied Behavior Analysis,* 1968, *1,* 47–53.

CHAPTER 4

Atthowe, J. Ward 113: Incentives and costs—A manual for patients. Unpublished manuscript, Veterans Administration Hospital, Palo Alto, California, 1964.

Atthowe, J. *The token economy: Its utility and limitations.* Unpublished paper presented to the Western Psychological Association, Long Beach, California, April, 1966.

Atthowe, J., and Krasner, L. Preliminary report on the application of contingent reinforcement procedure (token economy) on a "chronic" psychiatric ward. *Journal of Abnormal Psychology,* 1968, *73,* 371143.

Atthowe, J. Token economies come of age. *Behavior Therapy,* 1973, *4,* 646–654.

Ayllon, T., and Azrin, N. The measurement and reinforcement of behavior of psychotics. *Journal of the Experimental Analysis of Behavior,* 1965, *8,* 357–383.

Ayllon, T., and Azrin, N. *The token economy: A motivational system for therapy and rehabilitation.* New York: Appleton-Century-Crofts, 1968.

Axelrod, S. Comparison of individual and group contingencies in two special classes. *Behavior Therapy,* 1973, *4,* 83–90.

Bandura, A., and Perloff, B. The efficacy of self-monitoring reinforcement systems. *Journal of Personality and Social Psychology,* 1967, *7,* 111–116.

Bandura, A. *Principles of behavior modification.* New York: Holt, 1969.

Barrish, H., Saunders, M., and Wolf, M. Good behavior game: Effects of individual contingencies for group consequences on disruptive behavior in a classroom. *Journal of Applied Behavior Analysis,* 1969, *2,* 119–124.

Becker, W. *Parents are teachers.* Champaign, Ill.: Research Press, 1971.

Birnbrauer, J., and Lawler, J. Token reinforcement for learning. *Mental Retardation,* 1964, *2,* 275–279.

Bronfenbrenner, U. Soviet methods of character education: Some implications for research. *American Psychologist,* 1962, *17,* 550–564.

Burchard, J., and Tyler, V. The modification of delinquent behavior through operant conditioning. *Behavior Research and Therapy,* 1965, *2,* 245–250.

Burchard, J., and Barrera, F. An analysis of time-out and response cost in a programmed environment. *Journal of Applied Behavior Analysis,* 1972, *5,* 271–282.

Cohen, H. Educational therapy: The design of learning improvements. In J. M. Shlien (Ed.), *Research in psychotherapy.* Vol. III. Washington, D.C.: American Psychological Association, 1968.

Drabman, R., Spitalnik, R., and Spitalnik, K. Sociometric and disruptive behavior as a function of four types of token reinforcement programs. *Journal of Applied Behavior Analysis,* 1974, *7,* 93–101.

Fairweather, G. W. (Ed.). *Social psychology in treating mental illness: An experimental approach.* New York: Wiley, 1964.

Felixbrod, J., and O'Leary, K. Effects of reinforcement on children's academic behavior as a function of self-determined and externally imposed contingencies. *Journal of Applied Behavior Analysis.* 1973, *6,* 241–250.

Ferster, C., and Skinner, B. *Schedules of reinforcement.* New York: Appleton-Century-Crofts, 1957.

Frederikson, L. W., and Frederikson, C. B. Teacher-determined and self-determined token reinforcement in a special education classroom. *Behavior Therapy,* 1975, *6,* 310–314.

Glynn, E. Classroom applications of self-determined reinforcement. *Journal of Applied Behavior Analysis,* 1970, *3,* 123–132.

Girardeau, F., and Spradlin, J. Token rewards in a cottage program. *Mental Retardation*, 1964, *2*, 345–351.

Grabowski, J., and Thompson, T. A behavior modification program for behaviorally retarded institutionalized males. In J. Grabowski and T. Thompson (Eds.), *Behavior modification of the mentally retarded*. New York: Oxford University Press, 1972.

Hanf, C. A two-stage program for modifying maternal controlling during mother-child (M-C) interaction. Paper read at Western Psychological Association Meeting, Vancouver, B.C., 1969.

Haring, N., and Hauck, M. Improved learning conditions in the establishment of reading skills with disabled readers. *Exceptional Children*, 1969, *35*, 341–352.

Henderson, J., and Scoles, P. A community-based behavioral operant environment for psychotic men. *Behavior Therapy*, 1970, *1*, 245–251.

Jones, R. T., and Kazdin, A. Programming response maintenance after withdrawing token reinforcement. *Behavior Therapy*, 1975, *6*, 153–164.

Kale, R., Zoutnick, R., and Hopkins, B. Patient contributions to a therapeutic environment. *Michigan Mental Health Research Bulletin*, 1968, *11*, 33–38.

Kanfer, F., and Marston, A. Conditioning of self-reinforcing responses: An analogue to self-confidence training. *Psychological Reports*, 1063(a), *13*, 63–70.

Kanfer, F., and Marston, A. Determinants of self-reinforcement in human learning. *Journal of Experimental Psychology*, 1963(b), *66*, 245–254.

Kaufman, K., and O'Leary, K. Reward cost and self-evaluation procedures for disruptive adolescents in a psychiatric hospital school. *Journal of Applied Behavior Analysis*, 1972, *5*, 293–309.

Kazdin, A. *Behavior modification in applied settings*. Homewood, Ill.: Dorsey, 1975.

Kazdin, A., and Bootzin, R. The token economy: An evaluative review. *Journal of Applied Behavior Analysis*, 1972, *5*, 343–372.

Kazdin, A. E., and Klock, J. The effect of non-verbal teacher approval on student attentive behavior. *Journal of Applied Behavior Analysis*, 1973, *6*, 643–654.

Legum, L., and Nay, W. A color-coded discriminative stimulus in a successive stage token economy program for retardates. Paper presented at the Southeastern Psychological Association Meeting, New Orleans, 1973.

Long, R., Hammack, J., May, F., and Campbell, B. Intermittent reinforcement of operant behavior in children. *Journal of Experimental Analysis of Behavior*, 1958, *1*, 315–339.

Lovitt, T., and Curtiss, K. Academic response rate as a function of teacher and self-imposed contingencies. *Journal of Applied Behavior Analysis*, 1969, *2*, 49–53.

Madsen, C., Jr., Becker, W., and Thomas, D. Rules, praise and ignoring: Elements of elementary classroom control. *Journal of Applied Behavior Analysis*, 1968, *1*, 139–150.

Marks, J., Sonoda, B., and Schalock, R. Reinforcement vs. Relationship therapy for schizophrenics. *Journal of Abnormal Psychology*, 1968, *73*, 397–402.

McLaughlin, T., and Malaby, J. Reducing and measuring inappropriate verbalizations in a token classroom. *Journal of Applied Behavior Analysis*, 1972, *5*, 329–333.

Meichenbaum, D., Bowers, K., and Ross, R. Modification of classroom behavior of institutionalized female adolescent offenders. *Behavior Research and Therapy*, 1968, *6*, 343–353.

Meichenbaum, D. The nature and modification of impulsive children: Training impulsive children to talk to themselves. *Research Report No. 23*, Department of Psychology, University of Waterloo, Ontario, Canada, 1971 (a).

Meichenbaum, D. Cognitive factors in behavior modification. *Research Report No. 25*, Department of Psychology, University of Waterloo, Ontario, Canada, 1971 (b).

Nay, W. Written lecture, modeling and modeling roleplaying as instructional technique for parents. Paper presented to Southeastern Psychological Association Meeting, Atlanta, April, 1972.

Nay, W, Comprehensive behavioral treatment in a training school for delinquents. In K. Calhoun, H. Adams, and K. Mitchell (Eds.), *Innovative treatment methods in psychopathology*. New York: Wiley, 1974, pp. 203–243.

Nay, W. R., Northen, T., Melvin, J., and Lawrence, T. Introduction of levels to a token economy for delinquent adolescents: Outcomes and issues. Unpublished manuscript, Virginia Commonwealth University, 1975.

O'Leary, K., and Becker, W. Behavior modification of an adjustment class: A token reinforcement program. *Exceptional Children*, 1967, *9*, 637–642.

O'Leary, K., Becker, W., Evans, M., and Saudargas, R. A token reinforcement program in a public school: A replication and systematic analysis. *Journal of Applied Behavior Analysis*, 1969, *2*, 3–13.

O'Leary, K., and Drabman, R. Token reinforcement programs in the classroom: A review. *Psychological Bulletin*, 1971, *75*, 379–398.

Osborn, J. Free-time as a reinforcer in the management of classroom behavior. *Journal of Applied Behavior Analysis*, 1969, *2*, 113–118.

Packard, R. The control of "classroom attention": A group contingency for complex behavior. *Journal of Applied Behavior Analysis*, 1970, *3*, 13–28.

Panyan, M., Boozer, H., and Morris, N. Feedback to attendants as a reinforcer for applying operant techniques. *Journal of Applied Behavior Analysis*, 1970, *3*, 1–4.

Phillips, E. Achievement place: Token reinforcement procedures in a home-style rehabilitation setting for "pre-delinquent" boys. *Journal of Applied Behavior Analysis*, 1969, *1*, 213–223.

Phillips, E., Phillips, E., Fixen, D., and Wolf, M. Achievement place: Modification of the behaviors of pre-delinquent boys within a token economy. *Journal of Applied Behavior Analysis*, 1971, *4*, 45–59.

Phillips, E., Phillips, E., Wolf, M., and Fixen, D. Achievement place: Development of the elected manager system. *Journal of Applied Behavior Analysis*, 1973, *6*, 541–561.

Richard, H., Clements, C., and Willis, J. Effects of contingent and noncontingent token reinforcement upon classroom performance. *Psychological Reports*, 1970, *27*, 903–908.

Rimm, D., and Masters, J. *Behavior therapy*. New York: Academic Press, 1974.

Rosenbaum, A., O'Leary, K. D., and Jacob, R. Behavioral intervention with hyperactive children: Group consequences as a supplement to individual contingencies. *Behavior Therapy*, 1975, *6*, 315–323.

Ruskin, R., and Maley, R. Item preference in a token economy ward store. *Journal of Applied Behavior Analysis*, 1972, *5*, 373–378.

Santogrossi, D., O'Leary, K., Romanczyk, R., and Kaufman, K. Self-evaluation by adolescents in a psychiatric hospital school token program. *Journal of Applied Behavior Analysis*, 1973, *6*, 277–287.

Schaefer, H., and Martin, P. Behavior therapy for "apathy" of hospitalized schizophrenics. *Psychological Reports*, 1966, *19*, 1147–1158.

Schaefer, H., and Martin, P. *Behavior therapy*. New York: McGraw-Hill, 1969.

Schmidt, G., and Ulrich, R. Effects of group contingent events upon classroom noise. *Journal of Applied Behavior Analysis*, 1969, *2*, 171–179.

Sloggett, B. Use of group activities and team rewards to increase individual classroom productivity. *Teaching Exceptional Children*, Winter 1971, 54–66.

Tanner, B. A., Parrino, J. J., and Daniels, A. C. A token economy with "automated" data collection. *Behavior Therapy*, 1975, *6*, 111–118.

Taulbee, W., and Wright, H. Attitude therapy: A behavior modification program in a psychiatric hospital. In H. C. Richard (Ed.), *Behavioral intervention in human problems*. New York: Pergamon, 1971, pp. 335–362.

Tyler, V., and Brown, G. Token reinforcement of academic performance with institutionalized delinquent boys. *Journal of Educational Psychology*, 1968, *59*, 164–168.

Walker, H., and Buckley, N. The use of positive reinforcement in conditioning attending behavior. *Journal of Applied Behavior Analysis*, 1968, *1*, 245–252.

Walker, H., and Buckley, N. Programming generalization and maintenance of treatment effects across time and across settings. *Journal of Applied Behavior Analysis*, 1972, *5*, 209–224.

Zimmerman, J., Stuckey, T., Garlick, B., and Miller, M. Effects of token reinforcement on productivity in multiple handicapped clients in a sheltered workshop. *Rehabilitation Literature*, 1969, *30*, 34–41.

CHAPTER 5

Anant, S. Comment on "A follow-up of alcoholics treated by behavior therapy." *Behavior Research and Therapy*, 1968, *6*, 133.

Bandura, A., and Kupers, C. Transmission of aptterns of self-reinforcement through modeling. *Journal of Abnormal and Social Psychology*, 1964, *69*, 1–9.

Barlow, D., Leitenberg, H., and Agras, W. Preliminary report on the experimental control of sexual deviation by manipulation of the US in covert sensitization. Paper read at the Eastern Psychological Association Convention, Washington, D.C., April, 1968.

Bernstein, A. Covert reinforcement techniques: A consideration of intracranial contingencies. Unpublished manuscript, Virginia Commonwealth University, 1974.

Binder, C. V. A note on covert processes and the natural environment. *Behavior Therapy*, 1975, *6*, 568.

Blanchard, E., and Draper, D. Treatment of rodent phobia by covert reinforcement. *Behavior Therapy*, 1973, *4*, 559–564.

Borkovec, T. The effects of instructional suggestion and physiological cues on analogue fear. *Behavior Therapy*, 1973(a), *4*, 185–192.

Borkovec, T. The role of expectancy and physiological feedback in fear research: A review with special reference to subject characteristics. *Behavior Therapy*, 1973(b), *4*, 491–505.

Breger, L., and McGaugh, J. Learning theory and behavior therapy: A reply to Rachman and Eyesenck. *Psychological Bulletin*, 1966, *65*, 170–173.

Cautela, J. Treatment of compulsive behavior by covert sensitization. *Psychological Record*, 1966, *16*, 33–41.

Cautela, J. Covert sensitization. *Psychological Reports*, 1967, *20*, 459–468.

Cautela, J., and Kastenbaum, R. A reinforcement survey schedule for use in therapy, training and research. *Psychological Reports*, 1967, *20*, 1115–1120.

Cautela, J., and Wisocki, P. The use of imagery in the modification of attitudes toward the elderly. *Journal of Psychology*, 1969, *73*, 193–199.

Cautela, J. Covert negative reinforcement. *Journal of Behavior Therapy and Experimental Psychiatry,* 1970, *1,* 273–278.

Cautela, J., Walsh, K., and Wish, P. The use of covert reinforcement in the modification of attitudes toward the mentally retarded. Unpublished manuscript, Boston College, 1970.

Cautela, J. Covert conditioning. In A. Jacobs and L. Sachs (Eds.), *The psychology of private events.* New York: Academic Press, 1971.

Cautela, J. Treatment of overeating by covert conditioning. *Psychotherapy: Theory, Research and Practice,* 1972, *9,* 211–216.

Cautela, J., Flannery, R., and Hanley, S. Covert modeling: An experimental test. *Behavior Therapy,* 1974, *5,* 492–502.

Davison, D.G. Systematic desensitization as counterconditioning process. *Journal of Abnormal Psychology,* 1968, *73,* 91–99.

Diament, C., and Wilson, G. T. An experimental investigation of the effects of covert sensitization in an analogue eating situation. *Behavior Therapy,* 1975, *6,* 499–509.

Dorsey, T., Kanfer, R., and Duerfeldt, P. Task difficulty and noncontingent reinforcement as factors in self-reinforcement. *Journal of General Psychology,* 1971, *29,* 128–35.

Foreyt, J. P., and Hagen, R. L. Covert sensitization: Conditioning or suggestion? *Journal of Abnormal Psychology,* 1973, *82,* 17–23.

Gold, S., and Neufeld, I. A learning approach to the treatment of homosexuality. *Behavior Research and Therapy,* 1965, *2,* 201–204.

Gotestam, D., and Melin, L. Covert extinction with amphetamine addiction. *Behavior Therapy,* 1974, *5,* 90–92.

Guthrie, E. *The psychology of learning.* New York: Harper, 1935.

Hall, S. Self-control and therapist control in behavioral treatment of over-weight women. *Behavior Research and Therapy,* 1972, *10,* 59–68.

Harris, M. Self-directed program for weight control: A pilot study. *Journal of Abnormal Psychology,* 1969, *74,* 263–270.

Hill, W. Sources of evaluative reinforcement. *Psychological Bulletin,* 1968, *69,* 132–146.

Homme, L. Control of coverants: The operants of the mind. *Psychological Record,* 1965, *15,* 501–511.

Horan, J., and Johnson, R. Coverant conditioning through a self-management application of the Premack principle: An examination of its effect on weight reduction. *Journal of Behavior Therapy and Experimental Psychiatry,* 1971, *2,* 243–249.

Hull, C. *A behavior system.* New Haven: Yale University Press, 1952.

Jackson, B. Treatment of depression by self-reinforcement. *Behavior Therapy,* 1972, *3,* 293–307.

Jacobs, A., and Sachs, L. (Eds.). *The psychology of private events.* New York: Academic Press, 1971.

James, W. What is emotion? *Mind,* IX, 1884, 188–204.

Janda, L., and Rimm, D. Covert sensitization in the treatment of obesity. *Journal of Abnormal Psychology,* 1972, *80,* 37–42.

Johnson, S., and White, G. Self-observation as an agent of behavior change. *Behavior Therapy,* 1971, *2,* 488–497.

Kanfer, F., and Marston, A. Determinants of self-reinforcement in human learning. *Journal of Experimental Psychology,* 1963, *66,* 245–254.

Kanfer, F., and Duerfeldt, P. Age, class standing and commitment as determinants of cheating in children. *Child Development,* 1968, *39,* 545–557.

Karoly, R., and Kanfer, F. Situational and historical determinants of self-reinforcement. *Behavior Therapy*, 1974, *5*, 381–390.

Kazdin, A. Covert modeling, model similarity and reduction of avoidance behavior. *Behavior Therapy*, 1974, *5*, 325–340.

Kendrick, S., and McCullough, J. Sequential phases of covert reinforcement and covert sensitization in the treatment of homosexuality. *Journal of Behavior Therapy and Experimental Psychology*, 1972, *3*, 229–231.

Lang, P. The mechanics of desensitization and the laboratory study of human fear. In C. M. Franks (Ed.), *Behavior therapy: Appraisal and status*. New York: McGraw-Hill, 1969.

Lazarus, A., and Abramovitz, A. The use of "emotive imagery" in the treatment of children's phobias. *Journal of Mental Science*, 1962, *108*, 191–195.

Lewinsohm P. Clinical and theoretical aspects of depression. In K. Calhoun, H. Adams, and K. Mitchell (Eds.), *Innovative treatment methods in psychopathology*. New York: Wiley, 1974, pp. 63–120.

Mahoney, M. Research issues in self-management. *Behavior Therapy*, 1972, *3*, 45–63.

Mahoney, M. Self-reward and self-monitoring techniques for weight control. *Behavior Therapy*, 1974, *5*, 48–57.

Mahoney, M., Moura, N., and Wade, T. The relative efficacy of self-reward, self-punishment, and self-monitoring techniques for weight loss. *Journal of Consulting and Clinical Psychology*, in press.

Maletzky, B. "Assisted" covert sensitization: A preliminary report. *Behavior Therapy*, 1973, *4*, 117–119.

Manno, B., and Marston, A. Weight reduction as a function of negative covert reinforcement (sensitization) versus positive covert reinforcement. *Behavior Research and Therapy*, 1972, *10*, 201–207.

Marston, A. Dealing with low self-confidence. *Educational Research*, 1969, *63*, 134–138.

McFall, R. Effects of self-monitoring on normal smoking behavior. *Journal of Consulting and Clinical Psychology*, 1970, *35*, 135–142.

Mischel, W., and Liebert, R. Effects of discrepancies between observed and imposed reward criteria on their acquisition and transmission. *Journal of Personality and Social Psychology*, 1966, *3*, 45–53.

Nelson, C., and McReynolds, W. Self-recording and control of behavior: A reply to Simkins. *Behavior Therapy*, 1971, *2*, 594–597.

Rehm, L., and Marston, H. Reduction of social anxiety through modification of self-reinforcement. *Journal of Consulting and Clinical Psychology*, 1971, *36*, 410–421.

Rimm, D., and Masters, J. *Behavior therapy*. New York: Academic Press, 1974.

Sachs, L., Bean, H., and Manow, J. Comparison of smoking treatments. *Behavior Therapy*, 1970, *1*, 465–472.

Simkins, L. The reliability of self-recorded behaviors. *Behavior Therapy*, 1971, *2*, 83–87.

Skinner, B. *Science and human behavior*. New York: Macmillan, 1953.

Solomon, R. Punishment. *American Psychologist*, 1964, *19*, 239–253.

Titchener, E. The postulates of a structured psychology. *Philosophical Review VII*, 1898, 449–465.

Todd, F. Coverant control of self-evaluative responses in the treatment of depression: A new use for an old principle. *Behavior Therapy*, 1972, *3*, 91–94.

Tolman, E. *Purposive behavior in men and animals*. New York: Appleton, 1932.

Tyler, V., and Straughan, J. Coverant control and breath holding as techniques for the treatment of obesity. *Psychological Record*, 1970, *20*, 473–478.

Watson, J. *Psychology from the standpoint of a behaviorist*. Philadelphia: Lippincott, 1930.

Weitzman, B. Behavior therapy and psychotherapy. *Psychological Review*, 1967, *74*, 300–317.

Wiest, W. Some recent criticism of behaviorism and learning theory with special reference to Breger and McGaugh and to Chomsky. *Psychological Bulletin*, 1967, *67*, 214–225.

Wilkins, W. Desensitization: Social and cognitive factors underlying the effectiveness of Wolpe's procedure. *Psychological Bulletin*, 1971, *76*, 311–317.

Wisocki, P. The successful treatment of heroin addiction by covert conditioning techniques. In D. Upper and D. Goodenbough (Eds), *Behavior modification with the individual patient*. Nutley, N.J.: Roche Laboratories, 1972.

Wisocki, P. A covert reinforcement program for the treatment of test anxiety. *Behavior Therapy*, 1973, *4*, 264–266.

Wolpe, J. *Psychotherapy by reciprocal inhibition*. Stanford: Stanford University Press, 1958.

Wolpe, J., and Lang, P. A fear survey schedule for use in behavior therapy. *Behavior Research and Therapy*, 1964, *2*, 27–30.

Wundt, W. *Principles of physiological psychology*. (German, 1873) English, New York: Macmillan, 1910.

CHAPTER 6

Bandura, A. Social learning through imitation. In M. R. Jones (Ed.), *Nebraska symposium on motivation: 1962*. Lincoln: University of Nebraska Press, 1962, 211–269.

Bandura, A. Influence of model's reinforcement contingencies on the acquisition of imitative responses. *Journal of Personality and Social Psychology*, 1965, *1*, 589–595.

Bandura, A. *Principles of behavior modification*. New York: Holt, 1969.

Bandura, A., Blanchard, E., and Ritter, B. Relative efficacy of desensitization and modeling approaches for inducing behavioral, affective and attitudinal changes. *Journal of Personality and Social Psychology*, 1969, *13*, 173–199.

Bandura, A., Grusic, J., and Menlove, F. Vicarious extinction of avoidance behavior. *Journal of Personality and Social Psychology*, 1967, *5*, 16–23.

Bandura, A., and Kuypers, C. Transmission of patterns of self-reinforcement through modeling. *Journal of Abnormal and Social Psychology*, 1964, *69*, 1–9.

Bandura, A., and Menlove, F. Factors determining vicarious extinction of avoidance behavior through symbolic modeling. *Journal of Personality and Social Psychology*, 1968, *8*, 99–108.

Bandura, A., and Mischel, W. Modification of self-imposed delay of reward through exposure to live and symbolic models. *Journal of Personality and Social Psychology*, 1965, *2*, 698–705.

Bandura, A., and Rosenthal, T. Vicarious classical conditioning as a function of arousal level. *Journal of Personality and Social Psychology*, 1966, *3*, 54–62.

Bandura, A., Ross, D., and Ross, S. Imitation of film-mediated aggressive models. *Journal of Abnormal and Social Psychology*, 1963, *66*, 3–11.

Bandura, A., and Walters, R. *Social learning and personality development.* New York: Holt, 1963.

Bandura, A., and Whalen, C. The influence of antecedent reinforcement and divergent modeling cues on patterns of self-reward. *Journal of Personality and Social Psychology,* 1966, *3,* 373–382.

Baron, R. Attraction toward the model and model's competence as determinants of adult imitative behavior. *Journal of Personality and Social Psychology,* 1970, *14,* 345–351.

Berger, S. Conditioning through vicarious instigation. *Psychological Review,* 1962, *69,* 450–466.

Bishop, B., and Beckman, L. Conformity and imitation among hospitalized patients. *Journal of Clinical Psychology,* 1971, *27,* 529–532.

Blanchard, E. Relative contributions of modeling, informational influences, and physical contact in extinction of phobic behavior. *Journal of Abnormal Psychology,* 1970, *76,* 55–61.

Burchard, J., and Barrera, F. An analysis of time-out and response cost in a programmed environment. *Journal of Applied Behavior Analysis,* 1972, *5,* 271–282.

Eisler, R., Miller, P., and Hersen, M. Components of assertive behavior. *Journal of Clinical Psychology,* 1973, *29,* 295–299.

Hawkins, R., Peterson, R., Schweid, E., and Bijou, S. Behavior therapy in the home: Amelioration of a problem in parent-child relations with the parent in a therapeutic role. *Journal of Experimental Child Psychology,* 1966, *4,* 99–107.

Hersen, M., Eisler, R., Miller, P., Johnson, M., and Pinkston, S. Effects of practice, instruction and modeling on components of assertive behavior. *Behavior Research and Therapy,* 1973, *11,* 443–451.

Hicks, D. Imitation and retention of film mediated aggressive peer and adult models. *Journal of Personality and Social Psychology,* 1965, *2,* 97–100.

Hill, J., Liebert, R., and Mott, D. Vicarious extinction of avoidance behavior through films: An initial test. *Psychological Reports,* 1968, *22,* 192.

Janis, I., and Hoffman, D. Facilitating effects of daily contact between partners who make a decision to cut down on smoking. *Journal of Personality and Social Psychology,* 1970, *17,* 25–35.

Johnson, S., and Brown, R. Producing behavior change in parents of disturbed children. *Journal of Child Psychology and Psychiatry,* 1969, *10,* 107–121.

Lahey, B. Modification of the frequency of descriptive adjectives in the speech of head start children through modeling without reinforcement. *Journal of Applied Behavior Analysis,* 1971, *4,* 19–22.

Lira, F. Modeling for behavior change: A survey of research in underlying factors and clinical application. Unpublished manuscript, Virginia Commonwealth University, 1972.

Meichenbaum, D. Examination of model characteristics in reducing avoidance behavior. *Journal of Personality and Social Psychology,* 1971, *17,* 298–307.

Miller, N., and Dollard, J. *Social learning and imitation.* New Haven: Yale University Press, 1941.

Mischel, W., and Grusec, J. Determinants of the rehearsal and transmission of neutral and aversive behaviors. *Journal of Personality and Social Psychology,* 1966, *3,* 197–205.

Mischel, W., and Liebert, R. The role of power in the adoption of self-reward patterns. *Child Development,* 1967, *38,* 673–683.

Mowrer, O. *Learning theory and the symbolic process.* New York: Wiley, 1960.

Nay, W. Written, lecture, modeling and modeling-roleplaying as instructional techniques for parents. Paper presented to Southeastern Psychological Association, Atlanta, April 1972.

Nay, W. Comprehensive bheavioral treatment in a training school for delinquents. In K. Calhoun, H. Adams, and K. Mitchell (Eds.), *Innovative treatment methods in psychopathology*. New York: Wiley, 1974, Pp. 203–243.

Nay, W. R. A systematic comparison of instructional techniques for parents. *Behavior Therapy*, 1975, *6*, 14–21.

O'Brien, F., and Azrin, N. Developing proper mealtime behaviors of the institutional retarded. *Journal of Applied Behavior Analysis*, 1972, *5*, 389–399.

O'Leary, K., Becker, W., Evans, M., and Saudargas, R. A token reinforcement program in a public school: A replication and systematic analysis. *Journal of Applied Behavior Analysis*, 1969, *2*, 3–13.

Ritter, B. The group desensitization of children's snake phobias using vicarious and contact desensitization procedures. *Behavior, Research, and Therapy*, 1968, *6*, 1–6.

Ritter, B. Treatment of acrophobia with contact desensitization. *Behavior, Research and Therapy*, 1969, *7*, 41–45.

Rosekrans, M. Imitation in children as a function of perceived similarity to a social model. *Journal of Personality and Social Psychology*, 1967, *7*, 306–315.

Ross, D. Relationship between dependency, intentional learning, and incidental learning in preschool children. *Journal of Personality and Social Psychology*, 1966, *4*, 374–381.

Stumphauzer, J. Increased delay of gratification in young prison inmates through imitation of high-delay peer models. *Journal of Personality and Social Psychology*, 1972, *21*, 10–17.

Wolpe, J. *Psychotherapy by reciprocal inhibition*. Stanford, California: Stanford University Press, 1958.

Wolpe, J., and Lazarus, A. A. *Behavior therapy techniques*. Oxford: Pergamon, 1966.

CHAPTER 7

Bailey, K., and Sowder, T. Audiotape and videotape self-confrontation in psychotherapy. *Psychological Bulletin*, 1970, *77*:2, 127–137.

Bandura, A. *Principles of behavior modification*. New York: Holt, 1969.

Bandura, A., and Walters, R. *Social learning and personality development*. New York: Holt, 1963.

Boyd, H., and Sisney, V. Immediate self image confrontation and change in self concept. *Journal of Consulting Psychology*, 1967, *31*, 291–294.

Corbin, C. B. The effects of covert rehearsal on the development of a complex motor skill. *Journal of General Psychology*, 1967, *76*, 143–150.

Danet, B. Self-confrontation by videotape in group psychotherapy. Unpublished doctoral dissertation, University of Minnesota, 1967.

Eisler, R., Hersen, M., and Agras, W. Effects of videotape and instructional feedback on nonverbal marital interaction: An analog study. *Behavior Therapy*, 1973, *4*, 551–558.

Eisler, R., Miller, P., and Hersen, M. Components of assertive behavior. *Journal of Clinical Psychology*, 1973, *29*, 295–299.

Festinger, L., and Carlsmith, J. Cognitive consequences of forced compliance. *Journal of Abnormal and Social Psychology*, 1959, *58*, 203–210.

Geersman, R., and Revich, R. Auditory and visual dimensions of externally mediated self observation. *Journal of Nervous and Mental Disease*, 1969, *148*, 210–233.

Goldstein, A., Martens, J., Hubben, J., Van Belle, H., Schaaf, W., Wiersma, H., and Goodhait, A. The use of modeling to increase independent behavior. *Behavior Research and Therapy*, 1973, *11*, 31–42.

Goldstein, A., and Simonson, N. Social psychological approaches to psychotherapy research. In A. E. Bergin and S. H. Garfield (Eds.), *Handbook of psychotherapy and behavior change*. New York: Wiley, 1971.

Greenwald, A., and Albert, R. Acceptance and recall of improvised arguments. *Journal of Personality and Social Psychology*, 1968, *8*, 31–34.

Gutride, M., Goldstein, A., and Hunter, G. The use of modeling and roleplaying to increase social interaction among asocial psychiatric patients. *Journal of Consulting and Clinical Psychology*, 1973, *40*, 408–415.

Janis, J. L., and King, B. The influence of role-playing on opinion change. *Journal of Abnormal and Social Psychology*, 1954, *49*, 211–218.

Kanfer, F., and Phillips, J. *Learning foundations of behavior therapy*. New York: Wiley, 1970.

Karst, T. O., and Trexler, L. D. Initial study using fixed role and rational emotive therapy in treating public speaking anxiety. *Journal of Consulting and Clinical Psychology*, 1970, *24*, 360–366.

Kelly, G. *The Psychology of Personal Constructs: Vol. II Clinical Diagnosis and Psychotherapy*. New York: Norton, 1955.

Lazarus, A. A. Behavioral rehearsal vs. non-directive therapy vs. advice in effecting behavioral change. *Behavior Research and Therapy*, 1966, *4*, 209–212.

Lira, F., Nay, W. R., McCullough, J. P., and Etkin, M. The relative effects of modeling and roleplaying in reducing avoidance behaviors. *Journal of Consulting and Clinical Psychology*, 1975, *43*, 608–618.

Longin, H. E., and Rooney, W. M. Assertion training as a programatic intervention for hospitalized mental patients. Paper presented at the Meeting of the American Psychological Association, Montreal, Canada, 1973.

McFall, R. M., and Lillesand, D. B. Behavioral rehearsal with modeling and coaching in assertion training. *Journal of Abnormal Psychology*, 1971, *77*, 313–323.

McFall, R. M., and Marston, A. R. An experimental investigation of behavior rehearsal in assertive training. *Journal of Abnormal Psychology*, 1970, *76*, 295–303.

McFall, R. M., and Twentyman, C. T. Four experiments on the relative contributions of rehearsal, modeling and coaching to assertion training. *Journal of Abnormal Psychology*, 1973, *81*, 199–218.

Meichenbaum, D. Cognitive factors in behavior modification: Modifying what clients say to themselves. In C. Franks and G. T. Wilson (Eds.), *Annual review of behavior therapy: Theory and practice*. New York: Bruner/Mazel, 1973.

Meichenbaum, D. Self-instructional methods. In F. H. Kanfer and A. P. Goldstein (Eds.), *Helping people change*. New York: Pergamon, 1975.

Meichenbaum, D., and Cameron, R. Training schizophrenics to talk to themselves: A means of developing attentional controls. *Behavior Therapy*, 1973, *4*, 515–534.

Moreno, J. L. *Who shall survive?* Beacon, N.Y.: Beacon Press, 1953.

Morris, R. An inexpensive, easily built "Bug-in-the-ear" criterion system for training therapists in behavior modification techniques. *Behavior Therapy*, 1974, *5*, 685–688.

Mushala, P. Role play: A review of the techniques and a critical evaluation of its components. Unpublished manuscript, Virginia Commonwealth University, 1974.

Nay, W. R. A systematic comparison of instructional techniques for parents. *Behavior Therapy*, 1975, *6*, 1421.

Nay, W. R. Analogue measures. In T. Seminaro, K. Calhoun, and H. Adams (Eds.), *Handbook for behavioral assessment*. New York: Wiley, 1976.

Nay, W. R., Lira, F. T., and Etkin, M. Covert versus overt rehearsal in reducing avoidance behavior: The role of instructions and locus of control. Unpublished manuscript, Virginia Commonwealth University, 1976.

Paredes, A., Gottheil, E., Tausig, T., and Cornelision, F. Behavioral changes as a function of repeated self observation. *Journal of Nervous Disease*, 1969, *148*, 244–250.

Pollock, D., Nay, W. R., and Bailey, K. G. Behavioral and self-concept changes in group interaction with and without videotape feedback. Paper presented at Southeastern Psychological Association Meeting, New Orleans, April, 1973.

Schulman, J., and Nay, W. R. Videotape playback in psychotherapy: Current status, 1973. Unpublished manuscript, Virginia Commonwealth University, 1973.

Sturm, I. A behavioral outline of psychodrama. *Psychotherapy: Theory, Research, and Practice*, 1970, *7*, 245–247.

Underwood, B. Studies of distributed practice: XII. Retention of following varying degrees of original learning. *Journal of Experimental Psychology*, 1954, *47*, 294–300.

Welch, R. A highly efficient method of parental counseling: A mechanical third ear. Paper read at Rocky Mountain Psychological Convention, Albuquerque, New Mexico, 1966.

Wolkon, G. Ego strength, role-position salience and community tenure of the psychiatric patient. *Psychological Reports*, 1970, *26*, 951–953.

Wolpe, J. *The practice of behavior therapy*. New York: Pergamon Press, 1969.

Zimbardo, P. The effects of effort and improvisation on self persuasion produced by role play. *Journal of Experimental and Social Psychology*, 1965, *1*, 103–120.

CHAPTER 8

Bandura, A. *Principles of behavior modification*. New York: Holt, 1969.

Breger, L., and McGaugh, J. Critique and reformulation of "learning theory" approaches to psychotherapy and neurosis. *Psychological Bulletin*, 1965, *63*, 338–358.

Cautela, J. Treatment of compulsive behavior by covert sensitization. *Psychological Record*, 1966, *16*, 33–41.

Chapman, R., Smith, J., and Layden, T. Elimination of cigarette smoking by punishment and self-management training. *Behaviour Research and Therapy*, 1971, *9*, 255–264.

Crisp, A., Douglas, J., Ross, J., and Stonehill, E. Some developmental aspects of disorders of weight. *Journal of Psychosomatic Research*, 1970, *14*, 313–320.

Ferster, C., Nurnberger, J., and Levitt, E. The control of eating. *Journal of Mathematics*, 1962, *1*, 87–109.

Ferster, C. Classification of behavioral pathology. In L. Krasner and L. Ullmann

(Eds.), *Research in behavior modification: New developments nad implications.* New York: Holt, 1965.

Freud, S. *New introductory lectures on psycho-analysis.* New York: Norton, 1933.

Fromm, E. *Escape from freedom.* New York: Holt, 1941.

Goldfried, M., and Merbaum, M. (Eds.). *Behavior change through self-control.* New York: Holt, 1973.

Goldiamond, I. Self-control procedures in personal behavior problems. *Psychological Reports,* 1965, *17,* 851–868.

Gottman, J., and McFall, R. Self-monitoring effects in a program for potential high school dropouts: A time-series analysis. *Journal of Consulting and Clinical Psychology,* 1972, *39,* 273–281.

Hall, S. Self-control and therapist control in the behavioral treatment of over-weight women. *Behaviour Research and Therapy,* 1972, *10,* 59–68.

Hall, S., and Hall, R. Outcome and methodological considerations in behavioral treatment of obesity. *Behavior Therapy,* 1974, *5,* 352–364.

Harris, M. Self-directed program for weight control: A pilot study *Journal of Abnormal Psychology,* 1969, *74,* 263–270.

Homme, L. Perspectives in psychology: XXIV, Control of coverants, the operants of the mind. *Psychological Record,* 1965, *15,* 501–511.

Jeffrey, D., and Christensen, E. The relative efficacy of behavior therapy, will power and no-treatment control procedures for weight loss. *Research and Development Report #36,* University of Utah, 1972. Paper presented at the Association for Advancement of Behavior Therapy, New York, 1972.

Jung, C. *Two essays on analytical psychology.* London: Bailliere, Tondall, and Cox, 1928.

Kanfer, F. H. Self-regulation: Research, issues and speculations. In C. Neuringer and J. Michael (Eds.), *Behavior modification in clinical psychology.* New York: Appleton-Century-Crofts, 1970.

Kanfer, F. H. Self-management methods. In F. H. Kanfer and A. P. Goldstein (Eds.), *Helping people change.* New York: Pergamon, 1975.

Kanfer, F., and Karoly, P. Self-control: A behavioristic excursion into the lion's den. *Behavior Therapy,* 1972, *3,* 398–416.

Kanfer, F., and Phillips, J. *Learning foundations of behavior therapy.* New York: Wiley, 1970.

Kelly, G. Man's construction of his alternatives. In G. Lindsey (Ed.), *Assessment of human motives.* New York: Rinehart, 1958, pp. 33–64.

Keutzer, C., Lichtenstein, E., and Mees, H. Modification of smoking behavior: A review. *Psychological Bulletin,* 1968, *70,* 520–533.

Mahoney, M. Research issues in self-management. *Behavior Therapy,* 1972, *3,* 45–63.

Mahoney, M. Self-reward and self-monitoring techniques for weight control. *Dissertation Abstracts International,* 1973, *33*(8-B), 3951–3952.

Mahoney, M. Self-reward and self-monitoring techniques for weight control. *Behavior Therapy,* 1974(a), *5,* 48–57.

Mahoney, M. J. *Cognition and behavior modification.* Cambridge, Mass.: Ballinger, 1974(b).

Mahoney, M. J. Fat fiction. *Behavior Therapy,* 1975, *6,* 416–418.

Mahoney, M., Moura, N., and Wade, T. Relative efficacy of self-reward, self-punishment, and self-monitoring techniques for weight control. *Journal of Consulting and Clinical Psychology,* 1973, *40,* 404–407.

Mann, R. The behavior-therapeutic use of contingency contracting to control an adult behavior problem: Weight control. *Journal of Applied Behavior Analysis,* 1972, *5,* 99–109.

Manno, B., and Marston, A. Weight reduction as a function of negative covert reinforcement (sensitization) versus positive covert reinforcement. *Behavior Research and Therapy*, 1972, *10*, 201–207.

Mayer, J. *Overweight*. Englewood Cliffs, N.J.: Prentice Hall, 1968.

McFall, R. Effects of self-monitoring on normal smoking behavior. *Journal of Consulting and Clinical Psychology*, 1970, *35*, 135–142.

McFall, R., and Hammen, E. Motivation, structure and self-monitoring: Role of nonspecific factors in smoking reduction. *Journal of Consulting and Clinical Psychology*, 1971, *37*, 80–86.

McNamara, J. The use of self-monitoring techniques to treat nailbiting. *Behaviour Research and Therapy*, 1972, *10*, 193–194.

Mees, H. Sadistic fantasies modified by aversive conditioning and substitution: A case study. *Behaviour Research and Therapy*, 1966, *4*, 317–321.

Meichenbaum, D. Cognitive factors in behavior modification: Modifying what clients say to themselves. In C. Franks and T. Wilson (Eds.), *Annual review of behavior therapy: Theory and practice*. New York: Bruner-Mazel, 1973.

Meichenbaum, D. *Cognitive behavior modification*. Morristown, N.J.: General Learning Press, 1974.

Meichenbaum, D. Self-instructional methods. In F. H. Kanfer and A. P. Goldstein (Eds.), *Helping people change*. New York: Pergamon, 1975.

Meichenbaum, D., and Cameron, R. Training schizophrenics to talk to themselves: A means of developing attentional controls. *Behavior Therapy*, 1973, *4*, 515–534.

Morganstern, K. Cigarette smoke as a noxious stimulus in self-managed aversion therapy for compulsive eating: Technique and case illustration. *Behavior Therapy*, 1974, *5*, 255–260.

Ober, D. Modification of smoking behavior. *Journal of Consulting and Clinical Psychology*, 1968, *32*, 354–549.

Pratt, S., and Tooley, J. Contract psychology: Some methodological consideration and the research contract. Mimeo, Wichita State University, 1964.

Rogers, C. *Cleint-centered therapy*. Boston: Houghton Mifflin, 1951.

Rutner, I. The modification of smoking behavior through techniques of self-control. Unpublished master's thesis, Wichita State University, 1967.

Skinner, B. *Science and human behavior*. New York: Macmillan, 1953.

Stollak, G. Weight loss obtained under different experimental procedures. *Psychotherapy: Theory, Research and Practice*, 1967, *4*, 61–64.

Stuart, R., and Davis, B. Slim chance in a fat world: Behavioral control of obesity. Champaign, Ill.: Research Press, 1972.

Sullivan, H. *Conceptions of modern psychiatry*. Washington, D.C.: William Alanson White Psychiatric Foundation, 1947.

Thoreson, C. E., and Mahoney, M. J. *Behavioral self-control*. New York: Holt, 1974.

Tooley, J., and Pratt, S. An experimental procedure for the extinction of smoking behavior. *Psychological Reports*, 1967, *17*, 209–217.

Tracey, V., and Harper, J. Infantile obesity and respiratory infections. *British Medicine*, 1971, *1*, 16.

Ullmann, L., and Krasner, L. *A psychological approach to abnormal behavior*. Englewood Cliffs, N.J.: Prentice Hall, 1967.

United States Public Health Service. *Obesity and health*. Washington, D.C.: U.S. Government Printing Office, 1970.

Watson, D., and Tharp, R. *Self-directed behavior: Self-modification for personal adjustment*. Belmont, Calif.: Brooks/Cole, 1972.

Whitman, T. Modification of chronic smoking behavior: A comparison of three approaches. *Behaviour Research and Therapy*, 1969, *7*, 257–263.

Whitman, T. Aversive control of smoking behavior in a group context. *Behavior Research and Therapy*, 1972, *10*, 97–104.

Yates, A. *Behavior therapy*. New York: Wiley, 1970.

CHAPTER 9

Ayer, W. Implosive therapy: A review. *Psychotherapy: Theory, Research and Practice*, 1972, *9*, 242–250.

Bandura, A., Blanchard, E., and Ritter, R. The relative efficacy of desensitization and modeling approaches for inducing behavioral, affective, and attitudinal changes. *Journal of Personality and Social Psychology*, 1969, *13*, 173–199.

Bandura, A., Grusec, J. E., and Menlove, F. L. Vicarious extinction of avoidance behavior. *Journal of Personality and Social Psychology*, 1967, *5*, 16–23.

Barlow, D., Leitenberg, H., Agras, W., and Wincze, J. The transfer gap in systematic desensitization: An analogue study. *Behavior Research and Therapy*, 1969, *7*, 191–196.

Barrett, C. Systematic desensitization versus implosive therapy. *Journal of Abnormal Psychology*, 1969, *74*, 587–592.

Bernstein, D. A., and Borkovec, T. D. *Progressive relaxation training: A manual for the helping professions*. Champaign, Ill.: Research Press Co., 1974.

Bernstein, D. A., and Neitzel, M. T. Procedural variation in behavioral avoidance tests. *Journal of Consulting and Clinical Psychology*, 1973, *41*, 165–174.

Bernstein, D. A., and Paul, G. L. Some comments on therapy analogue research with small animal "phobias." *Journal of Behavior Therapy and Experimental Psychiatry*, 1971, *2*, 225–237.

Borkovec, T. Effects of expectancy on the outcome of systematic desensitization and implosive treatments for analogue anxiety. *Behavior Therapy*, 1972, *3*, 29–40.

Borkovec, T. D. The role of expectancy and physiological feedback in fear research: A review with special reference to subject characteristics. *Behavior Therapy*, 1973, *4*, 491–505.

Borkovec, T. D., Kaloupek, D. G., and Slama, K. M. The facilitative effect of muscle tension release in the relaxation treatment of sleep disturbance. *Behavior Therapy*, 1975, *6*, 301–309.

Boudywns, P. Flooding and implosive therapy with situation specific and non-situation specific anxiety. Paper presented at meeting of the Association for the Advancement of Behavior Therapy, Miami, December, 1973.

Boulougouris, J., Marks, I., and Marset, P. Superiority of flooding (implosion) desensitization for reducing pathological fear. *Behavior Research and Therapy*, 1971, *9*, 7–16.

Bruno, R. D., and McCullough, J. P. Systematic desensitization of an oral examination phobia. *Journal of Behavior Therapy and Experimental Psychiatry*, 1973, *4*, 187–189.

Cooke, G. The efficacy of two desensitization procedures: An analogue study. *Behavior Research and herapy*, 1966, *4*, 17–24.

Cooke, G. Evaluation of the efficacy of the components of reciprocal inhibition psychotherapy. *Journal of Abnormal Psychology*, 1968, *73*, 464–467.

Cooper, A., Furst, J., and Bridger, W. A brief commentary on the usefulness of studying fears of snakes. *Journal of Abnormal Psychology*, 1969, *74*. 413–414.

Craig, K. Physiological arousal as a function of imagined, vicarious, and direct stress experiences. *Journal of Abnormal Psychology*, 1968, *73*, 513–520.

Davis, D., McLemore, G., and London, P. The role of visual imagery in desensitization. *Behavior Research and Therapy*, 1970, *8*, 11–13.

Davison, G. Systematic desensitization as a counter-conditioning process. *Journal of Abnormal Psychology*, 1968, *73*, 91–99.

Davison, G., and Wilson, G. Critique of "Desensitization: Social and cognitive factors underlying the effectiveness of Wolpe's procedure." *Psychological Bulletin*, 1972, *78*, 28–31.

Davison, G., and Wilson, G. T. Processes of fear-reduction in systematic desensitization: Cognitive and social reinforcement factors in humans. *Behavior Therapy*, 1973, *4*, 1–21.

Donner, L., and Guerney, B., Jr. Automated group desensitization for test anxiety. *Behavior Research and Therapy*, 1969, *7*, 1–13.

Emery, J., and Krumboltz, J. Standard versus individual hierarchies in desensitization to reduce test anxiety. *Journal of Counseling Psychology*, 1967, *14*, 204–209.

Evans, M. B. Procedures for a high demand behavioral avoidance test and for a diagnosis/treatment subject expectancy manipulation: Brief note. *Behavior Therapy*, 1975, *6*, 72–77.

Everaerd, W., Rijken, H. M., and Emmelkamp, P. A comparison of flooding and "successive approximations" in the treatment of agoraphobia. *Behavior Research and Therapy*, 1973, *11*, 105–117.

Fazio, A. Treatment components in implosive therapy. *Journal of Abnormal Psychology*, 1970, *76*, 211–219.

Geer, J. H. Fear and autonomic arousal. *Journal of Abnormal Psychology*, 1966, *71*, 253–255.

Gilner, F., Lipsitz, D., and Davenport, D. Drive level and incentive in systematic desensitization. Paper presented at the American Association of Behavior Therapists, Miami, 1973.

Grossberg, J., and Wilson, H. Physiological changes accompanying visualization of fearful and neutral situations. *Journal of Personality and Social Psychology*, 1968, *10*, 124–133.

Guapp, L. A., Stern, R. M., and Galbraith, G. G. False heart-rate feedback and reciprocal inhibition by aversive relief in the treatment of snake avoidance behavior. *Behavior Therapy*, 1972, *3*, 7–20.

Hoenig, J., and Reed, G. F. The objective assessment of desensitization. *British Journal of Psychiatry*, 1966, *112*, 1279–1283.

Hogan, R. Implosive therapy in the short term treatment of psychotics. *Psychotherapy: Theory, Research and Practice*. 1966, *3*, 25–31.

Hogan, R., and Kirchner, J. A preliminary report of the extinction of learned fears via short term implosive therapy. *Journal of Abnormal Psychology*, 1967, *72*, 106–111.

Hogan, R., and Kirchner, J. Implosive, eclectic verbal and bibliotherapy in the treatment of fears of snakes. *Bheavior Research and Therapy*, 1968, *6*, 167–171.

Hyman, E. Physiological processes during systematic desensitization. *Dissertation Abstracts International*, 1971, *31* (12-B), 7599.

Jacobson, E. *Progressive relaxation*. Chicago: University of Chicago Press, 1938.

Jacobson, E. Variation of blood pressure with skeletal muscle tension and relaxation. *Annuals of Internal Medicine*, 1939, *12*, 1194.

Jones, M. Elimination of children's fears. *Journal of Experimental Psychology*, 1924, *7*, 382.

Jones, M. A laboratory study of fear. The case of Peter. *Journal of Genetic Psychology*, 1924, *31*, 308.

Jones, D. An examination of the role of mental imagery ability in the treatment of snake fear by systematic desensitization. *Dissertation Abstracts International*, 1972, *32*, (7-B), 4219–4222.

Kanfer, F., and Phillips, J. *Learning foundations of behavior therapy*. New York: Wiley, 1970.

Kirchner, J., and Hogan, R. The therapist variable in the implosion of phobias. *Psychotherapy: Theory, Research and Practice*, 1966, *3*, 102–104.

Kirsch, I., Wolpin, M., and Knutson, J. L. A comparison of *in vivo* methods for rapid reduction of "stage fright" in the college classroom: A field experiment. *Behavior Therapy*, 1975, *6*, 165–171.

Klein, M., Dittman, A., Parloff, M., and Gill, M. Behavior therapy: Observations and reflections. *Journal of Consulting and Clinical Psychology*, 1969, *33*, 259–266.

Koenig, K. P. False emotional feedback and the modification of anxiety. *Behavior Therapy*, 1973, *4*, 193–202.

Krause, M. S., Fitzsimmons, M., and Wolf, N. Focusing on the client's expectations of treatment. *Psychological Reports*, 1969, *24*, 973–974.

Lang, P. The mechanics of desensitization and the laboratory study of human fear. In C. M. Franks (Ed.), *Behavior therapy: Appraisal and status*. New York: McGraw-Hill, 1969.

Lang, P., and Lazovik, A. Experimental desensitization of a phobia. *Journal of Abnormal and Social Psychology*, 1963, *66*, 519–525.

Lang, P., Lazovik, A., and Reynolds, D. Desensitization, suggestibility, and pseudotherapy. *Journal of Abnormal Psychology*, 1965, *70*, 395–402.

Lang, P., Melamed, B., and Hart, J. A psychophysiological analysis of fear modification using an automated desensitization procedure. *Journal of Abnormal Psychology*, 1970, *76*, 220–234.

Lazarus, A. Group therapy of phobic disorders by systematic desensitization. *Journal of Abnormal and Social Psychology*, 1961, *63*, 505–510.

Lehrer, P. Physiological effects of relaxation in a double-blind analog of desensitization. *Behavior Therapy*, 1972, *3*, 193–208.

Leitenberg, H., Agras, W., Thompson, L., and Wright, D. Feedback in behavior modification: An experimental analysis in two phobic cases. *Journal of Applied Behavior Analysis*, 1968, *1*, 131–137.

Leitenberg, H., Agras, W., Barlow, D., and Oliveau, D. The contribution of selective positive reinforcement and therapeutic instructions to systematic therapy. *Journal of Abnormal Psychology*, 1969, *74*, 113–118.

Levis, D., and Carrera, R. Effects of 10 hours of implosive therapy in the treatment of outpatients. A preliminary report. *Journal of Abnormal Psychology*, 1967, *72*, 504–508.

Liberman, D. Therapist warmth and subject expectation in systematic desensitization therapy. *Dissertation Abstracts International*, 1972, *32* (10-D), 6054.

Lindsley, O. Training teachers and parents in behavior modification. Paper presented at Behavioral Technology Conference, University of Oregon, July, 1968.

Lira, F. T., Nay, W. R., McCullough, J. P., and Etkin, M. W. Relative effects of modeling and role playing in the treatment of avoidance behaviors. *Journal of Consulting and Clinical Psychology*, 1975, *43*, 608–618.

Lomont, J., and Edwards, J. The role of relaxation in systematic desensitization. *Behavior Research and Therapy*, 1967, *5*, 11–25.

Lomont, J., and Brock, L. Stimulus hierarchy generalization in systematic desensitization. *Behavior Research and Therapy*, 1971, *9*, 197–208.

London, P. *The modes and morals of psychotherapy.* New York: Holt, 1964.

Marks, I. M. Flooding (implosion) and allied treatments. In W. S. Agras (Ed.), *Behavior modification: Principles and clinical applications.* Boston: Little, Brown, 1972.

Marquis, J., and Morgan, W. *A guidebook for systematic desensitization.* Palo Alto, Calif.: Veterans Administration Hospital, 1969.

Mathews, A. Psychophysiological approaches to the investigation of desensitization and related procedures. *Psychological Bulletin,* 1971, *76,* 73–91.

Mathews, A. M., and Gelder, M. G. Psychophysiological investigations of brief relaxation training. *Journal of Psychosomatic Research,* 1969, 13, 1–12.

McGlynn, F., Reynolds, E., and Lindner, L. Experimental desensitization following therapeutically oriented instructions. *Journal of Behavior Therapy and Experimental Psychiatry,* 1972, *2,* 13–18.

McGlynn, F. Experimental desensitization following three types of instructions. *Behavior Research and Therapy,* 1971, *9,* 367–369.

McLemore, C. Imagery and desensitization. *Behavior Research and Therapy,* 1972, *10,* 51–57.

McNamara, J. Systematic desensitization versus implosive therapy: Issues in outcomes. *Psychotherapy: Theory, Research and Practice,* 1972, *9,* 13–16.

McReynolds, W., and Tori, C. A further assessment of attention-placebo effects and demand characteristics in studies of systematic desensitization. *Journal of Consulting and Clinical Psychology,* 1972, *38,* 261–264.

Moore, N. Behavior therapy in bronchial asthma: A controlled study. *Journal of Psychosomatic Research,* 1965, *9,* 257.

Morganstern, K. Implosive therapy and flooding procedures: A critical review. *Psychological Bulletin,* 1973, *79,* 318–334.

Munjack, D. J. Overcoming obstacles to desensitization using *in vivo* stimuli and Brevital. *Behavior Therapy,* 1975, *6,* 543–546.

Murray, E. J., and Jacobson, L. I. The nature of learning in traditional and behavioral psychotherapy. In A. Bergin and S. Garfield (Eds.), *Handbook of psychotherapy and behavior change.* New York: Wiley, 1971.

Nay, W. R., Gottlieb, J., and Bailey, K. G. A systematic comparison of three modalities of videotape feedback. Unpublished manuscript, Virginia Commonwealth University, 1974.

Nay, W. R., Pollock, D., and Bailey, K. G. Behavioral and self-concept changes in group interaction with and without videotape feedback. Paper presented at Southeastern Psychological Association, New Orleans, April, 1973.

Oliveau, D., Agras, W., Leitenberg, H., Moore, R., and Wright, D. Systematic desensitization, therapeutically oriented instructions and selective positive reinforcement. *Behavior Research and Therapy,* 1969, *7,* 27–33.

O'Neil, D., and Howell, R. Three modes of hierarchy presentation in systematic desensitization therapy. *Behavior Research and Therapy,* 1969, *7,* 289–294.

Osgood, C. E., Suci, G. J., and Tannenbaum, P. H. *The measurement of meaning.* Urbana, Ill.: University of Illinois Press, 1957.

Paul, G. *Insight versus desensitization in psychotherapy: An experiment in anxiety reduction.* Standford: Stanford University Press, 1966.

Paul, G. Physiological effects of relaxation training and hypnotic suggestion. *Journal of Abnormal Psychology,* 1969, *74,* 425–437.

Paul, G. Inhibition of physiological response to stressful imagery by relaxation training and hypnotically suggested relaxation. *Behavior Research and Therapy,* 1969, *7,* 249–256.

Paul, G., and Trimble, R. Recorded versus "live" relaxation training and hypnotic suggestion: Comparative effectiveness for reducing physiological arousal and inhibiting stress response. *Behavior Therapy,* 1970, *1,* 285–302.

Rachman, S. The role of muscular relaxation in desensitizing therapy. *Behavior Research and Therapy,* 1968, *6,* 159–166.

Richardson, A. *Mental imagery.* New York: Springer, 1969.

Rimm, D., and Masters, J. *Behavior therapy.* New York: Academic Press, 1974.

Ross, S. M., and Proctor, S. Frequency and duration of hierarchy item exposure in a systematic desensitization analogue. *Behavior Research and Therapy,* 1973, *11,* 303–312.

Rubin, S. E., Lawlis, G. F., Tasto, D. L., and Namenek, T. Factor analysis of the 122-item fear survey schedule. *Behaviour Research and Therapy,* 1969, *7,* 381–386.

Rutner, I. T. The effects of feedback and instructions on phobic behavior. *Behavior Therapy,* 1973, *4,* 338–348.

Ryan, V. C., and Gizynski, A. Behavior therapy in retrospect: Patients' feelings about their behavior therapies. *Journal of Consulting and Clinical Psychology,* 1971, *37,* 1–9.

Sherman, R. Two year follow-up of training in relaxation as a behavioral self-management skill. *Behavior Therapy,* 1975, *6,* 419–420.

Sherrington, C. *Integrative action of the nervous sytem.* New Haven, Conn.: Yale University Press, 1906.

Smith, R., Dixon, A., and Sheppard, L. Review of flooding procedures (implosion) in animals and man. *Perceptual and Motor Skills,* 1973, *37,* 351–374.

Spielberger, C., Gorsuch, R., and Lushene, R. *State-trait anxiety inventory.* Palo Alto, Calif.: Consulting Press, 1970.

Stampfl, T., and Levis, D. Essentials of implosive therapy: A learning theory-based psychodynamic behavioral therapy. *Journal of Abnormal Psychology,* 1967, *72,* 496–503.

Stampfl, T., and Levis, D. Implosive therapy: A behavioral therapy? *Behavior Research and Therapy,* 1968, *6,* 31–36.

Staub, E. Duration of stimulus-exposure as determinant of the efficacy of flooding procedures in the elimination of fear. *Behavior Research and Therapy,* 1968, *6,* 131–132.

Sushinsky, L., and Bootzin, R. Cognitive desensitization as a model of systematic desensitization. *Behavior Research and Therapy,* 1970, *8,* 29–34.

Tasto, D., Hickson, R., and Rubin, S. Scaled profile analysis of fear survey schedule factors. *Behavior Therapy,* 1971, *2,* 543–549.

Valins, S., and Ray, A. Effects of cognitive desensitization on avoidance behavior. *Journal of Personality and Social Psychology,* 1967, *7,* 345–350.

Walk, R. D. Self-ratings of fear in a fear evoking situation. *Journal of Abnormal and Social Psychology,* 1956, *52,* 171–178.

Watson, J. P., Gaind, R., and Marks, I. M. Prolonged exposure: A rapid treatment for phobias. *British Medical Journal,* 1971, *1,* 13–15.

Weil, G., and Goldfried, M. Treatment of insomnia in an eleven year old child through self-relaxation. *Behavior Therapy,* 1973, *4,* 282–294.

Willis, R., and Edwards, J. A study of the comparative effectiveness of systematic desensitization and implosive therapy. *Behaviour Research and Therapy,* 1969, *7,* 387–395.

Wilkins, W. Desensitization: Social and cognitive factors underlying the effectiveness of Wolpe's procedure. *Psychological Bulletin,* 1971, *76,* 311–317.

Wilkins, W. Desensitization: Getting it together with Davison and Wilson, *Psychological Bulletin,* 1972, *78,* 32–36.

Wilkins, W. Expectancy of therapeutic gain: An empirical and conceptual critique. *Journal of Consulting and Clinical Psychology*, 1973, *40*, 69–77.

Wilson, G. Efficacy of "flooding" procedures in desensitization of fear: A theoretical note. *Behavior Research and Therapy*, 1967, *5*, 138.

Wilson, G. T. Innovations in the modification of phobic behaviors in two clinical cases. *Behavior Therapy*, 1973, *4*, 426–430.

Wolpe, J. *Psychotherapy by reciprocal inhibition.* Stanfrod: Stanford University Press, 1958.

Wolpe, J., and Lang, P. A fear survey for use in behavior therapy. *Behaviour Research and Therapy*, 1964, *2*, 27–30.

Wolpe, J. *The practice of behavior therapy.* New York: Pergamon, 1969, 1973.

Wolpin, M., and Pearsall, L. Rapid deconditioning of a fear of snakes. *Behaviour Research and Therapy*, 1965, *3*, 107.

CHAPTER 10

Allen, A. Case study: Implementation of behavior modification techniques in summer camp settings. *Behavior Therapy*, 1973, *4*, 570–575.

Becker, W. *Parents are teachers.* Champaign, Ill.: Research Press, 1971.

Bolstad, O. D., and Johnson, S. M. Self-regulation in the modification of disruptive classroom behavior. *Journal of Applied Behavior Analysis*, 1972, *5*, 443–454.

Boren, J. J., and Coleman, A. D. Some experiments on reinforcement principles within a psychiatric ward for delinquent soldiers. *Journal of Applied Behavior Analysis*, 1970, *3*, 29–37.

Brierton, S., Garms, R., and Metzger, R. Practical problems encountered in an aide administered token reward cottage program. *Mental Retardation*, 1969, *7*, 40–43.

Davison, G. The training of undergraduates as social reinforcers for artistic children. In L. P. Ullman and F. Krasner (Eds.), *Case studies in behavior modification.* New York: Holt, 1965.

Ferritor, D. E., Buckholdt, D., Hamblin, R. L., and Smith, L. The noneffects of contingent reinforcement for attending behavior on work accomplished. *Journal of Applied Behavior Analysis*, 1972, *5*, 7–17.

Gardner, J. Teaching behavior modification to nonprofessionals. *Journal of Applied Behavior Analysis*, 1972, *5*, 517–521.

Glickman, H., Plutchick, R., and Landau, H. Social and biological reinforcement in an open psychiatric ward. *Journal of Behavior Therapy and Experimental Psychiatry*, 1973, *4*, 121–124.

Gripp, R., and Magaro, P. A token economy program evaluation with untreated control ward comparisons. *Behavior Research and Therapy*, 1971, *9*, 137–149.

Haffey, V. Behavior modification utilizing a token economy program. *Journal of Psychiatric Nursing and Mental Health Services*, 1970, *8*, 31–35.

Hollander, M., and Plutchick, R. A reinforcement program for psychiatric attendants. *Journal of Behavior Therapy and Experimental Psychiatry*, 1972, *3*, 299–300.

Katz, R. C., Johnson, C. A., and Gelfand, S. Modifying the dispensing of reinforcers: Some implications for behavior modification with hospitalized patients. *Behavior Therapy*, 1972, *3*, 579–588.

Kaufman, K., and O'Leary, K. Reward, cost and self-evaluation procedures for disruptive adolescents in a psychiatric hospital school. *Journal of Applied Behavior Analysis,* 1972, *5,* 293–309.

Kazdin, A., and Bootzin, R. The token economy: An evaluative review. *Journal of Applied Behavior Analysis,* 1972, *5,* 343–372.

Lee, D., and Znachko, G. Training psychiatric aides in behavior modification techniques. *Journal of Psychiatric Nursing and Mental Health Services,* 1968, *6,* 7–11.

Loeber, R. Engineering the behavioral engineer. *Journal of Applied Behavior Analysis,* 1971, *4,* 321–326.

Martin, G. Teaching operant technology to psychiatric nurses, aides, and attendants. In F. W. Clarke, L. A. Evans, and L. A. Hammerlynck (Eds.), *Implementing behavioral programs for schools and clinics:* Proceedings of the Third Banff International Conference on Behavior Modification. Champaign: Research Press Co., 1972.

McLaughlin, T., and Malaby, J. Reducing and measuring inappropriate verbalizations in a token classroom. *Journal of Applied Behavior Analysis,* 1972, *5,* 329–333.

McNamara, J. Teacher and students as sources for behavior modification in the classroom. *Behavior Therapy,* 1971, *2,* 205–213.

Nay, W. Comprehensive behavioral treatment in a training school for delinquents. In K. Calhoun, H. Adams, and K. Mitchell (Eds.), *Innovative treatment methods in psychopathology.* New York: Wiley, 1974.

Nay, W. A systematic comparison of instructional techniques for parents. *Behavior Therapy,* 1975, *6,* 14–21.

Nay, W. R. Intra-institutional "roadblocks" to behavior modification programming. In D. Marholin (Ed.), *Child behavior therapy.* New York: Gardner Press, in press.

O'Brien, J., Raynes, A., and Patch, V. An operant reinforcement system to improve ward behavior in in-patient drug addicts. *Journal of Behavior Therapy and Experimental Psychiatry,* 1971, *2,* 239–242.

O'Leary, K., and Drabman, R. Token reinforcement programs in the classroom: A review. *Psychological Bulletin,* 1971, *75,* 379–398.

Panyon, M., Boozer, H., and Morris, N. Feedback to attendants as a reinforcer for applying operant techniques. *Journal of Applied Behavior Analysis,* 1970, *3,* 1–4.

Patterson, G., Cobb, J., and Ray, R. A social engineering technology for retraining aggressive boys. In H. E. Adams and I. P. Unikel (Eds.), *Issues and trends in behavior therapy.* Springfield, Ill.: Thomas, 1973.

Patterson, G., and Guillion, E. *Living with children.* Champaign, Ill.: Research Press, 1968.

Pizzat, F. *Behavior modification in residential treatment for children: A model program.* New York: Behavioral Publications, 1973.

Pomerleau, O., Bobrove, P., and Harris, L. Some observations on a controlled social environment for psychiatric patients. *Journal of Behavior Therapy and Experimental Psychiatry,* 1972, *3,* 5–21.

Poser, E. Training behavior change agents: A five year perspective. In F. W. Clark, D. R. Evans, and C. A. Hammerlynck (Eds.), *Implementing behavioral programs for school and clinics:* Proceedings of the Third Banff International Conference of Behavior Modification. Champaign, Ill.: Research Press, 1972.

Zimmerman, E., Zimmerman, J., and Russell, C. Differential effects of token reinforcement on instruction-following behavior in retarded students instructed as a group. *Journal of Applied Behavior Analysis,* 1969, *2,* 101–112.

CHAPTER 11

Ayllon, T., and Azrin, N. The measurement and reinforcement of behavior of psychotics. *Journal of the Experimental Analysis of Behavior*, 1965, *8*, 357–383.

Ayllon, T., and Azrin, N. *The token economy: A motivational system for therapy and rehabilitation*. New York: Appleton-Century-Crofts, 1968.

Atthowe, J., and Krasner, L. Preliminary report on the application of contingent reinforcement procedure (token economy) on a "chronic" psychiatric ward. *Journal of Abnormal Psychology*, 1968, *73*, 37–43.

Baer, D. Some remedial uses of the reinforcement contingency. In J. M. Shlein (Ed.), *Research in psychotherapy: Vol. III*. Washington, D.C.: American Psychological Association, 1968.

Braun, S. H. Ethical issues in behavior modification. *Behavior Therapy*, 1975, *6*, 51–62.

Breger, L., and McGaugh, J. Critique and reformulation of "learning theory" approaches to psychotherapy and neurosis. *Psychological Bulletin*, 1965, *63*, 338–358.

Carrera, F., and Adams, P. An ethical perspective on operant conditioning. *Journal of the American Academy of Child Psychiatry*, 1970, *9*, 607–623.

Clonce vs. Richardson, 379 F. Supp. 338 (W.D. Mo. 1974).

Covington vs. Harris, 491 F.2d 617 (D.C. Cir. 1969).

Ennis, B. Civil liberties and mental illness. *Criminal Law Bulletin*, 1971, *7*, 101, 122–123.

Goodall, K. Shapers at work. *Psychology Today*, 1972, *6*, 53–63.

In Re Gault, 387 U.S. 1 (1967).

Jobson vs. Henne, 355 F.2d 129, 132 N.E. (2nd Cir. 1966).

Judicial Council, American Medical Association. *Opinions and reports of the Judicial Council*. Chicago: American Medical Association, 1969.

Kaimowitz vs. Michigan Department of Mental Health, 42 U.S.L. Week 2063 (Mich. Cir. Ct., Wayne Cty. July 10, 1973).

Kazdin, A., and Bootzin, R. The token economy: An evaluation review. *Journal of Applied Behavior Analysis*, 1972, *5*, 343–372.

Knecht vs. Gilman, 488 F.2d. 1136 (8th Cir. 1973).

Krasner, L. Behavior modification—values and training: The perspective of a psychologist. In C. M. Franks (Ed.), *Behavior therapy appraisal and status*. New York: McGraw-Hill, 1969.

Lazo, J. A. (Ed.). *Biographical directory of the American Psychological Association*. Washington, D.C.: American Psychological Association, 1973.

Lee, A. L., and Jacobs, G. Workshop airs patient's rights. *Hospitals*, 1973, *47*, 39–43.

LeShan, E., and LeShan, L. A home is not a lab. *New York Times Magazine*. April 7, 1968, 197–207.

London, P. *The modes and morals of psychotherapy*. New York: Holt, 1964.

London, P. *Behavior control*. New York: Harper, 1969.

Mackey vs. Procunier, 477 F.2d. 877 (9th Cir. 1973).

Martin, R. *Legal challenges to behavior modification*. Champaign, Ill.: Research Press, 1975.

Mental Patient's Liberation Project. *Bill of rights for mental patients*. New York: Mental Patient's Liberation Project, 1971.

Miron, N. Issues and implications of operant conditioning: The primary ethical consideration. In R. Ulrich, T. Stachnik, and J. Mabry (Eds.), *Control of human behavior from cure to prevention, Vol. II.* Glenview, Ill.: Scott, Foresman, 1970.

Morales vs. Turman, 383 F. Supp. 53 (E.D. Tex. 1974).

Narrol, W. Experimental application of reinforcement principles to the analysis and treatment of hospital alcoholics. *Journal of Studies on Alcohol*, 1967, *105*, 08.

Pennsylvania Association for Retarded Children vs. Commonwealth of Pennsylvania, 334 F. Supp. 1257 (E.D. Pa. 1971).

Rogers, C. R. *Client-centered therapy.* Boston: Houghton Mifflin, 1951.

Rouse vs. Cameron, 373 F.2d. 451 (D.C. 1966).

Saslow, G. The use of a psychiatric unit in a general hospital. In A. F. Wessen (Ed.), *The psychiatric hospital as a social system.* Springfield, Ill.: Thomas, 1964.

Schaefer, H. H. Investigations in operant conditioning procedures in a mental hospital. In J. Fisher and R. Harris (Eds.), *Reinforcement theory in psychological treatment—A symposium 25, 26,* 1966 (California Mental Health Research Monograph No. 8).

Shoben, E., Jr. The therapeutic object: Men or machines? *Journal of Counseling Psychology*, 1963, *10*, 264–268.

Skinner, B. F. *Science and human behavior.* New York: Macmillan, 1953.

Skinner, B. F. *Beyond freedom and dignity.* New York: Knopf, 1971.

U.S. Adjutant General's Department. *Trials of war criminals before Nuremberg military tribunals under control council law, No. 10.* Washington, D.C., 1947, *2*, 181–183.

Weist, W. M. Some recent criticisms of behaviorism and learning theory with special reference to Breger and McGaugh and Chomsky. *Psychological Bulletin*, 1967, *67*, 214–225.

Wexler, D. Token and taboo: Behavior modification, token economies, and the law. *California Law Review*, 1973, *61*.

Williams vs. Robinson, 432 F.2d. 637 (D.C. 1970).

World Medical Association. *Declaration of Helsinki.* Helsinki, 1964.

Wyatt vs. Stickney, 344 F. Supp. 373, 380 (M.D. Ala. 1972).

Yates, A. *Behavior therapy.* New York: Wiley, 1970.

INDEX

PRODUCTION NOTE

Behavioral Intervention was photocomposed
in Baskerville and Optima types by
Cemar Graphic Designs Ltd of Rockville Centre, New York
The printing and binding were done by
Haddon Craftsmen of Scranton, Pa.